HomeBody

THEO PARISH

HOMEBODY

HARPER
alley

An Imprint of HarperCollinsPublishers

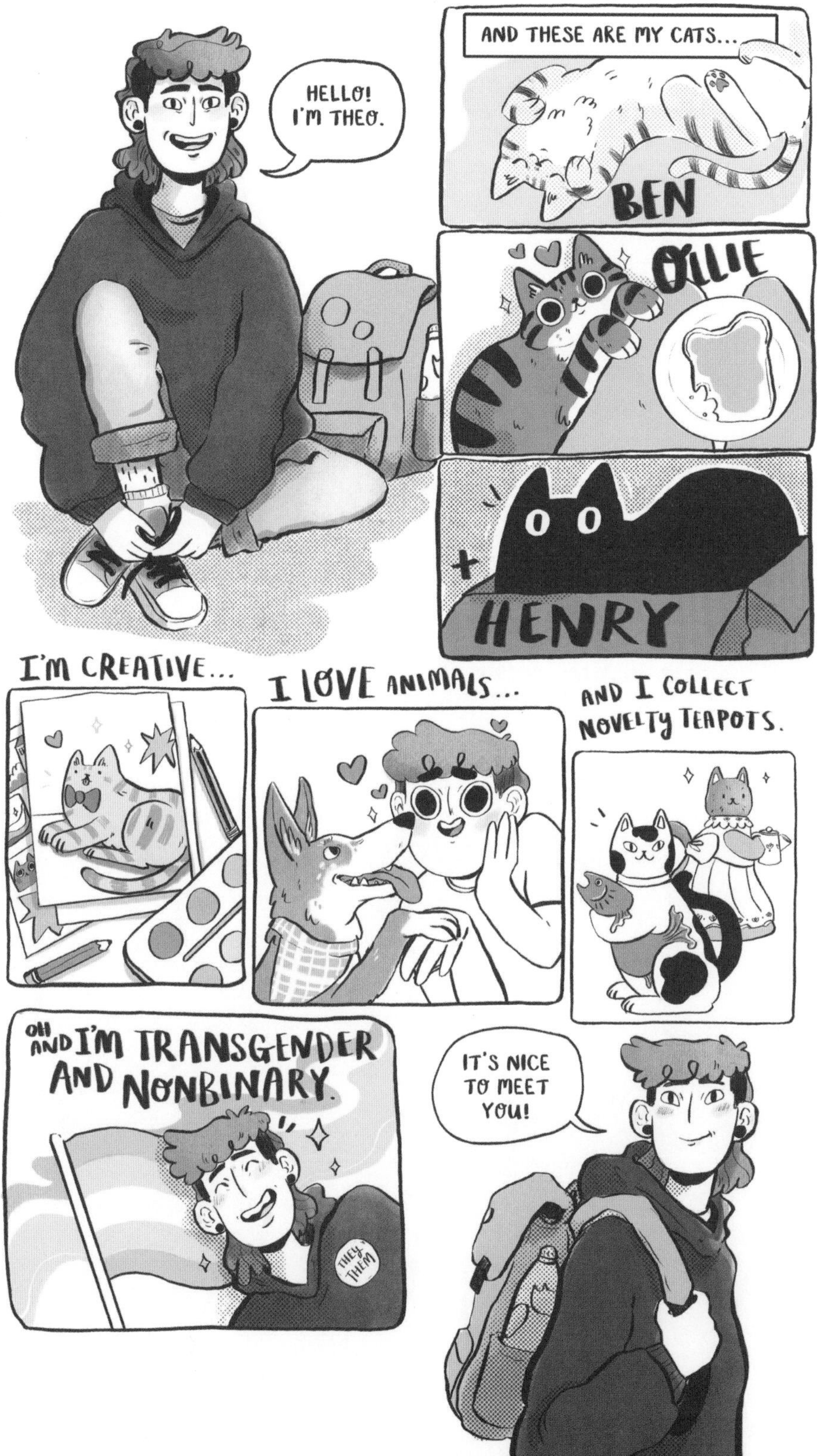
HELLO! I'M THEO.
AND THESE ARE MY CATS...
BEN
OLLIE
+
HENRY
I'M CREATIVE...
I LOVE ANIMALS...
AND I COLLECT NOVELTY TEAPOTS.
OH AND I'M TRANSGENDER AND NONBINARY.
THEY THEM
IT'S NICE TO MEET YOU!

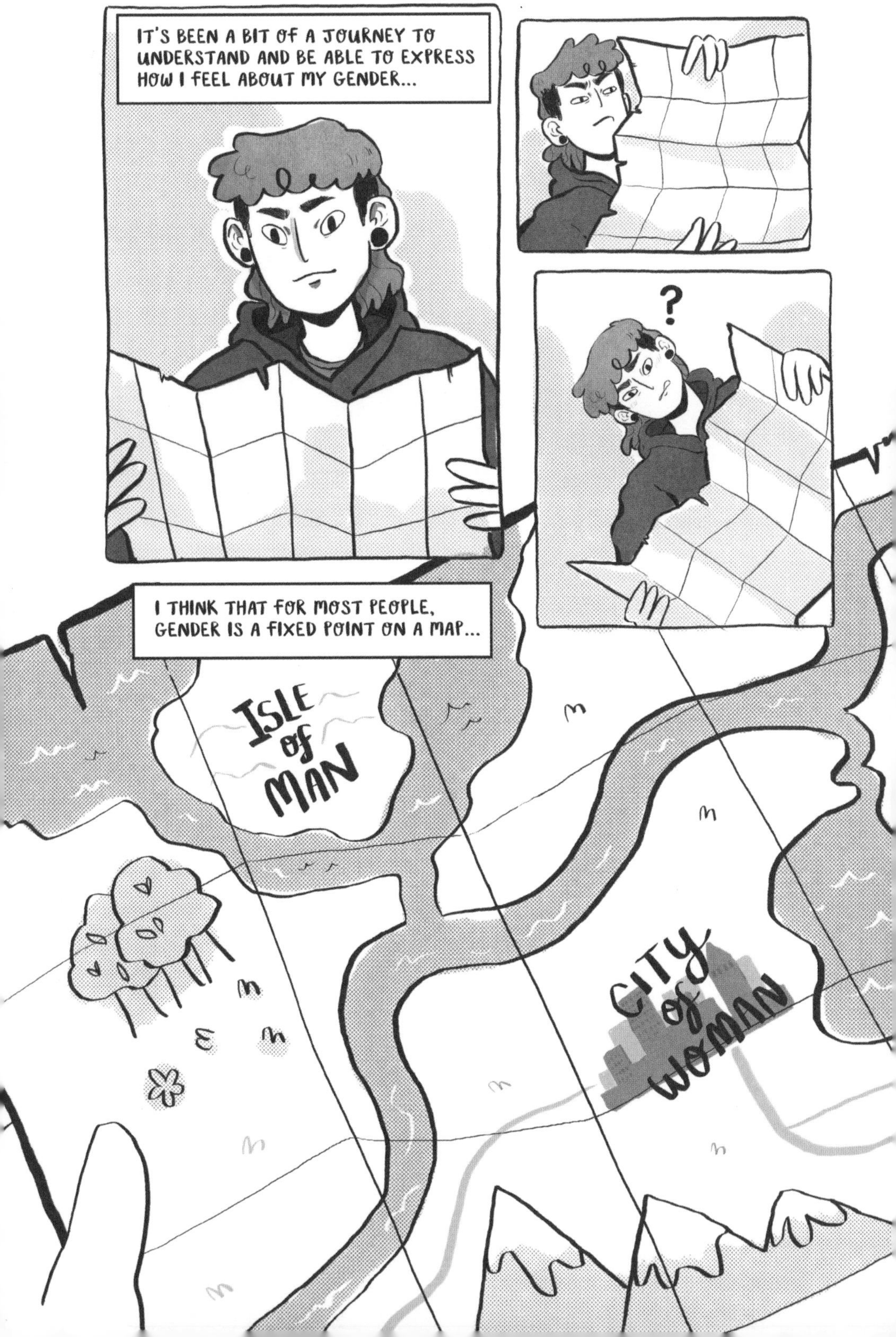
IT'S BEEN A BIT OF A JOURNEY TO UNDERSTAND AND BE ABLE TO EXPRESS HOW I FEEL ABOUT MY GENDER...
?
I THINK THAT FOR MOST PEOPLE, GENDER IS A FIXED POINT ON A MAP...
ISLE of MAN
CITY of WOMAN

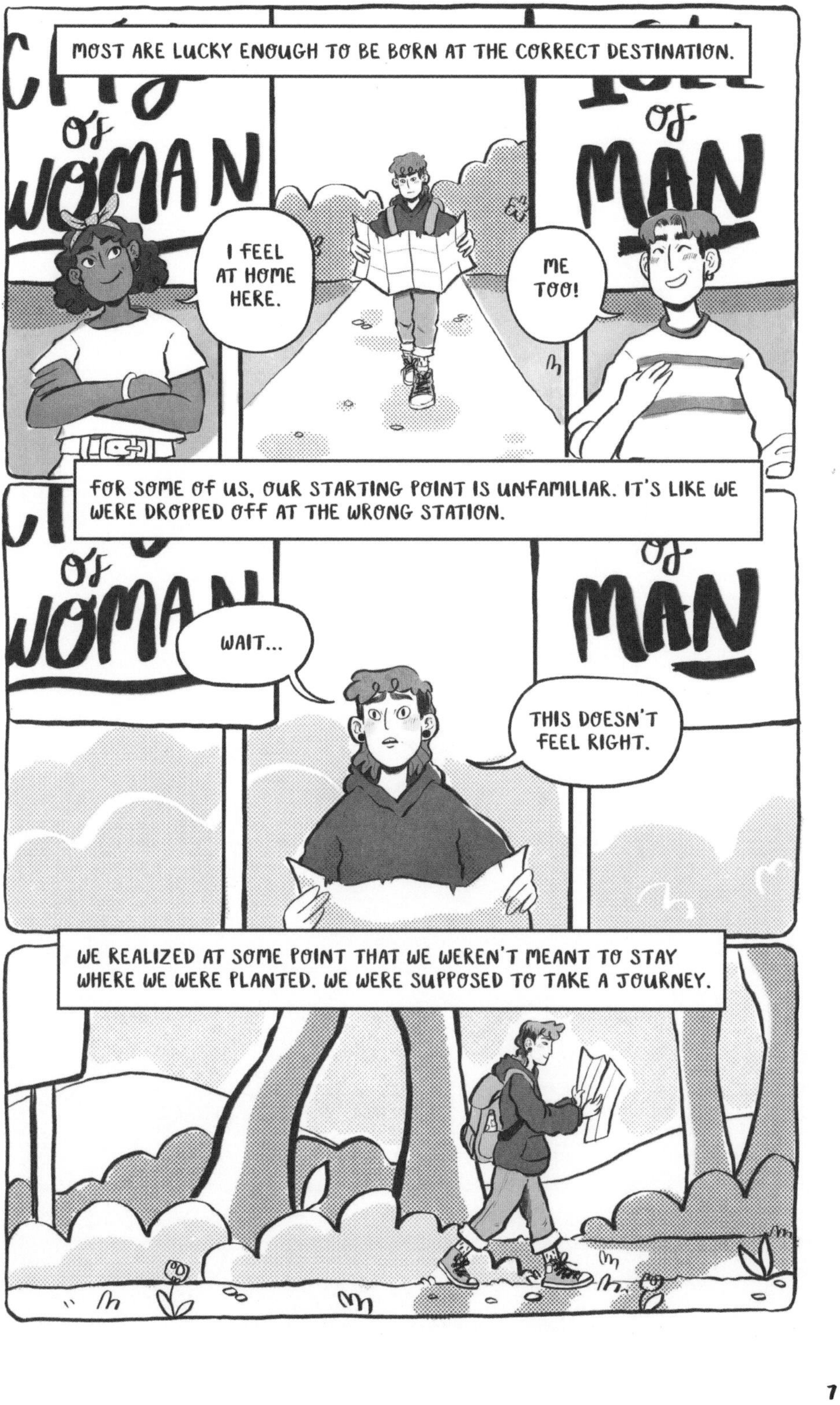
MOST ARE LUCKY ENOUGH TO BE BORN AT THE CORRECT DESTINATION.
OF WOMAN
I FEEL AT HOME HERE.
OF MAN
ME TOO!
FOR SOME OF US, OUR STARTING POINT IS UNFAMILIAR. IT'S LIKE WE WERE DROPPED OFF AT THE WRONG STATION.
OF WOMAN
OF MAN
WAIT...
THIS DOESN'T FEEL RIGHT.
WE REALIZED AT SOME POINT THAT WE WEREN'T MEANT TO STAY WHERE WE WERE PLANTED. WE WERE SUPPOSED TO TAKE A JOURNEY.

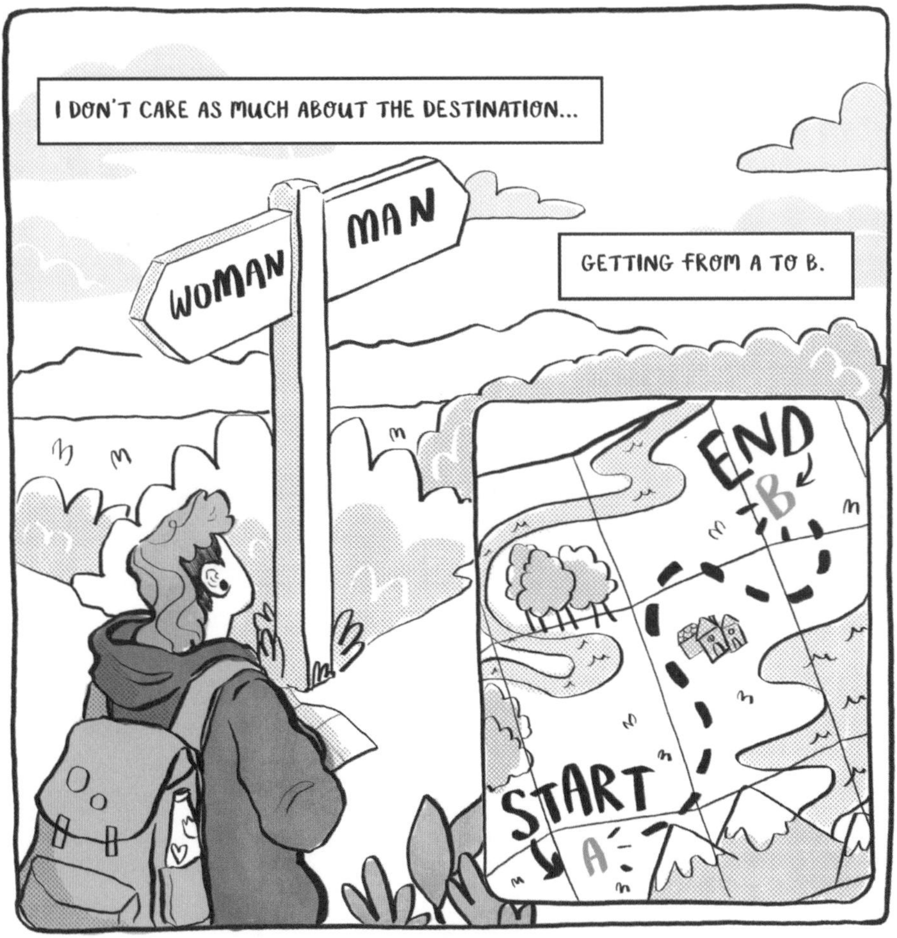
I DON'T CARE AS MUCH ABOUT THE DESTINATION...
WOMAN
MAN
GETTING FROM A TO B.
END
B
START
A

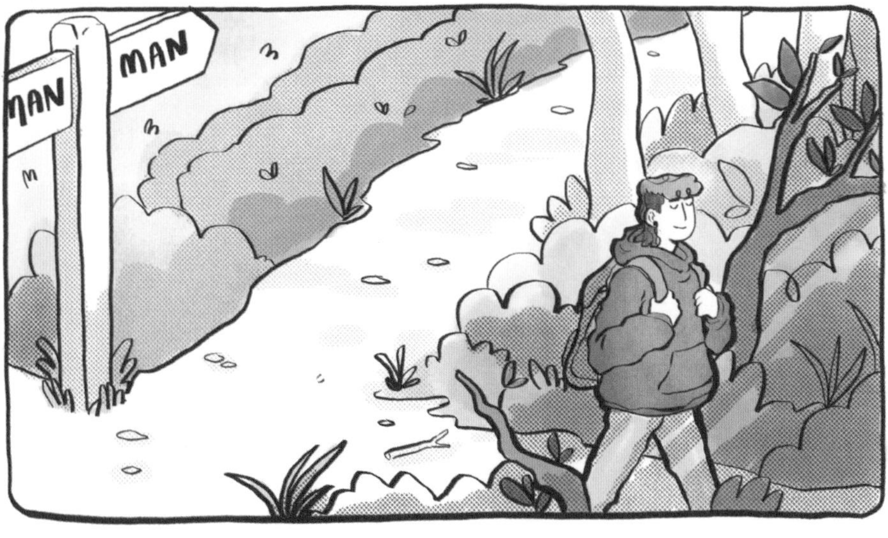
MAN
MAN

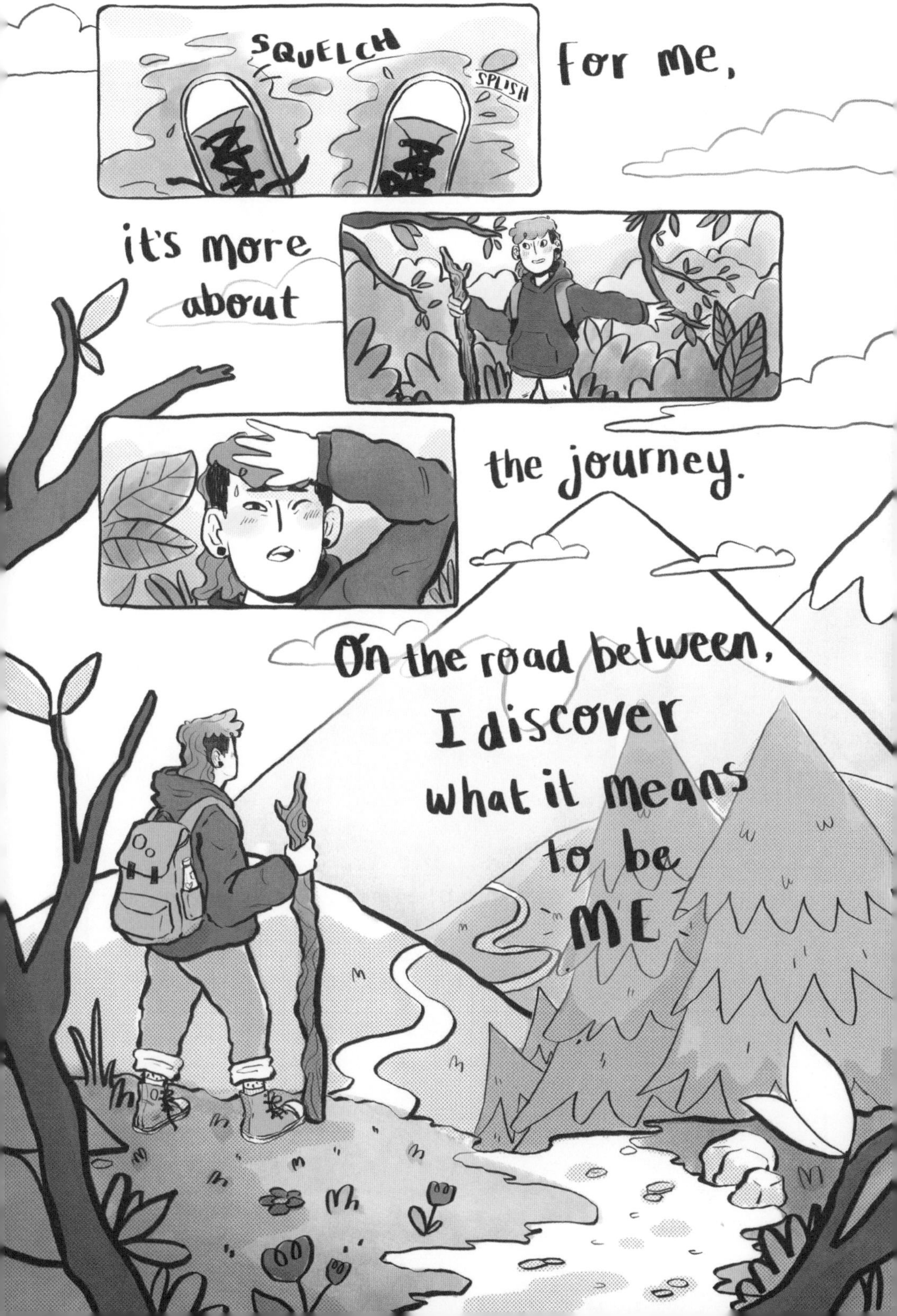
SQUELCH
SPLISH
for me,
it's more about
the journey.
On the road between,
I discover
what it means
to be
ME

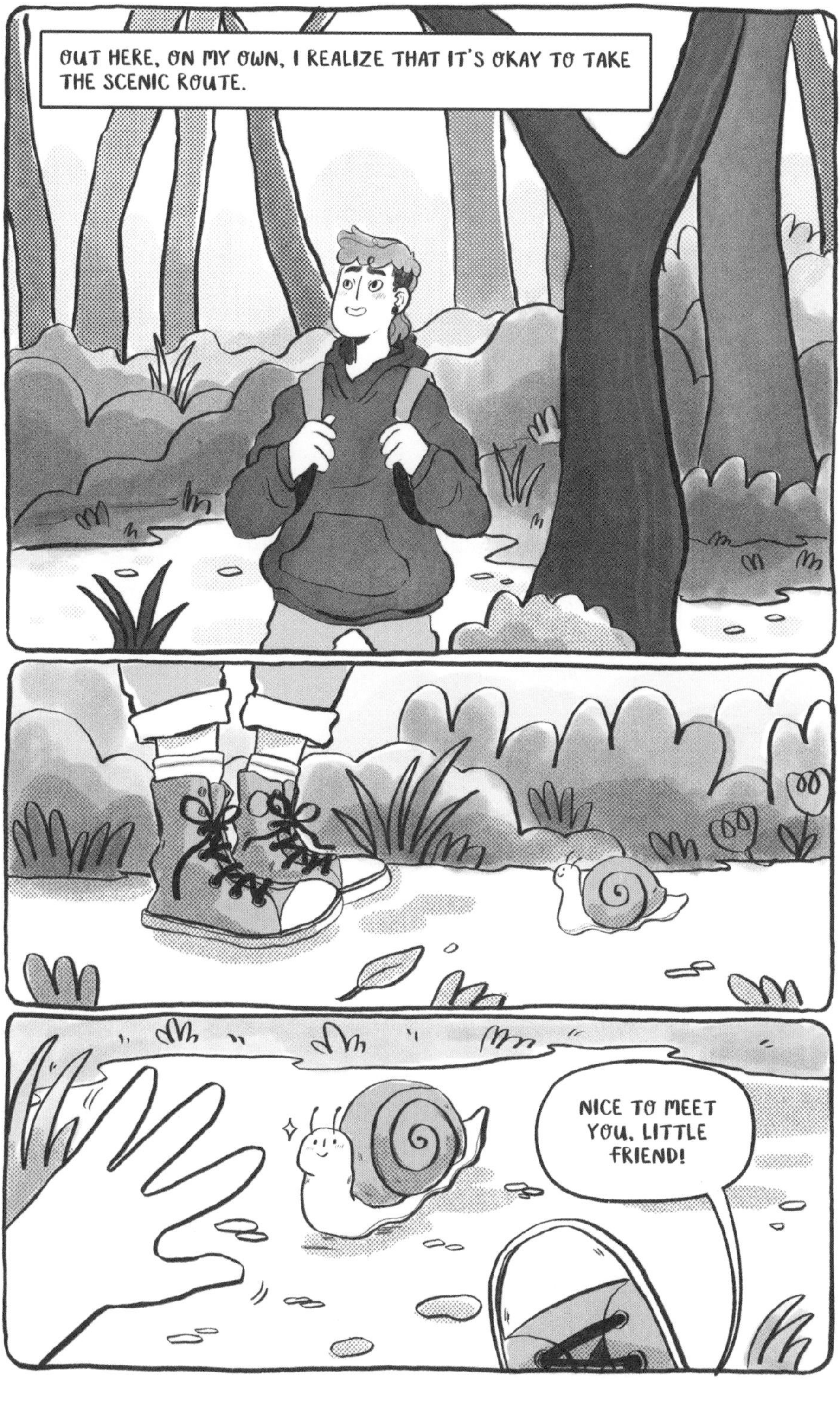
OUT HERE, ON MY OWN, I REALIZE THAT IT'S OKAY TO TAKE THE SCENIC ROUTE.
NICE TO MEET YOU, LITTLE FRIEND!

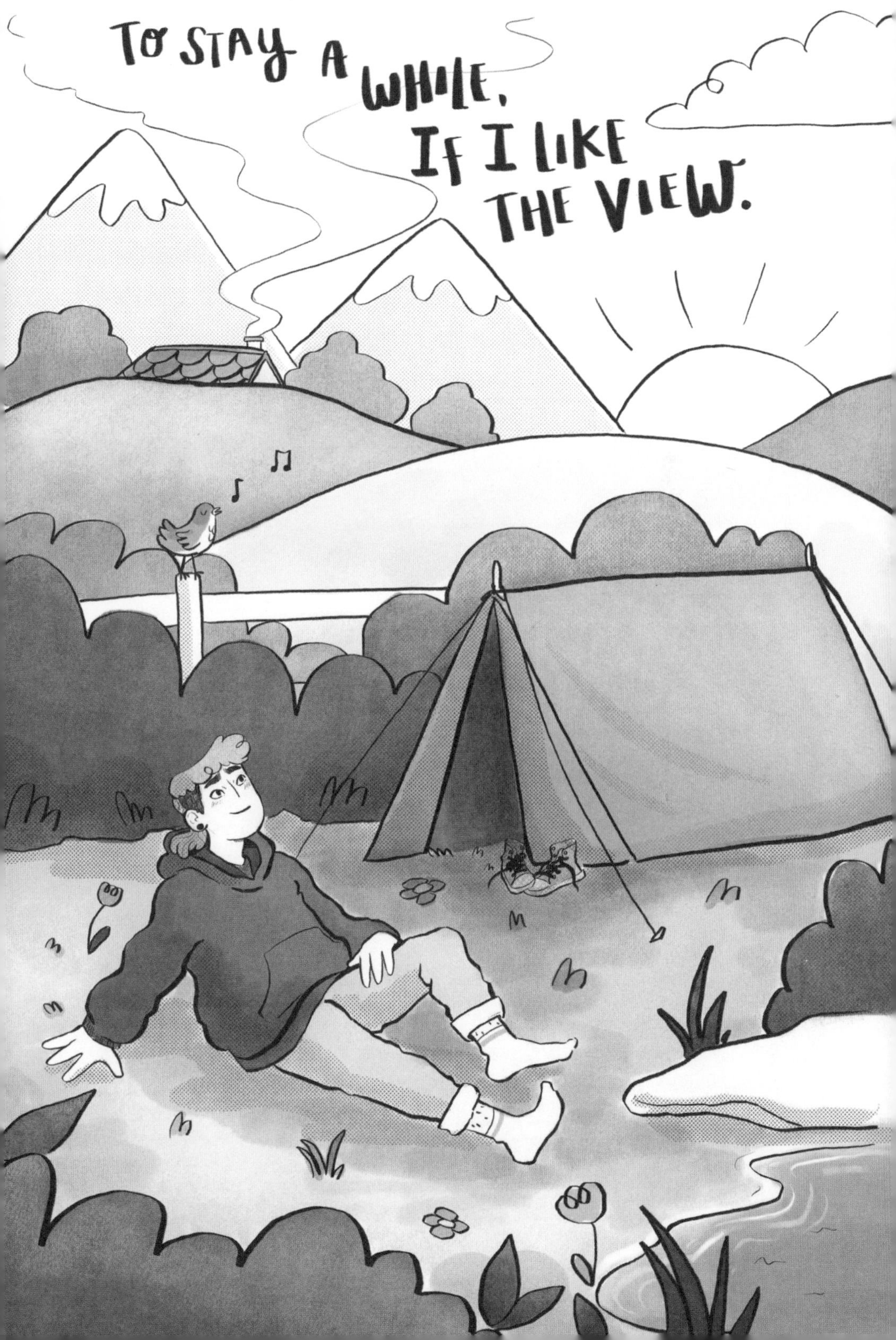
TO STAY A WHILE,
IF I LIKE
THE VIEW.

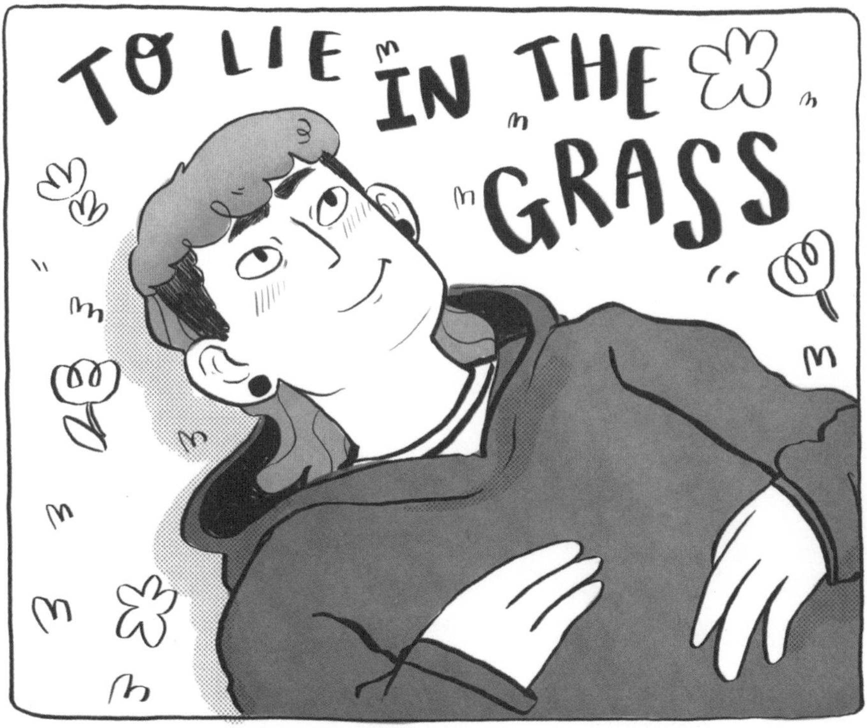
TO LIE IN THE GRASS

TAKE IN THE UNIVERSE
HANGING OVER ME

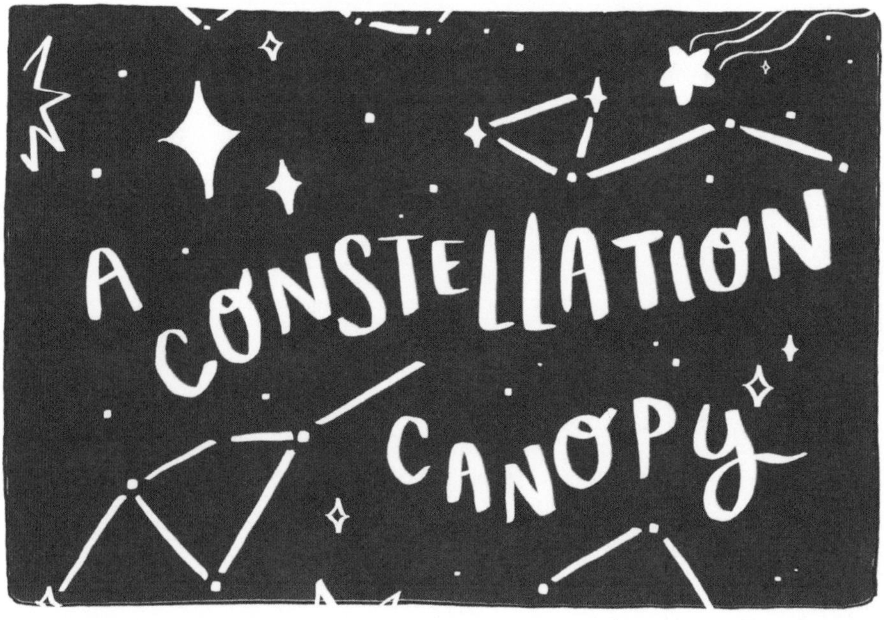
A CONSTELLATION CANOPY

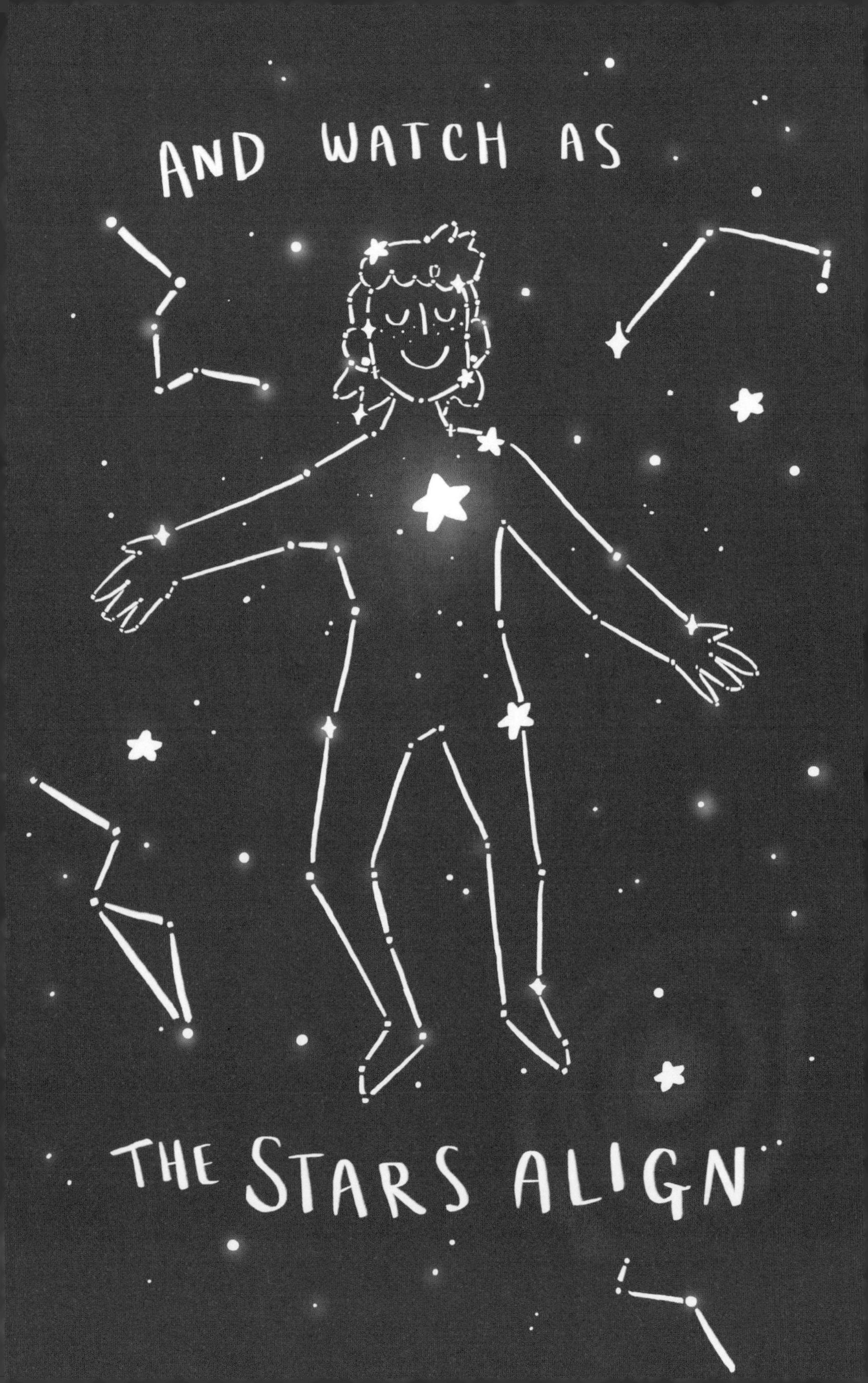
AND WATCH AS
THE STARS ALIGN

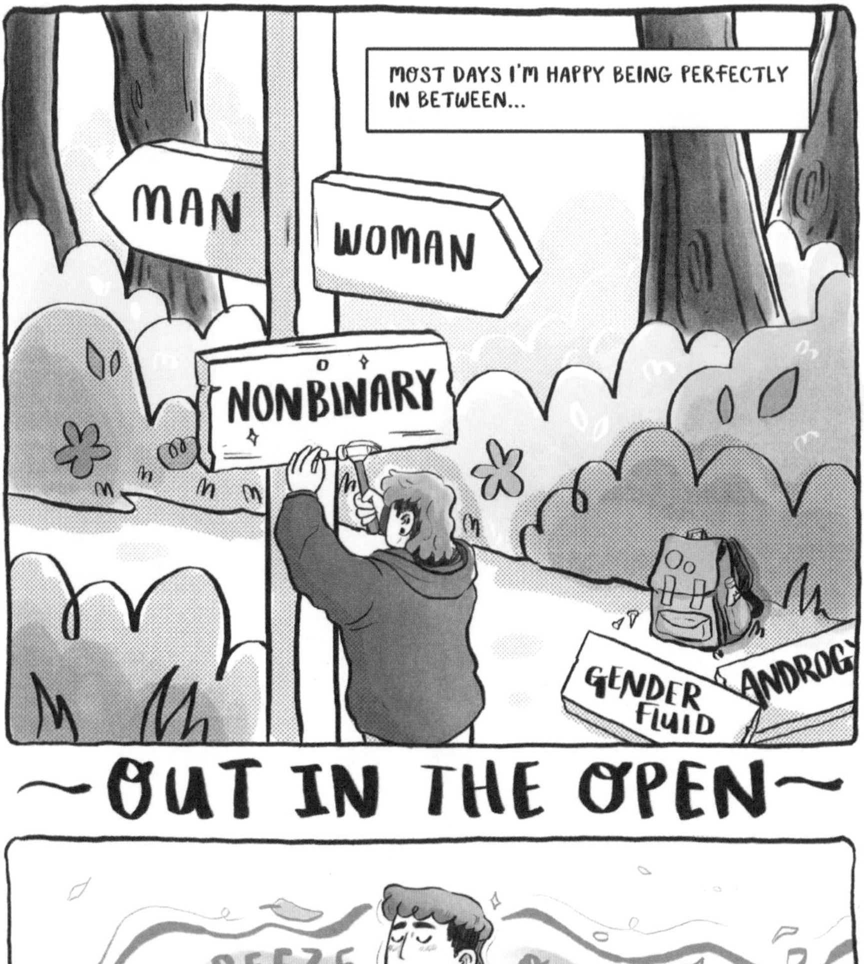
MOST DAYS I'M HAPPY BEING PERFECTLY IN BETWEEN...
MAN
WOMAN
NONBINARY
GENDER FLUID
ANDROGY

~OUT IN THE OPEN~

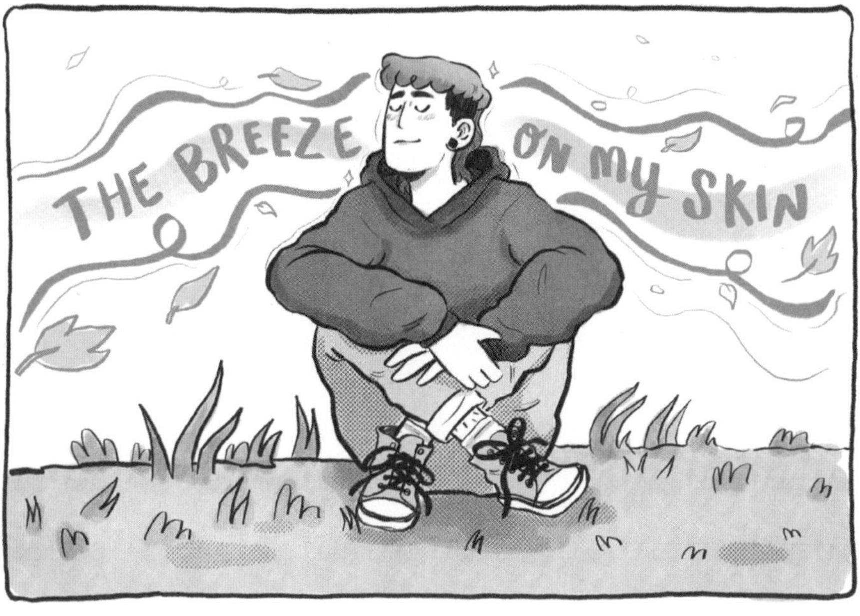
THE BREEZE ON MY SKIN

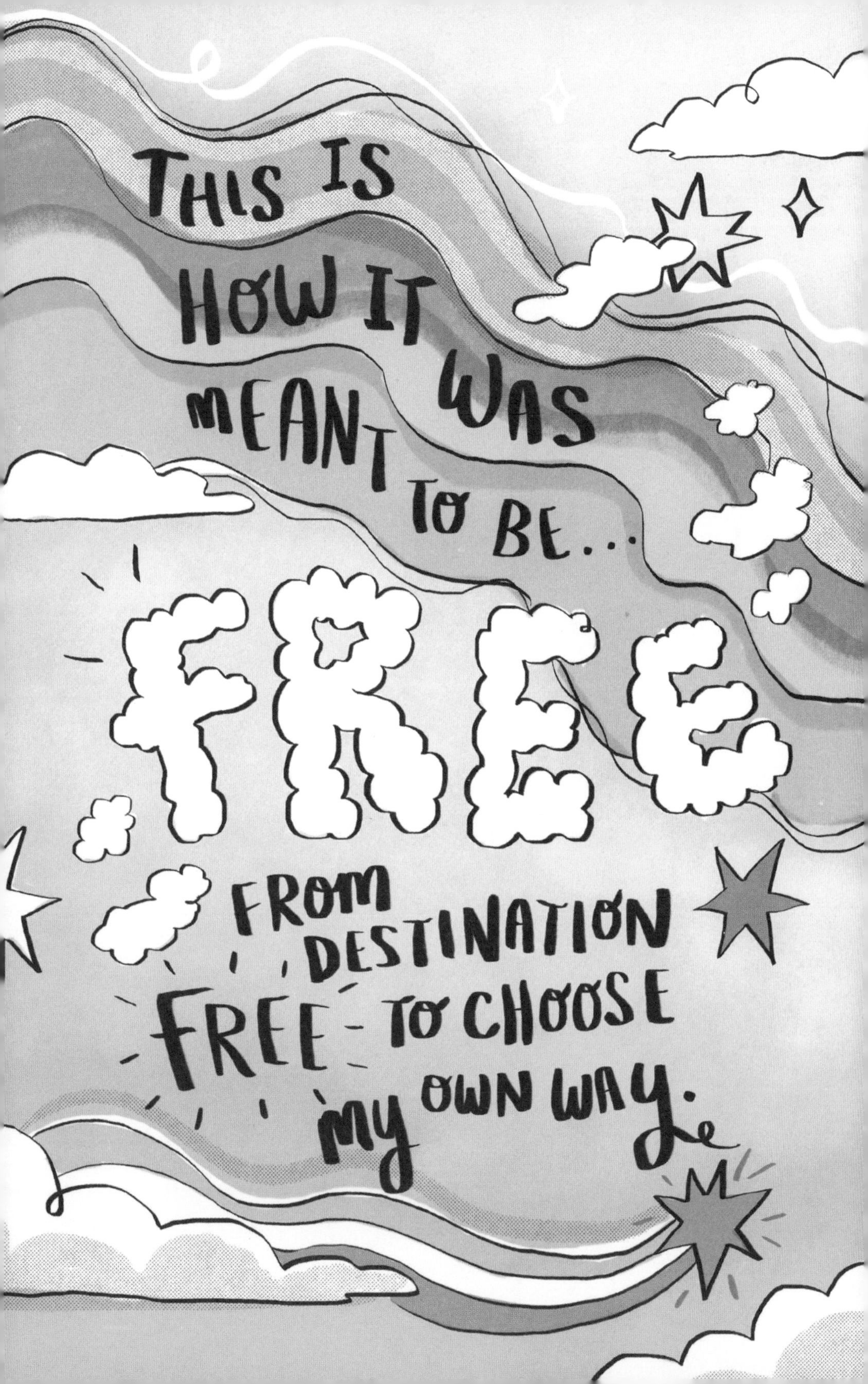
THIS IS HOW IT WAS MEANT TO BE...
FREE
FROM DESTINATION
FREE TO CHOOSE
MY OWN WAY.

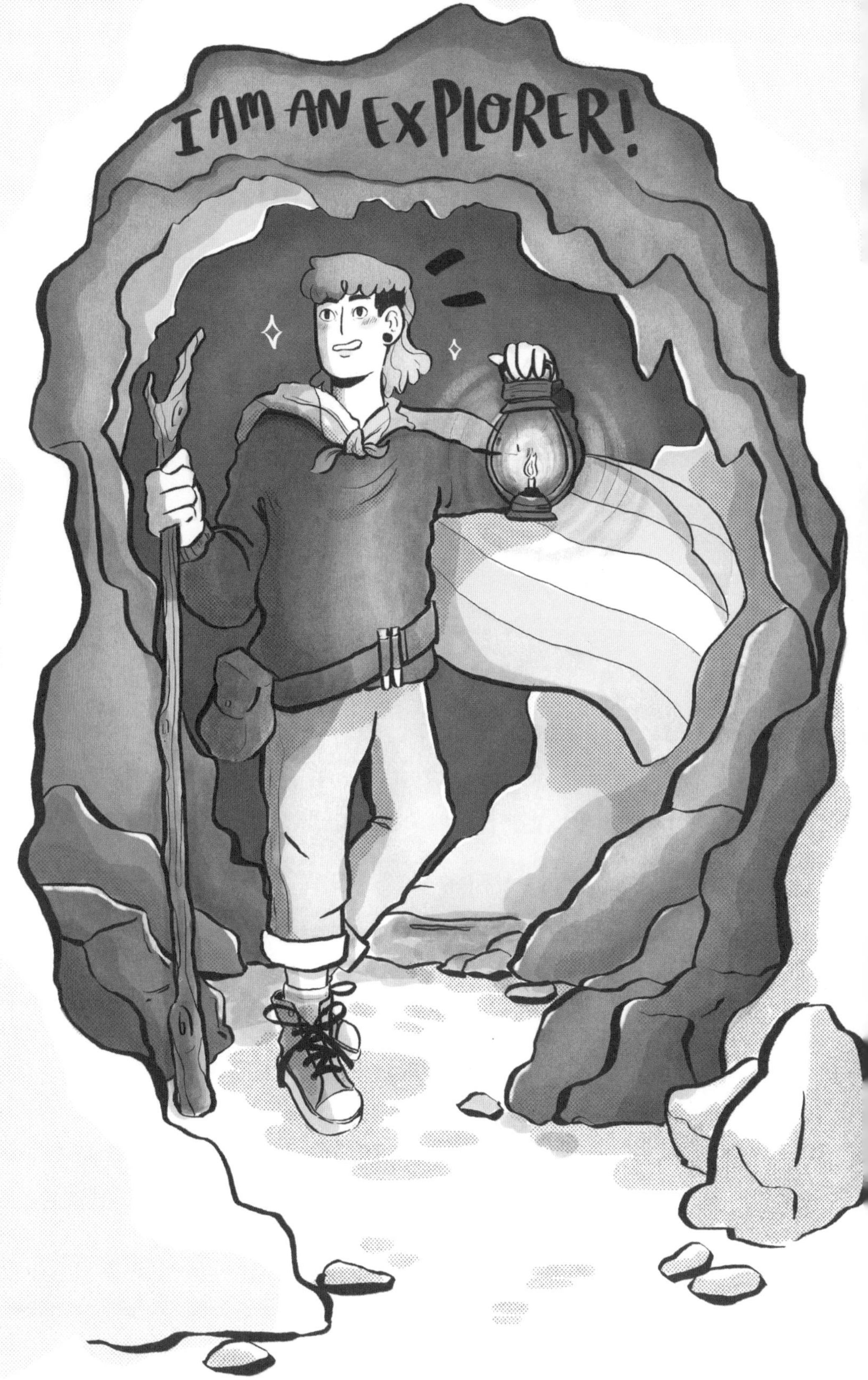
I AM AN EXPLORER!

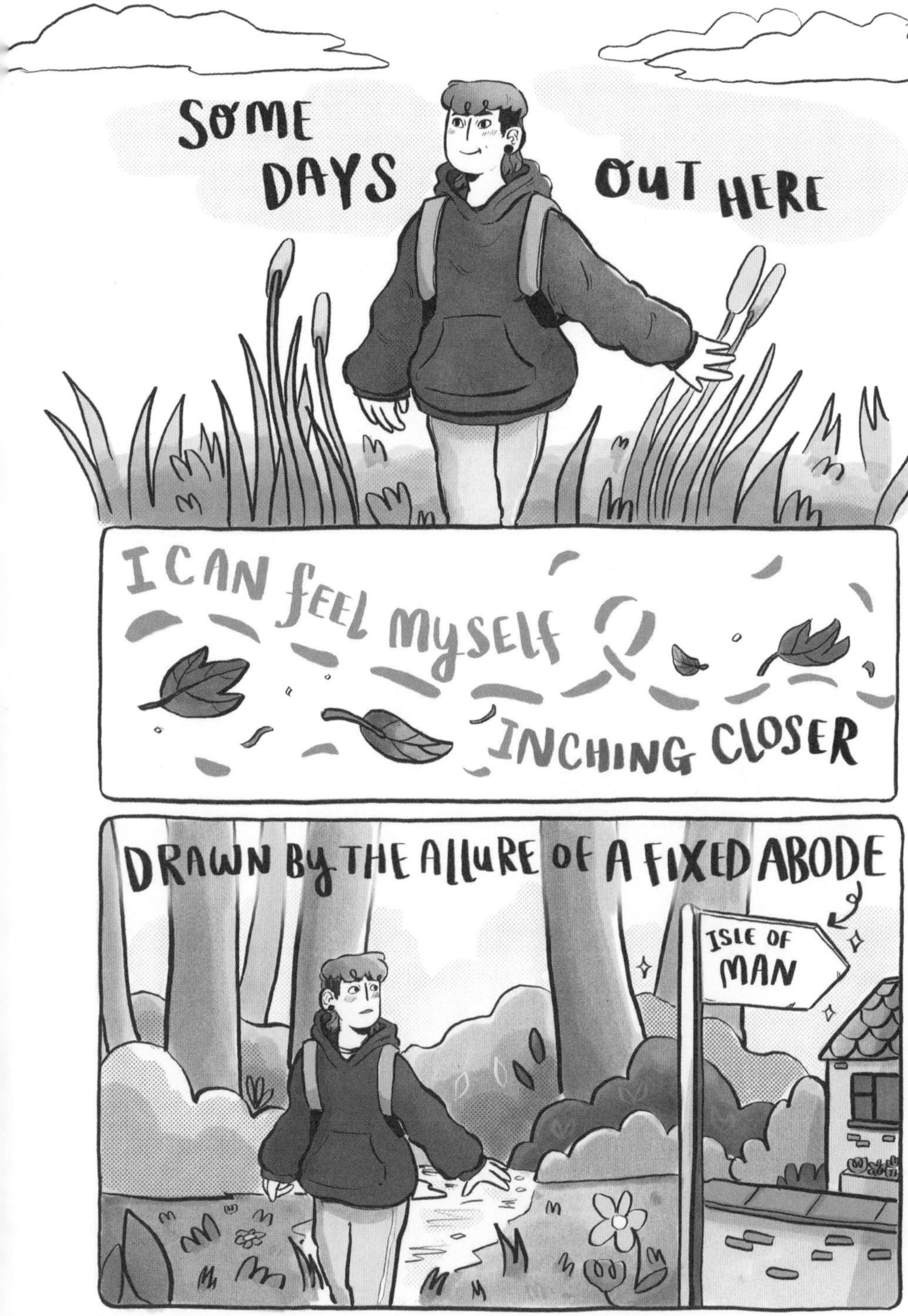
SOME DAYS OUT HERE
I CAN FEEL MYSELF
INCHING CLOSER
DRAWN BY THE ALLURE OF A FIXED ABODE
ISLE OF MAN

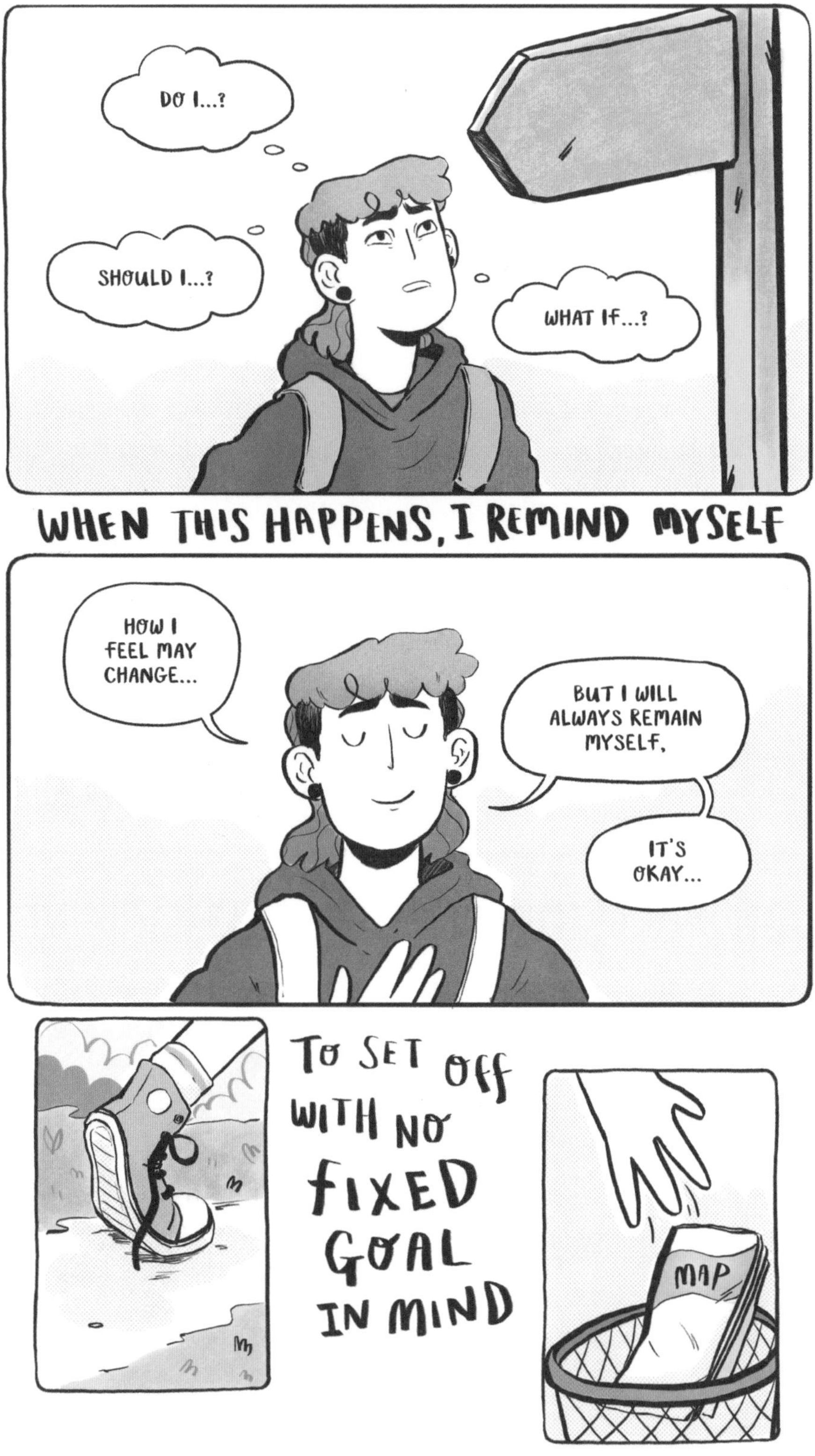
DO I...?
SHOULD I...?
WHAT IF...?
WHEN THIS HAPPENS, I REMIND MYSELF
HOW I FEEL MAY CHANGE...
BUT I WILL ALWAYS REMAIN MYSELF,
IT'S OKAY...
TO SET OFF WITH NO FIXED GOAL IN MIND
MAP

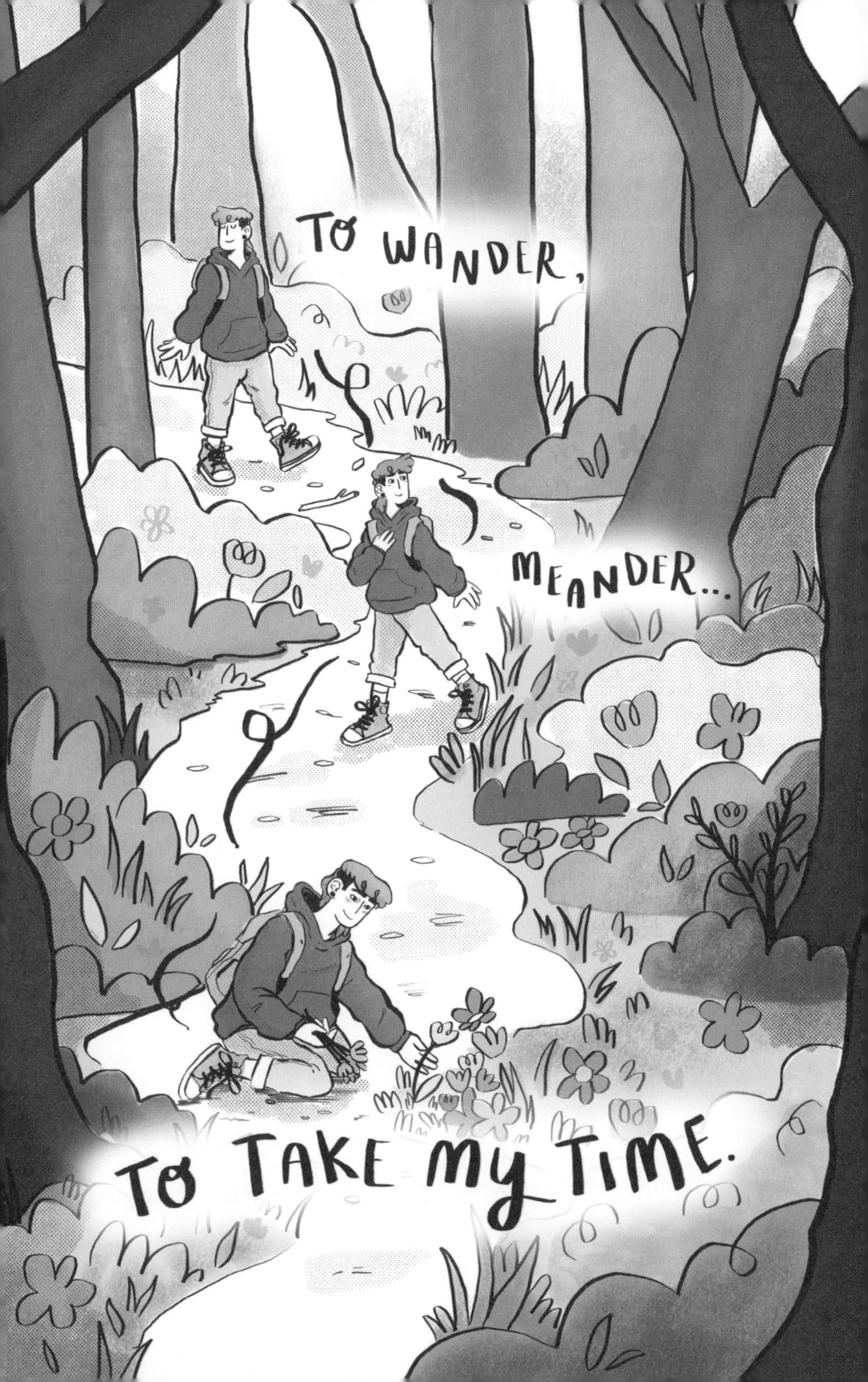
TO WANDER,
MEANDER...
TO TAKE MY TIME.

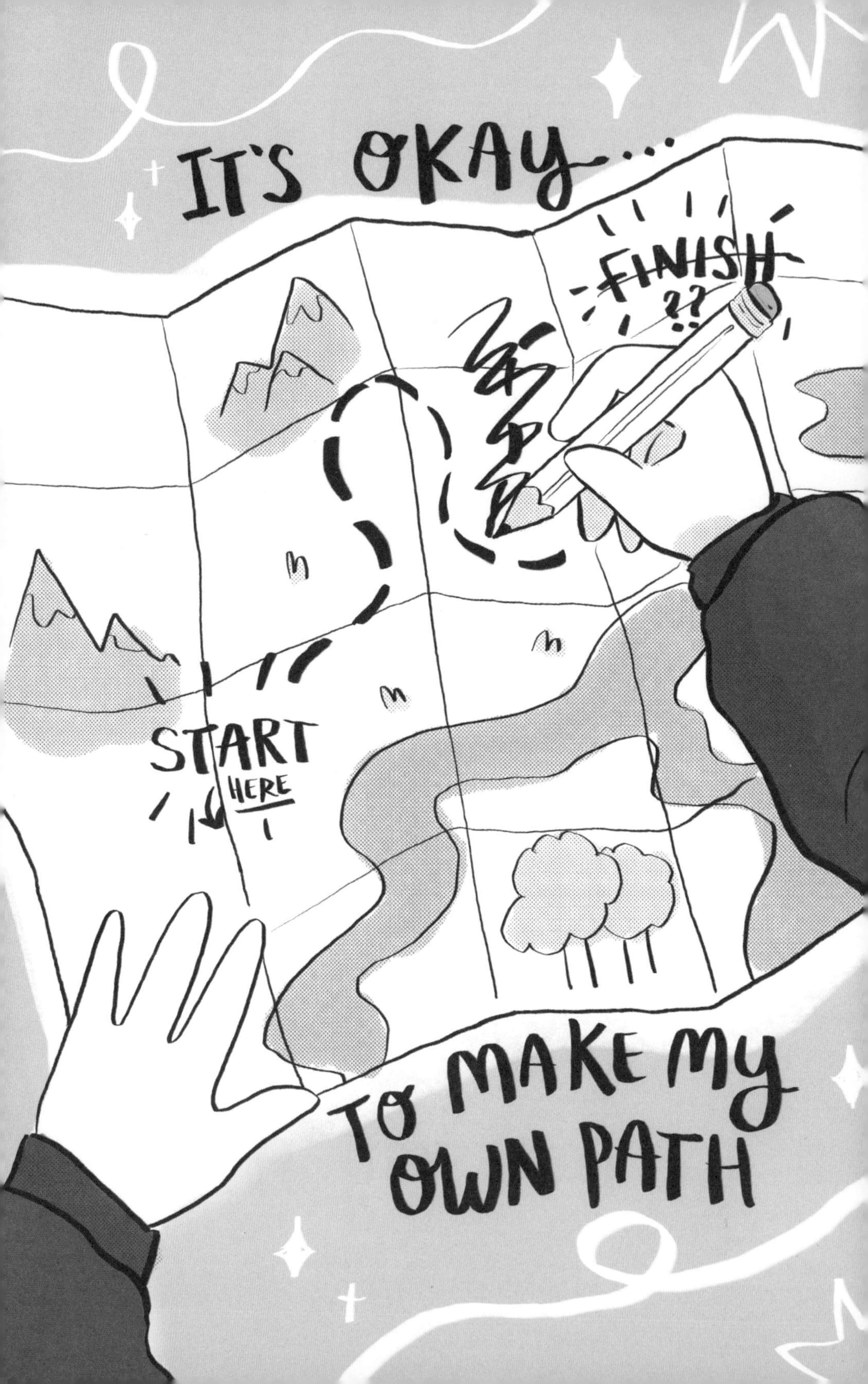
IT'S OKAY....
FINISH
??
START
HERE
TO MAKE MY
OWN PATH

TO BEGIN GOING SOMEWHERE...

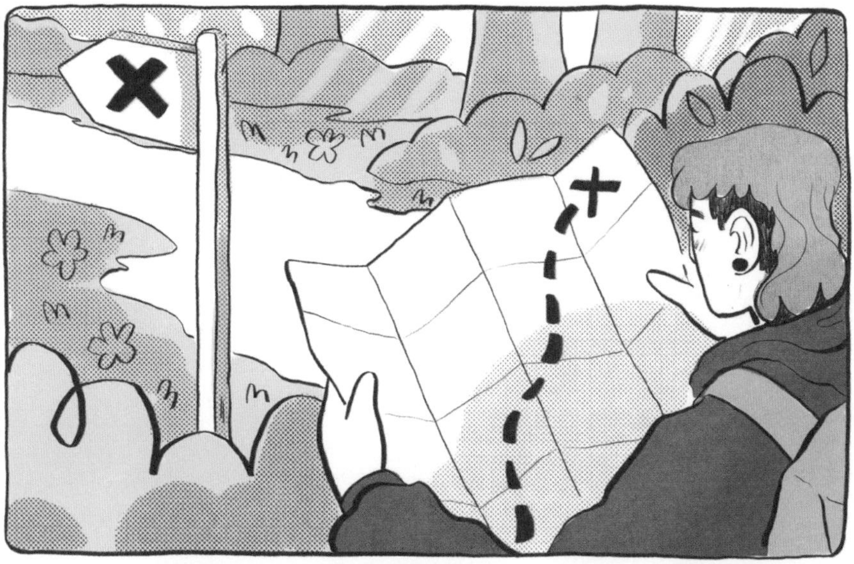

THEN CHANGE MY MIND.

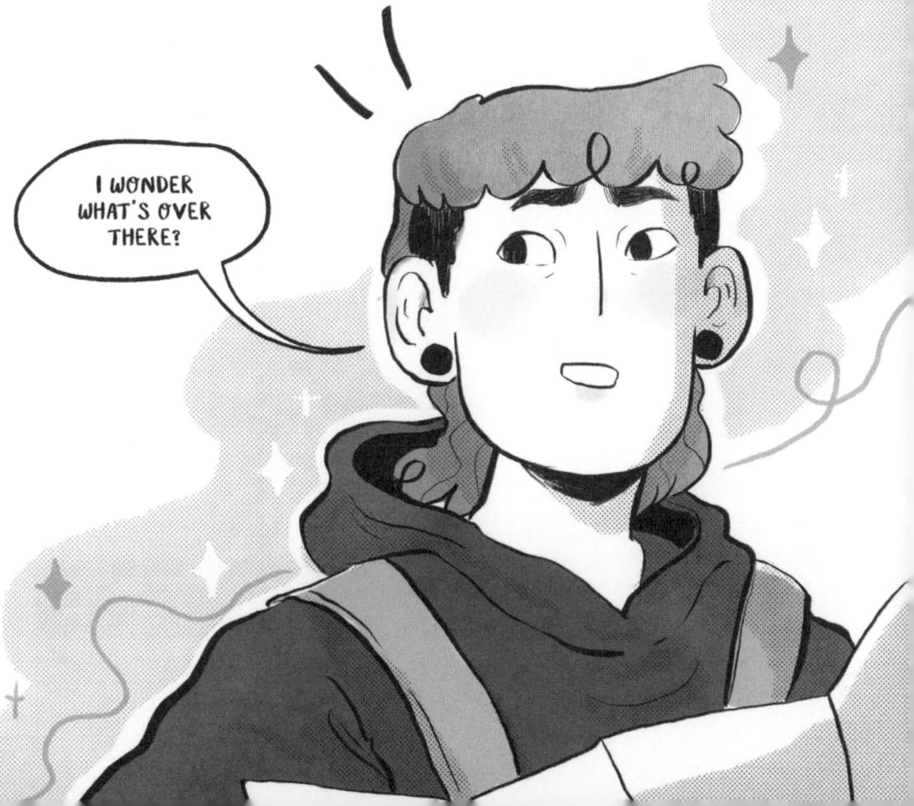
I WONDER WHAT'S OVER THERE?

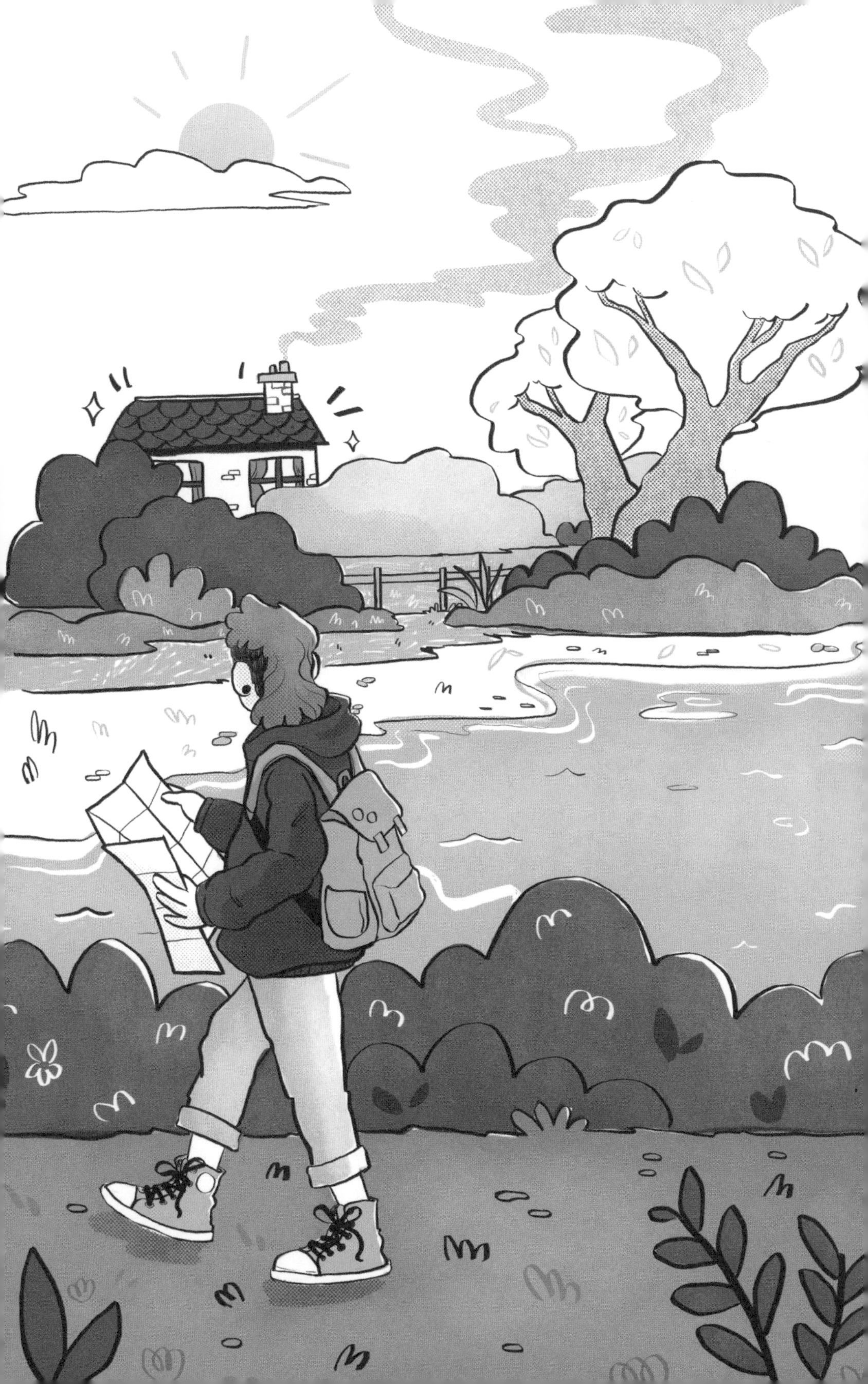

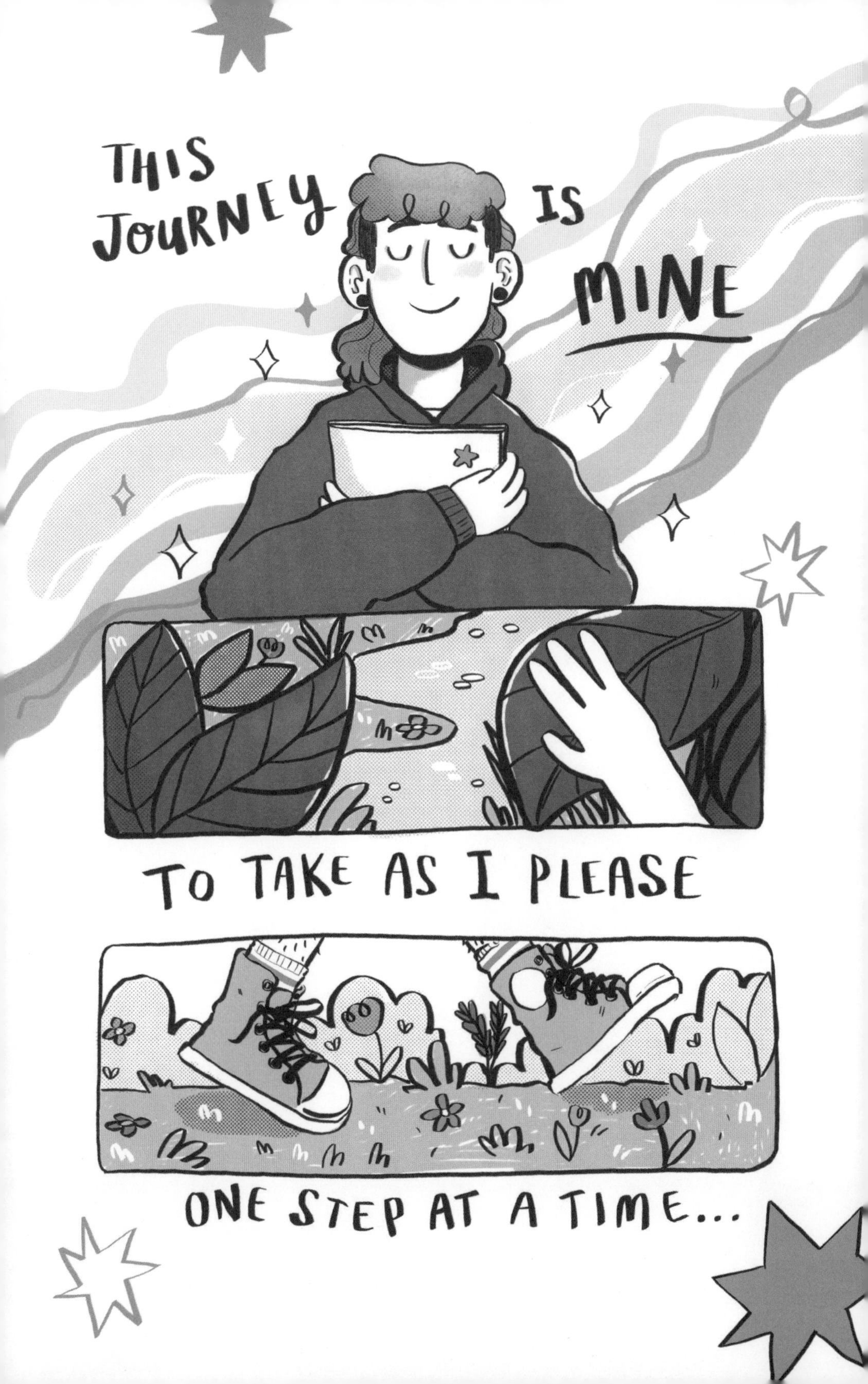
THIS JOURNEY IS MINE
TO TAKE AS I PLEASE
ONE STEP AT A TIME...

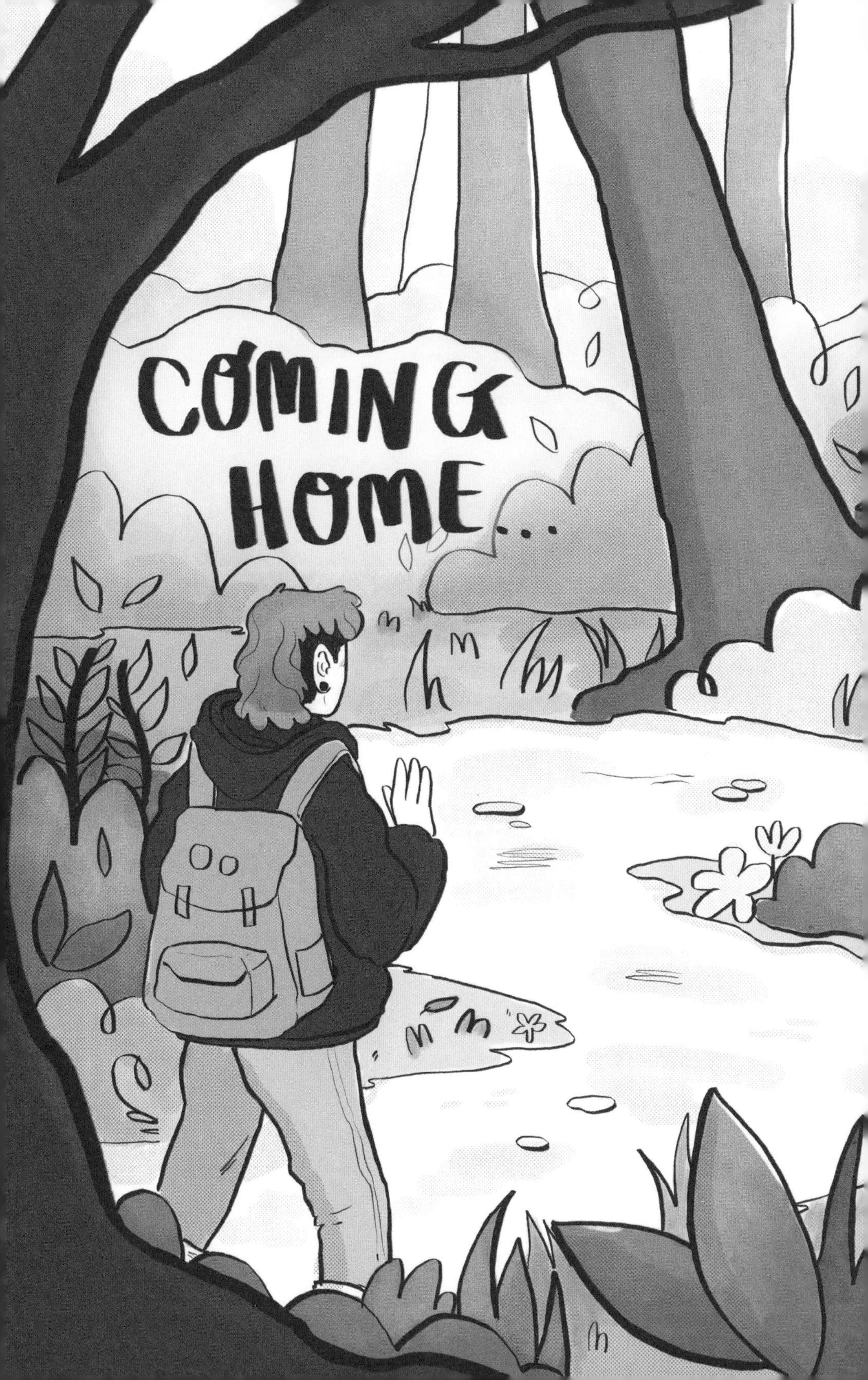
COMING HOME...

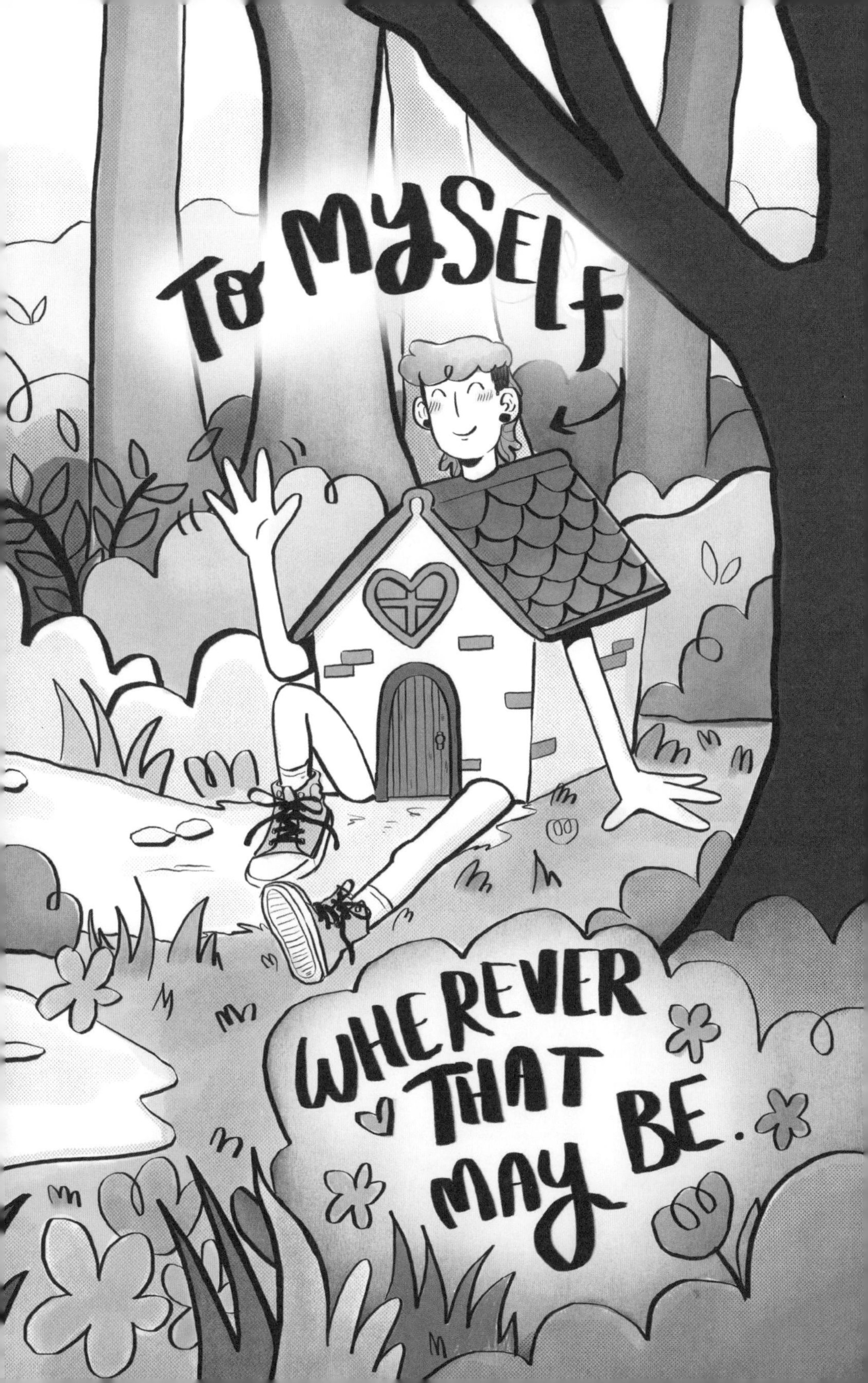
TO MYSELF
WHEREVER THAT MAY BE.

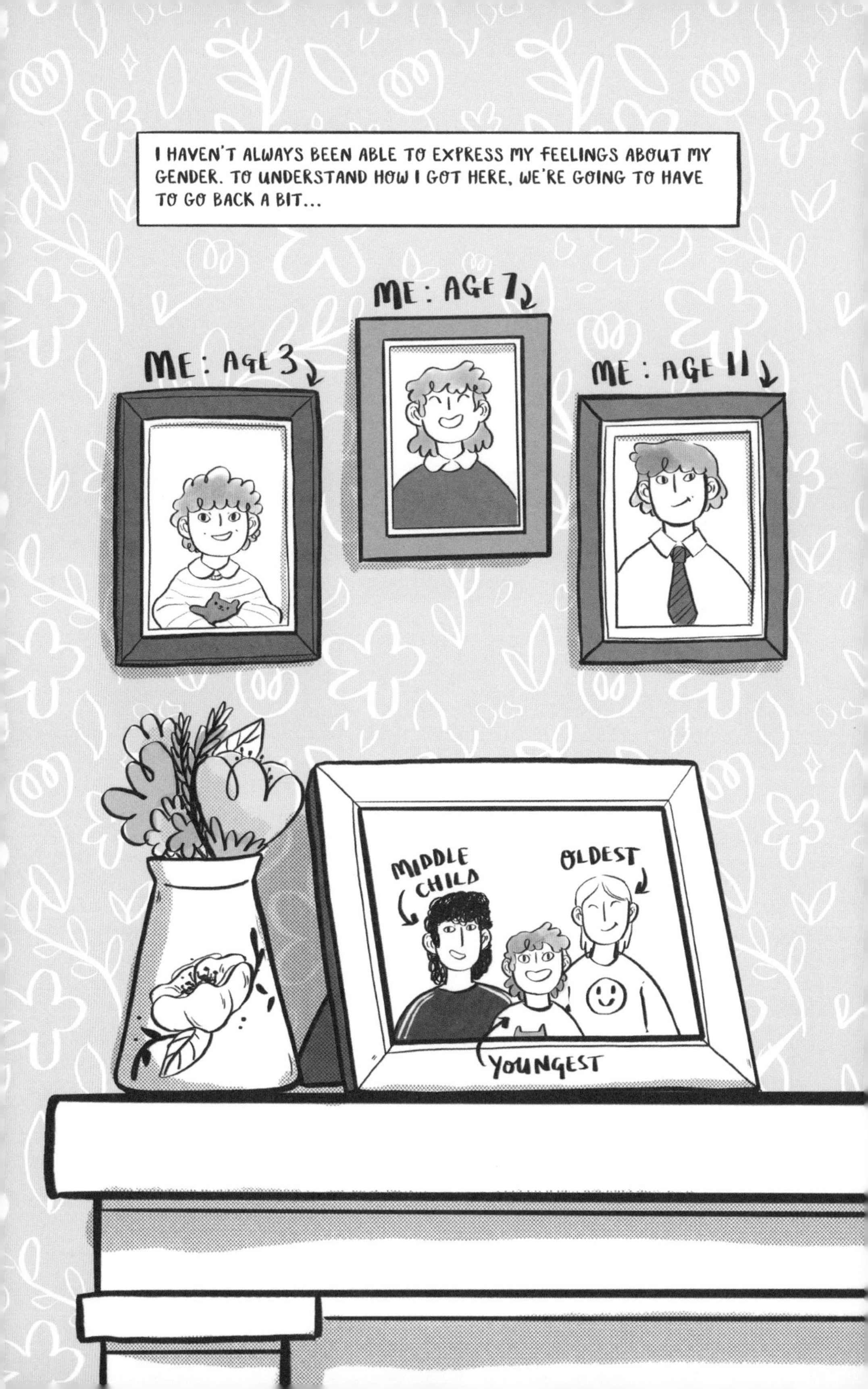
I HAVEN'T ALWAYS BEEN ABLE TO EXPRESS MY FEELINGS ABOUT MY GENDER. TO UNDERSTAND HOW I GOT HERE, WE'RE GOING TO HAVE TO GO BACK A BIT...
ME: AGE 3
ME: AGE 7
ME: AGE 11
MIDDLE CHILD
OLDEST
YOUNGEST

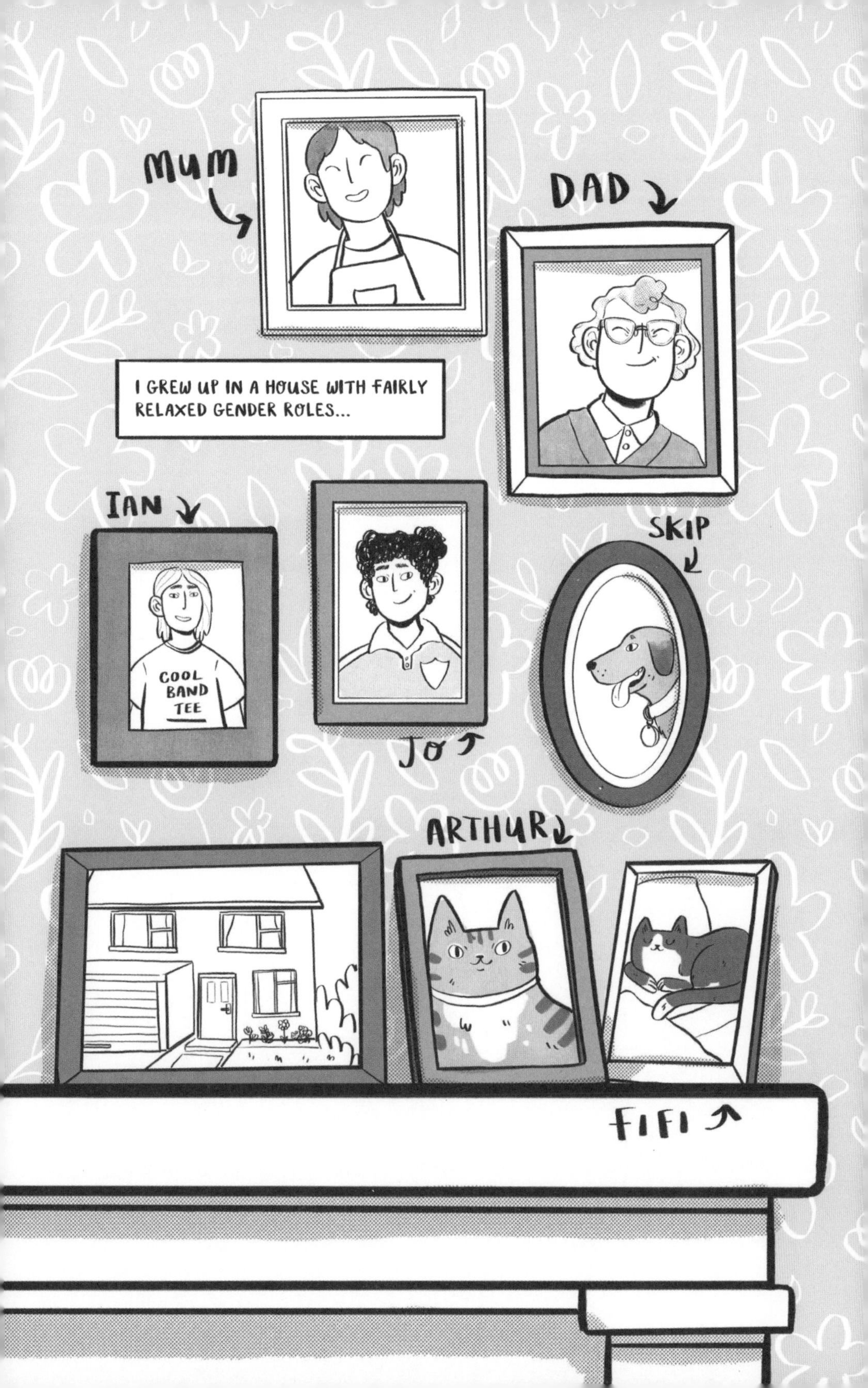
MUM
DAD
I GREW UP IN A HOUSE WITH FAIRLY RELAXED GENDER ROLES...
IAN
COOL BAND TEE
JO
SKIP
ARTHUR
FIFI

MY MUM IS PRACTICAL AND KIND.

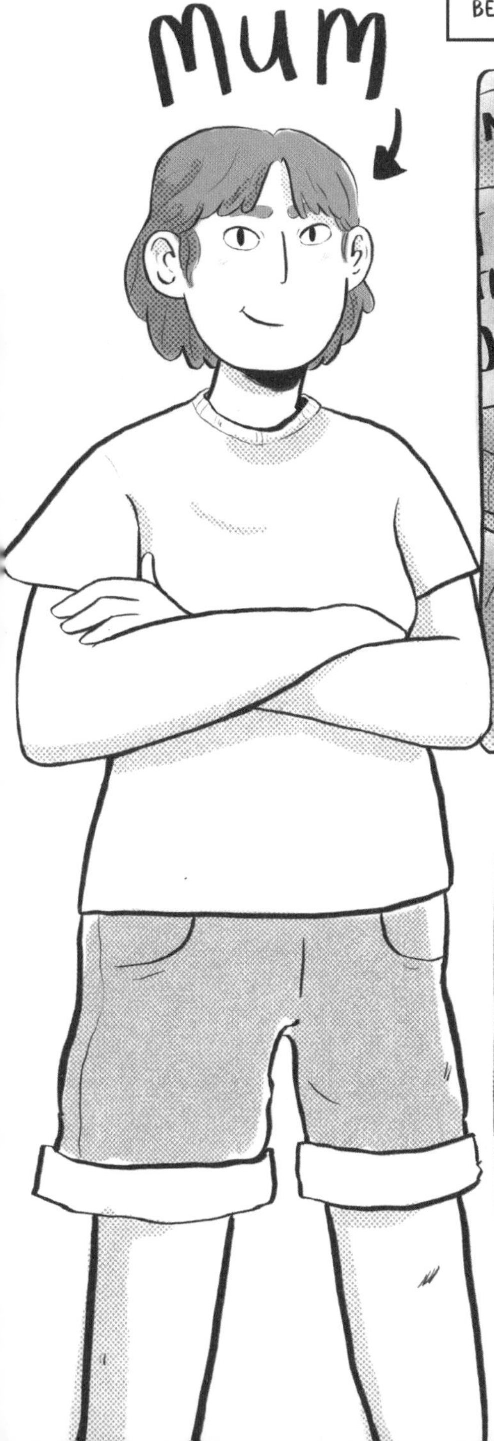
MUM

SHE ALWAYS STANDS UP FOR WHAT SHE BELIEVES IN.

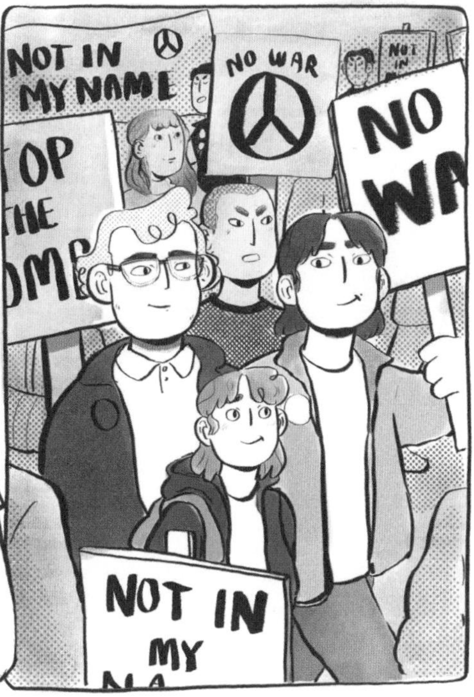
NOT IN MY NAME
NO WAR
NO WA
NOT IN MY

SHE LIKES GARDENING...

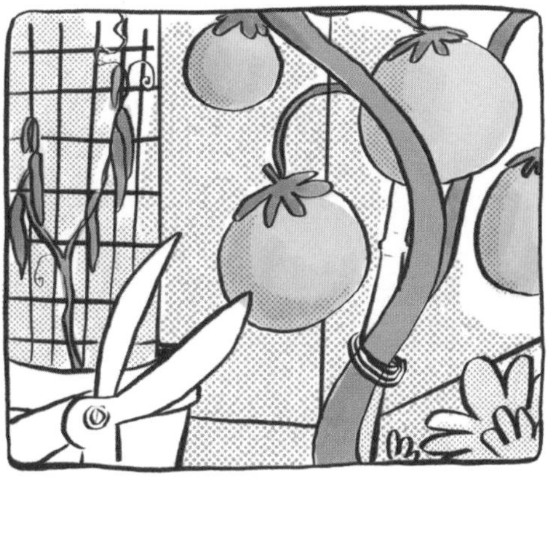

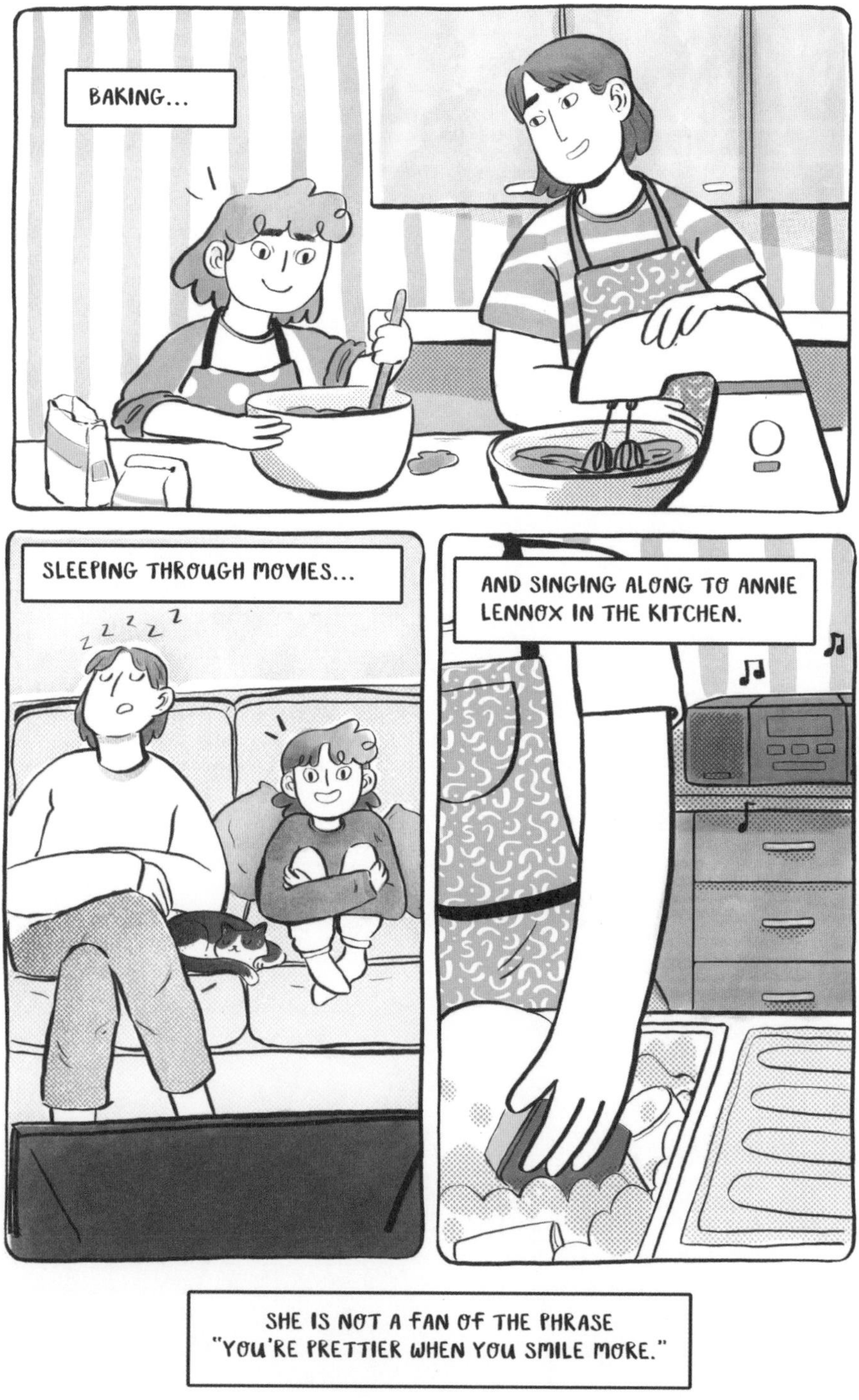
BAKING...
SLEEPING THROUGH MOVIES...
AND SINGING ALONG TO ANNIE LENNOX IN THE KITCHEN.
SHE IS NOT A FAN OF THE PHRASE "YOU'RE PRETTIER WHEN YOU SMILE MORE."

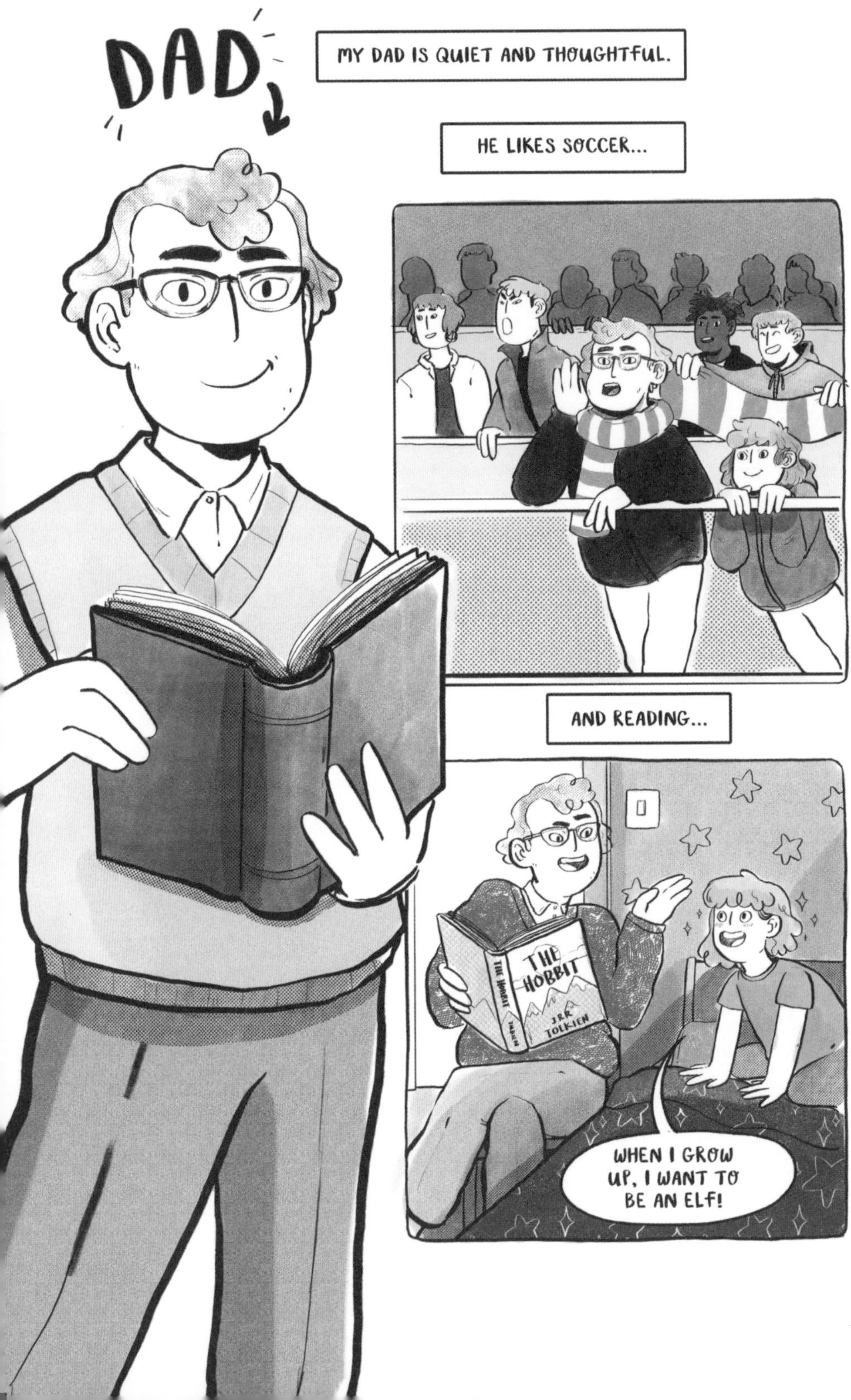
DAD
MY DAD IS QUIET AND THOUGHTFUL.
HE LIKES SOCCER...
AND READING...
THE HOBBIT
J.R.R. TOLKIEN
WHEN I GROW UP, I WANT TO BE AN ELF!

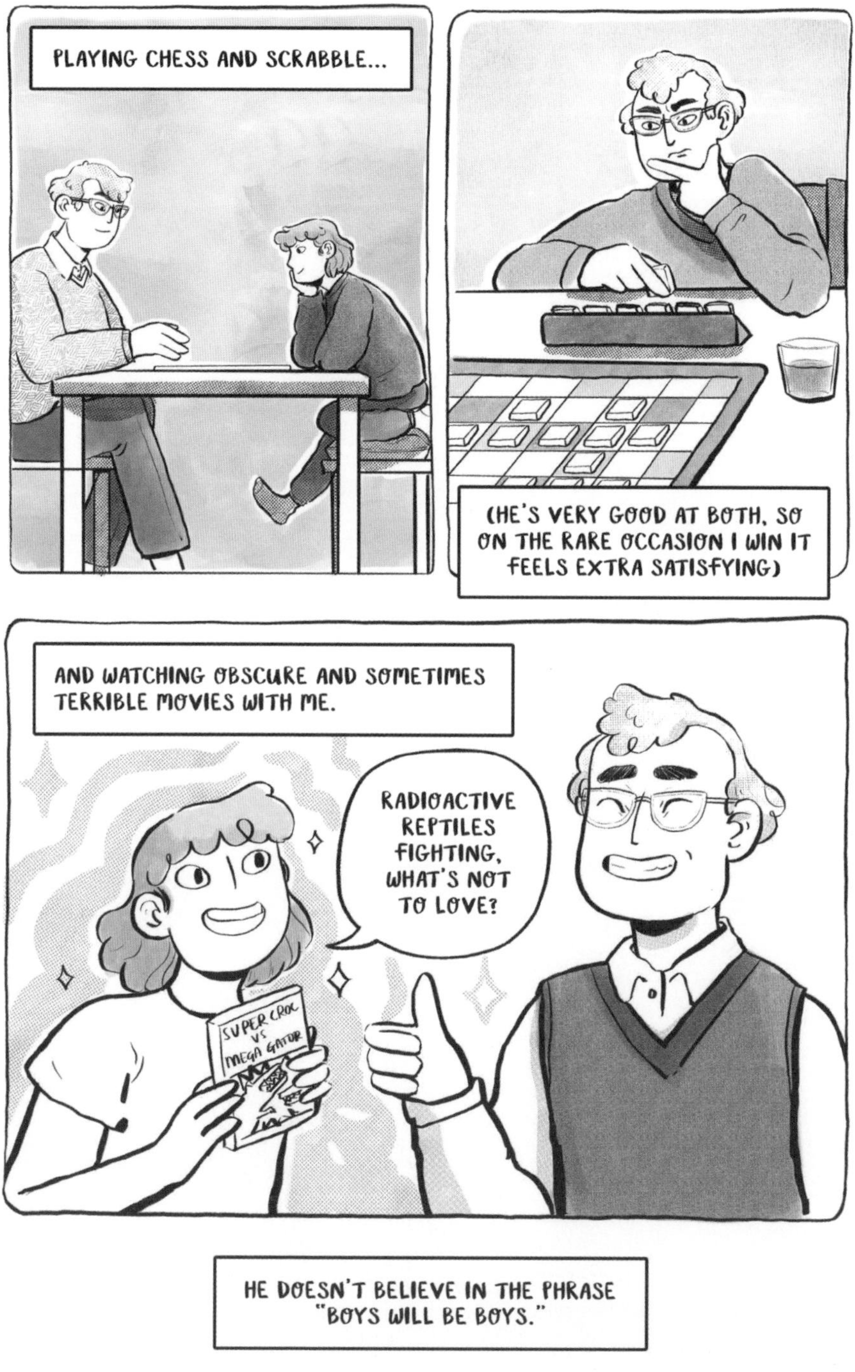
PLAYING CHESS AND SCRABBLE...
(HE'S VERY GOOD AT BOTH, SO ON THE RARE OCCASION I WIN IT FEELS EXTRA SATISFYING)
AND WATCHING OBSCURE AND SOMETIMES TERRIBLE MOVIES WITH ME.
RADIOACTIVE REPTILES FIGHTING, WHAT'S NOT TO LOVE?
SUPER CROC VS MEGA GATOR
HE DOESN'T BELIEVE IN THE PHRASE "BOYS WILL BE BOYS."

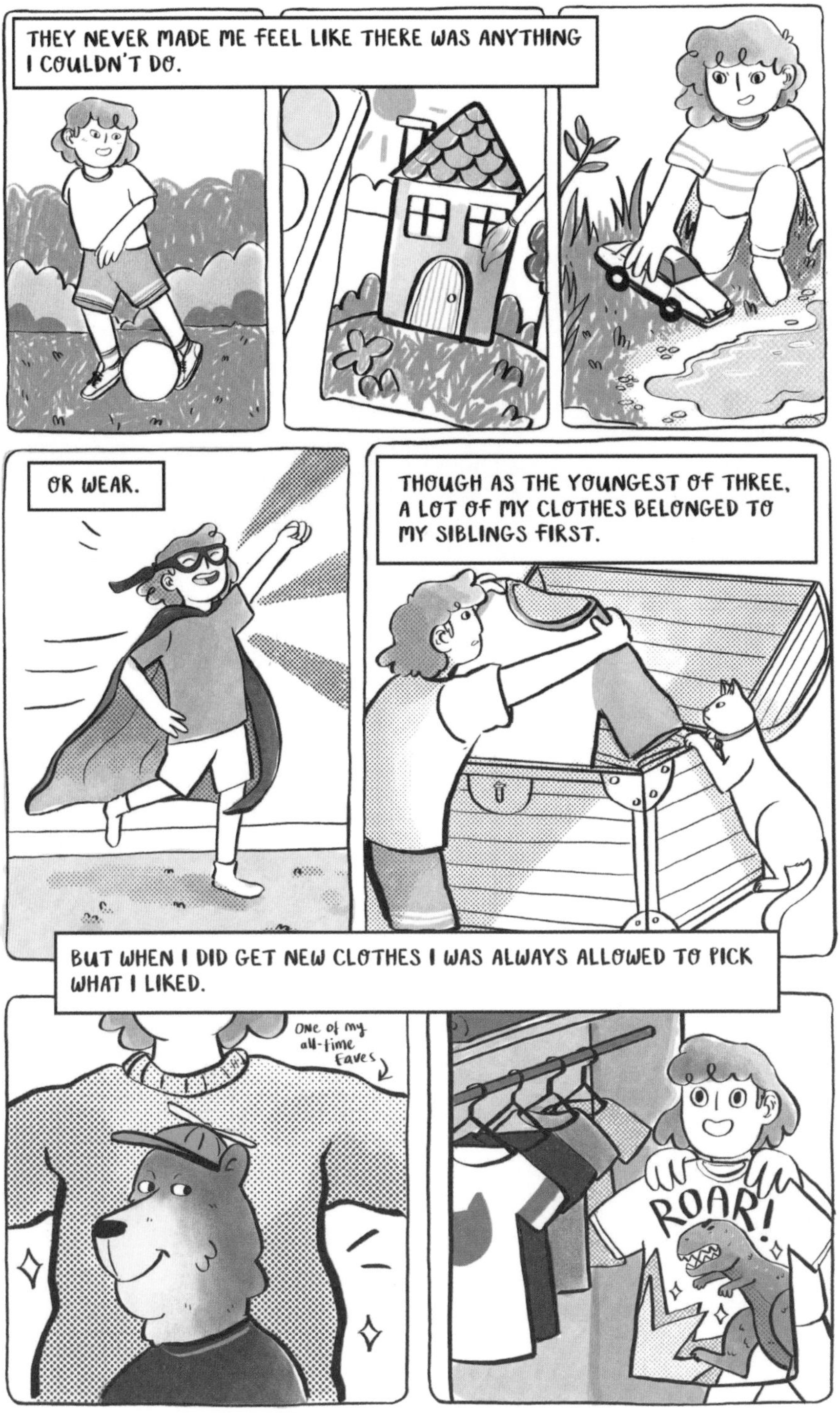

THEY NEVER MADE ME FEEL LIKE THERE WAS ANYTHING I COULDN'T DO.
OR WEAR.
THOUGH AS THE YOUNGEST OF THREE, A LOT OF MY CLOTHES BELONGED TO MY SIBLINGS FIRST.
BUT WHEN I DID GET NEW CLOTHES I WAS ALWAYS ALLOWED TO PICK WHAT I LIKED.
One of my all-time faves
ROAR!

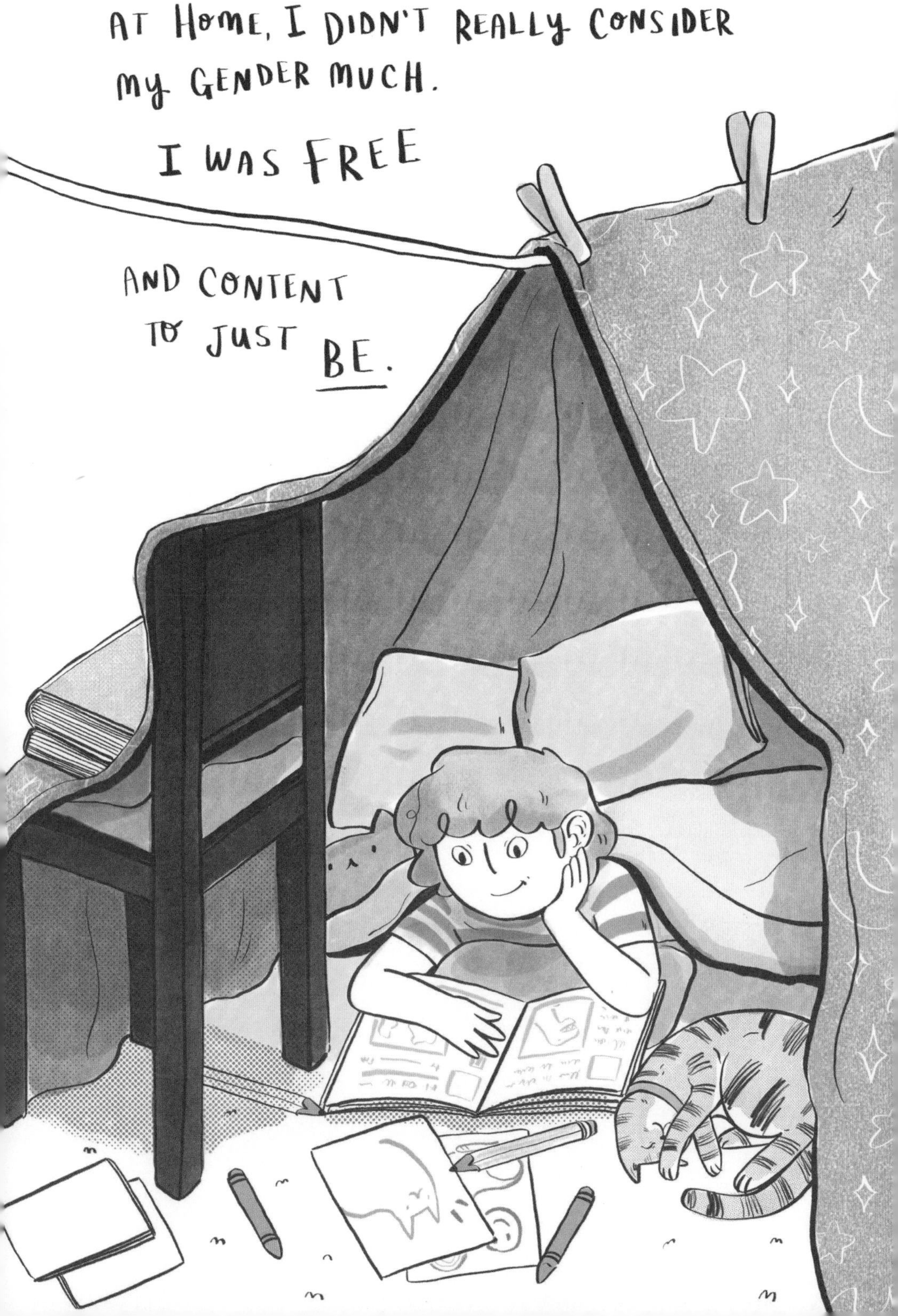
AT HOME, I DIDN'T REALLY CONSIDER MY GENDER MUCH.
I WAS FREE
AND CONTENT TO JUST BE.

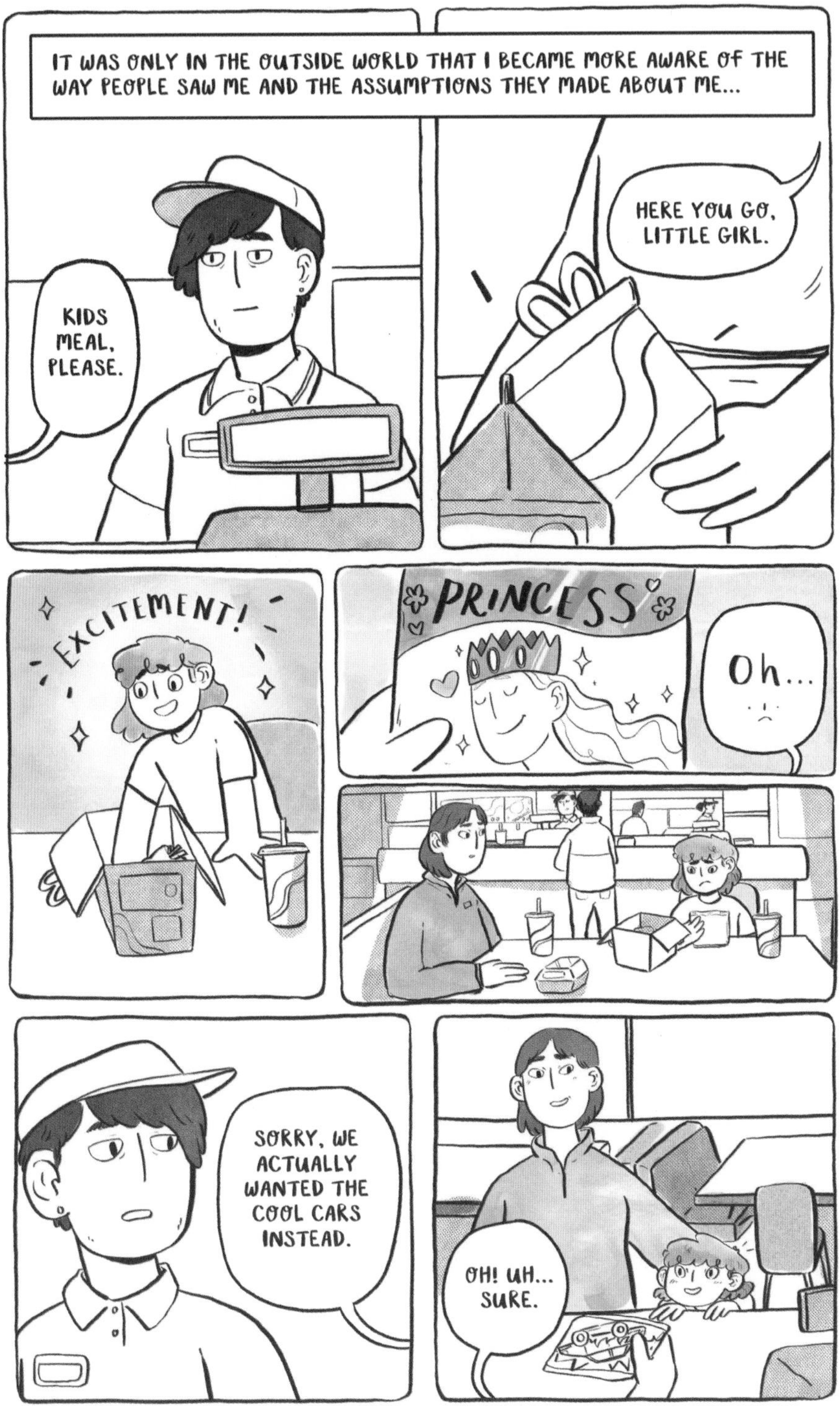
IT WAS ONLY IN THE OUTSIDE WORLD THAT I BECAME MORE AWARE OF THE WAY PEOPLE SAW ME AND THE ASSUMPTIONS THEY MADE ABOUT ME...
KIDS MEAL, PLEASE.
HERE YOU GO, LITTLE GIRL.
EXCITEMENT!
PRINCESS
Oh...
SORRY, WE ACTUALLY WANTED THE COOL CARS INSTEAD.
OH! UH... SURE.

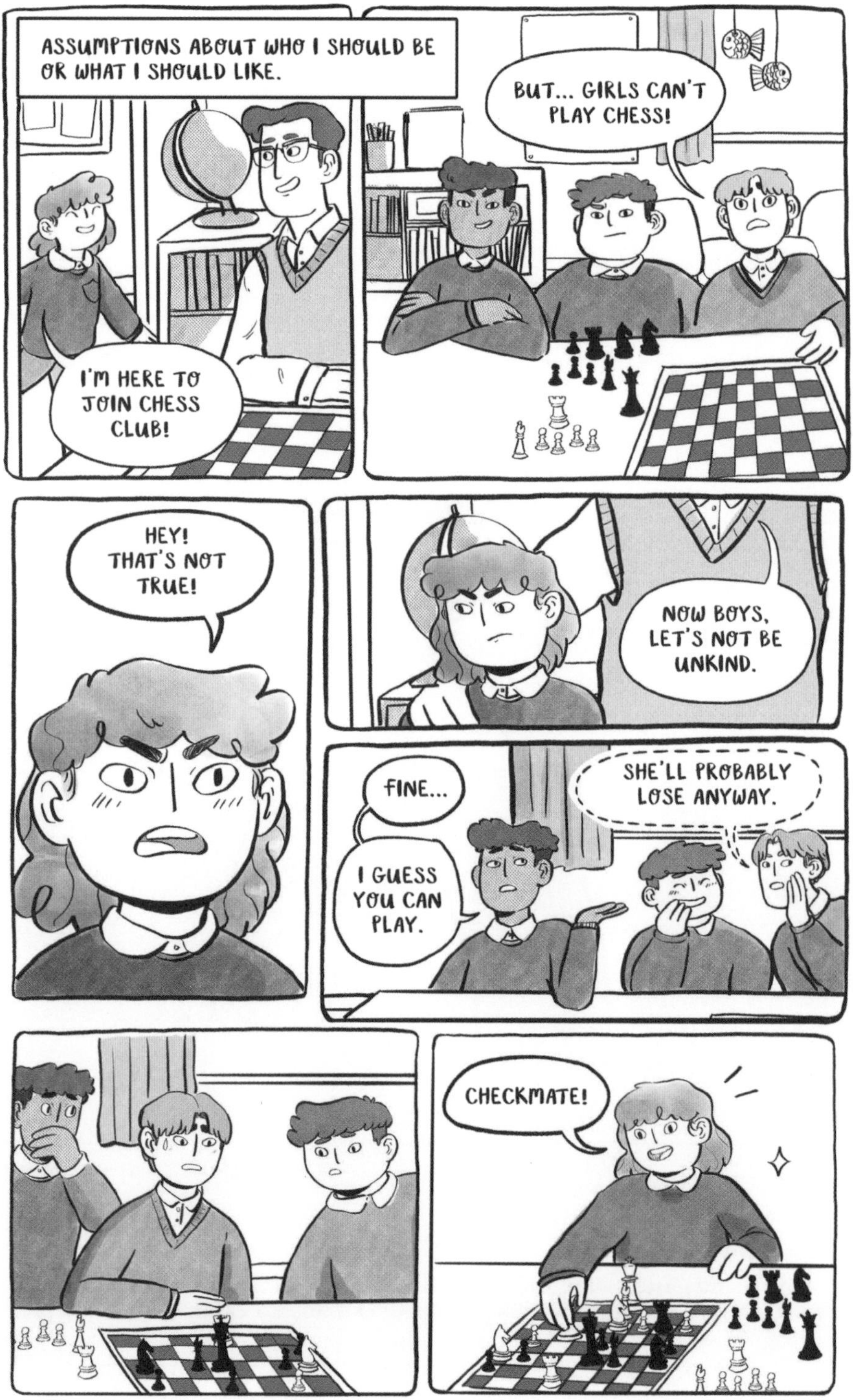
ASSUMPTIONS ABOUT WHO I SHOULD BE OR WHAT I SHOULD LIKE.
I'M HERE TO JOIN CHESS CLUB!
BUT... GIRLS CAN'T PLAY CHESS!
HEY! THAT'S NOT TRUE!
NOW BOYS, LET'S NOT BE UNKIND.
FINE...
I GUESS YOU CAN PLAY.
SHE'LL PROBABLY LOSE ANYWAY.
CHECKMATE!

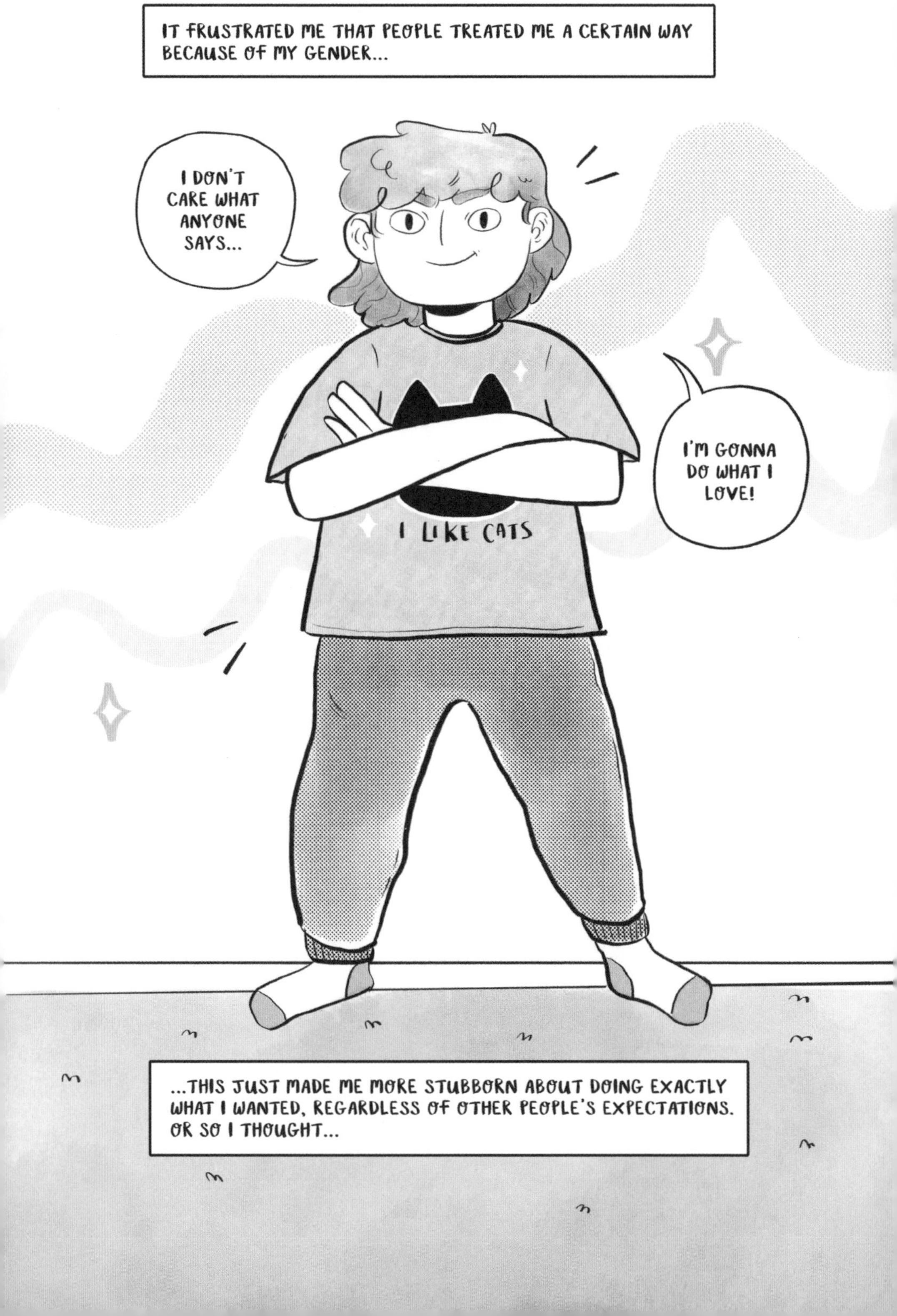
IT FRUSTRATED ME THAT PEOPLE TREATED ME A CERTAIN WAY BECAUSE OF MY GENDER...
I DON'T CARE WHAT ANYONE SAYS...
I'M GONNA DO WHAT I LOVE!
I LIKE CATS
...THIS JUST MADE ME MORE STUBBORN ABOUT DOING EXACTLY WHAT I WANTED, REGARDLESS OF OTHER PEOPLE'S EXPECTATIONS. OR SO I THOUGHT...

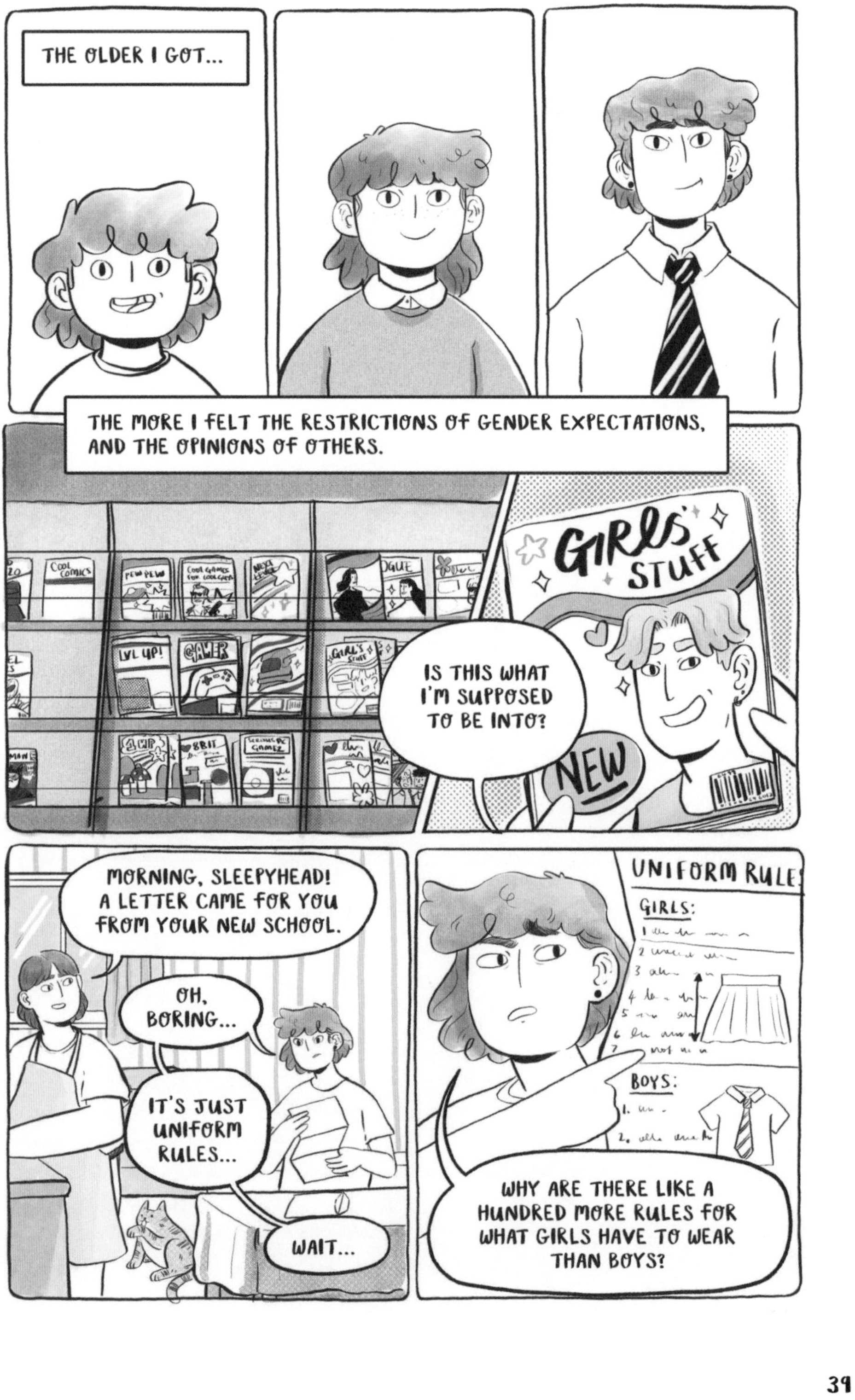
THE OLDER I GOT...
THE MORE I FELT THE RESTRICTIONS OF GENDER EXPECTATIONS, AND THE OPINIONS OF OTHERS.
COOL COMICS
PEW PEW
COOL GAMES FOR COOL GAMERS
NEXT LEVEL
LVL UP!
GAMER
GIRL'S STUFF
8BIT
SERIOUS PC GAMEZ
GIRLS' STUFF
NEW
IS THIS WHAT I'M SUPPOSED TO BE INTO?
MORNING, SLEEPYHEAD! A LETTER CAME FOR YOU FROM YOUR NEW SCHOOL.
OH, BORING...
IT'S JUST UNIFORM RULES...
WAIT...
UNIFORM RULES
GIRLS:
BOYS:
WHY ARE THERE LIKE A HUNDRED MORE RULES FOR WHAT GIRLS HAVE TO WEAR THAN BOYS?

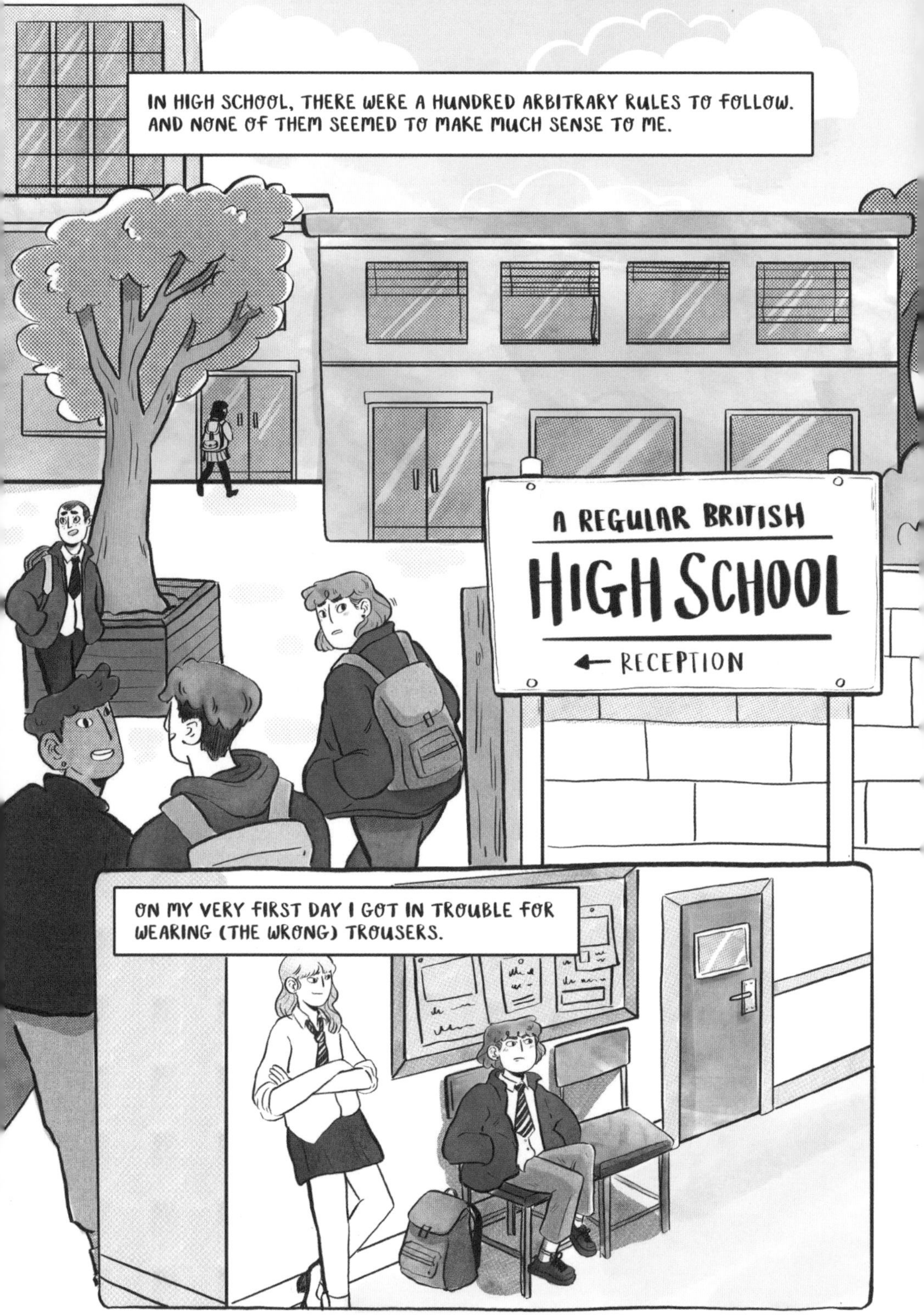
IN HIGH SCHOOL, THERE WERE A HUNDRED ARBITRARY RULES TO FOLLOW. AND NONE OF THEM SEEMED TO MAKE MUCH SENSE TO ME.
A REGULAR BRITISH
HIGH SCHOOL
← RECEPTION
ON MY VERY FIRST DAY I GOT IN TROUBLE FOR WEARING (THE WRONG) TROUSERS.

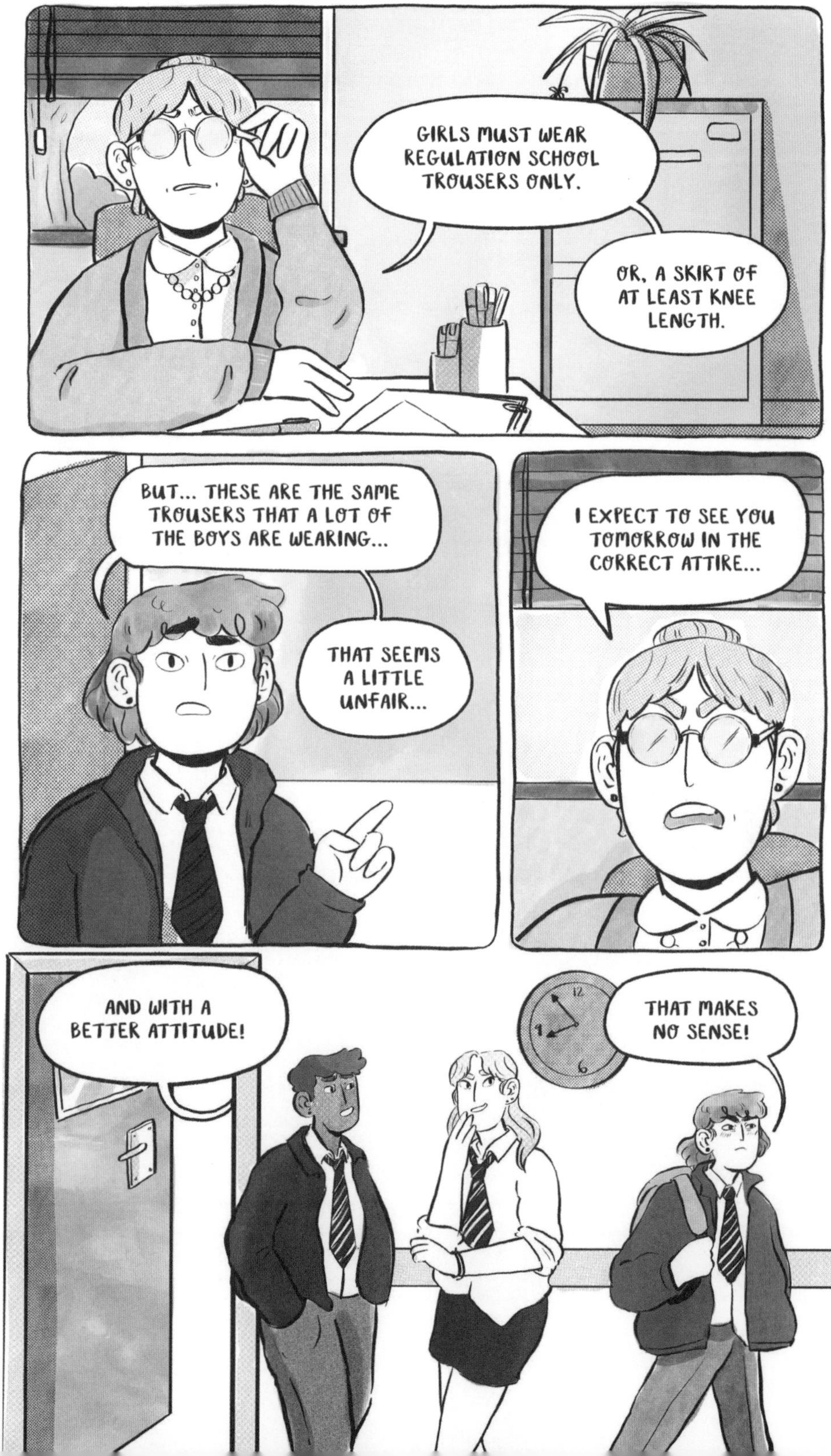
GIRLS MUST WEAR REGULATION SCHOOL TROUSERS ONLY.
OR, A SKIRT OF AT LEAST KNEE LENGTH.
BUT... THESE ARE THE SAME TROUSERS THAT A LOT OF THE BOYS ARE WEARING...
THAT SEEMS A LITTLE UNFAIR...
I EXPECT TO SEE YOU TOMORROW IN THE CORRECT ATTIRE...
AND WITH A BETTER ATTITUDE!
THAT MAKES NO SENSE!

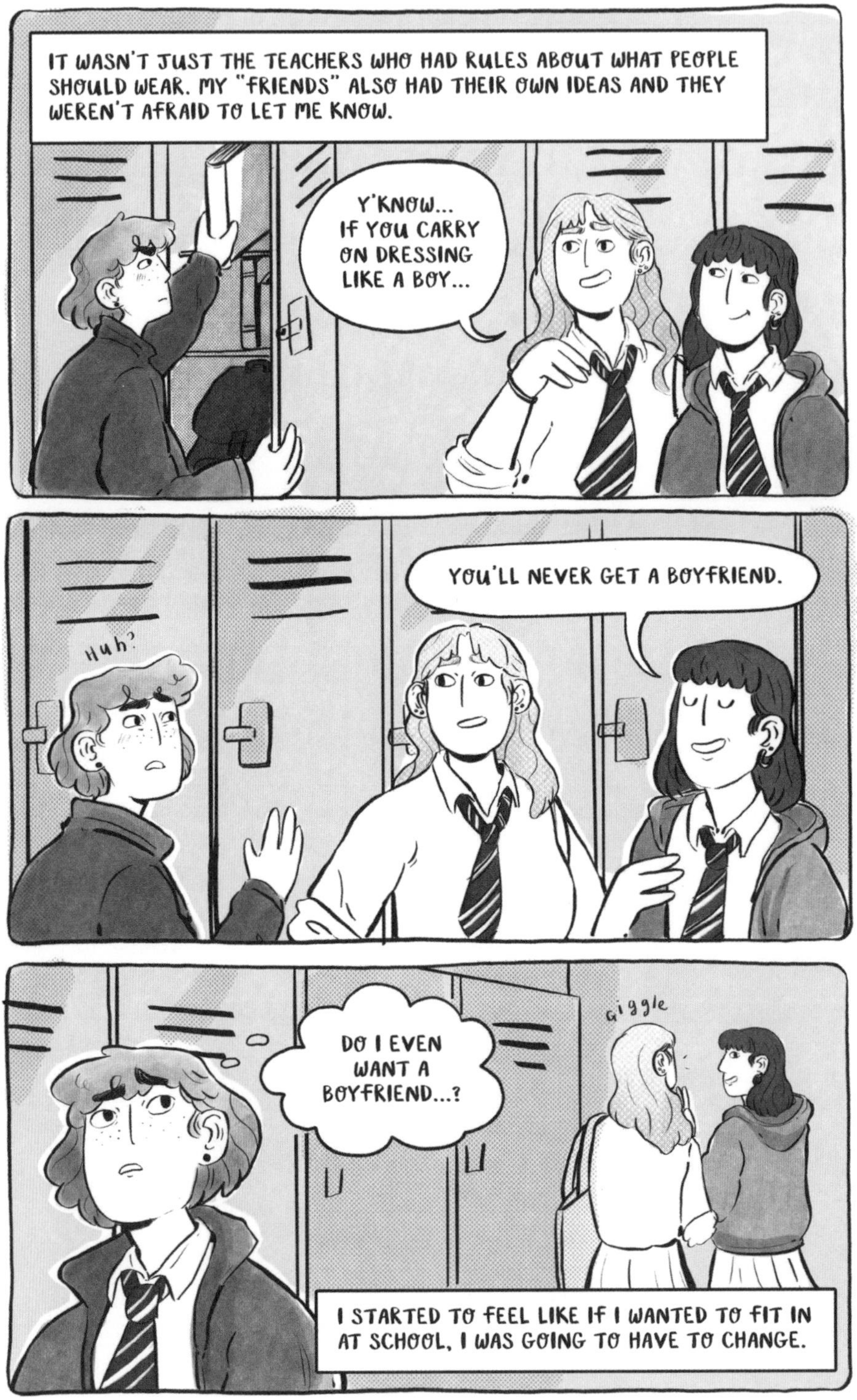
IT WASN'T JUST THE TEACHERS WHO HAD RULES ABOUT WHAT PEOPLE SHOULD WEAR. MY "FRIENDS" ALSO HAD THEIR OWN IDEAS AND THEY WEREN'T AFRAID TO LET ME KNOW.
Y'KNOW... IF YOU CARRY ON DRESSING LIKE A BOY...
YOU'LL NEVER GET A BOYFRIEND.
Huh?
DO I EVEN WANT A BOYFRIEND...?
giggle
I STARTED TO FEEL LIKE IF I WANTED TO FIT IN AT SCHOOL, I WAS GOING TO HAVE TO CHANGE.

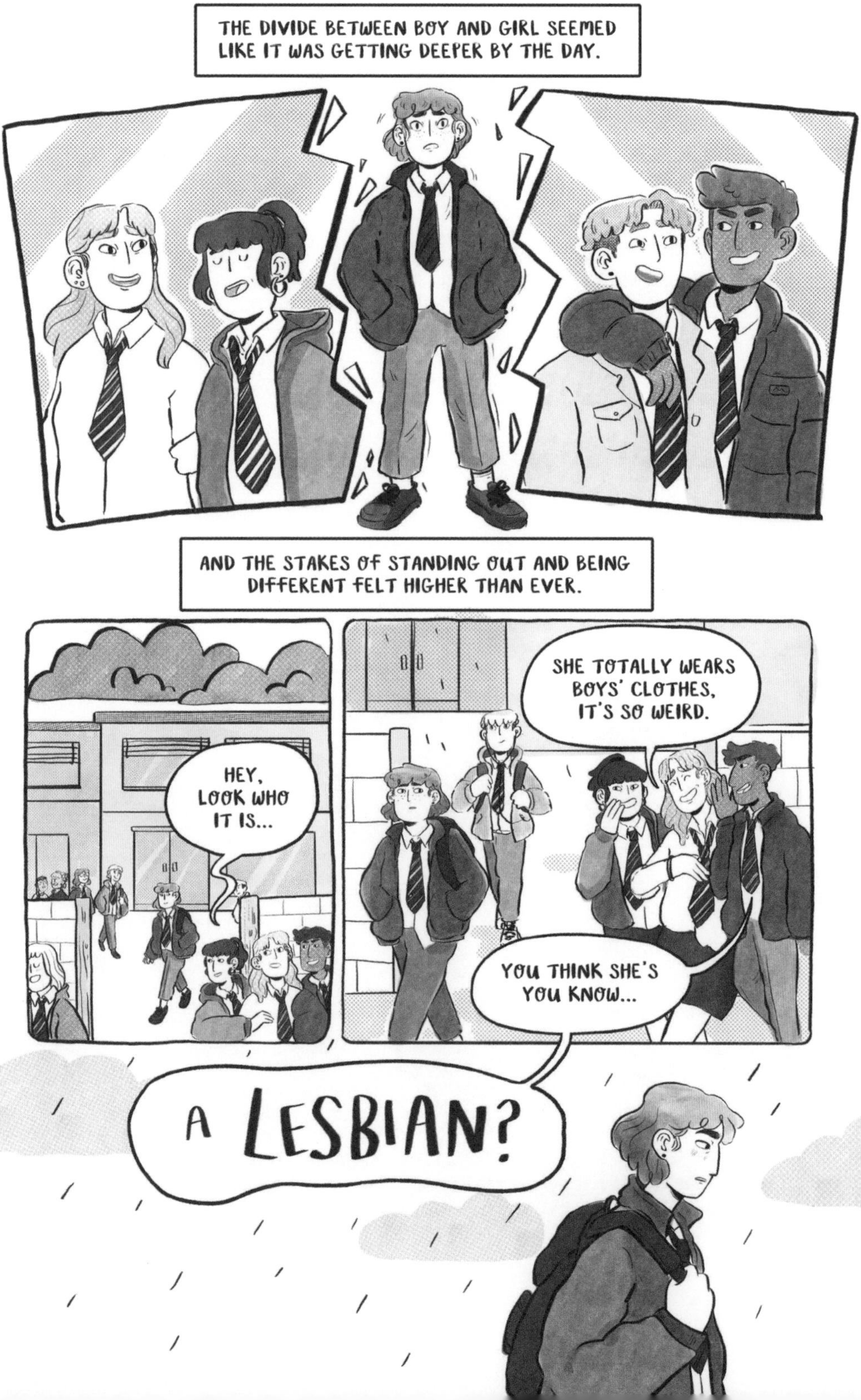
THE DIVIDE BETWEEN BOY AND GIRL SEEMED LIKE IT WAS GETTING DEEPER BY THE DAY.
AND THE STAKES OF STANDING OUT AND BEING DIFFERENT FELT HIGHER THAN EVER.
HEY, LOOK WHO IT IS...
SHE TOTALLY WEARS BOYS' CLOTHES, IT'S SO WEIRD.
YOU THINK SHE'S YOU KNOW...
A LESBIAN?

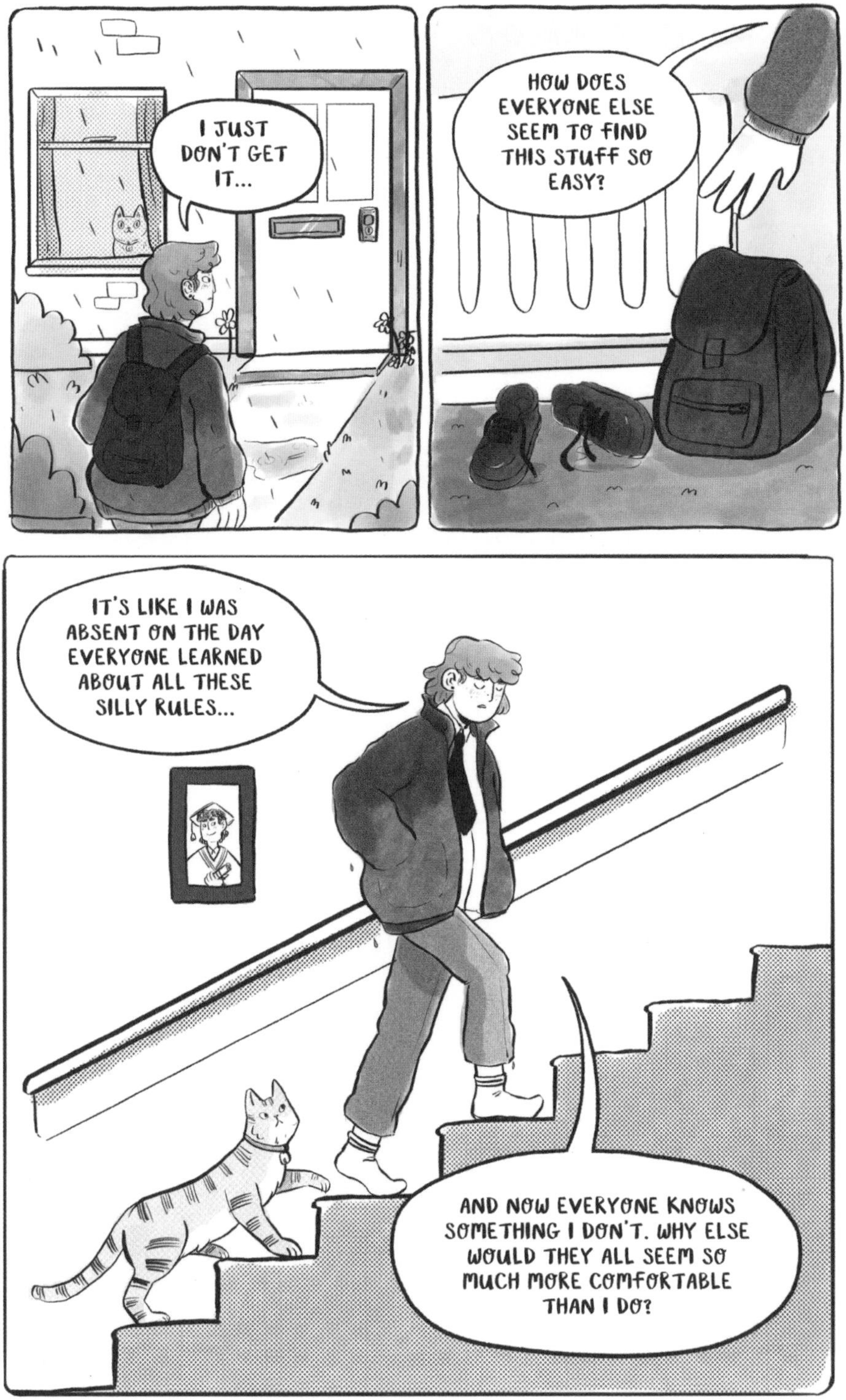
I JUST DON'T GET IT...
HOW DOES EVERYONE ELSE SEEM TO FIND THIS STUFF SO EASY?
IT'S LIKE I WAS ABSENT ON THE DAY EVERYONE LEARNED ABOUT ALL THESE SILLY RULES...
AND NOW EVERYONE KNOWS SOMETHING I DON'T. WHY ELSE WOULD THEY ALL SEEM SO MUCH MORE COMFORTABLE THAN I DO?

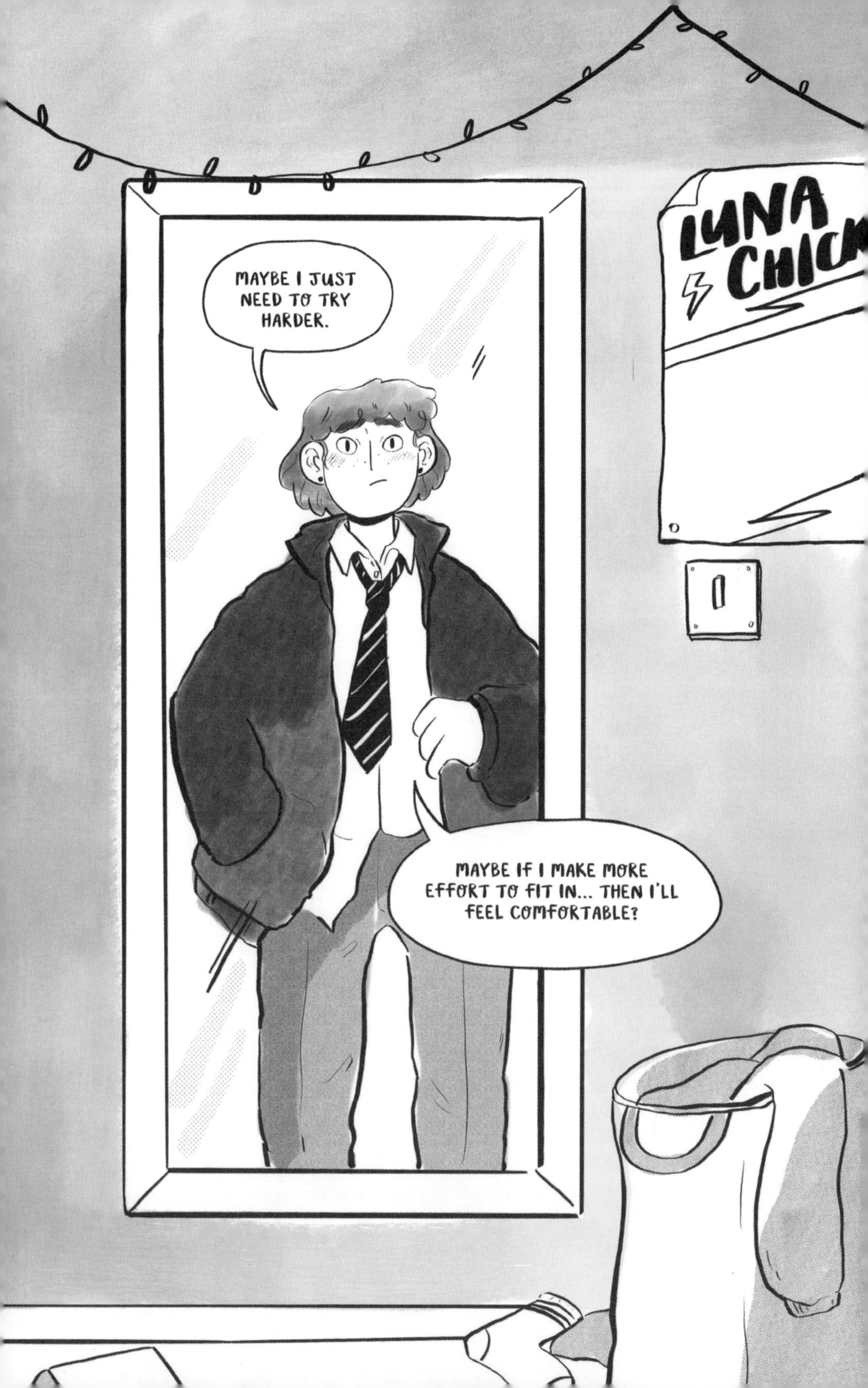
MAYBE I JUST NEED TO TRY HARDER.
LUNA CHICK
MAYBE IF I MAKE MORE EFFORT TO FIT IN... THEN I'LL FEEL COMFORTABLE?

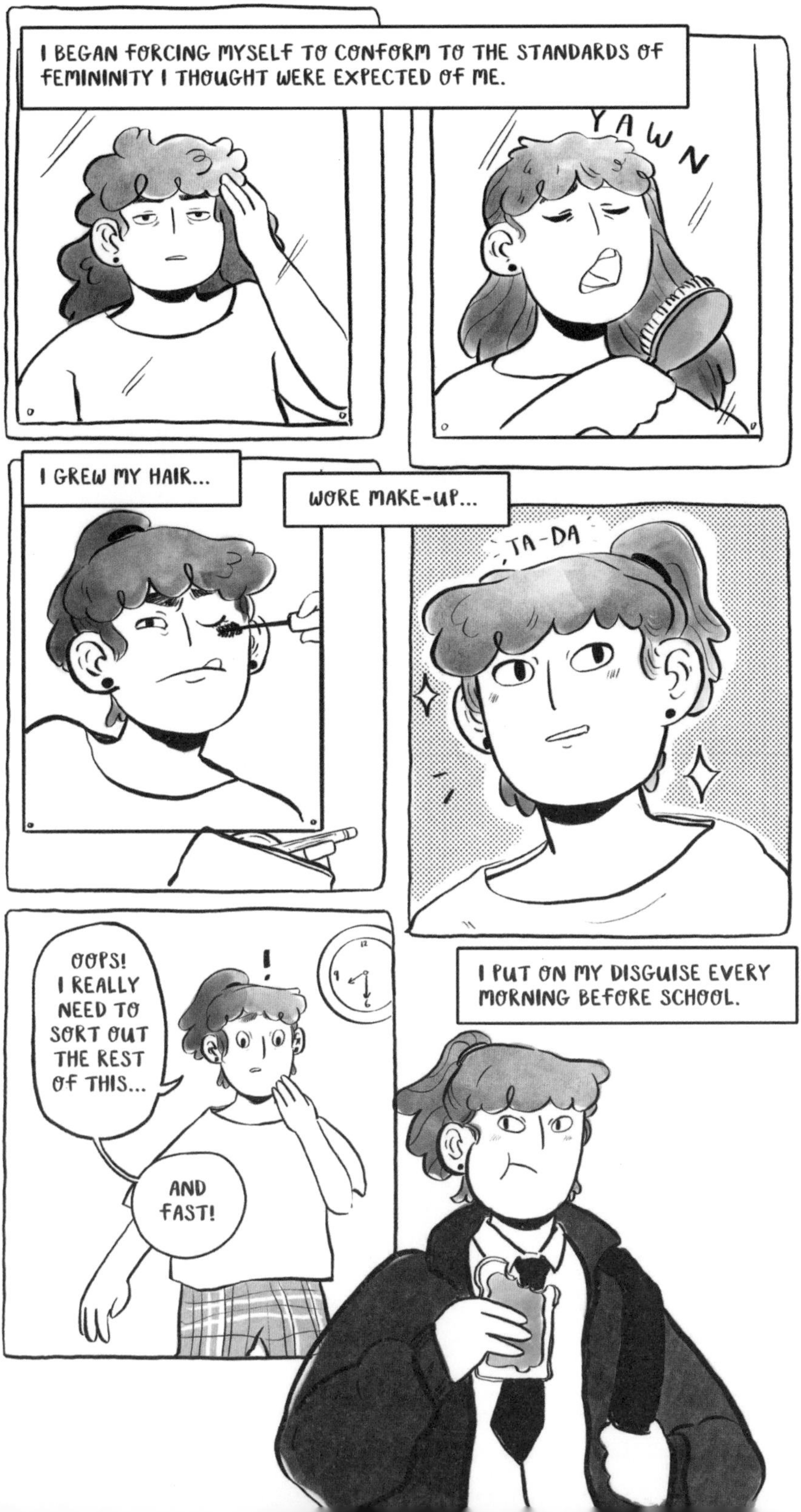

I BEGAN FORCING MYSELF TO CONFORM TO THE STANDARDS OF FEMININITY I THOUGHT WERE EXPECTED OF ME.
YAWN
I GREW MY HAIR...
WORE MAKE-UP...
TA-DA
OOPS! I REALLY NEED TO SORT OUT THE REST OF THIS...
!
AND FAST!
I PUT ON MY DISGUISE EVERY MORNING BEFORE SCHOOL.

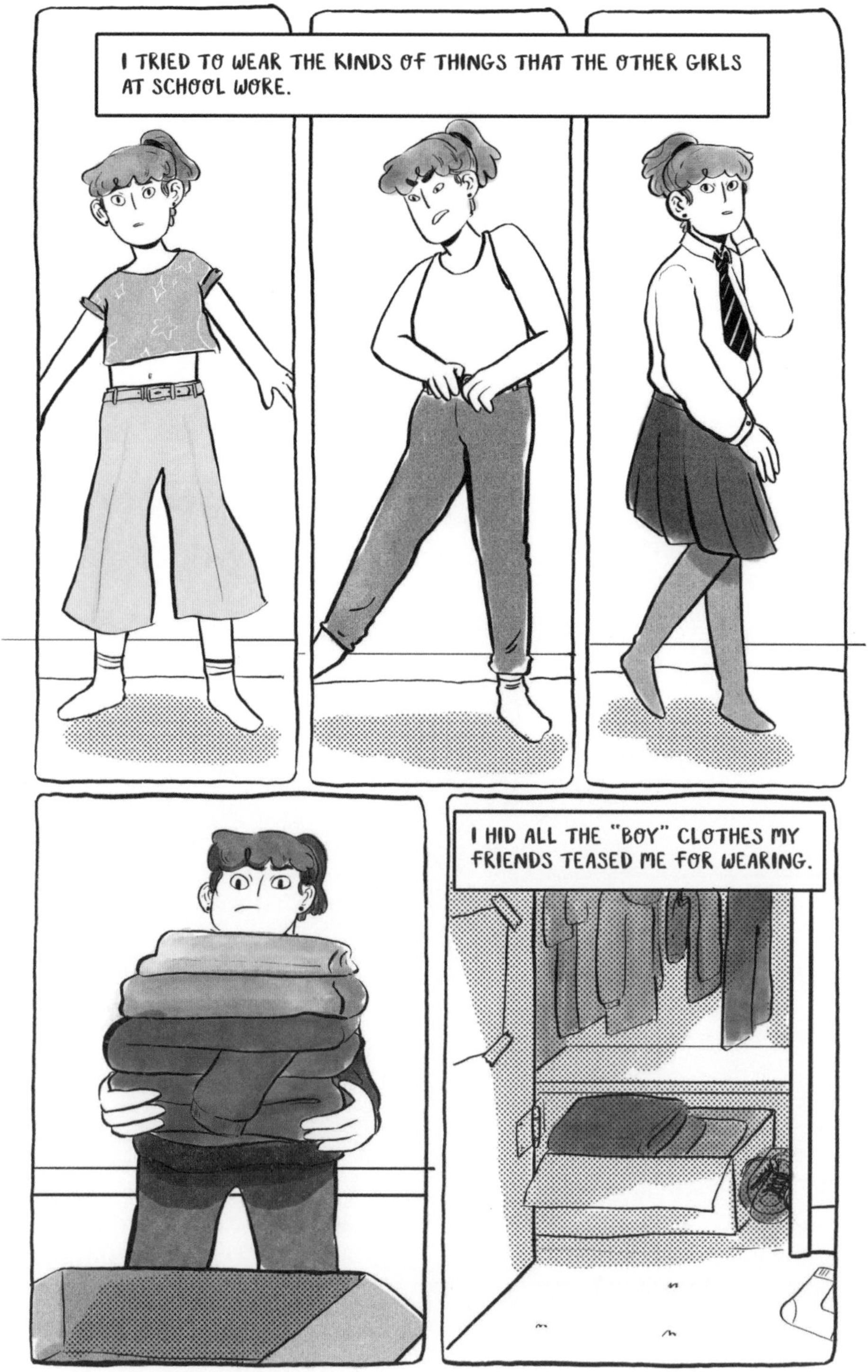
I TRIED TO WEAR THE KINDS OF THINGS THAT THE OTHER GIRLS AT SCHOOL WORE.
I HID ALL THE "BOY" CLOTHES MY FRIENDS TEASED ME FOR WEARING.

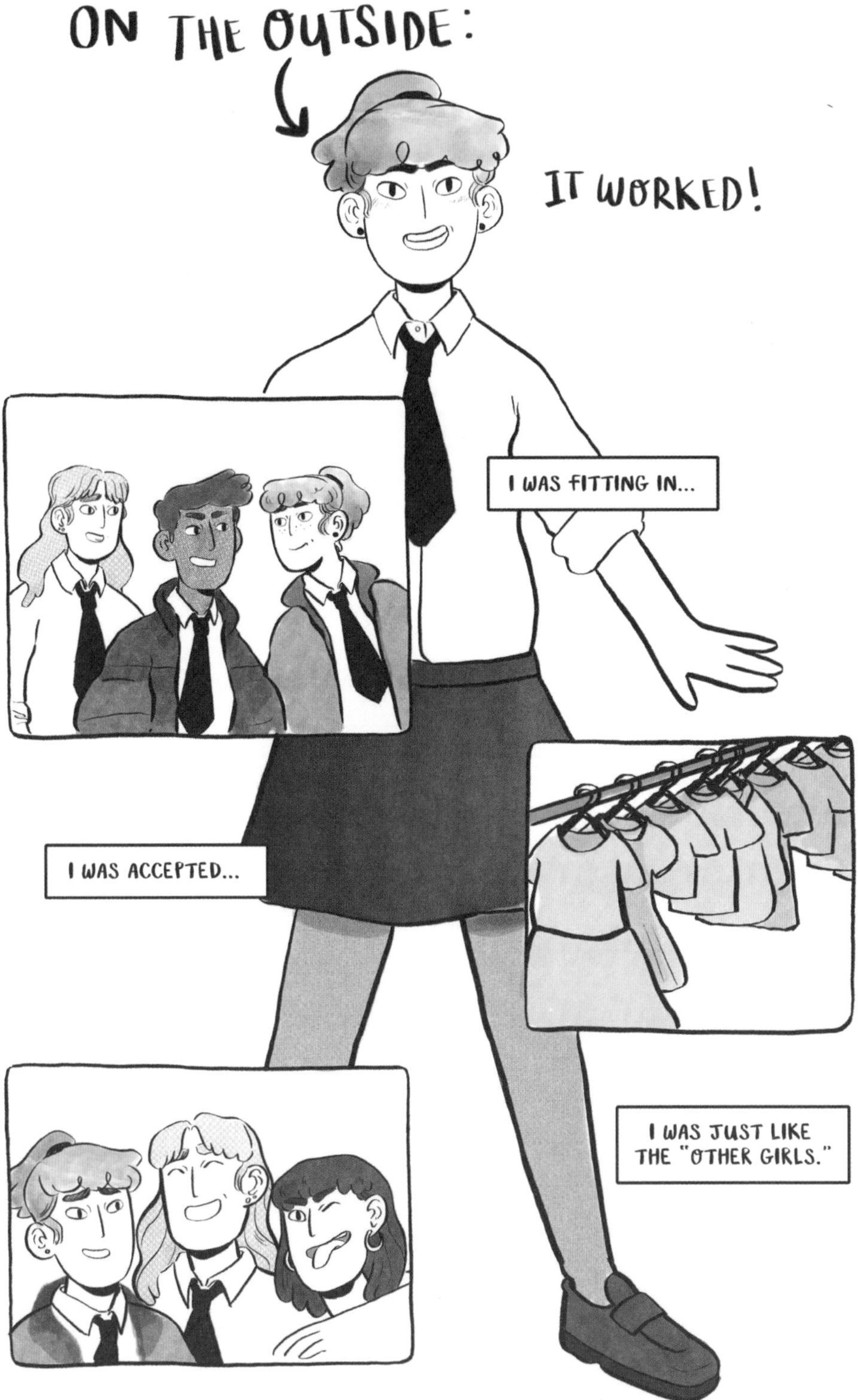

ON THE OUTSIDE:
IT WORKED!
I WAS FITTING IN...
I WAS ACCEPTED...
I WAS JUST LIKE THE "OTHER GIRLS."

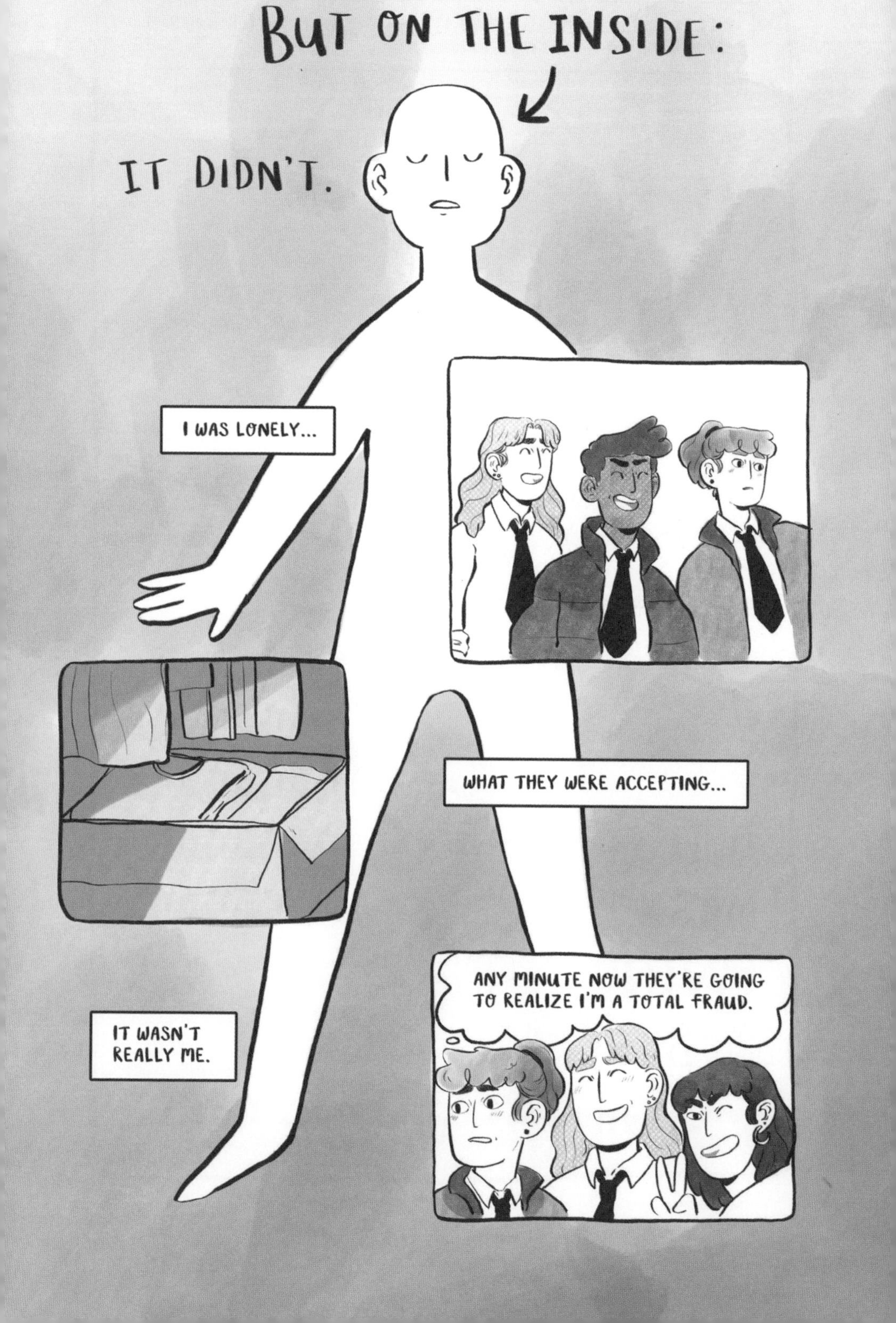
BUT ON THE INSIDE:
IT DIDN'T.
I WAS LONELY...
WHAT THEY WERE ACCEPTING...
IT WASN'T REALLY ME.
ANY MINUTE NOW THEY'RE GOING TO REALIZE I'M A TOTAL FRAUD.

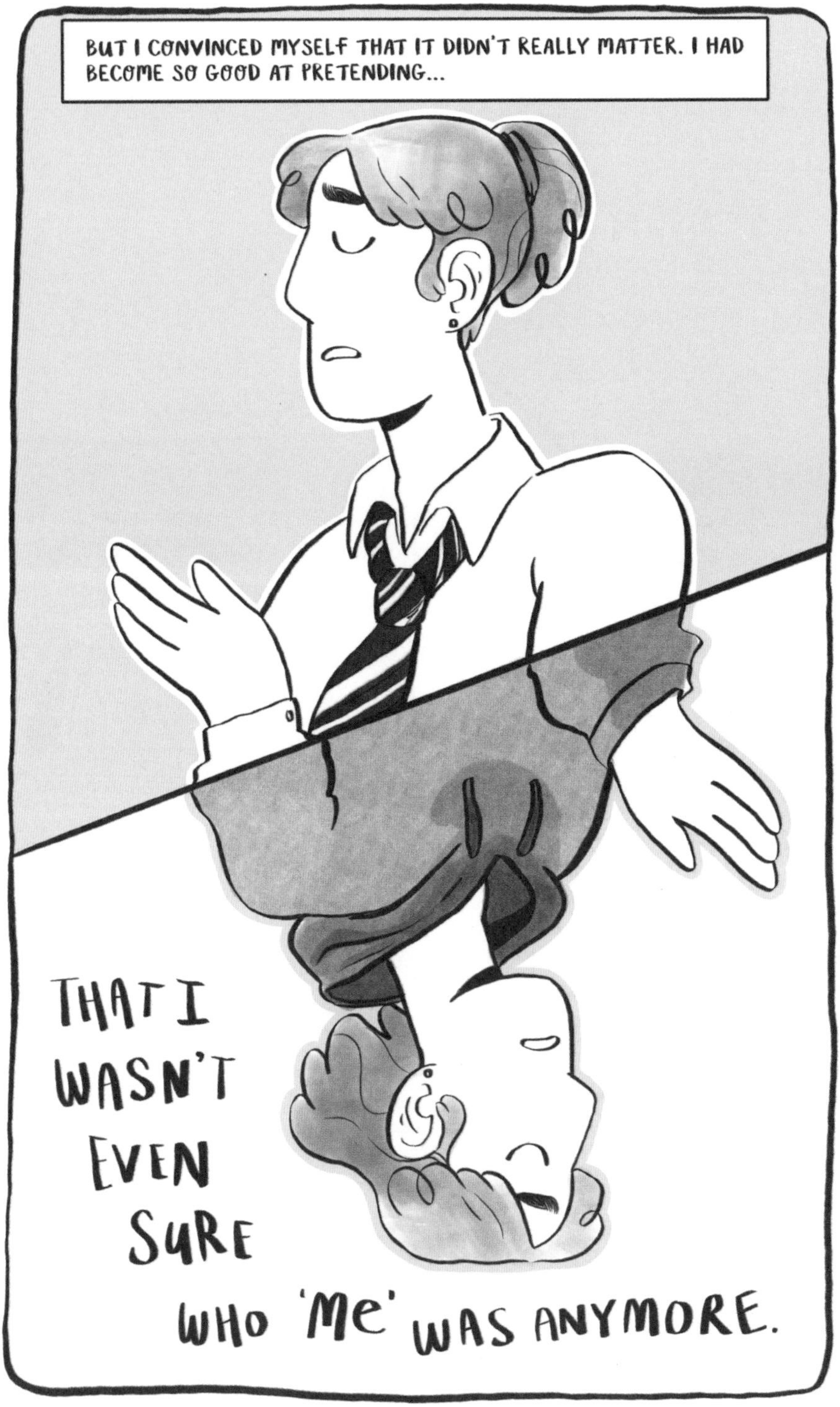
BUT I CONVINCED MYSELF THAT IT DIDN'T REALLY MATTER. I HAD BECOME SO GOOD AT PRETENDING...
THAT I WASN'T EVEN SURE WHO 'ME' WAS ANYMORE.

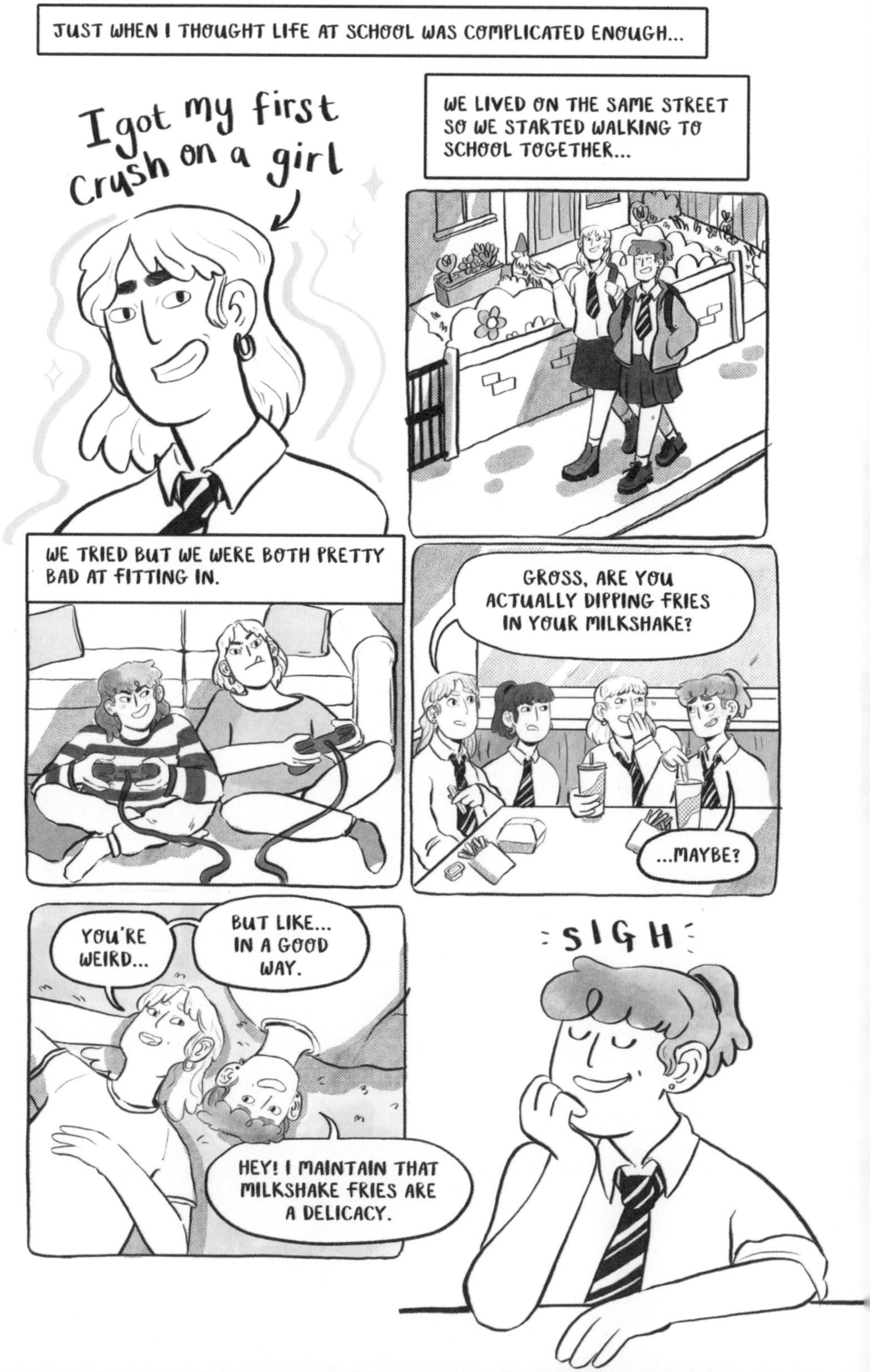
JUST WHEN I THOUGHT LIFE AT SCHOOL WAS COMPLICATED ENOUGH...
I got my first crush on a girl
WE LIVED ON THE SAME STREET SO WE STARTED WALKING TO SCHOOL TOGETHER...
WE TRIED BUT WE WERE BOTH PRETTY BAD AT FITTING IN.
GROSS, ARE YOU ACTUALLY DIPPING FRIES IN YOUR MILKSHAKE?
...MAYBE?
YOU'RE WEIRD...
BUT LIKE... IN A GOOD WAY.
HEY! I MAINTAIN THAT MILKSHAKE FRIES ARE A DELICACY.
SIGH

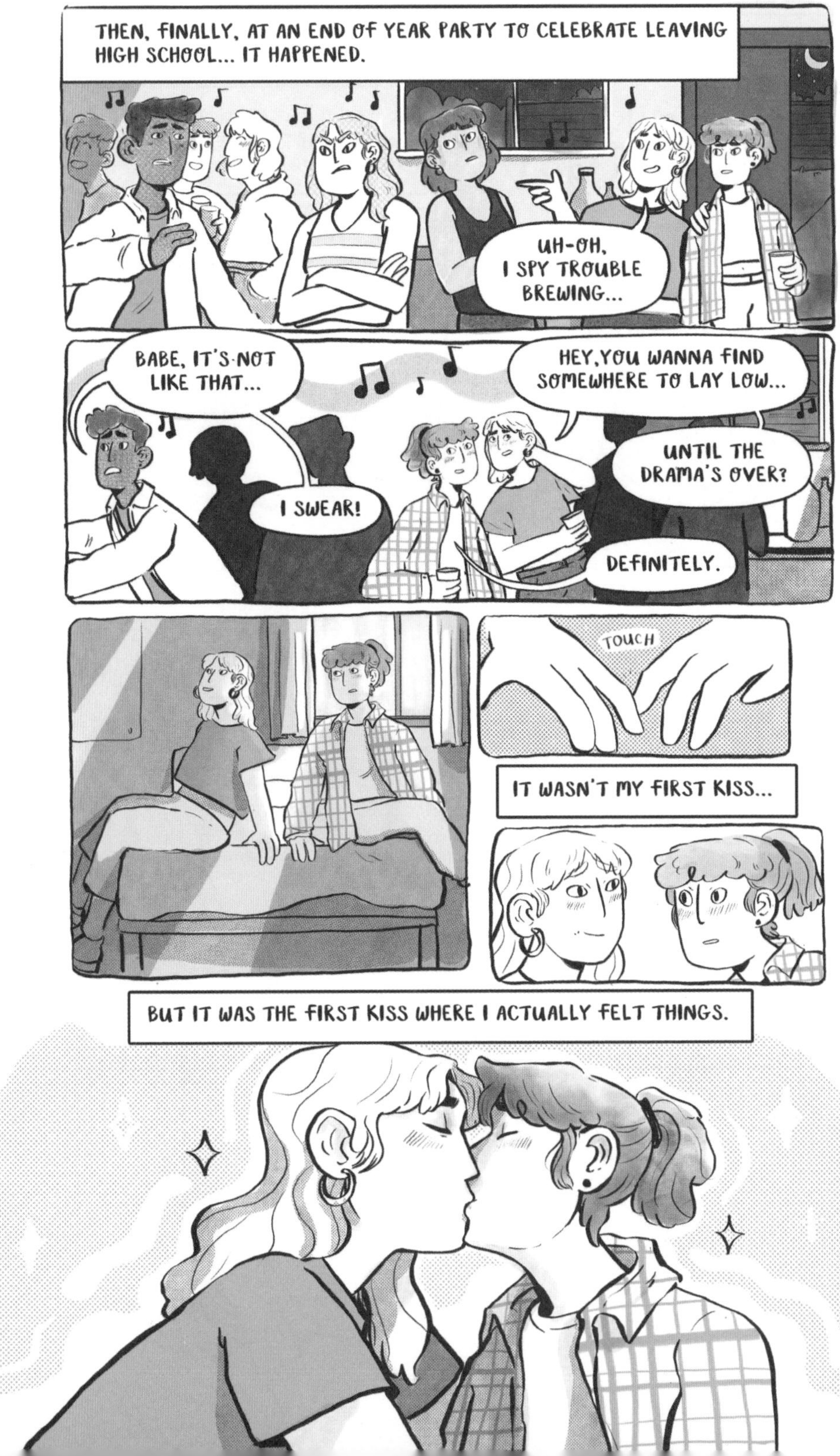
THEN, FINALLY, AT AN END OF YEAR PARTY TO CELEBRATE LEAVING HIGH SCHOOL... IT HAPPENED.
UH-OH, I SPY TROUBLE BREWING...
BABE, IT'S NOT LIKE THAT...
I SWEAR!
HEY, YOU WANNA FIND SOMEWHERE TO LAY LOW...
UNTIL THE DRAMA'S OVER?
DEFINITELY.
TOUCH
IT WASN'T MY FIRST KISS...
BUT IT WAS THE FIRST KISS WHERE I ACTUALLY FELT THINGS.

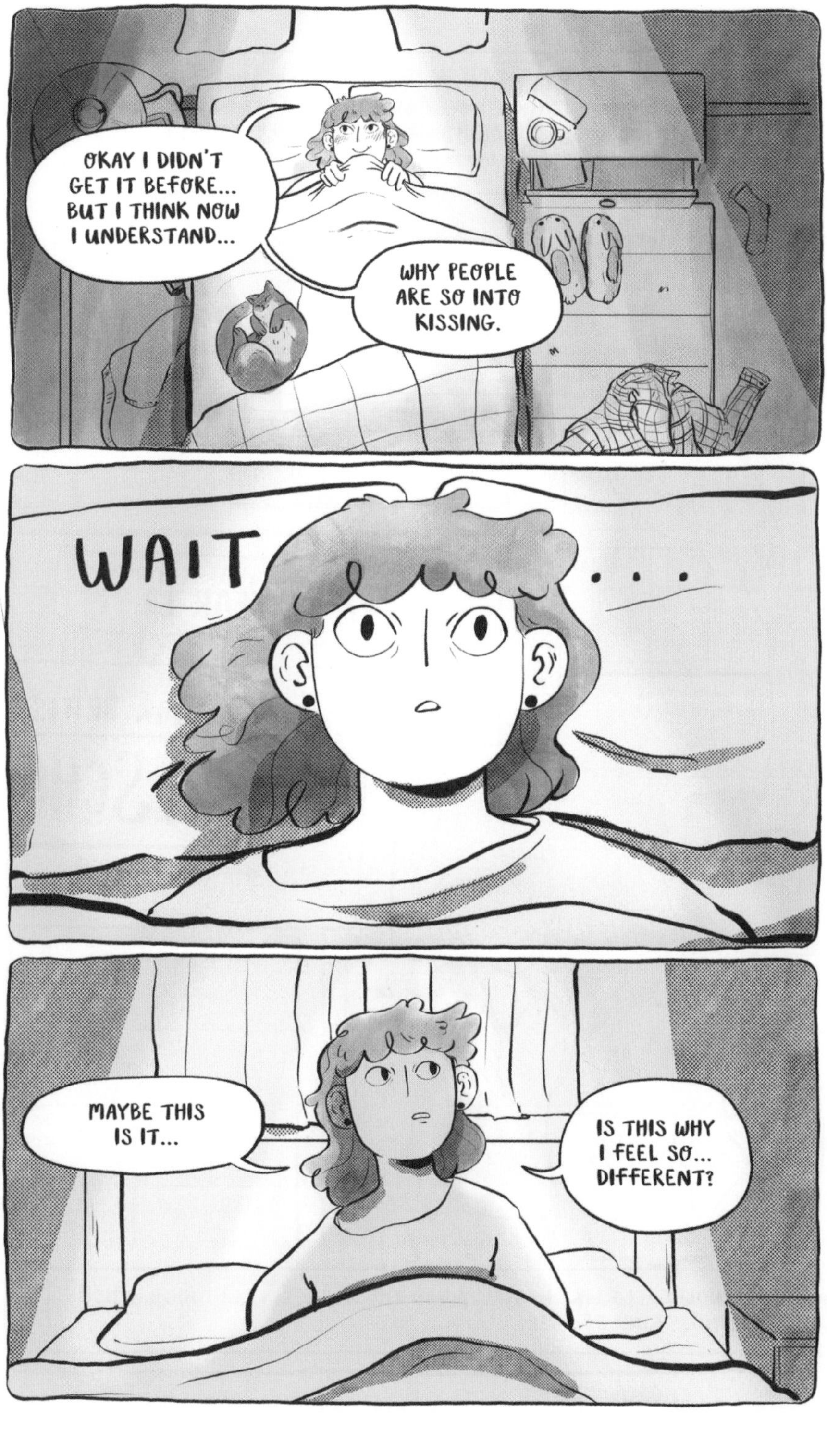
OKAY I DIDN'T GET IT BEFORE... BUT I THINK NOW I UNDERSTAND...
WHY PEOPLE ARE SO INTO KISSING.
WAIT . . .
MAYBE THIS IS IT...
IS THIS WHY I FEEL SO... DIFFERENT?

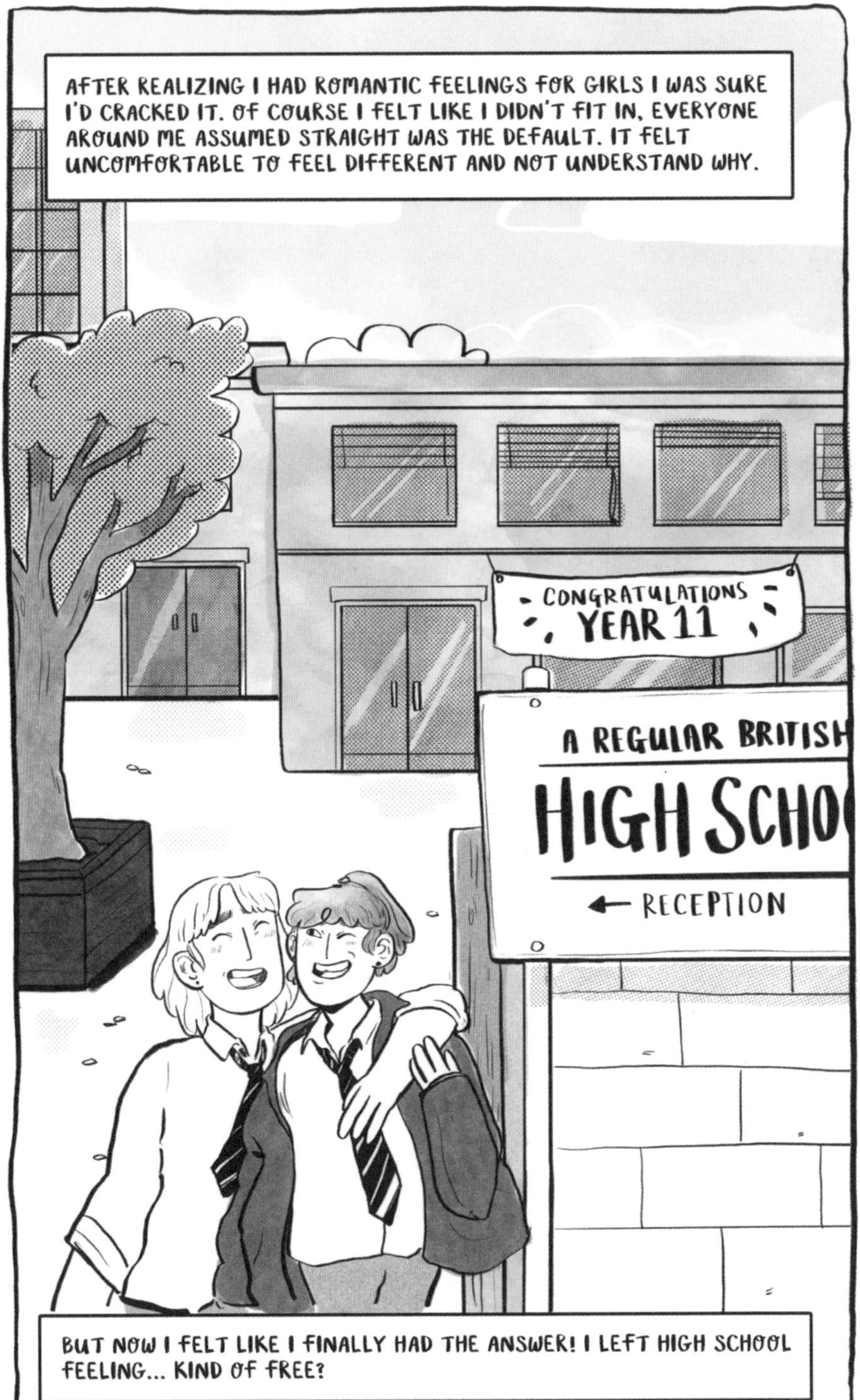
AFTER REALIZING I HAD ROMANTIC FEELINGS FOR GIRLS I WAS SURE I'D CRACKED IT. OF COURSE I FELT LIKE I DIDN'T FIT IN, EVERYONE AROUND ME ASSUMED STRAIGHT WAS THE DEFAULT. IT FELT UNCOMFORTABLE TO FEEL DIFFERENT AND NOT UNDERSTAND WHY.
CONGRATULATIONS YEAR 11
A REGULAR BRITISH
HIGH SCHO
← RECEPTION
BUT NOW I FELT LIKE I FINALLY HAD THE ANSWER! I LEFT HIGH SCHOOL FEELING... KIND OF FREE?

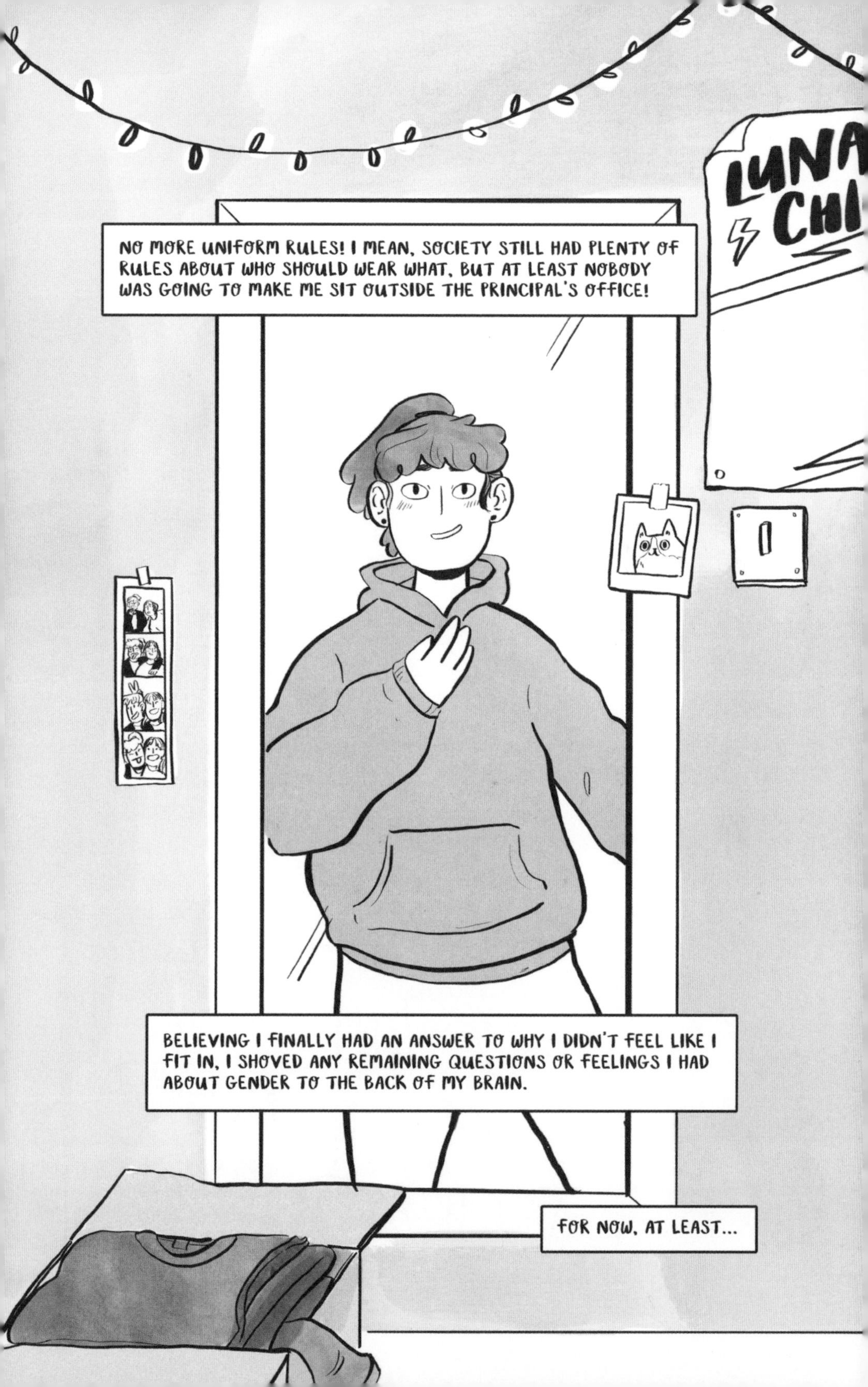

NO MORE UNIFORM RULES! I MEAN, SOCIETY STILL HAD PLENTY OF RULES ABOUT WHO SHOULD WEAR WHAT, BUT AT LEAST NOBODY WAS GOING TO MAKE ME SIT OUTSIDE THE PRINCIPAL'S OFFICE!
BELIEVING I FINALLY HAD AN ANSWER TO WHY I DIDN'T FEEL LIKE I FIT IN, I SHOVED ANY REMAINING QUESTIONS OR FEELINGS I HAD ABOUT GENDER TO THE BACK OF MY BRAIN.
FOR NOW, AT LEAST...

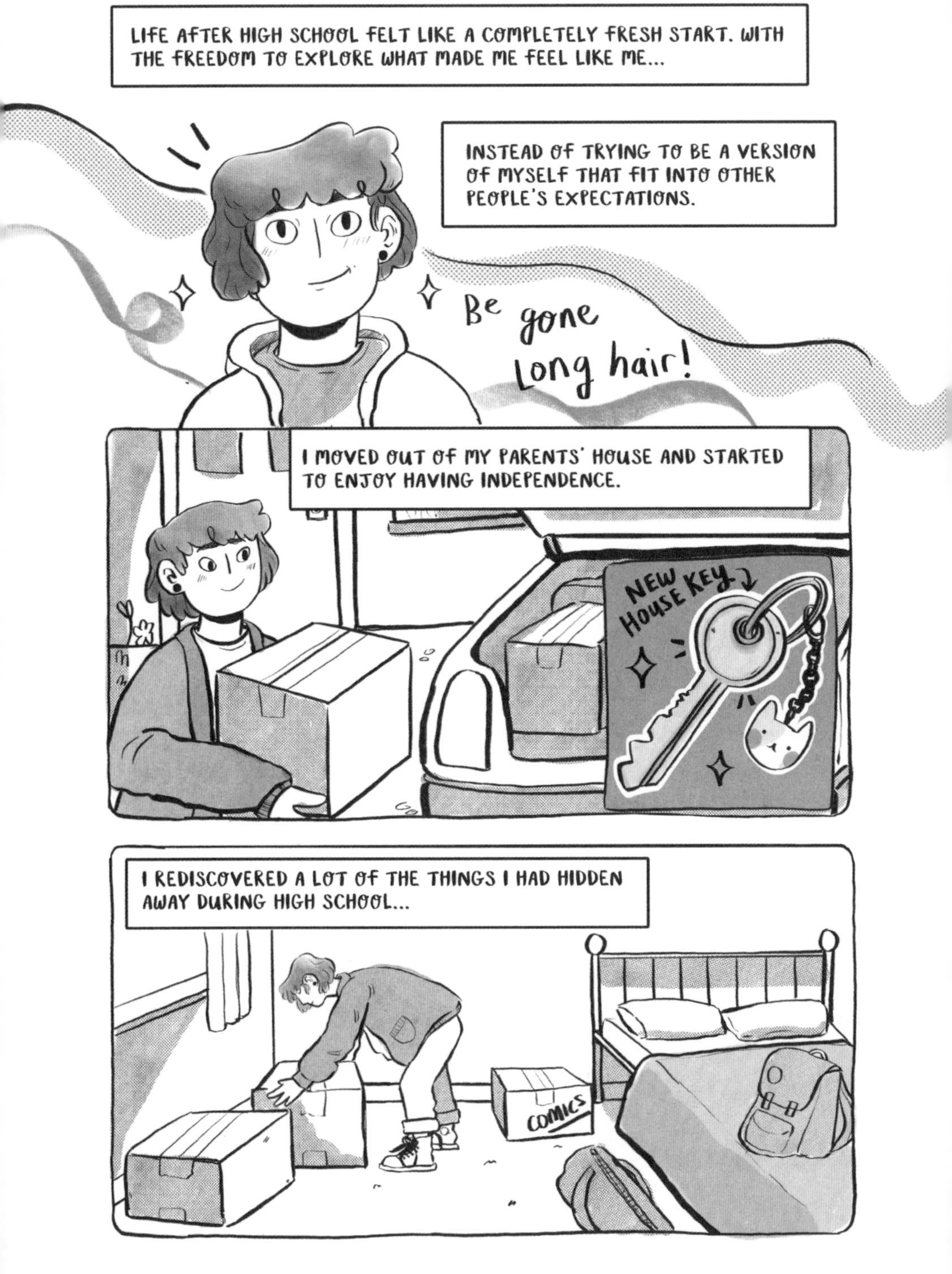
LIFE AFTER HIGH SCHOOL FELT LIKE A COMPLETELY FRESH START. WITH THE FREEDOM TO EXPLORE WHAT MADE ME FEEL LIKE ME...
INSTEAD OF TRYING TO BE A VERSION OF MYSELF THAT FIT INTO OTHER PEOPLE'S EXPECTATIONS.
Be gone long hair!
I MOVED OUT OF MY PARENTS' HOUSE AND STARTED TO ENJOY HAVING INDEPENDENCE.
NEW HOUSE KEY
I REDISCOVERED A LOT OF THE THINGS I HAD HIDDEN AWAY DURING HIGH SCHOOL...
COMICS

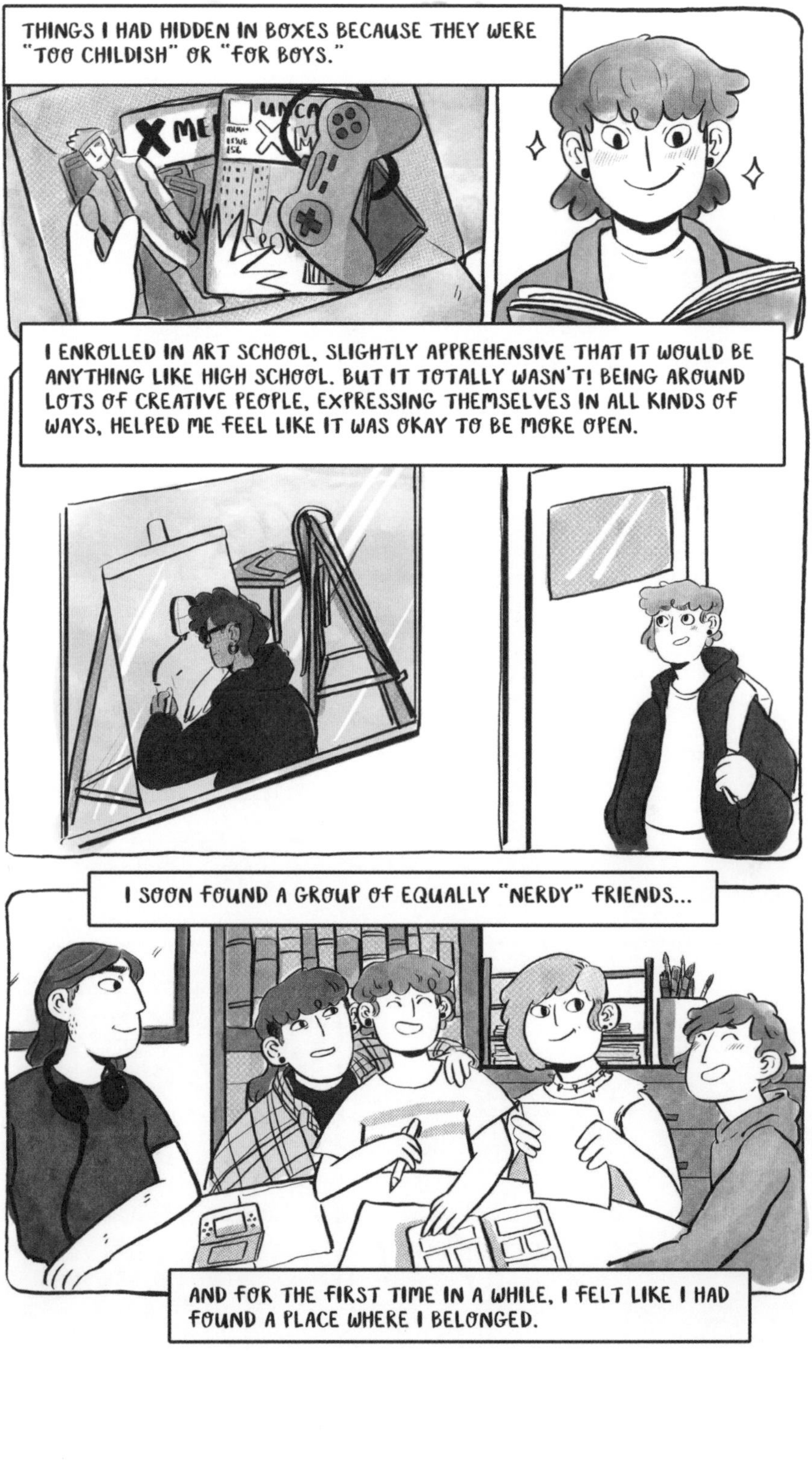
THINGS I HAD HIDDEN IN BOXES BECAUSE THEY WERE "TOO CHILDISH" OR "FOR BOYS."
I ENROLLED IN ART SCHOOL, SLIGHTLY APPREHENSIVE THAT IT WOULD BE ANYTHING LIKE HIGH SCHOOL. BUT IT TOTALLY WASN'T! BEING AROUND LOTS OF CREATIVE PEOPLE, EXPRESSING THEMSELVES IN ALL KINDS OF WAYS, HELPED ME FEEL LIKE IT WAS OKAY TO BE MORE OPEN.
I SOON FOUND A GROUP OF EQUALLY "NERDY" FRIENDS...
AND FOR THE FIRST TIME IN A WHILE, I FELT LIKE I HAD FOUND A PLACE WHERE I BELONGED.

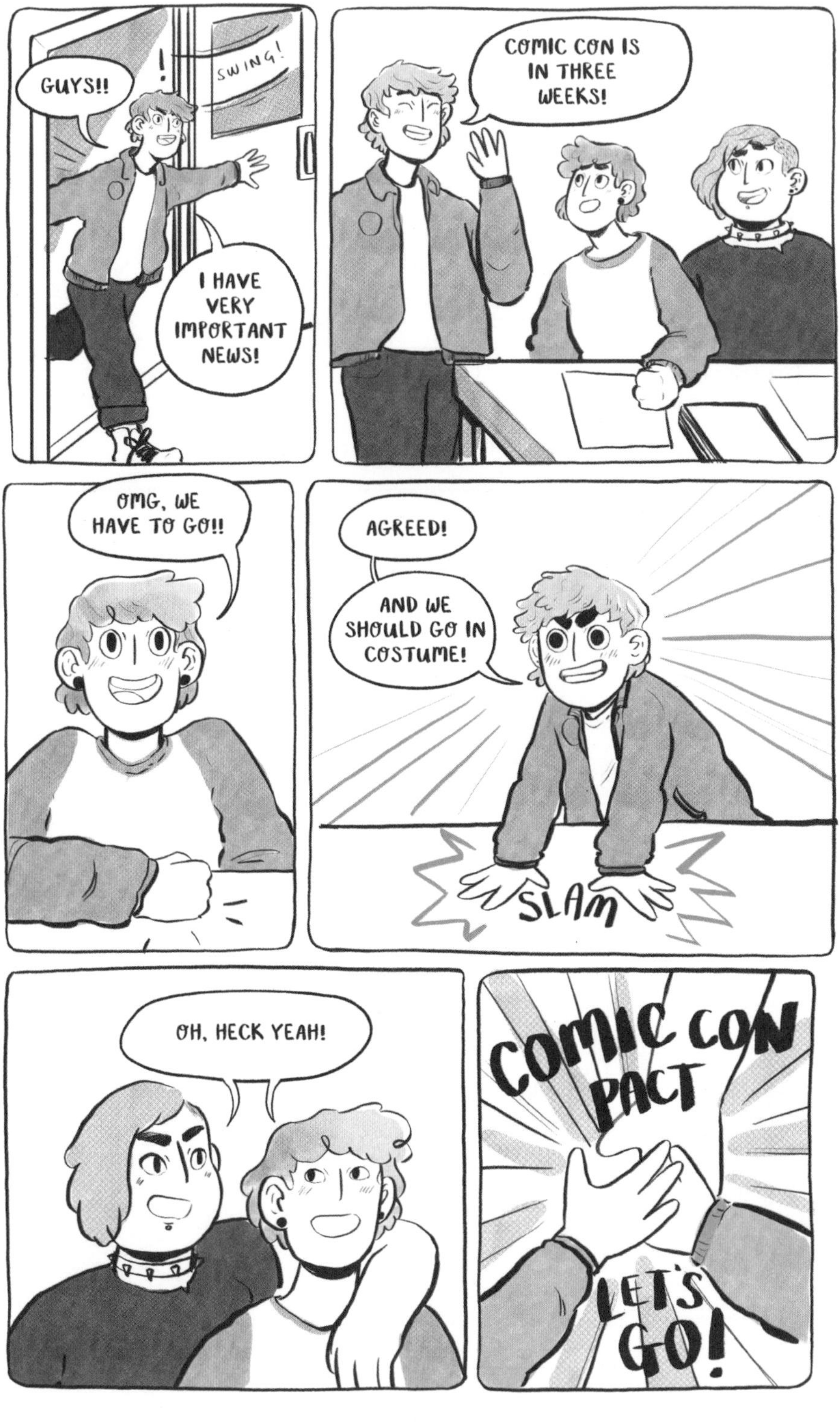
GUYS!!
!
SWING!
I HAVE VERY IMPORTANT NEWS!
COMIC CON IS IN THREE WEEKS!
OMG, WE HAVE TO GO!!
AGREED!
AND WE SHOULD GO IN COSTUME!
SLAM
OH, HECK YEAH!
COMIC CON PACT
LET'S GO!

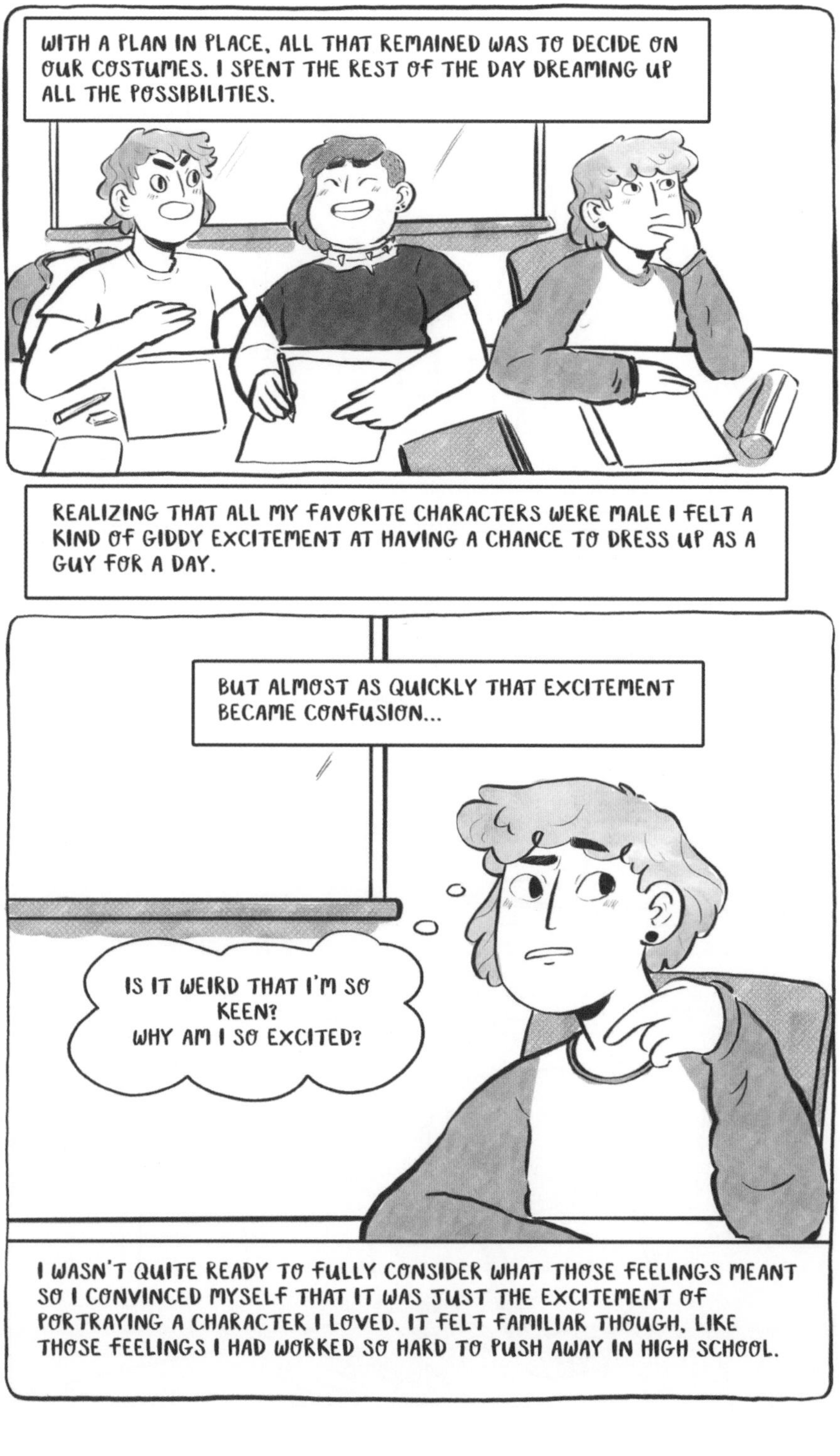
WITH A PLAN IN PLACE, ALL THAT REMAINED WAS TO DECIDE ON OUR COSTUMES. I SPENT THE REST OF THE DAY DREAMING UP ALL THE POSSIBILITIES.
REALIZING THAT ALL MY FAVORITE CHARACTERS WERE MALE I FELT A KIND OF GIDDY EXCITEMENT AT HAVING A CHANCE TO DRESS UP AS A GUY FOR A DAY.
BUT ALMOST AS QUICKLY THAT EXCITEMENT BECAME CONFUSION...
IS IT WEIRD THAT I'M SO KEEN? WHY AM I SO EXCITED?
I WASN'T QUITE READY TO FULLY CONSIDER WHAT THOSE FEELINGS MEANT SO I CONVINCED MYSELF THAT IT WAS JUST THE EXCITEMENT OF PORTRAYING A CHARACTER I LOVED. IT FELT FAMILIAR THOUGH, LIKE THOSE FEELINGS I HAD WORKED SO HARD TO PUSH AWAY IN HIGH SCHOOL.

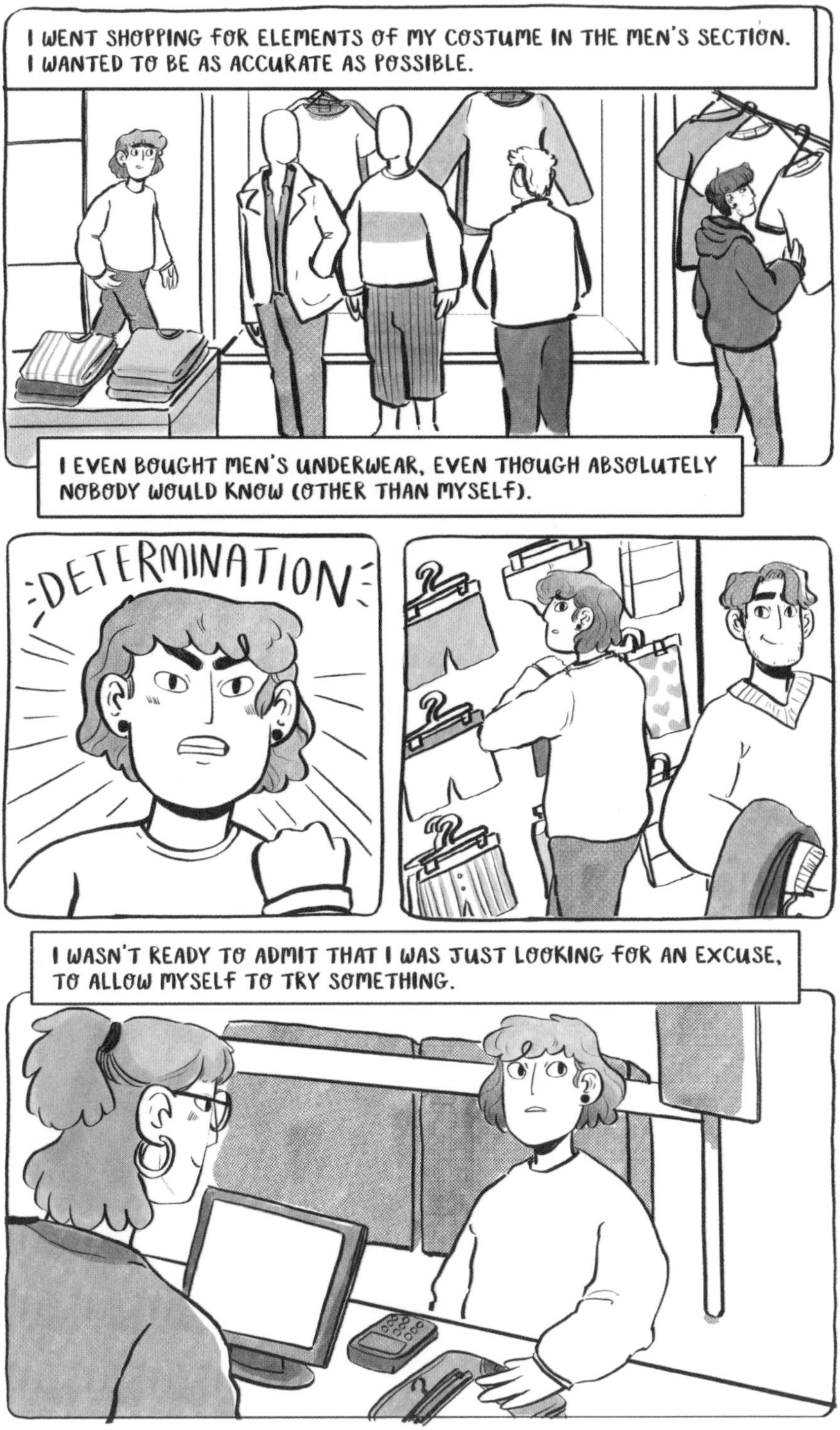
I WENT SHOPPING FOR ELEMENTS OF MY COSTUME IN THE MEN'S SECTION. I WANTED TO BE AS ACCURATE AS POSSIBLE.
I EVEN BOUGHT MEN'S UNDERWEAR, EVEN THOUGH ABSOLUTELY NOBODY WOULD KNOW (OTHER THAN MYSELF).
DETERMINATION
I WASN'T READY TO ADMIT THAT I WAS JUST LOOKING FOR AN EXCUSE, TO ALLOW MYSELF TO TRY SOMETHING.

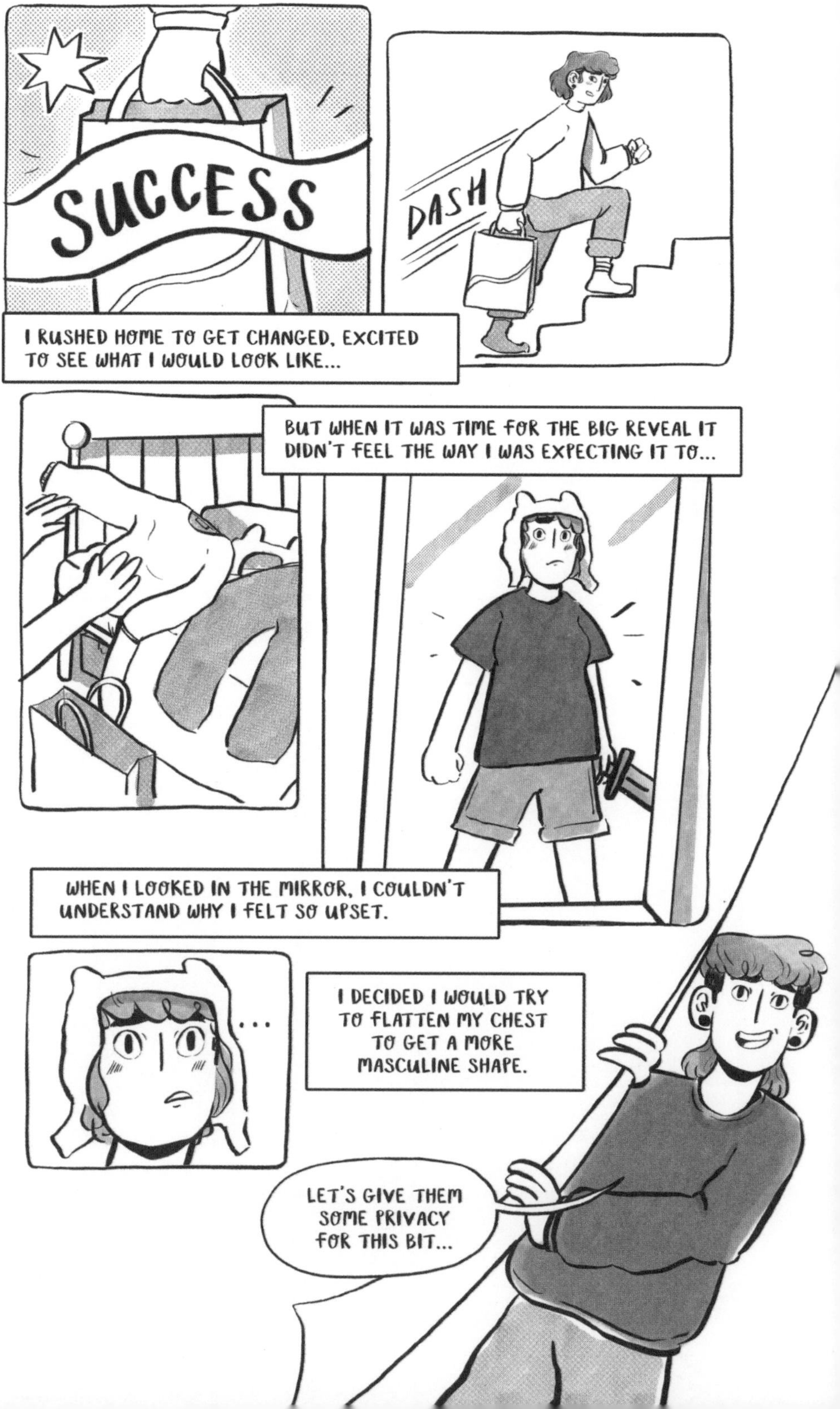
SUCCESS
DASH
I RUSHED HOME TO GET CHANGED, EXCITED TO SEE WHAT I WOULD LOOK LIKE...
BUT WHEN IT WAS TIME FOR THE BIG REVEAL IT DIDN'T FEEL THE WAY I WAS EXPECTING IT TO...
WHEN I LOOKED IN THE MIRROR, I COULDN'T UNDERSTAND WHY I FELT SO UPSET.
...
I DECIDED I WOULD TRY TO FLATTEN MY CHEST TO GET A MORE MASCULINE SHAPE.
LET'S GIVE THEM SOME PRIVACY FOR THIS BIT...

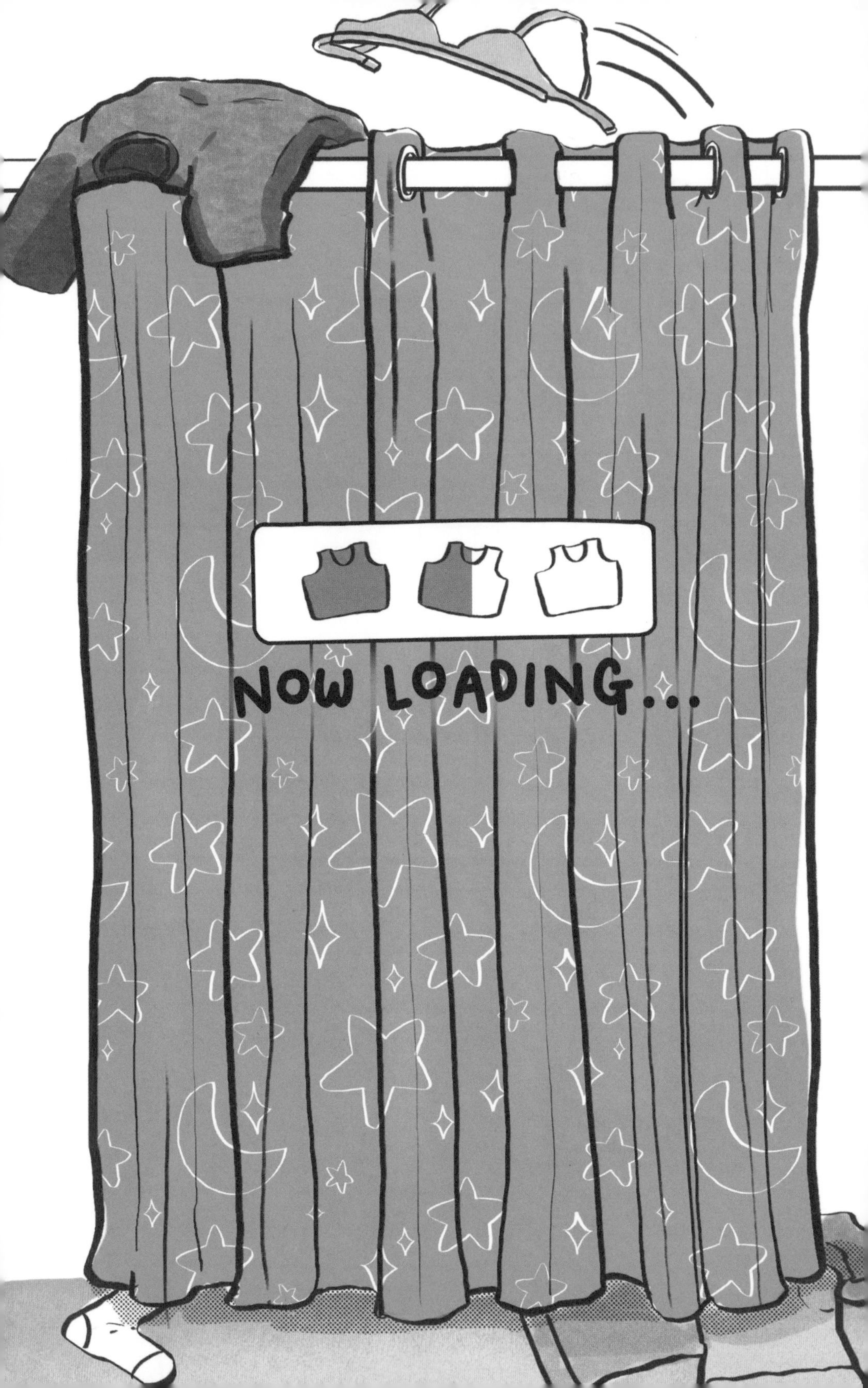
NOW LOADING...

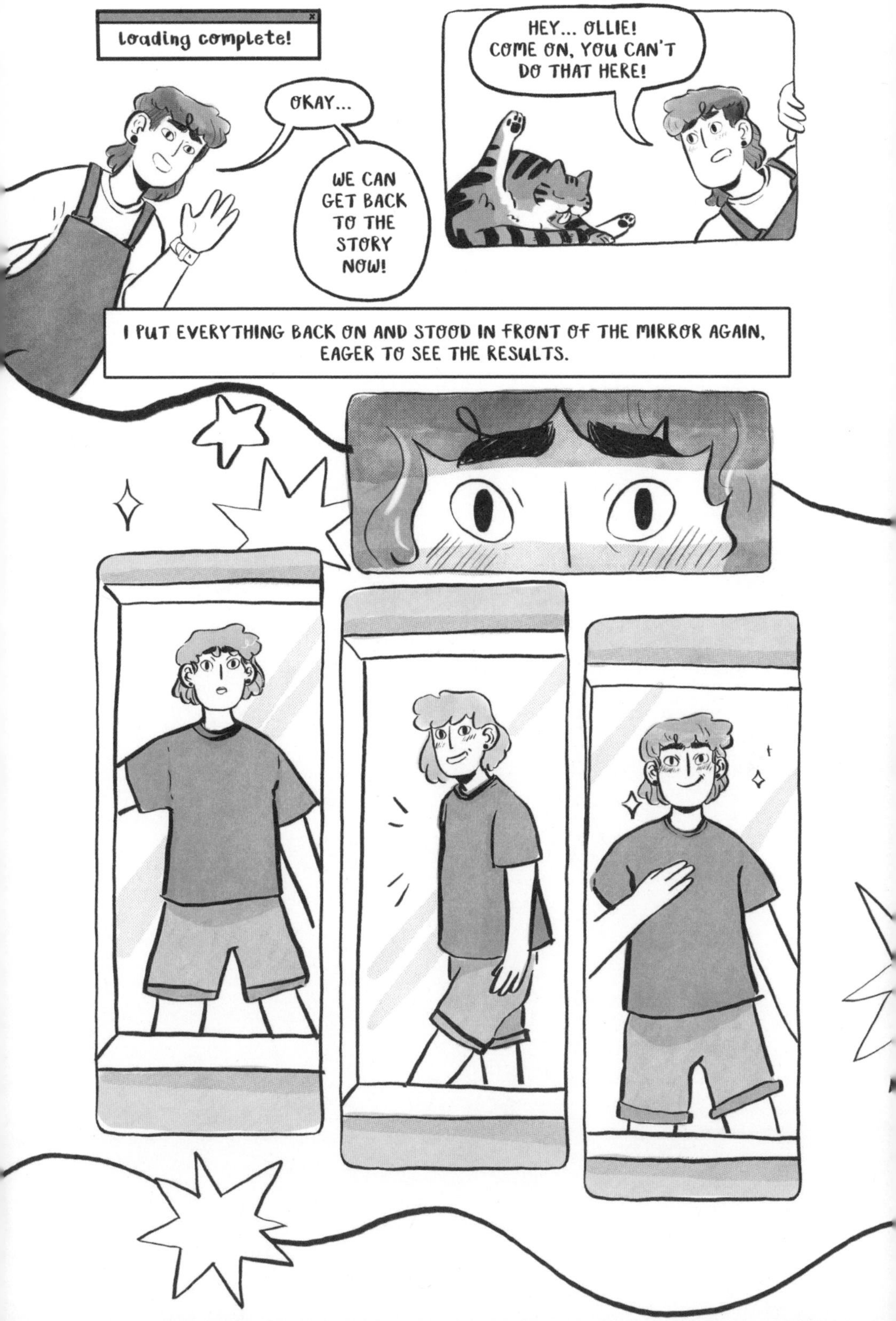
Loading complete!
OKAY...
WE CAN GET BACK TO THE STORY NOW!
HEY... OLLIE! COME ON, YOU CAN'T DO THAT HERE!
I PUT EVERYTHING BACK ON AND STOOD IN FRONT OF THE MIRROR AGAIN, EAGER TO SEE THE RESULTS.

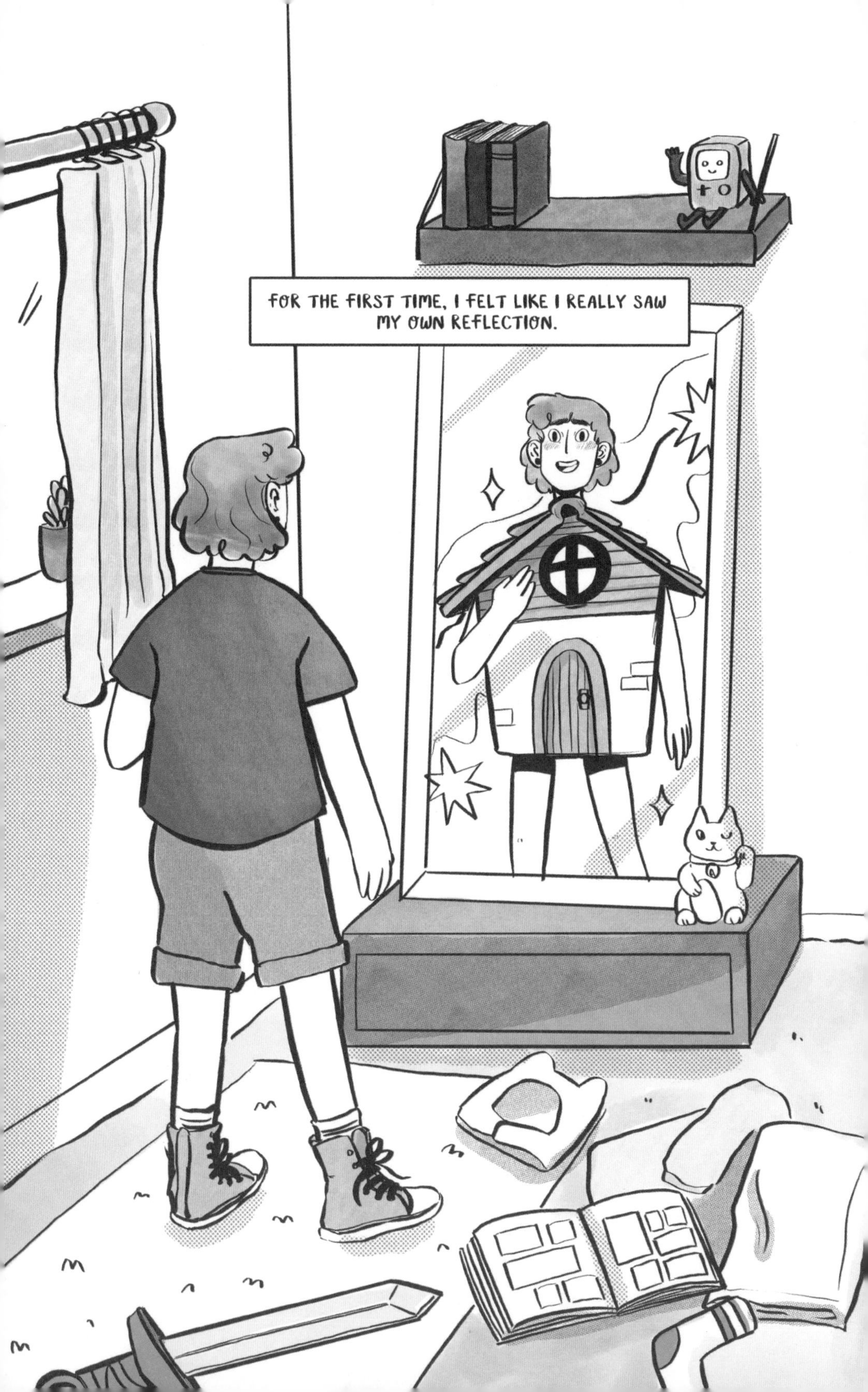
FOR THE FIRST TIME, I FELT LIKE I REALLY SAW MY OWN REFLECTION.

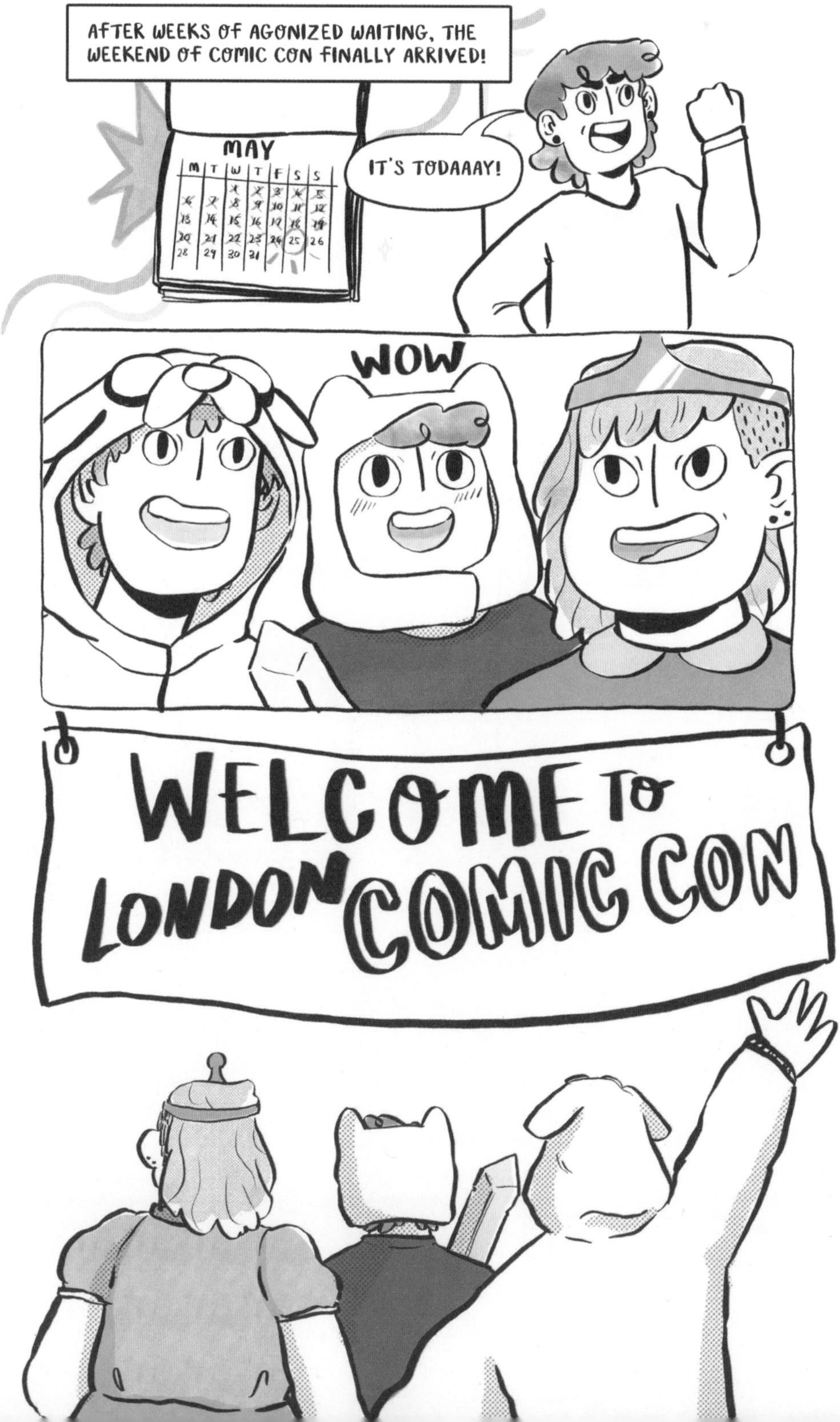
AFTER WEEKS OF AGONIZED WAITING, THE WEEKEND OF COMIC CON FINALLY ARRIVED!
MAY
M T W T F S S
IT'S TODAAAY!
WOW
WELCOME TO LONDON COMIC CON

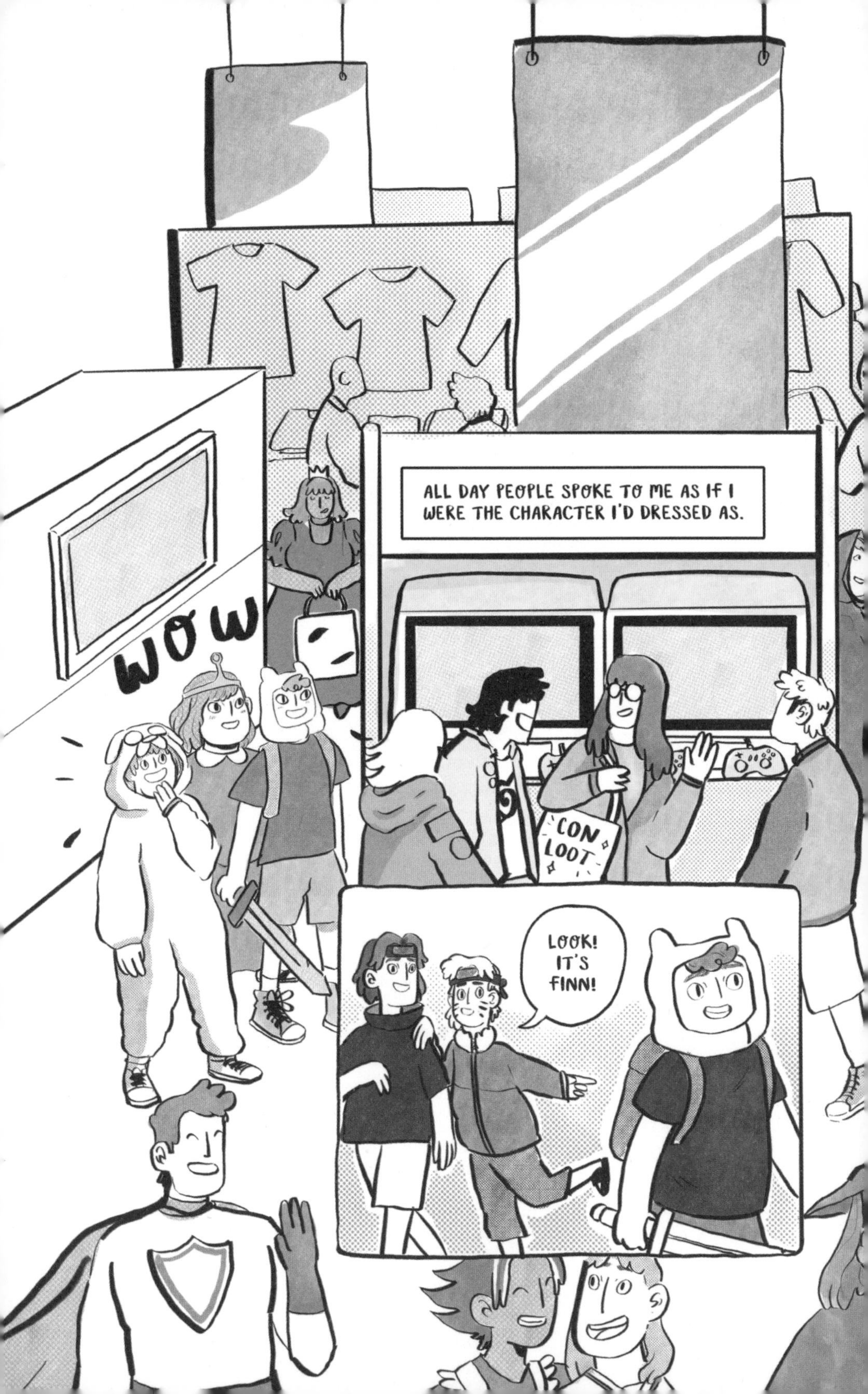
ALL DAY PEOPLE SPOKE TO ME AS IF I WERE THE CHARACTER I'D DRESSED AS.
WOW
CON LOOT
LOOK! IT'S FINN!

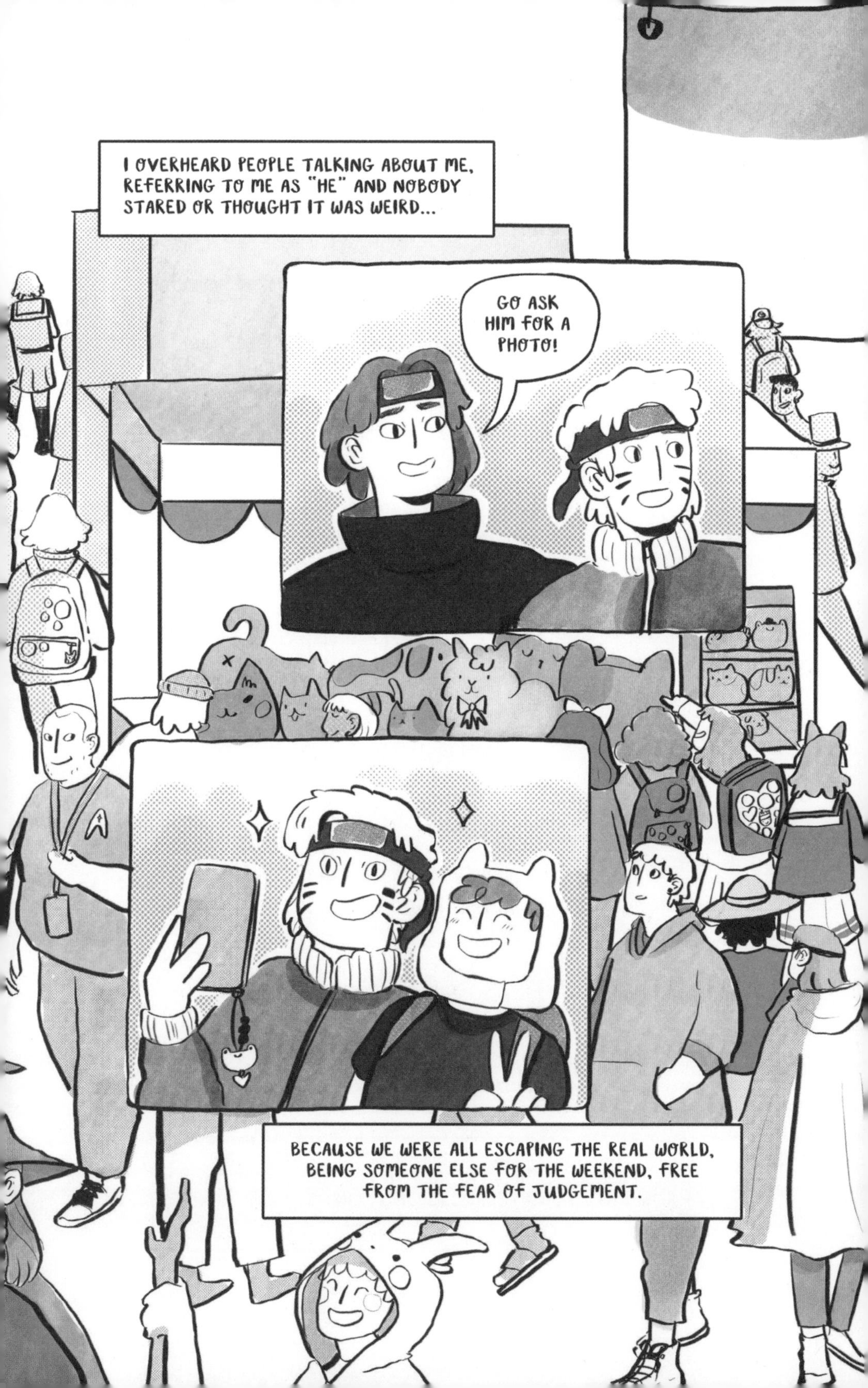
I OVERHEARD PEOPLE TALKING ABOUT ME, REFERRING TO ME AS "HE" AND NOBODY STARED OR THOUGHT IT WAS WEIRD...
GO ASK HIM FOR A PHOTO!
BECAUSE WE WERE ALL ESCAPING THE REAL WORLD, BEING SOMEONE ELSE FOR THE WEEKEND, FREE FROM THE FEAR OF JUDGEMENT.

THAT WAS AWESOME!
I CAN'T BELIEVE WE HAVE TO GO BACK TO REALITY TOMORROW!

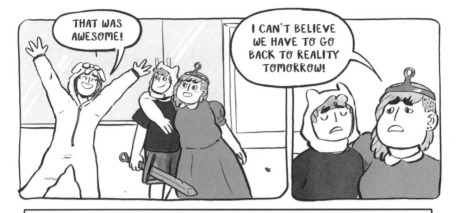

DRESSING UP AS A CHARACTER GAVE ME A CHANCE TO FEEL LIKE SOMEONE ELSE FOR THE DAY AND EXPERIMENT WITH HOW I PRESENTED MYSELF...

ALL WITHIN THE SAFETY OF A WELCOMING AND LIKE-MINDED COMMUNITY.

HE GAP

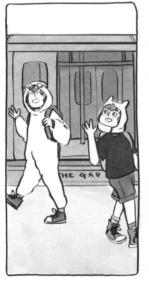

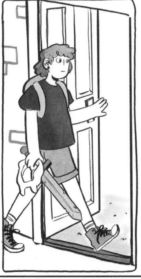

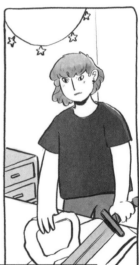

AT THE TIME I WASN'T READY TO CONSIDER WHY THIS FELT QUITE SO IMPORTANT TO ME, OR WHY I WAS SO DISAPPOINTED WHEN IT WAS OVER...

ALL I KNEW WAS THAT I NEEDED TO FIND MORE OPPORTUNITIES FOR THIS KIND OF ESCAPE. I DIDN'T WANT TO HAVE TO WAIT SIX MONTHS FOR THE NEXT COMIC CON TO FEEL LIKE THIS AGAIN!

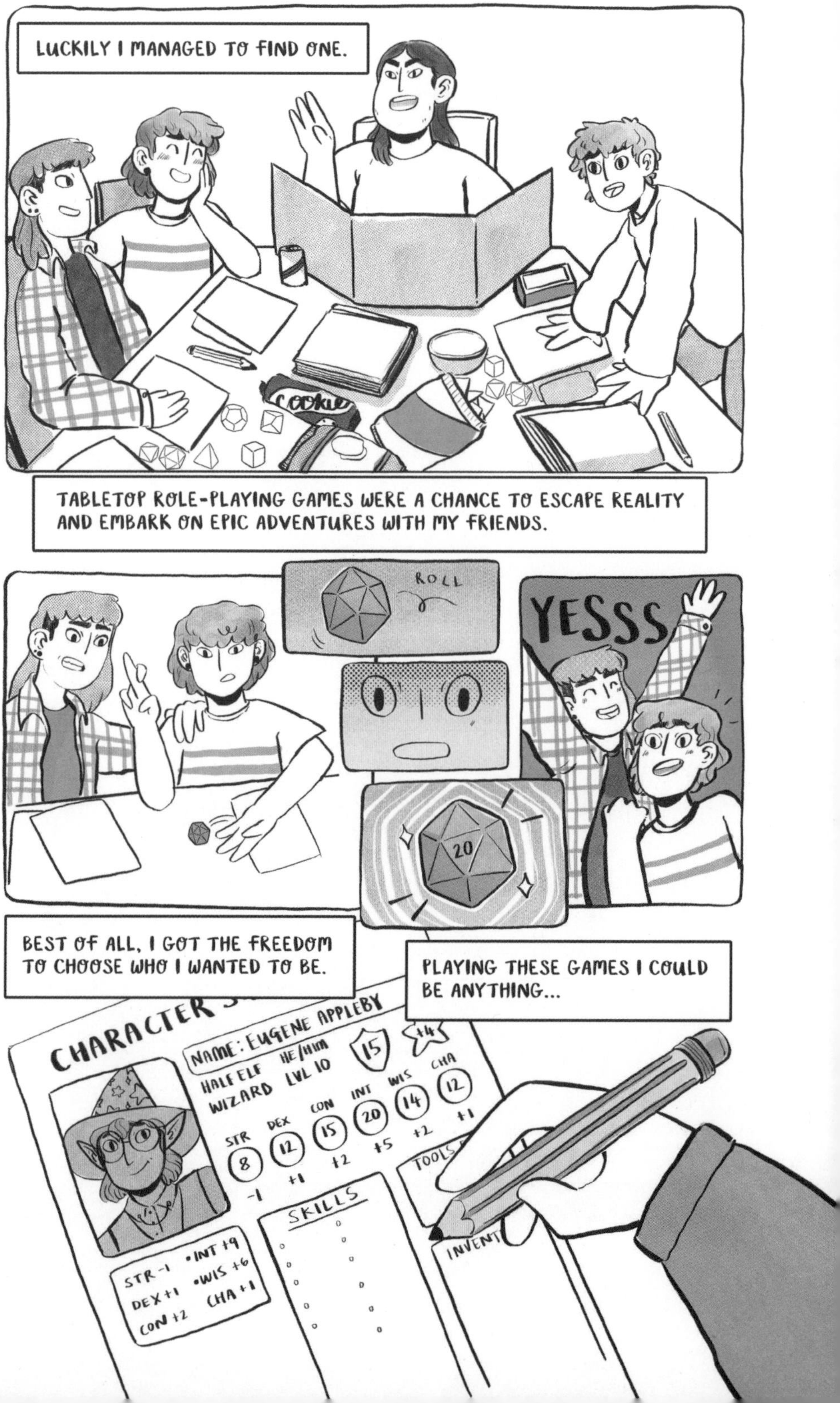
LUCKILY I MANAGED TO FIND ONE.
COOKIE
TABLETOP ROLE-PLAYING GAMES WERE A CHANCE TO ESCAPE REALITY AND EMBARK ON EPIC ADVENTURES WITH MY FRIENDS.
ROLL
20
YESSS
BEST OF ALL, I GOT THE FREEDOM TO CHOOSE WHO I WANTED TO BE.
PLAYING THESE GAMES I COULD BE ANYTHING...
CHARACTER
NAME: EUGENE APPLEBY
HALF ELF
HE/HIM
WIZARD
LVL 10
15
+4
STR 8 -1
DEX 12 +1
CON 15 +2
INT 20 +5
WIS 14 +2
CHA 12 +1
SKILLS
STR -1
DEX +1
CON +2
•INT +9
•WIS +6
CHA +1

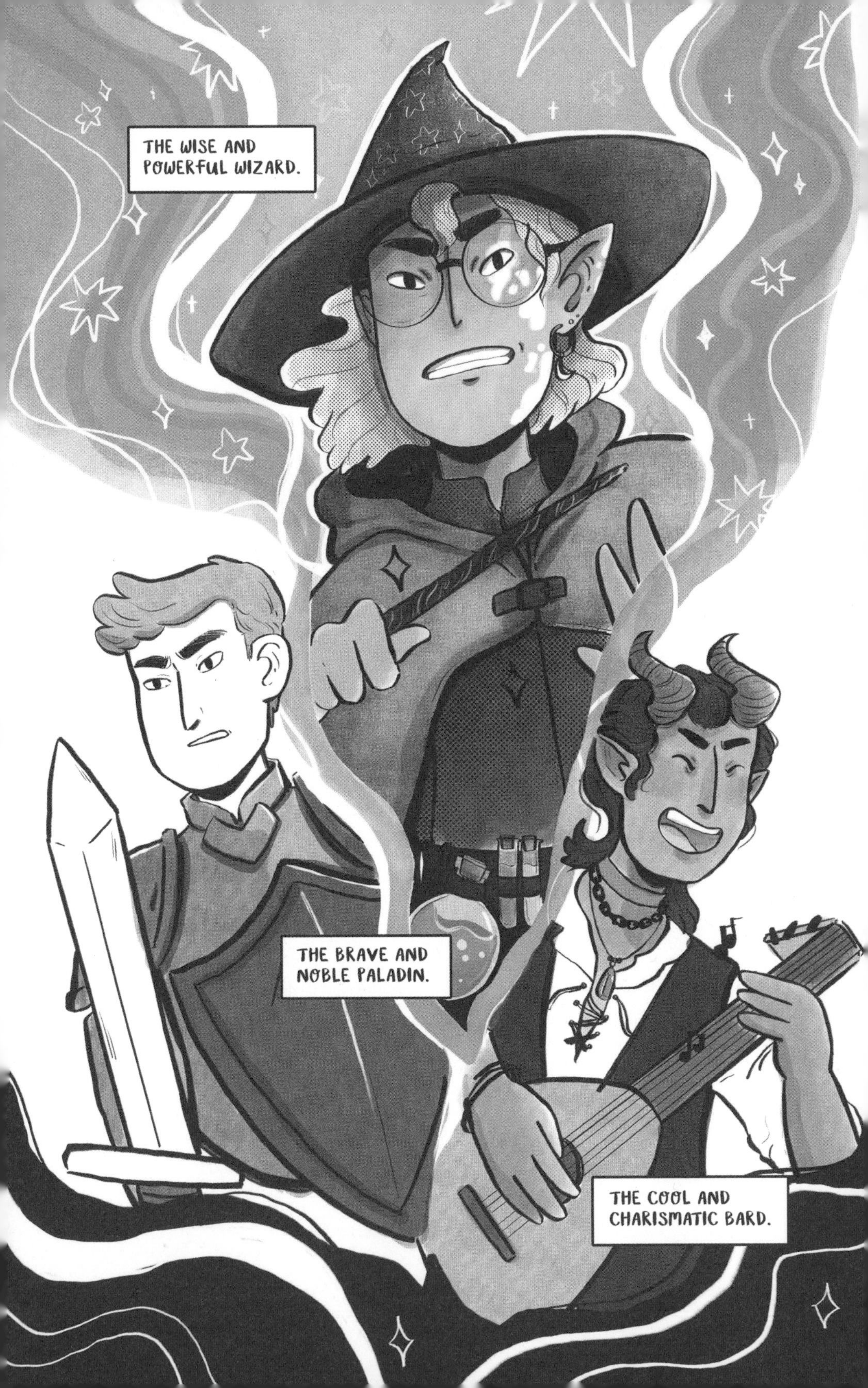
THE WISE AND POWERFUL WIZARD.
THE BRAVE AND NOBLE PALADIN.
THE COOL AND CHARISMATIC BARD.

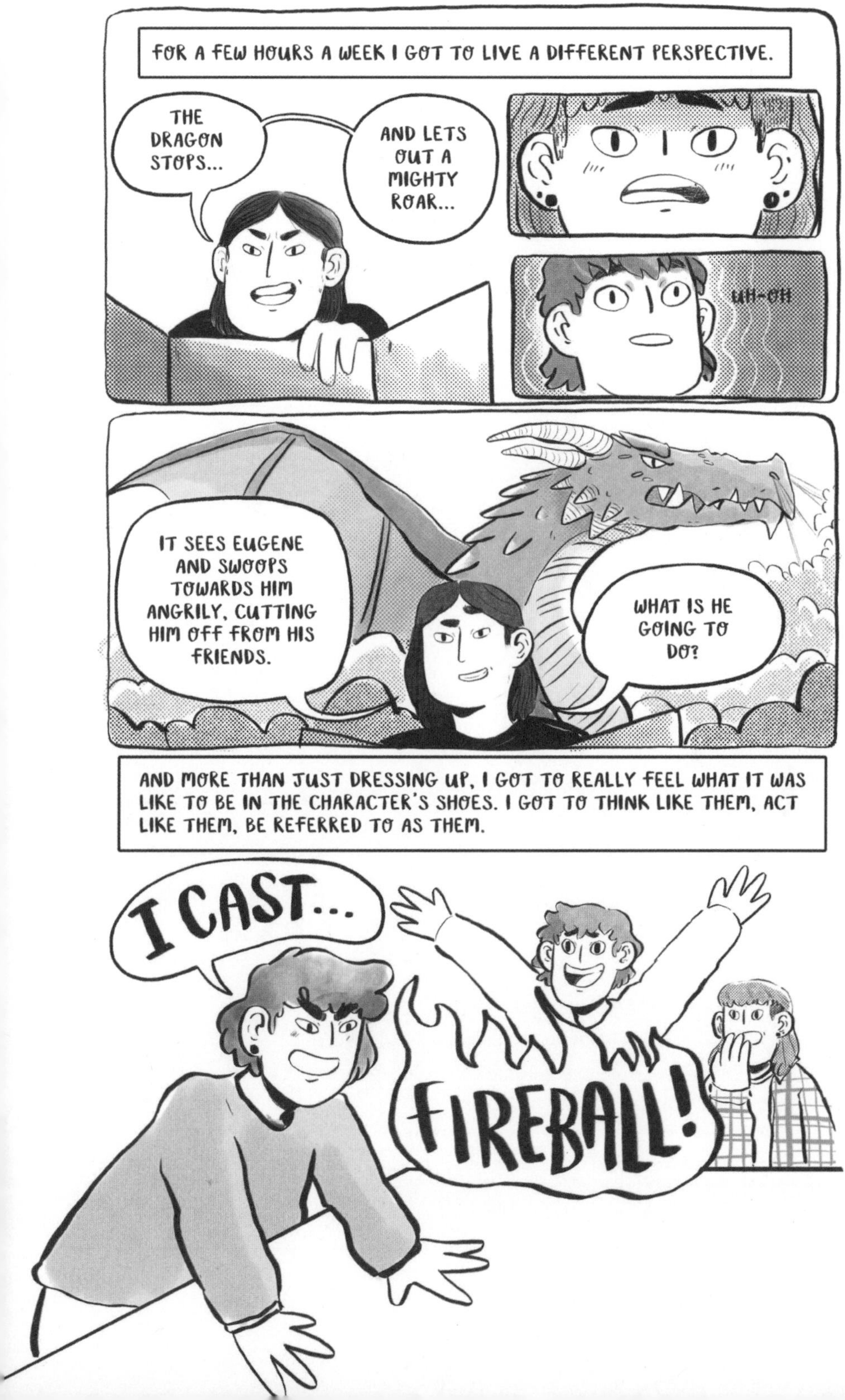
FOR A FEW HOURS A WEEK I GOT TO LIVE A DIFFERENT PERSPECTIVE.
THE DRAGON STOPS...
AND LETS OUT A MIGHTY ROAR...
UH-OH
IT SEES EUGENE AND SWOOPS TOWARDS HIM ANGRILY, CUTTING HIM OFF FROM HIS FRIENDS.
WHAT IS HE GOING TO DO?
AND MORE THAN JUST DRESSING UP, I GOT TO REALLY FEEL WHAT IT WAS LIKE TO BE IN THE CHARACTER'S SHOES. I GOT TO THINK LIKE THEM, ACT LIKE THEM, BE REFERRED TO AS THEM.
I CAST...
FIREBALL!

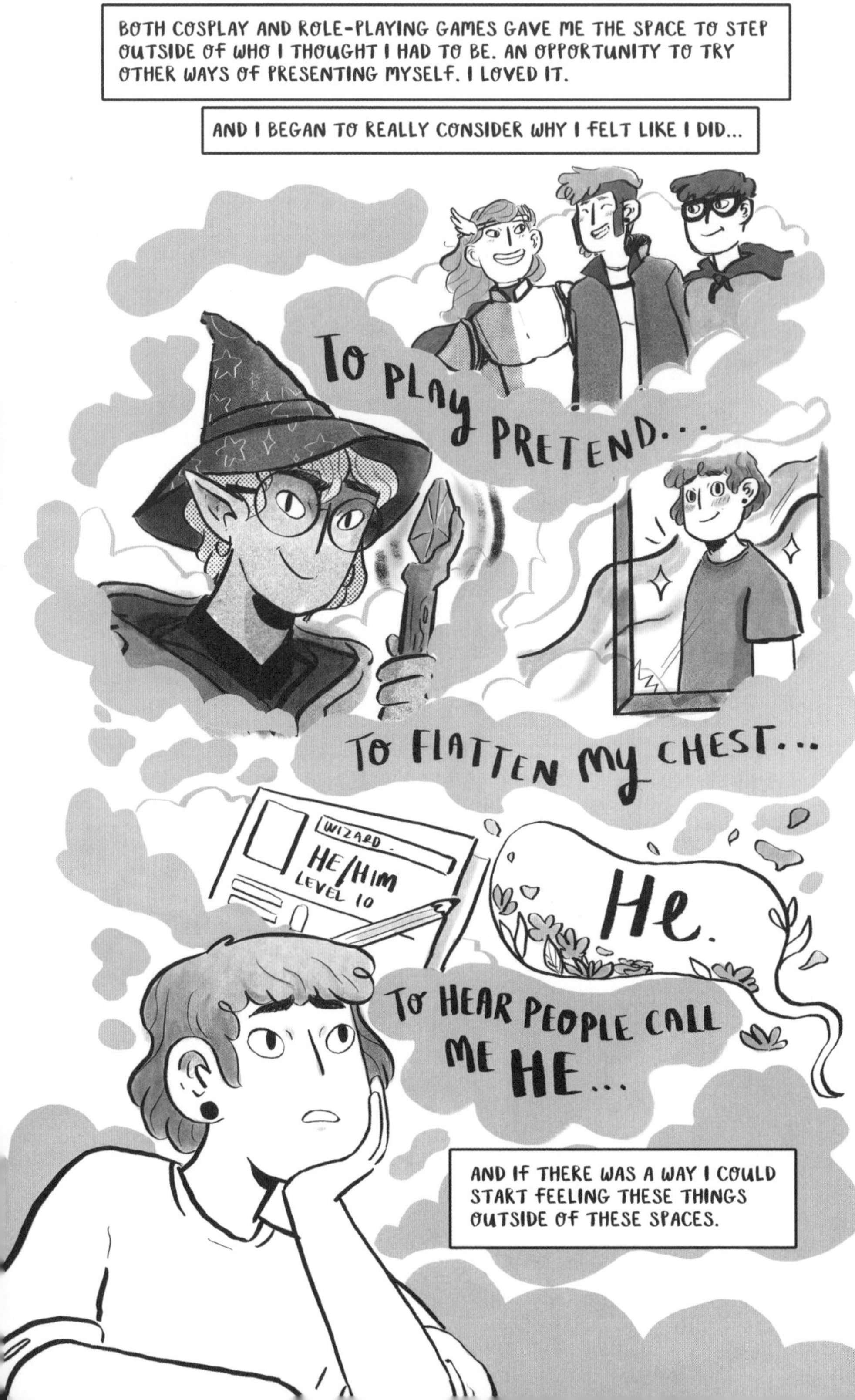
BOTH COSPLAY AND ROLE-PLAYING GAMES GAVE ME THE SPACE TO STEP OUTSIDE OF WHO I THOUGHT I HAD TO BE. AN OPPORTUNITY TO TRY OTHER WAYS OF PRESENTING MYSELF. I LOVED IT.
AND I BEGAN TO REALLY CONSIDER WHY I FELT LIKE I DID...
TO PLAY PRETEND...
TO FLATTEN MY CHEST...
WIZARD
HE/HIM
LEVEL 10
HE.
TO HEAR PEOPLE CALL ME HE...
AND IF THERE WAS A WAY I COULD START FEELING THESE THINGS OUTSIDE OF THESE SPACES.

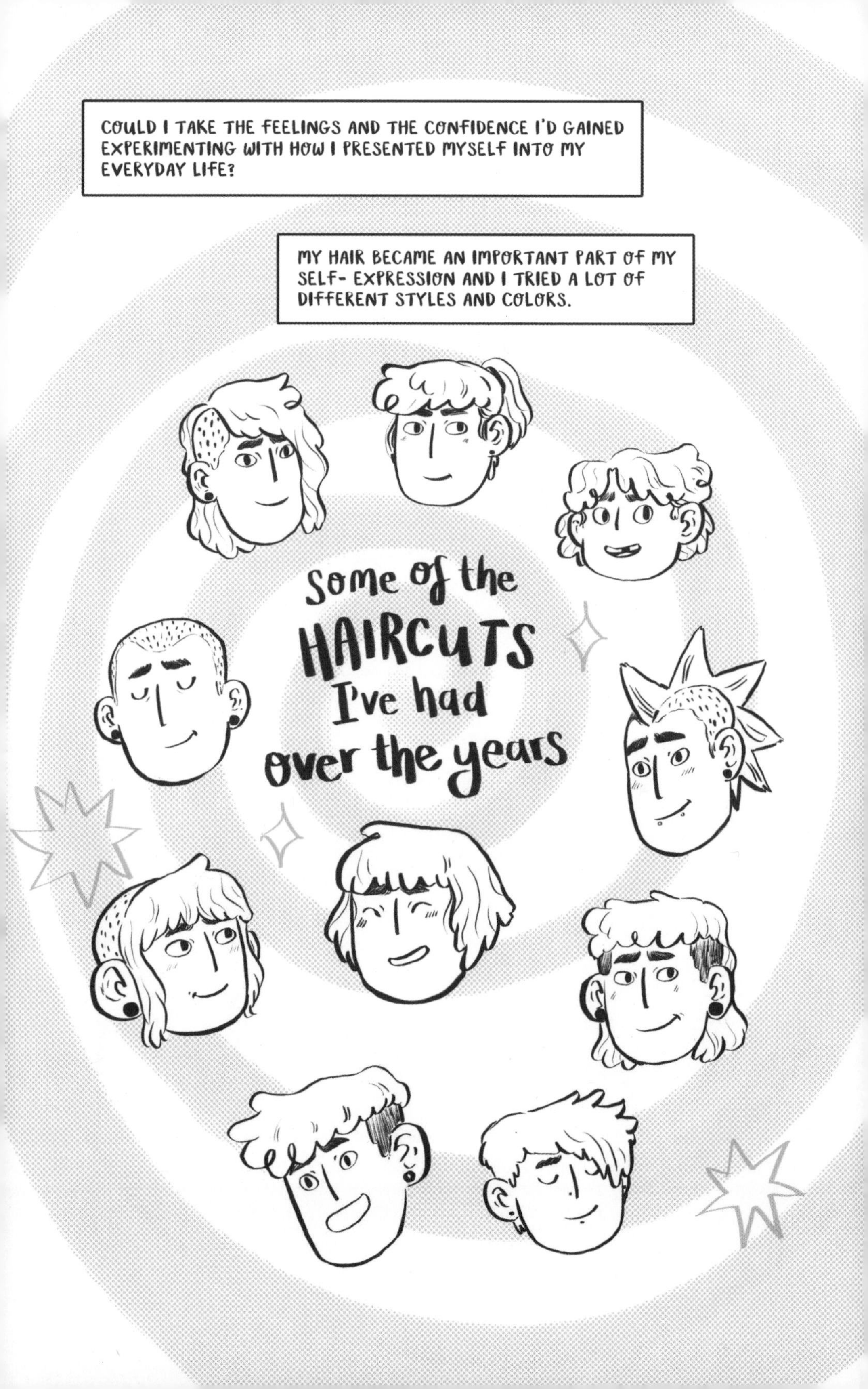
COULD I TAKE THE FEELINGS AND THE CONFIDENCE I'D GAINED EXPERIMENTING WITH HOW I PRESENTED MYSELF INTO MY EVERYDAY LIFE?
MY HAIR BECAME AN IMPORTANT PART OF MY SELF- EXPRESSION AND I TRIED A LOT OF DIFFERENT STYLES AND COLORS.
Some of the HAIRCUTS I've had over the years

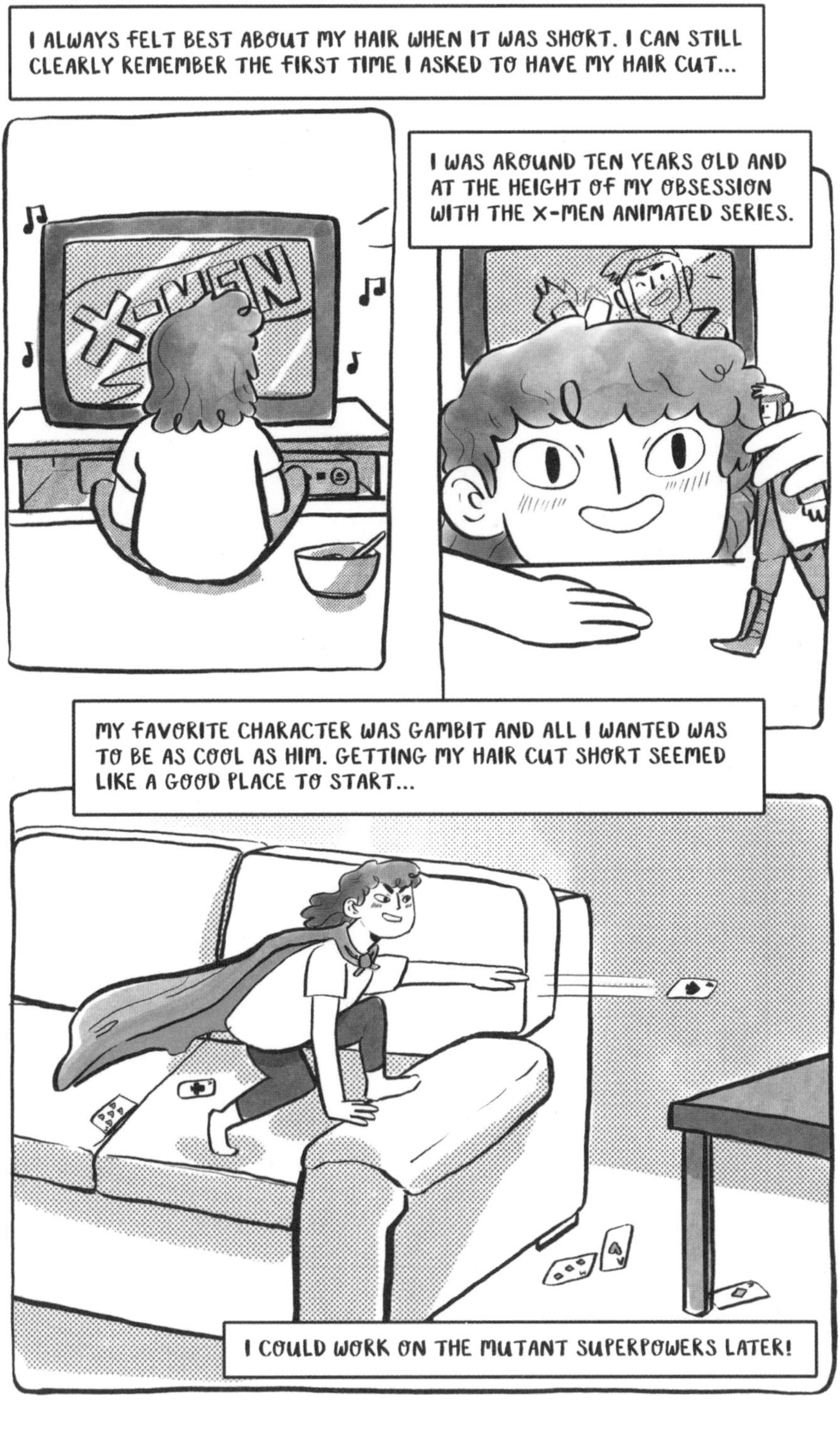
I ALWAYS FELT BEST ABOUT MY HAIR WHEN IT WAS SHORT. I CAN STILL CLEARLY REMEMBER THE FIRST TIME I ASKED TO HAVE MY HAIR CUT...
X-MEN
I WAS AROUND TEN YEARS OLD AND AT THE HEIGHT OF MY OBSESSION WITH THE X-MEN ANIMATED SERIES.
MY FAVORITE CHARACTER WAS GAMBIT AND ALL I WANTED WAS TO BE AS COOL AS HIM. GETTING MY HAIR CUT SHORT SEEMED LIKE A GOOD PLACE TO START...
I COULD WORK ON THE MUTANT SUPERPOWERS LATER!

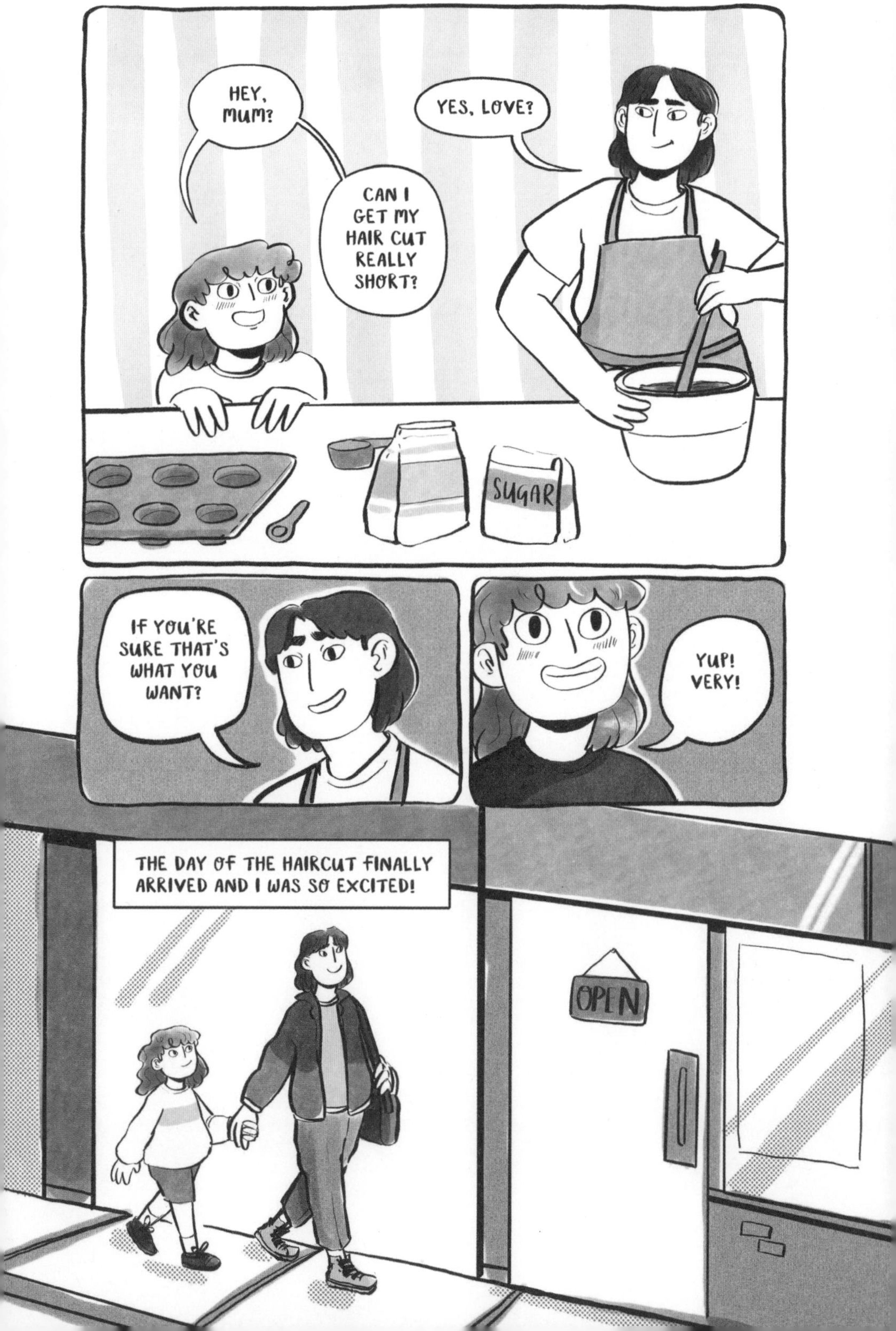

HEY, MUM?
YES, LOVE?
CAN I GET MY HAIR CUT REALLY SHORT?
SUGAR
IF YOU'RE SURE THAT'S WHAT YOU WANT?
YUP! VERY!
THE DAY OF THE HAIRCUT FINALLY ARRIVED AND I WAS SO EXCITED!
OPEN

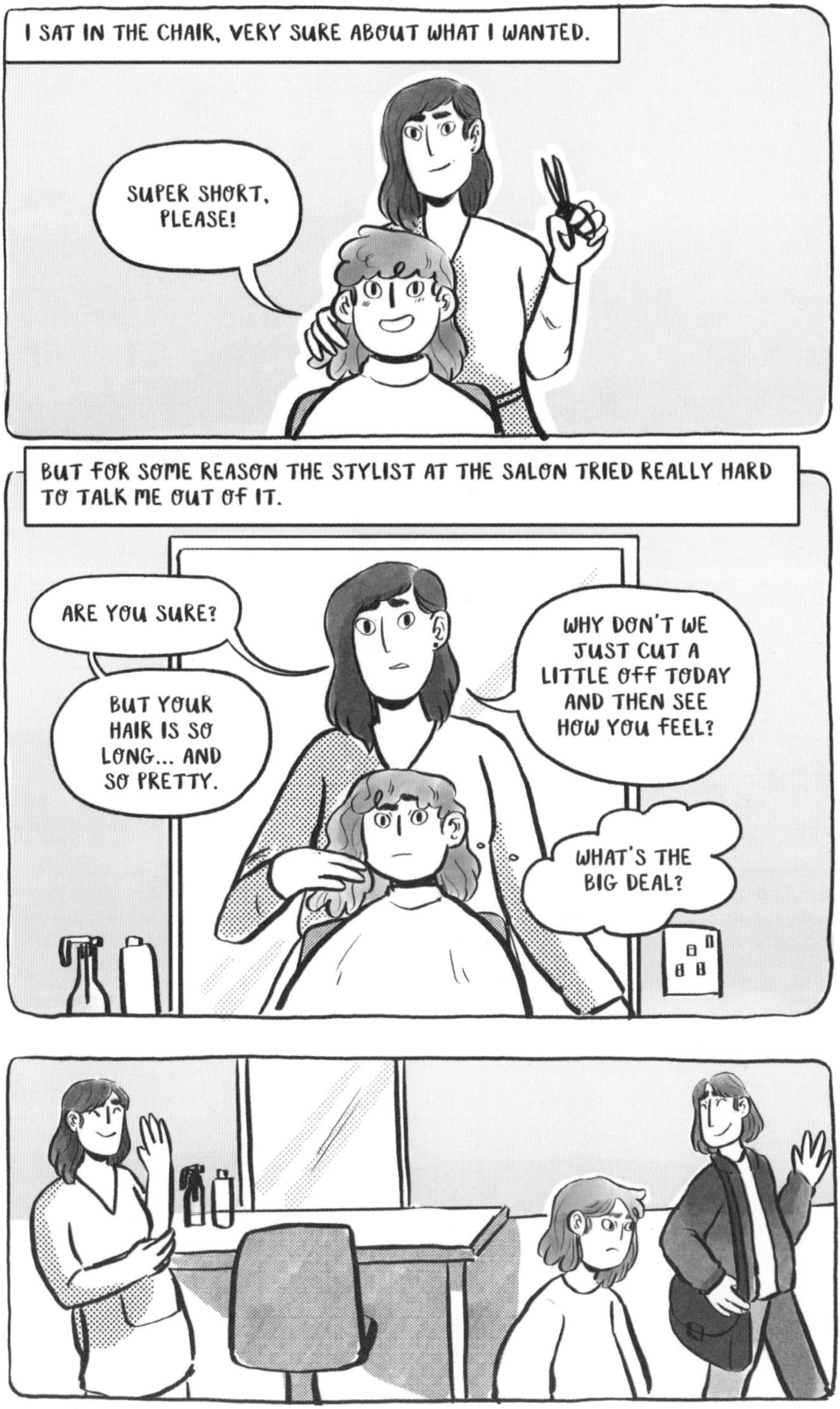
I SAT IN THE CHAIR, VERY SURE ABOUT WHAT I WANTED.
SUPER SHORT, PLEASE!
BUT FOR SOME REASON THE STYLIST AT THE SALON TRIED REALLY HARD TO TALK ME OUT OF IT.
ARE YOU SURE?
BUT YOUR HAIR IS SO LONG... AND SO PRETTY.
WHY DON'T WE JUST CUT A LITTLE OFF TODAY AND THEN SEE HOW YOU FEEL?
WHAT'S THE BIG DEAL?

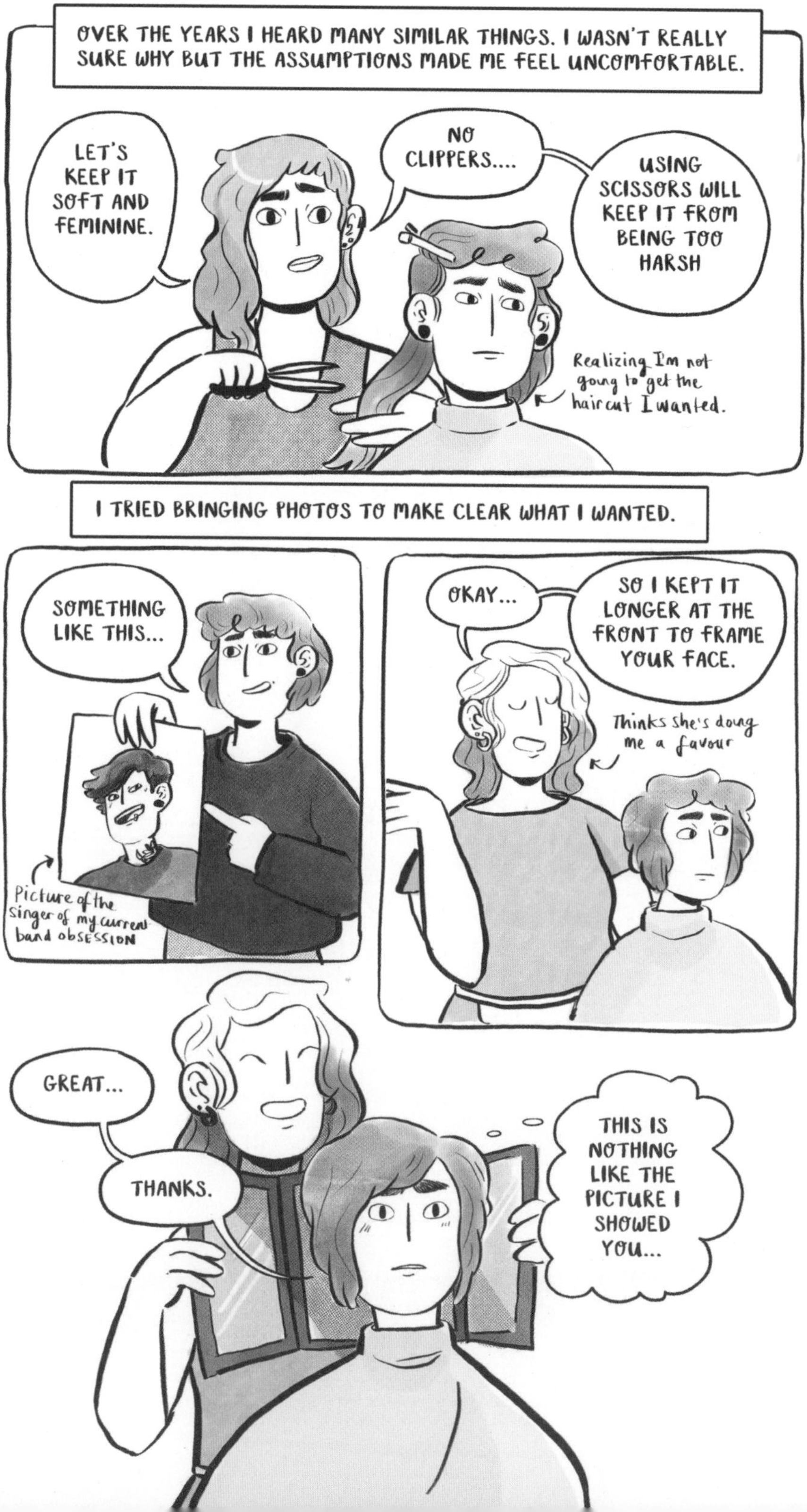

OVER THE YEARS I HEARD MANY SIMILAR THINGS. I WASN'T REALLY SURE WHY BUT THE ASSUMPTIONS MADE ME FEEL UNCOMFORTABLE.
LET'S KEEP IT SOFT AND FEMININE.
NO CLIPPERS....
USING SCISSORS WILL KEEP IT FROM BEING TOO HARSH
Realizing I'm not going to get the haircut I wanted.
I TRIED BRINGING PHOTOS TO MAKE CLEAR WHAT I WANTED.
SOMETHING LIKE THIS...
Picture of the singer of my current band obsession
OKAY...
SO I KEPT IT LONGER AT THE FRONT TO FRAME YOUR FACE.
Thinks she's doing me a favour
GREAT...
THANKS.
THIS IS NOTHING LIKE THE PICTURE I SHOWED YOU...

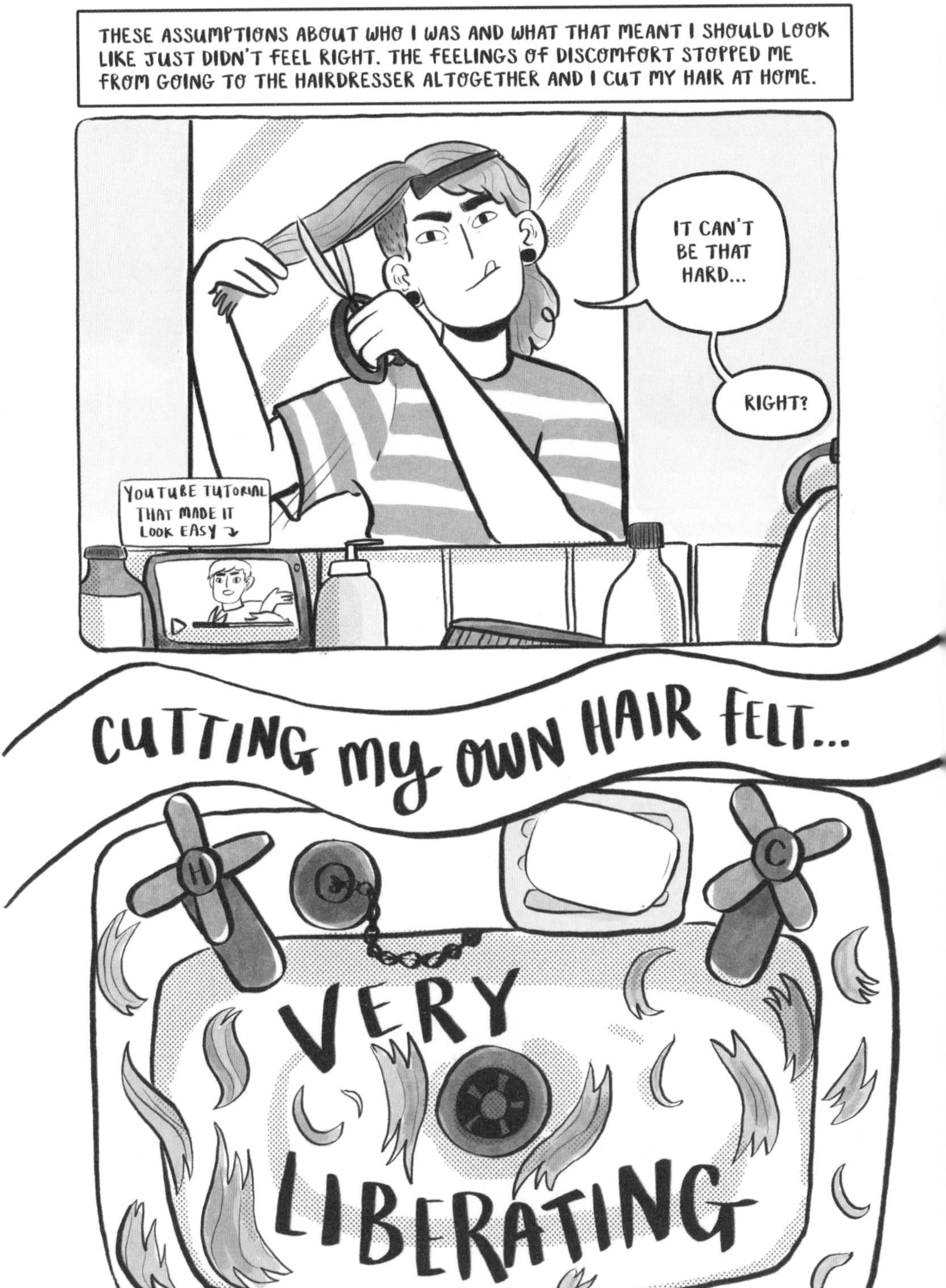
THESE ASSUMPTIONS ABOUT WHO I WAS AND WHAT THAT MEANT I SHOULD LOOK LIKE JUST DIDN'T FEEL RIGHT. THE FEELINGS OF DISCOMFORT STOPPED ME FROM GOING TO THE HAIRDRESSER ALTOGETHER AND I CUT MY HAIR AT HOME.
IT CAN'T BE THAT HARD...
RIGHT?
YOUTUBE TUTORIAL THAT MADE IT LOOK EASY
CUTTING MY OWN HAIR FELT...
H
C
VERY LIBERATING

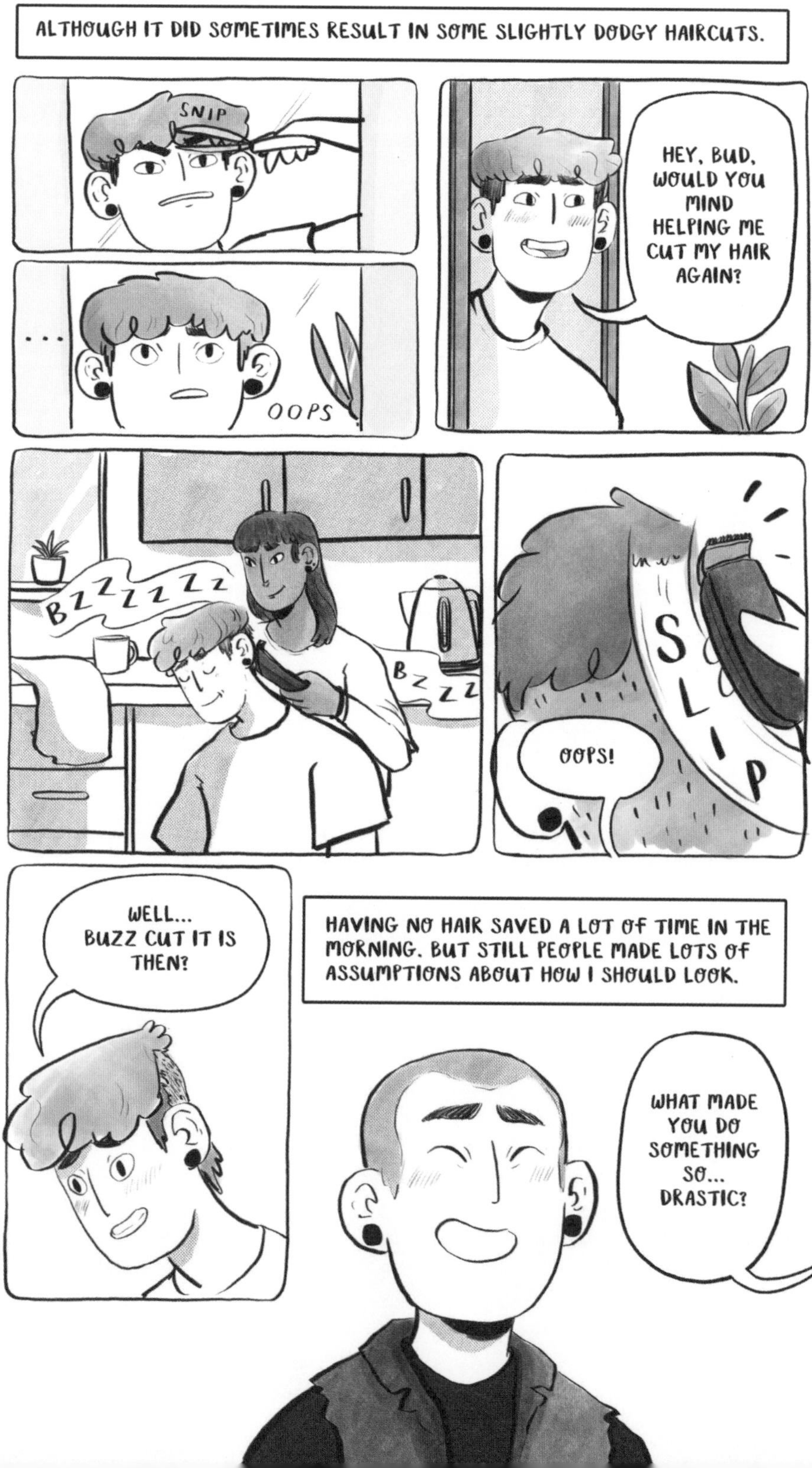
ALTHOUGH IT DID SOMETIMES RESULT IN SOME SLIGHTLY DODGY HAIRCUTS.
SNIP
...
OOPS
HEY, BUD, WOULD YOU MIND HELPING ME CUT MY HAIR AGAIN?
BZZZZZZZ
BZZZ
SLIP
OOPS!
WELL... BUZZ CUT IT IS THEN?
HAVING NO HAIR SAVED A LOT OF TIME IN THE MORNING. BUT STILL PEOPLE MADE LOTS OF ASSUMPTIONS ABOUT HOW I SHOULD LOOK.
WHAT MADE YOU DO SOMETHING SO... DRASTIC?

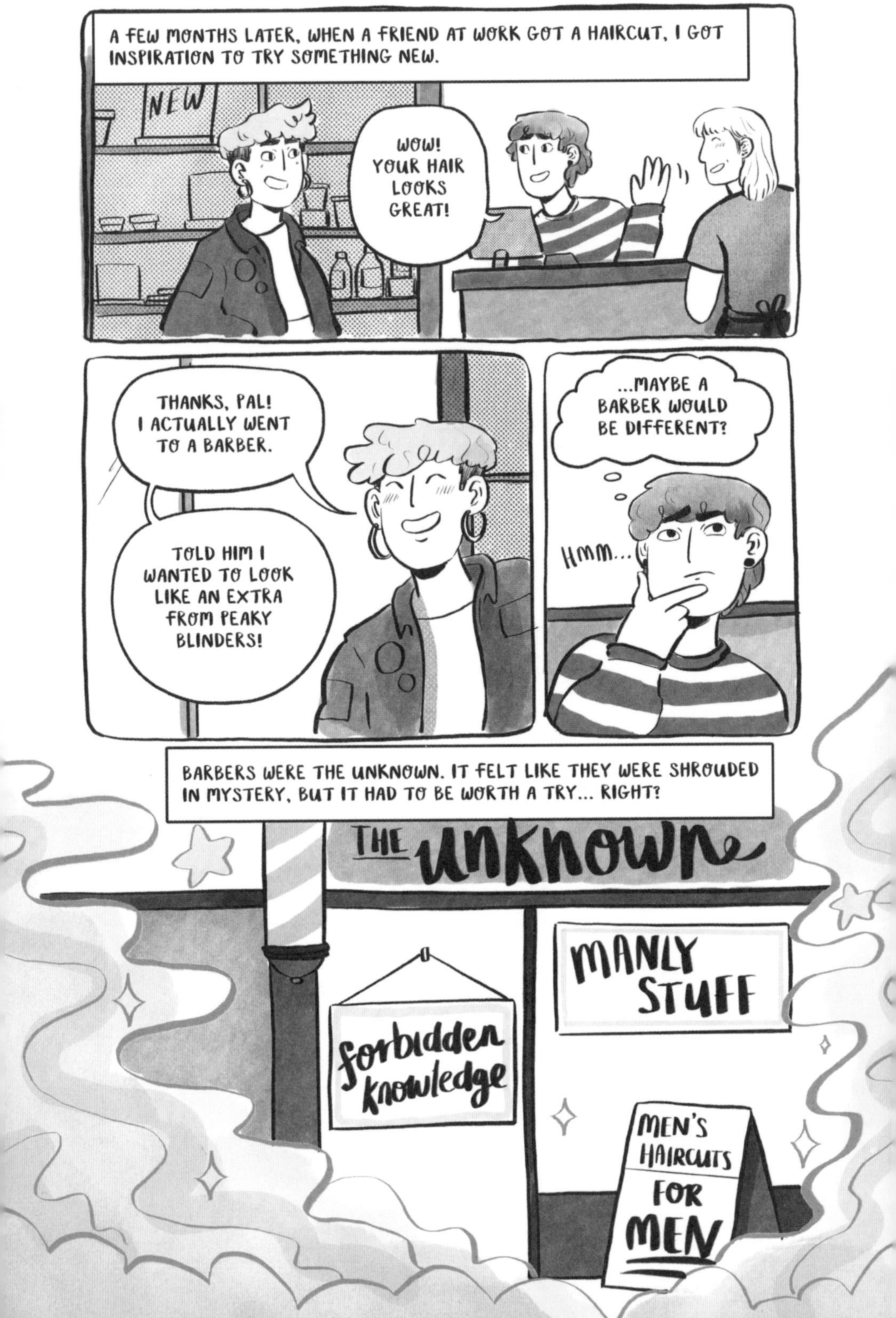
A FEW MONTHS LATER, WHEN A FRIEND AT WORK GOT A HAIRCUT, I GOT INSPIRATION TO TRY SOMETHING NEW.
NEW
WOW! YOUR HAIR LOOKS GREAT!
THANKS, PAL! I ACTUALLY WENT TO A BARBER.
TOLD HIM I WANTED TO LOOK LIKE AN EXTRA FROM PEAKY BLINDERS!
...MAYBE A BARBER WOULD BE DIFFERENT?
HMM...
BARBERS WERE THE UNKNOWN. IT FELT LIKE THEY WERE SHROUDED IN MYSTERY, BUT IT HAD TO BE WORTH A TRY... RIGHT?
THE UNKNOWN
MANLY STUFF
forbidden knowledge
MEN'S HAIRCUTS FOR MEN

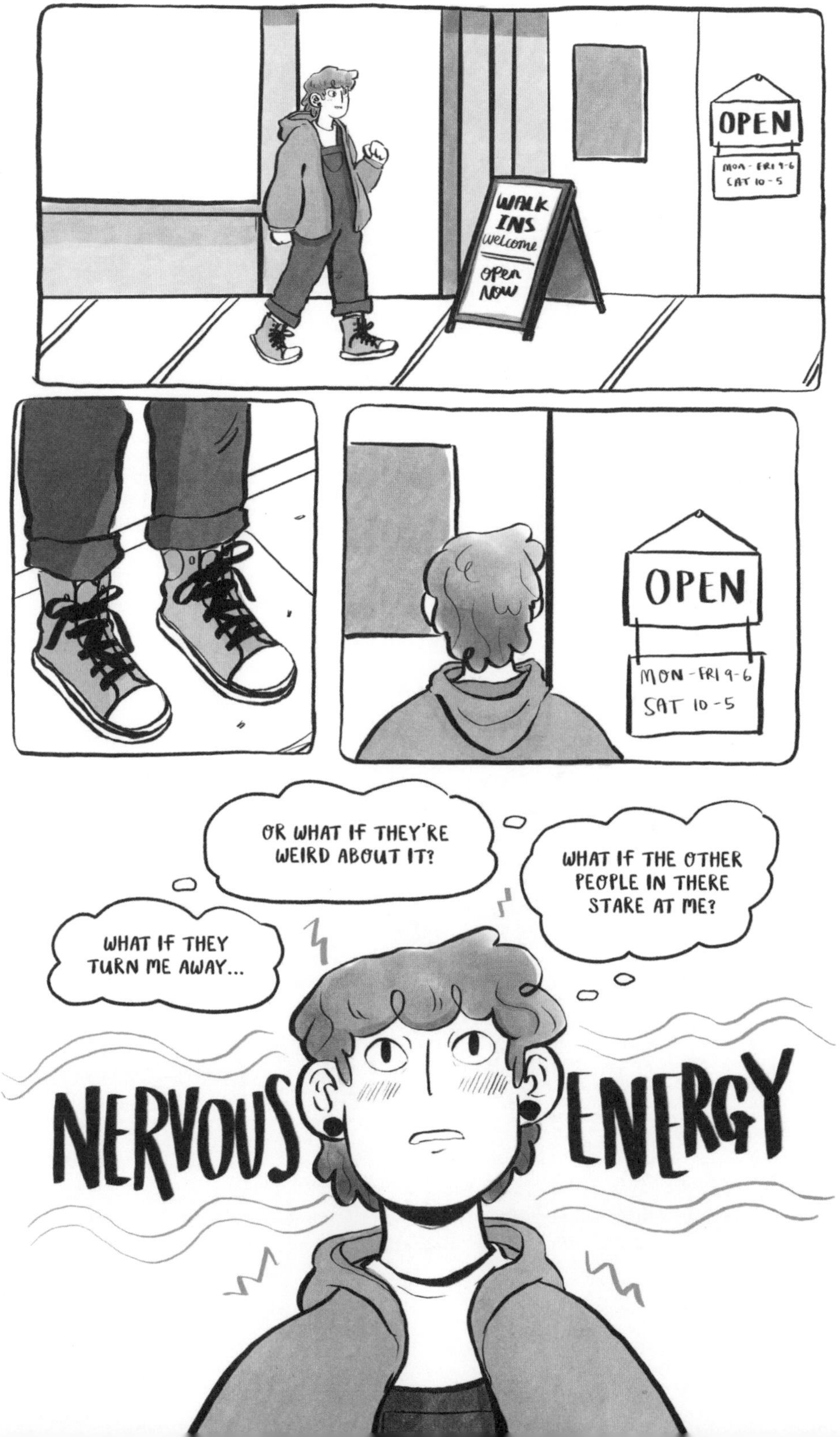
WALK INS welcome
open now
OPEN
MON-FRI 9-6
SAT 10-5
OPEN
MON-FRI 9-6
SAT 10-5
WHAT IF THEY TURN ME AWAY...
OR WHAT IF THEY'RE WEIRD ABOUT IT?
WHAT IF THE OTHER PEOPLE IN THERE STARE AT ME?
NERVOUS ENERGY

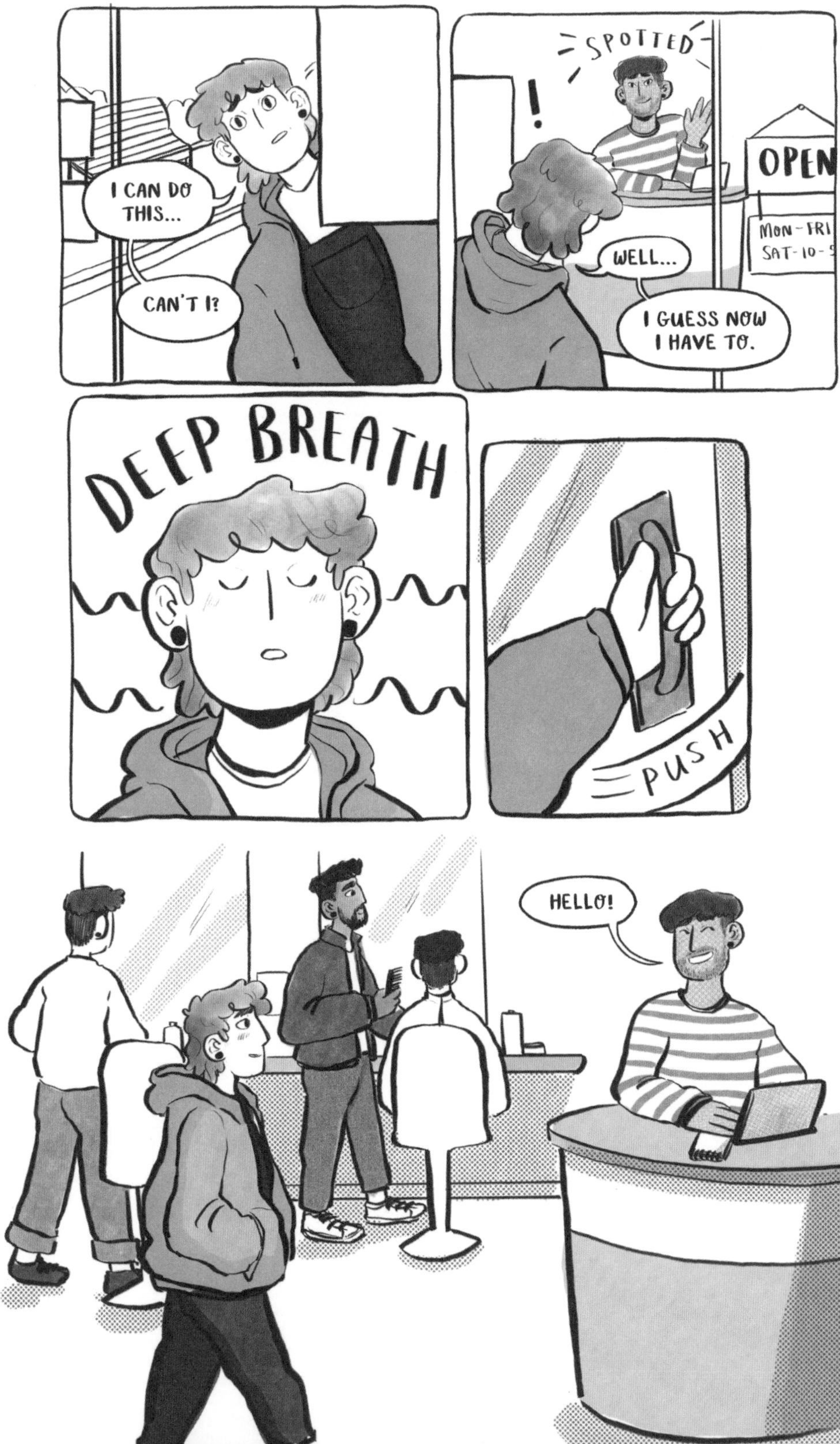
I CAN DO THIS...
CAN'T I?
SPOTTED
!
OPEN
MON-FRI
SAT-10-5
WELL...
I GUESS NOW I HAVE TO.
DEEP BREATH
PUSH
HELLO!

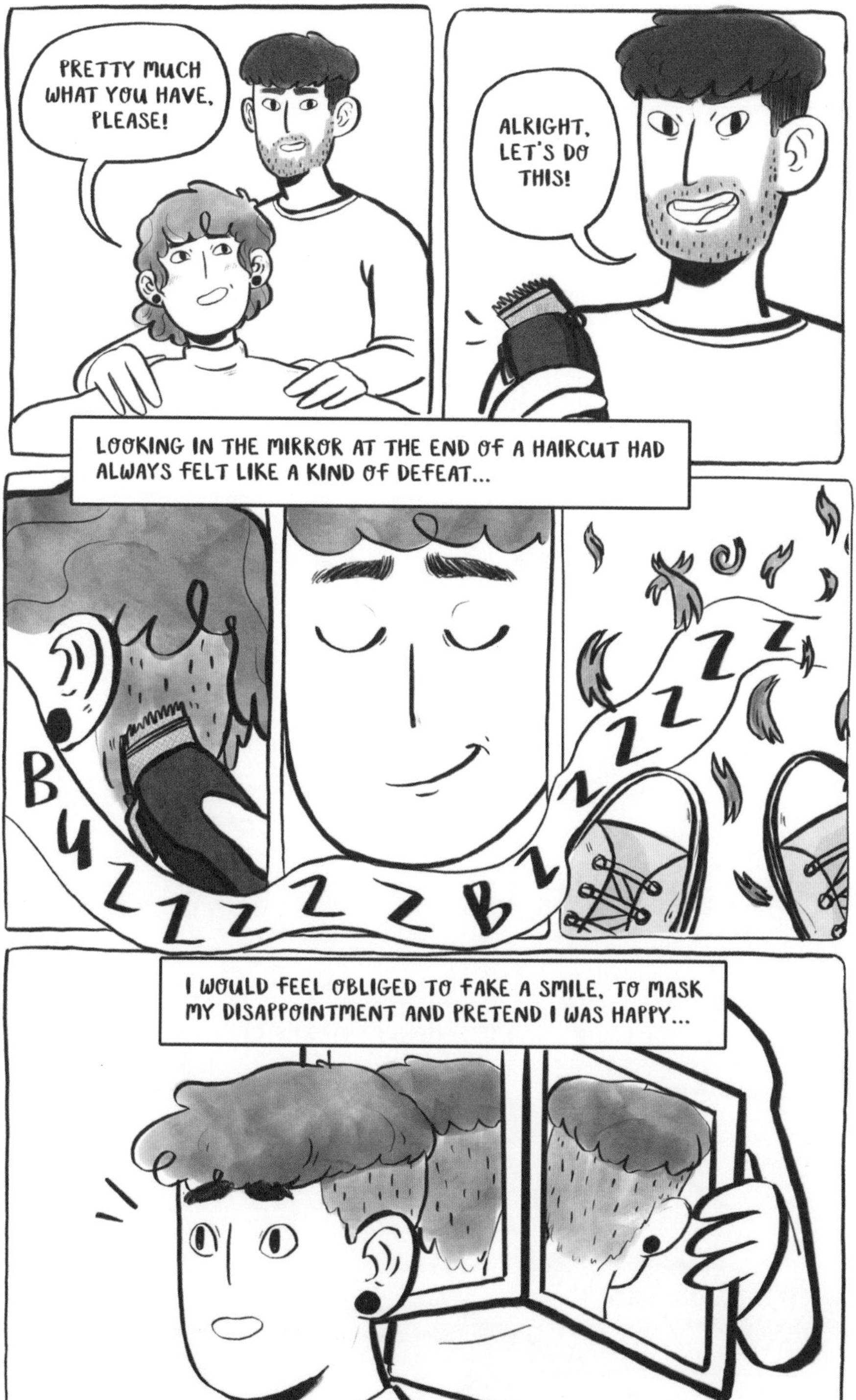
PRETTY MUCH WHAT YOU HAVE, PLEASE!
ALRIGHT, LET'S DO THIS!
LOOKING IN THE MIRROR AT THE END OF A HAIRCUT HAD ALWAYS FELT LIKE A KIND OF DEFEAT...
BUZZZZZ BZZZZZZZZ
I WOULD FEEL OBLIGED TO FAKE A SMILE, TO MASK MY DISAPPOINTMENT AND PRETEND I WAS HAPPY...

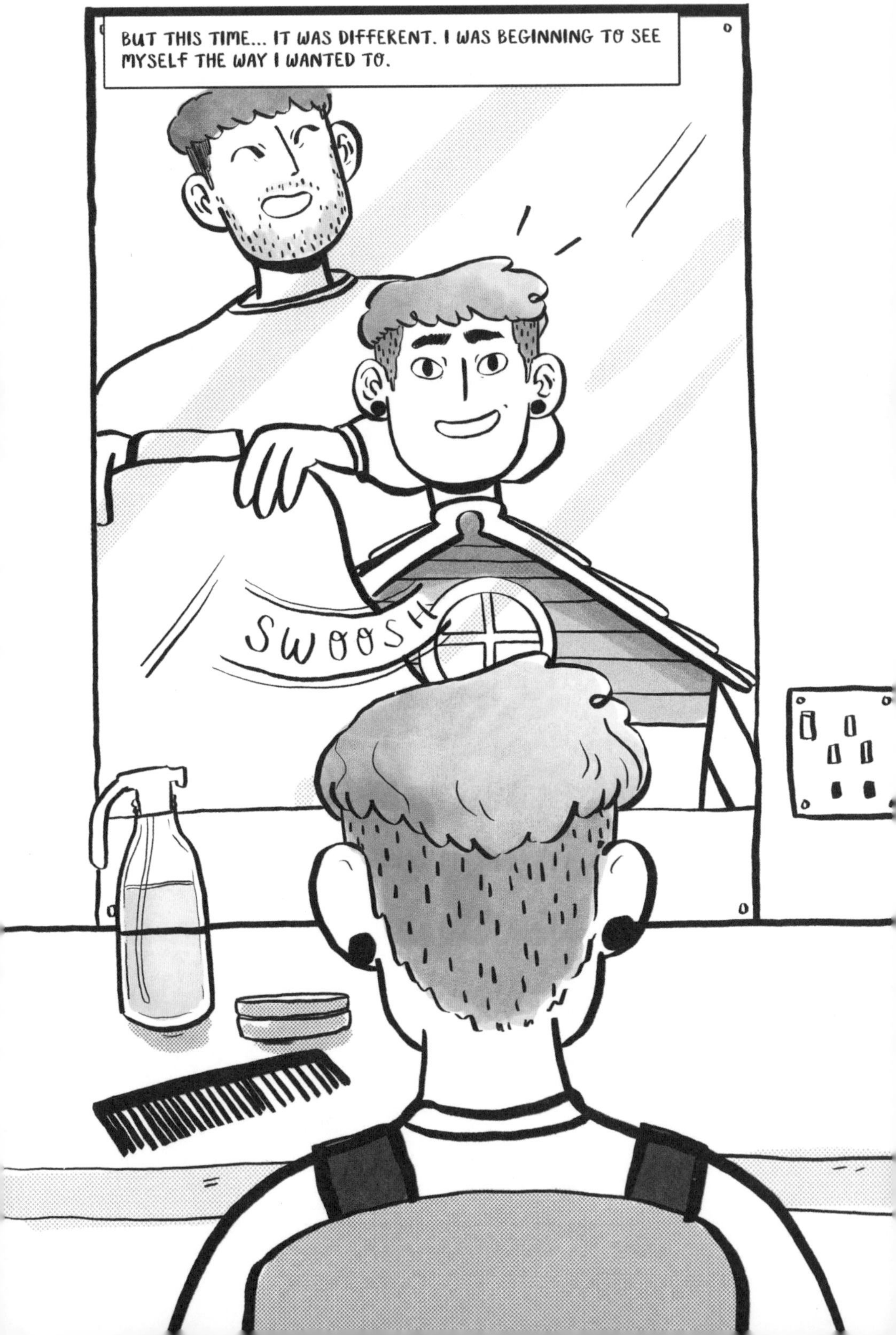
BUT THIS TIME... IT WAS DIFFERENT. I WAS BEGINNING TO SEE MYSELF THE WAY I WANTED TO.
SWOOSH

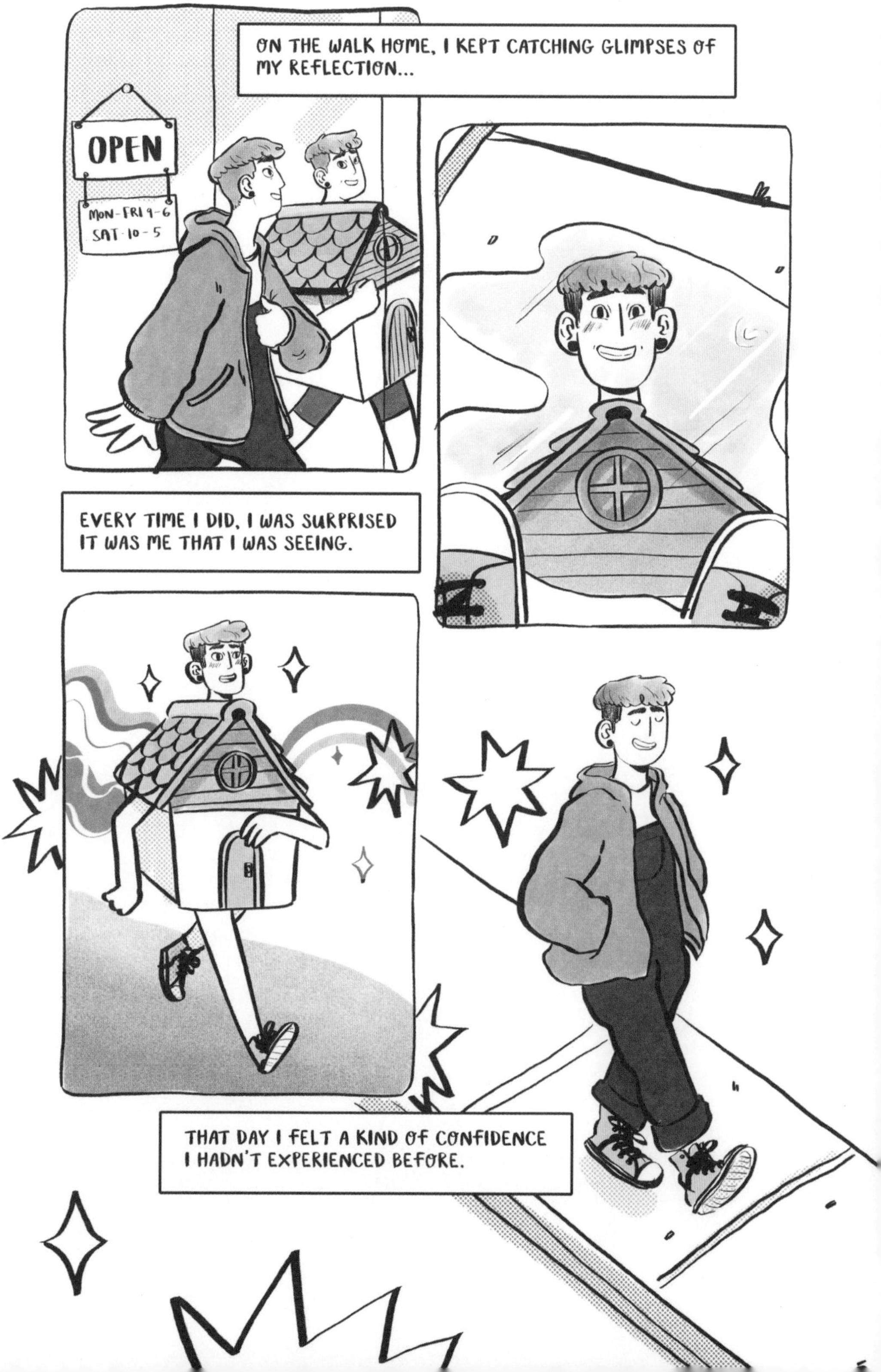
ON THE WALK HOME, I KEPT CATCHING GLIMPSES OF MY REFLECTION...
OPEN
MON-FRI 9-6
SAT 10-5
EVERY TIME I DID, I WAS SURPRISED IT WAS ME THAT I WAS SEEING.
THAT DAY I FELT A KIND OF CONFIDENCE I HADN'T EXPERIENCED BEFORE.

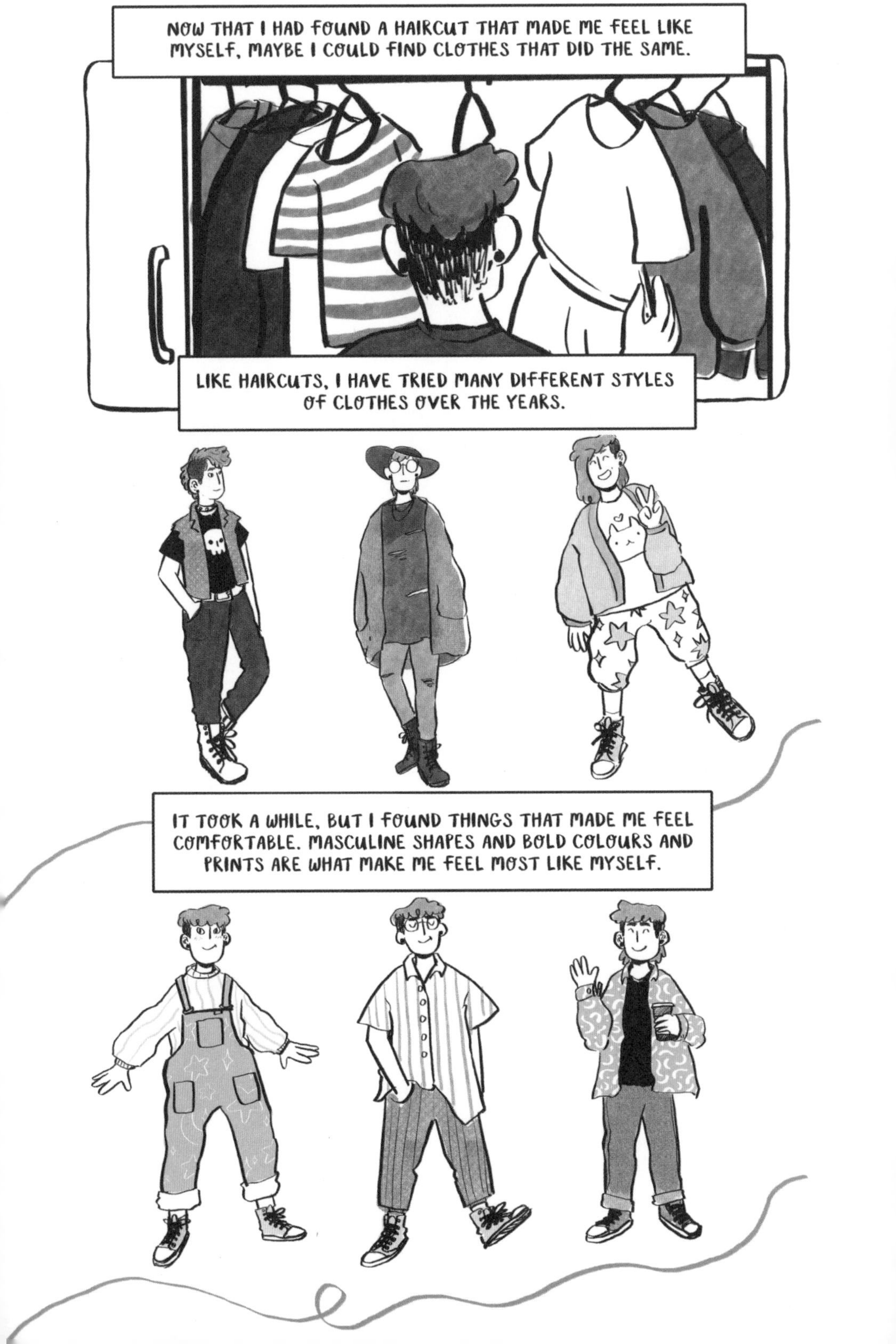
NOW THAT I HAD FOUND A HAIRCUT THAT MADE ME FEEL LIKE MYSELF, MAYBE I COULD FIND CLOTHES THAT DID THE SAME.
LIKE HAIRCUTS, I HAVE TRIED MANY DIFFERENT STYLES OF CLOTHES OVER THE YEARS.
IT TOOK A WHILE, BUT I FOUND THINGS THAT MADE ME FEEL COMFORTABLE. MASCULINE SHAPES AND BOLD COLOURS AND PRINTS ARE WHAT MAKE ME FEEL MOST LIKE MYSELF.

IT WAS COMPLICATED. I KNEW THAT CLOTHES HAD NO GENDER, BUT I ALSO KNEW THAT WHAT I WORE DICTATED HOW PEOPLE PERCEIVED ME.

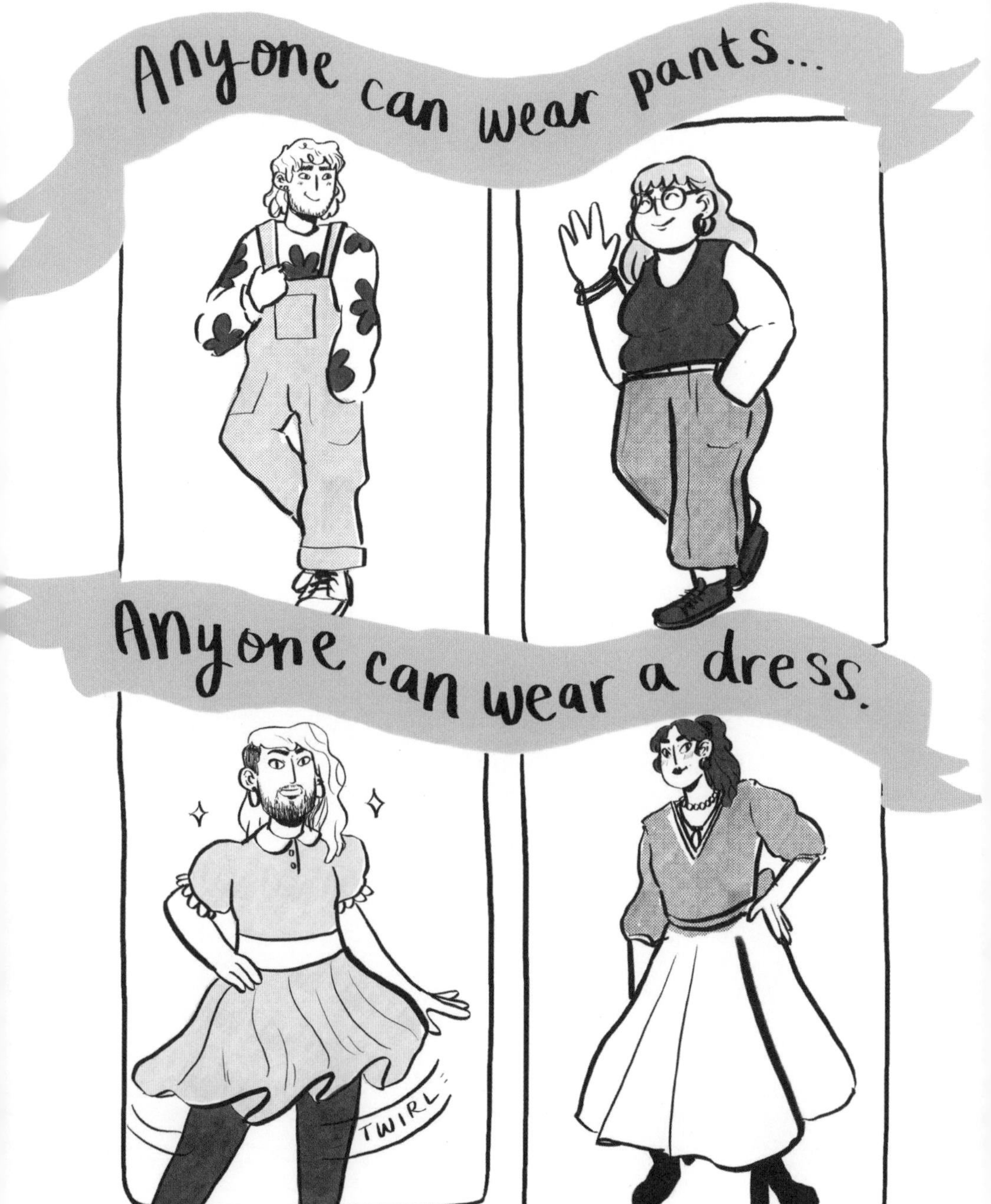
Anyone can wear pants...
Anyone can wear a dress.
TWIRL

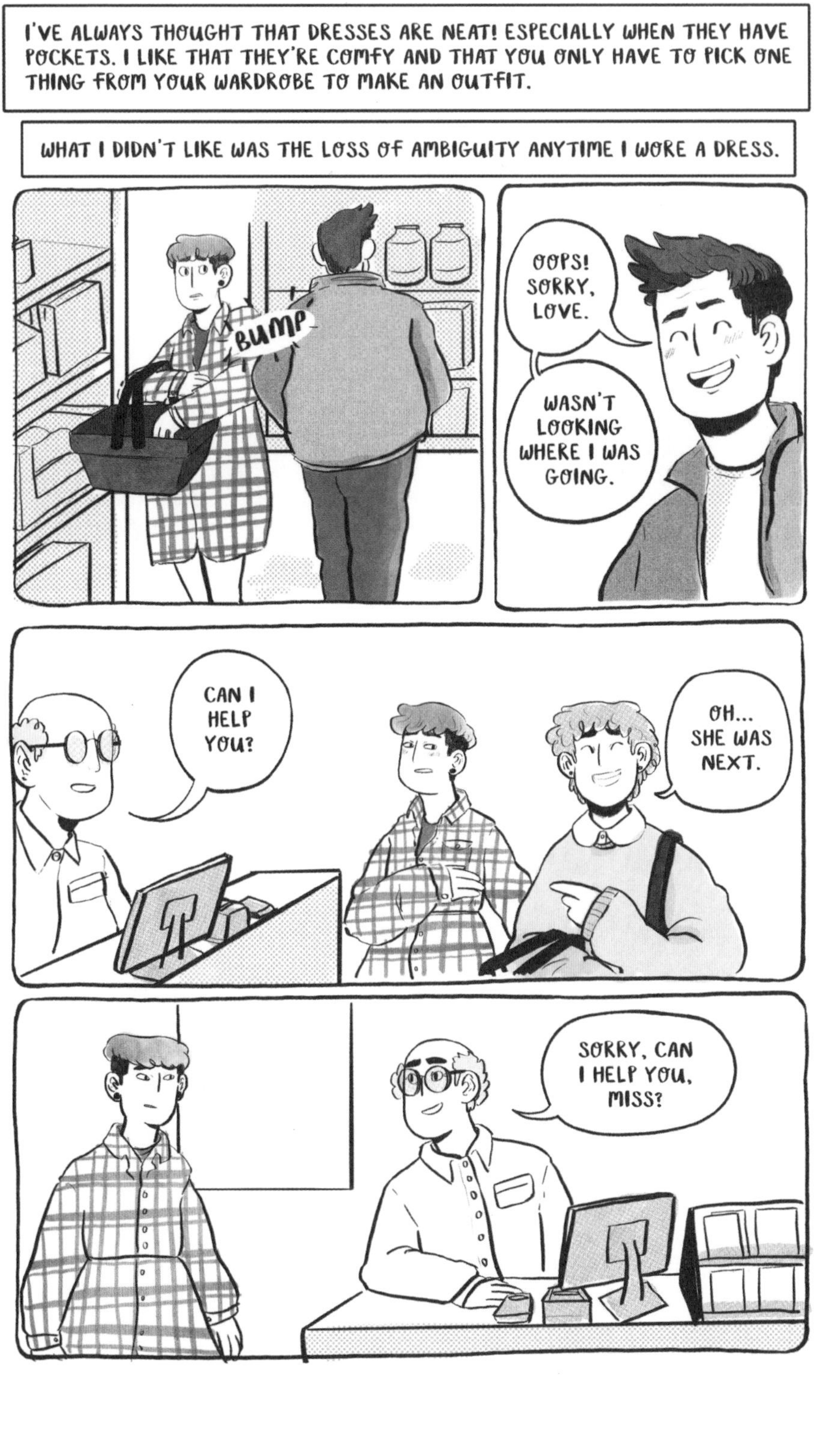
I'VE ALWAYS THOUGHT THAT DRESSES ARE NEAT! ESPECIALLY WHEN THEY HAVE POCKETS. I LIKE THAT THEY'RE COMFY AND THAT YOU ONLY HAVE TO PICK ONE THING FROM YOUR WARDROBE TO MAKE AN OUTFIT.
WHAT I DIDN'T LIKE WAS THE LOSS OF AMBIGUITY ANYTIME I WORE A DRESS.
BUMP
OOPS! SORRY, LOVE.
WASN'T LOOKING WHERE I WAS GOING.
CAN I HELP YOU?
OH... SHE WAS NEXT.
SORRY, CAN I HELP YOU, MISS?

I REALLY WISH PEOPLE DIDN'T JUST ASSUME...

AND I WISH IT DIDN'T BOTHER ME SO MUCH.

I WAS BEGINNING TO TRULY UNDERSTAND THAT THIS WAS ABOUT SO MUCH MORE THAN JUST HOW I LIKED TO DRESS OR HAVE MY HAIR.

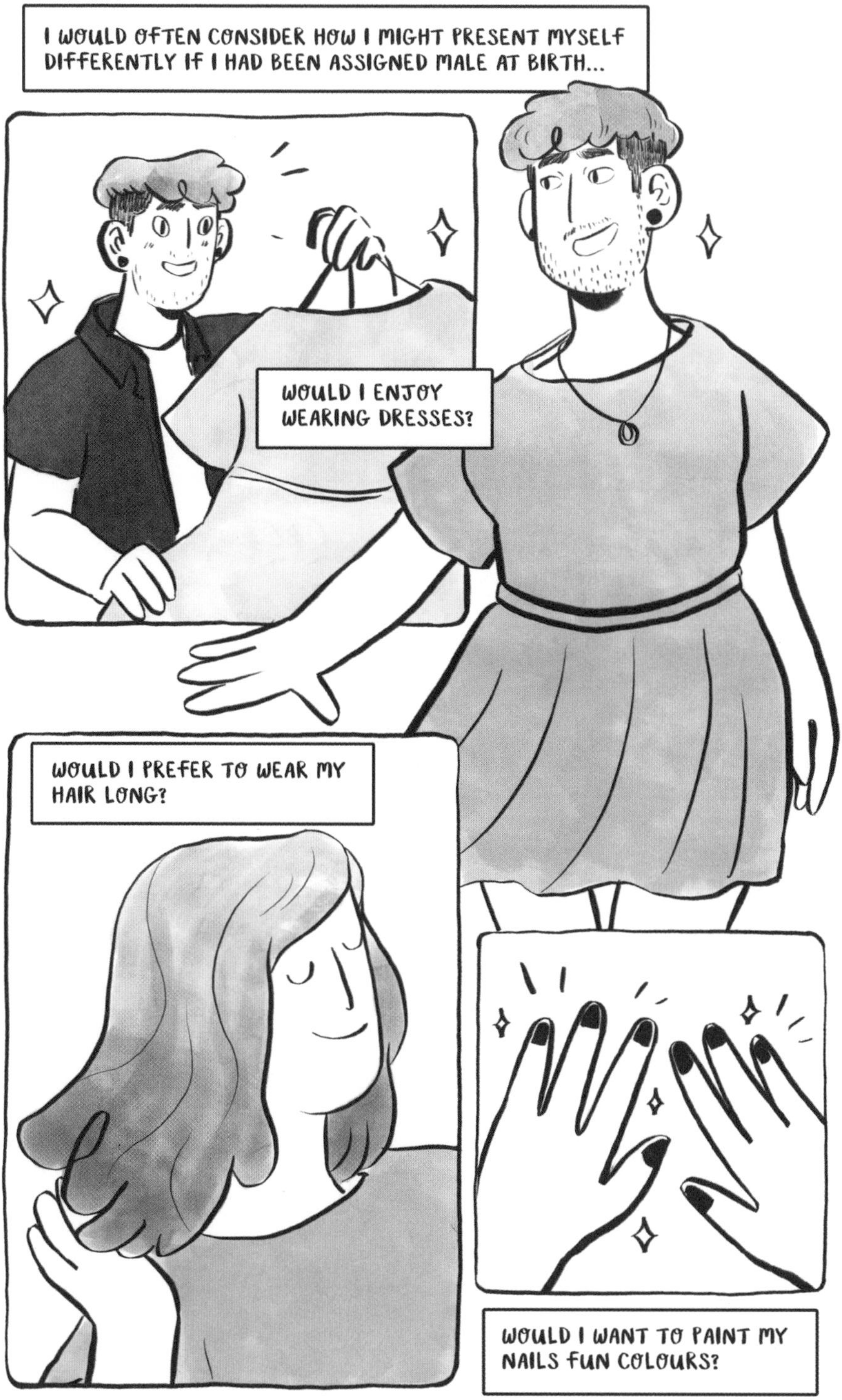
I WOULD OFTEN CONSIDER HOW I MIGHT PRESENT MYSELF DIFFERENTLY IF I HAD BEEN ASSIGNED MALE AT BIRTH...
WOULD I ENJOY WEARING DRESSES?
WOULD I PREFER TO WEAR MY HAIR LONG?
WOULD I WANT TO PAINT MY NAILS FUN COLOURS?

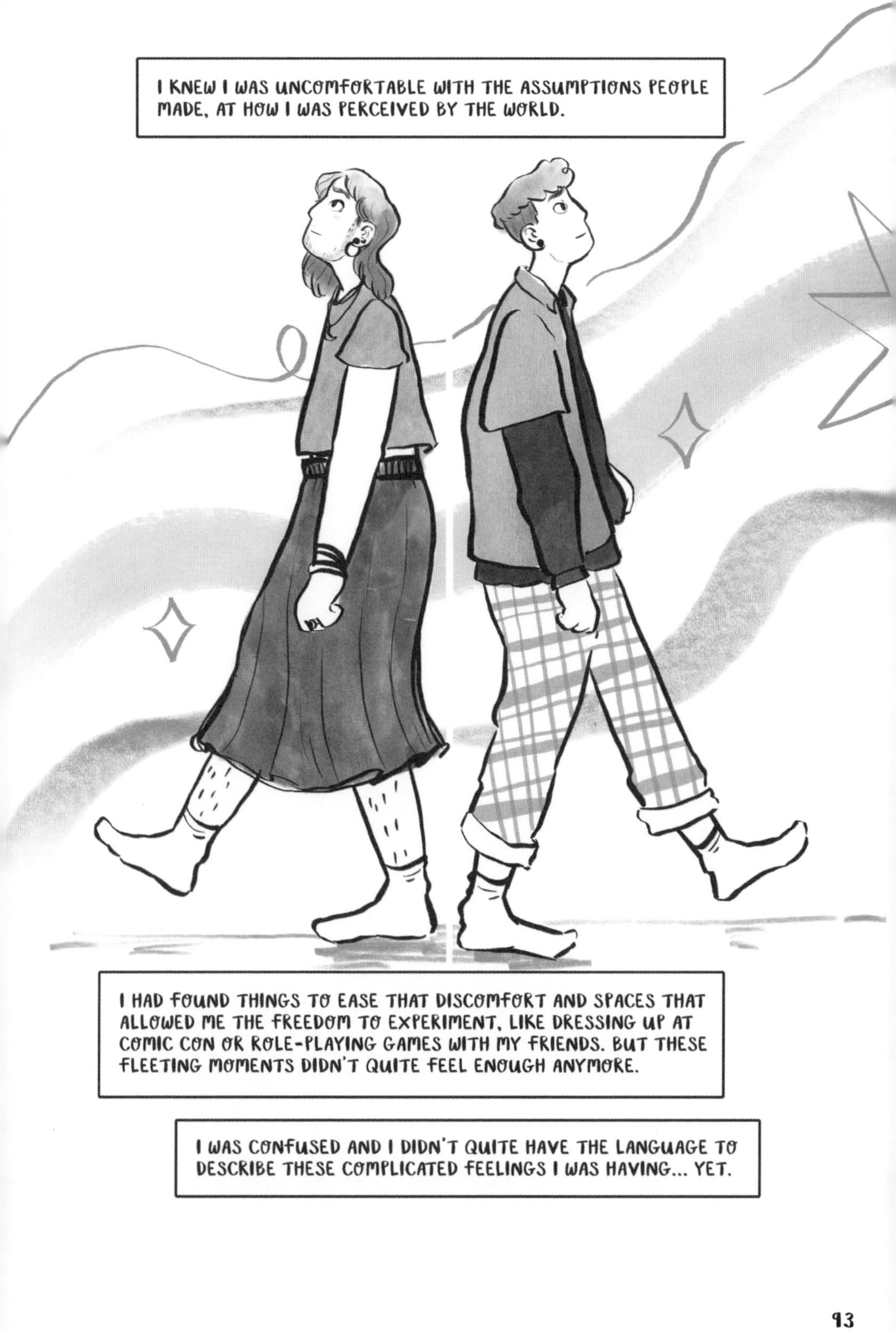
I KNEW I WAS UNCOMFORTABLE WITH THE ASSUMPTIONS PEOPLE MADE, AT HOW I WAS PERCEIVED BY THE WORLD.
I HAD FOUND THINGS TO EASE THAT DISCOMFORT AND SPACES THAT ALLOWED ME THE FREEDOM TO EXPERIMENT, LIKE DRESSING UP AT COMIC CON OR ROLE-PLAYING GAMES WITH MY FRIENDS. BUT THESE FLEETING MOMENTS DIDN'T QUITE FEEL ENOUGH ANYMORE.
I WAS CONFUSED AND I DIDN'T QUITE HAVE THE LANGUAGE TO DESCRIBE THESE COMPLICATED FEELINGS I WAS HAVING... YET.

WHEN I WAS GROWING UP I NEVER REALLY HEARD THE TERM "TRANSGENDER."

IT WASN'T SOMETHING THAT WAS TALKED ABOUT MUCH AND THERE WAS VERY LIMITED REPRESENTATION OF TRANS PEOPLE IN MOVIES OR ON TV.

WITHOUT KNOWING THE LANGUAGE TO DESCRIBE WHAT I WAS FEELING, I STARTED TO DO MY OWN RESEARCH...

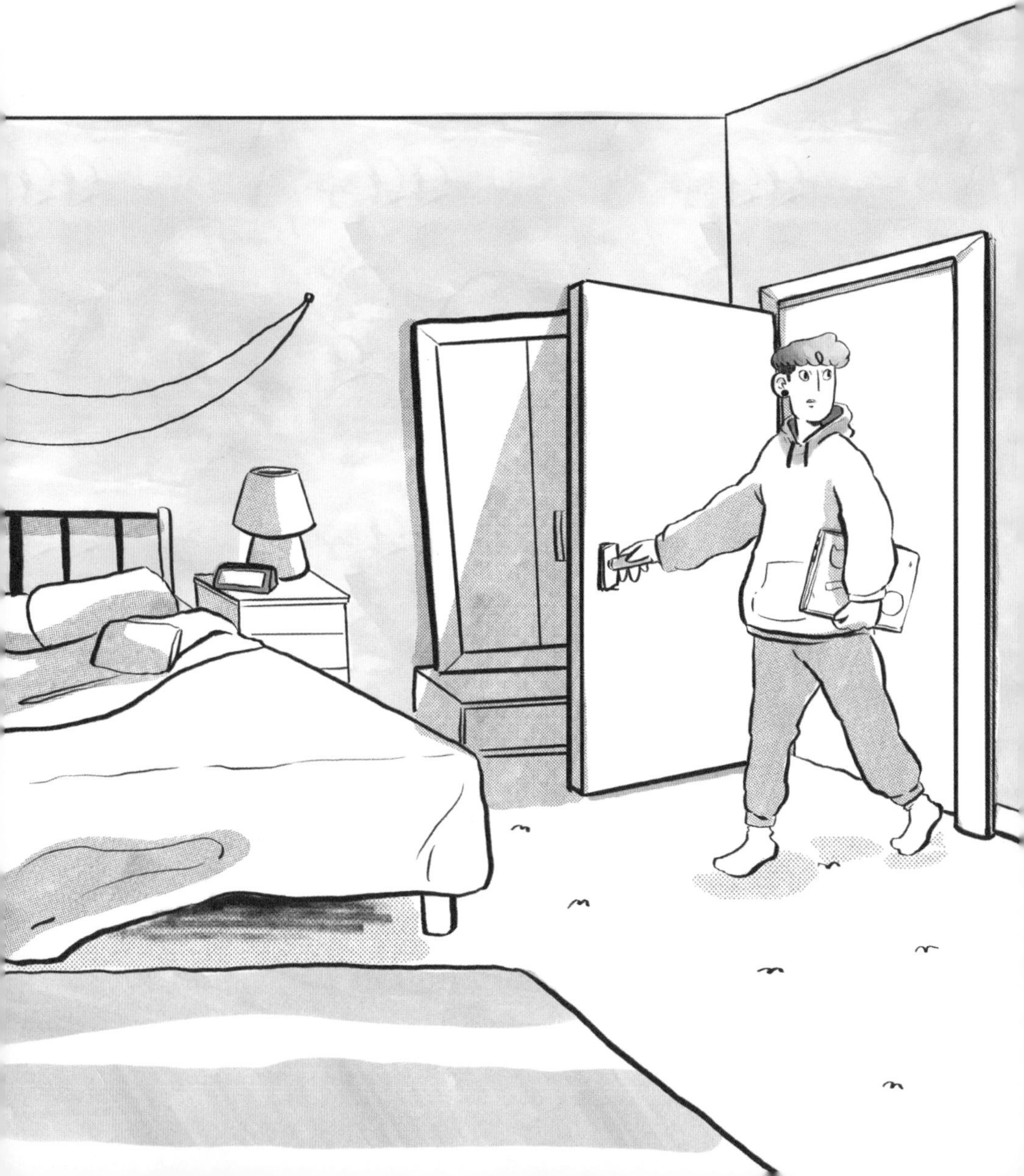

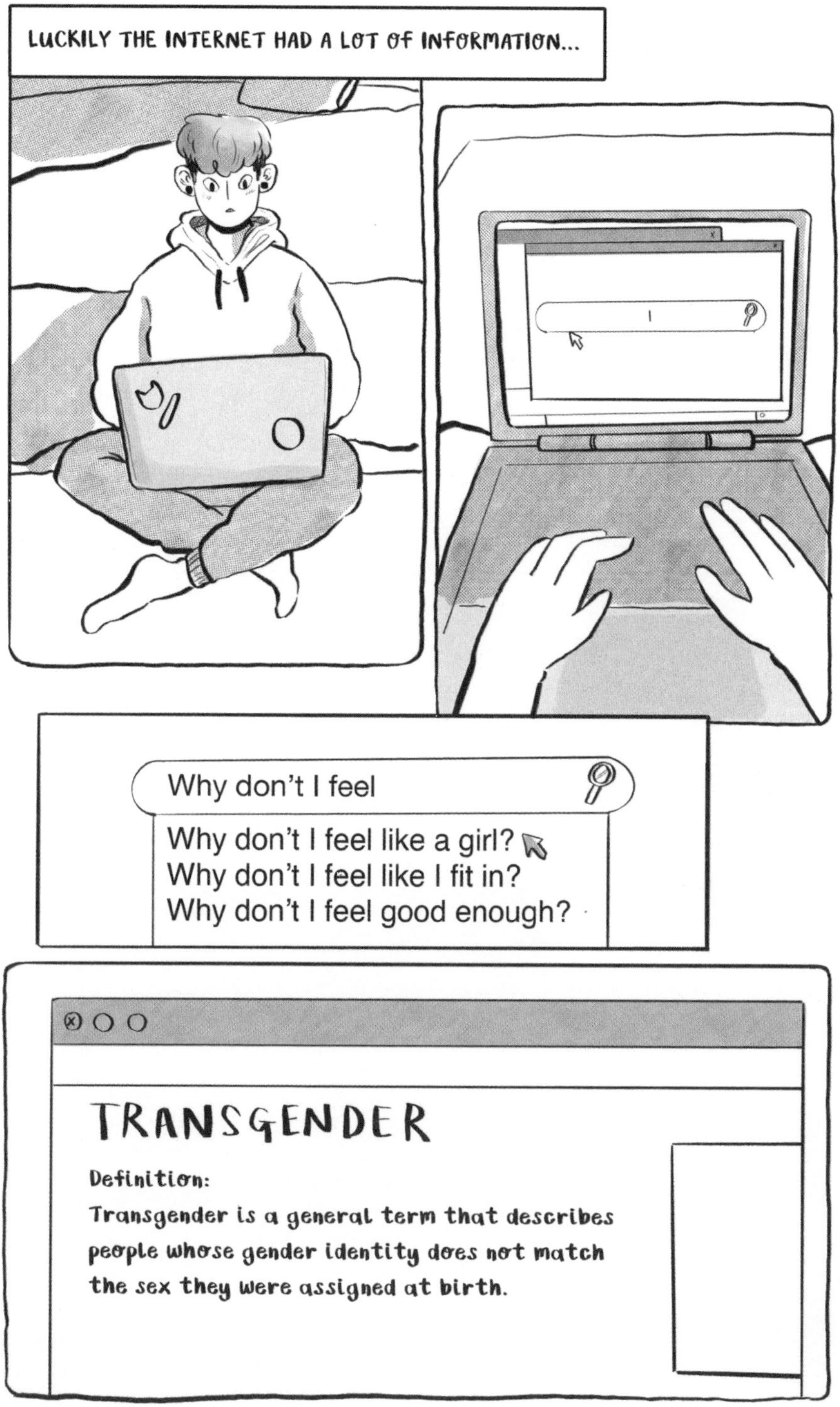
LUCKILY THE INTERNET HAD A LOT OF INFORMATION...
Why don't I feel
Why don't I feel like a girl?
Why don't I feel like I fit in?
Why don't I feel good enough?
TRANSGENDER
Definition:
Transgender is a general term that describes people whose gender identity does not match the sex they were assigned at birth.

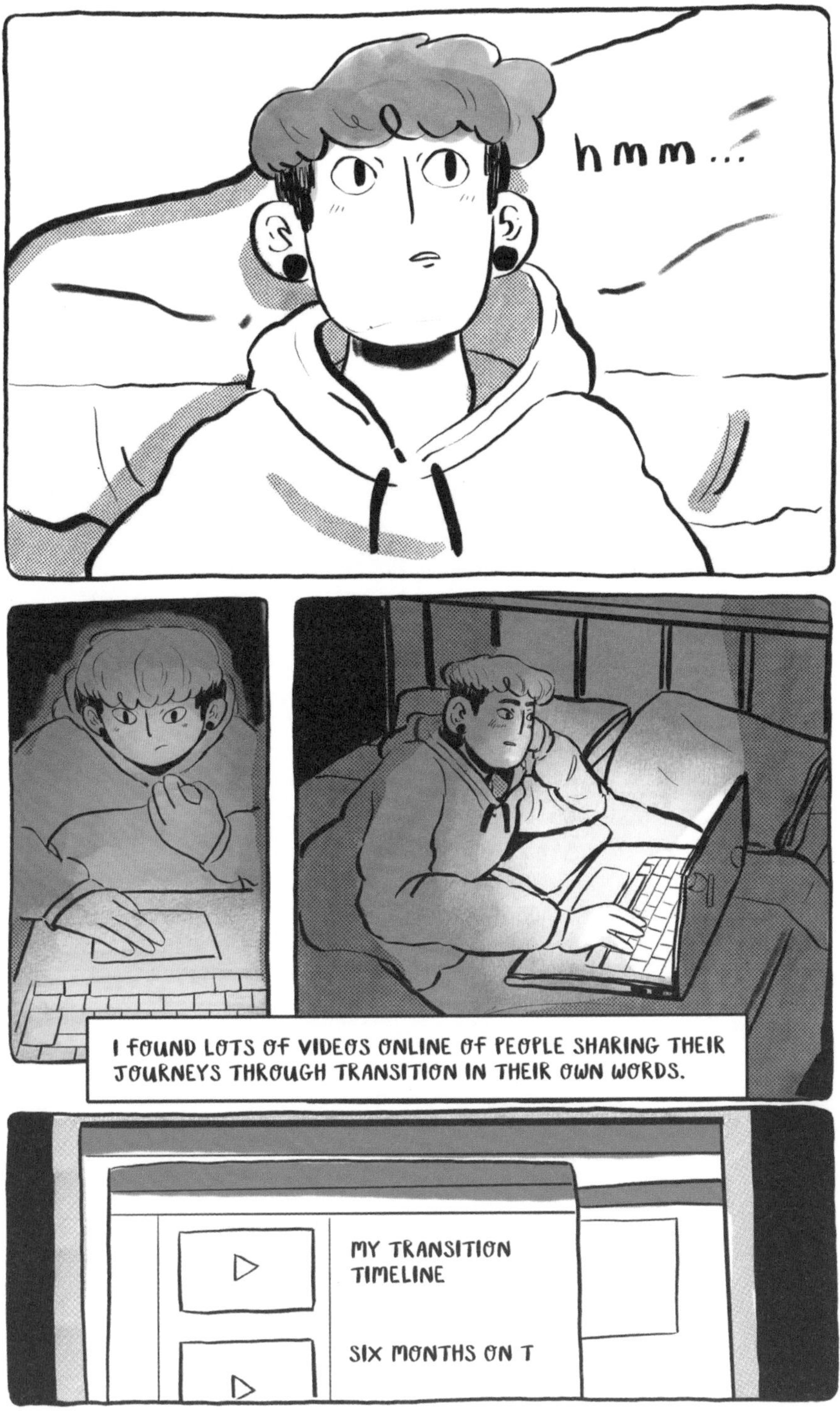
hmm...
I FOUND LOTS OF VIDEOS ONLINE OF PEOPLE SHARING THEIR JOURNEYS THROUGH TRANSITION IN THEIR OWN WORDS.
MY TRANSITION TIMELINE
SIX MONTHS ON T

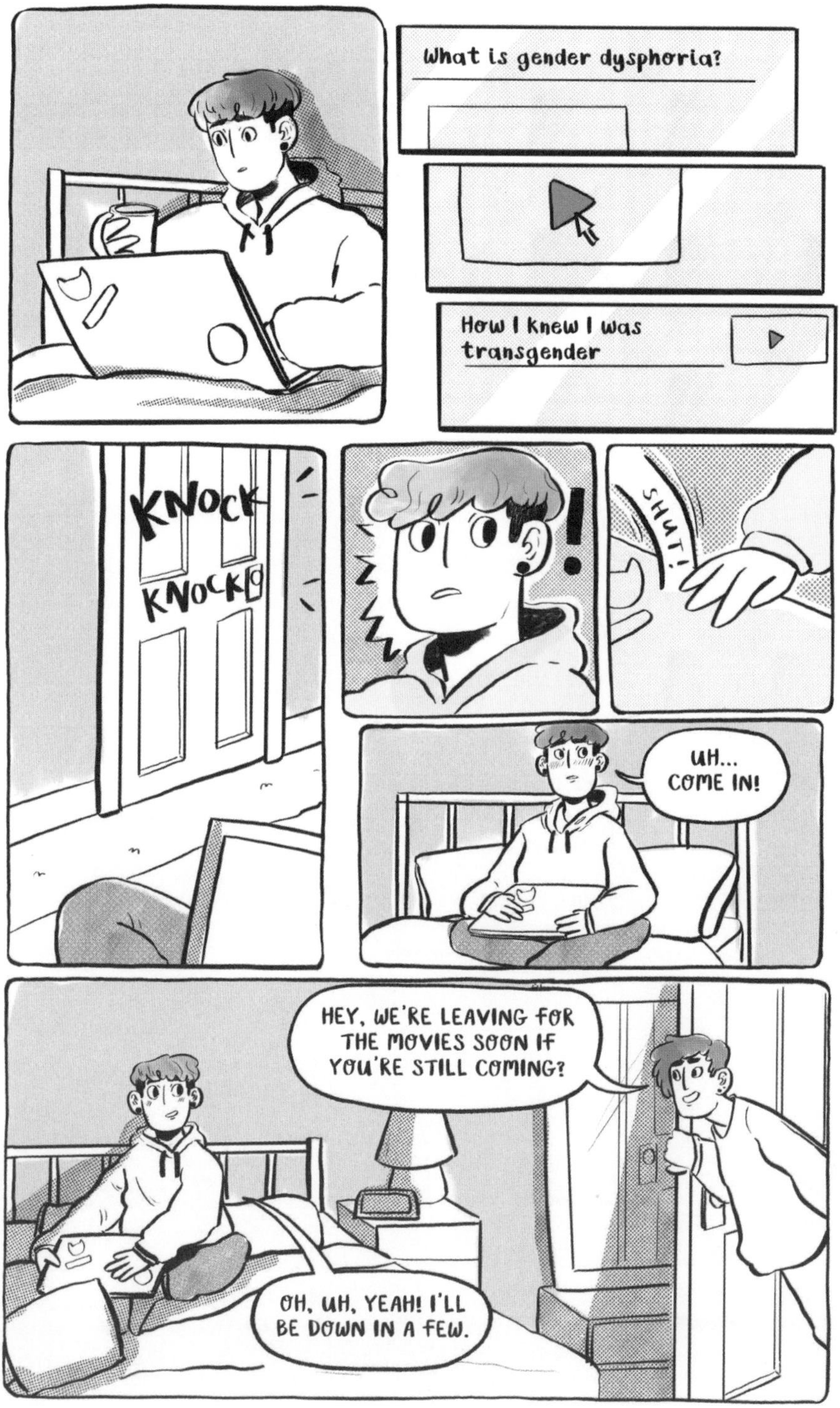
What is gender dysphoria?
How I knew I was transgender
KNOCK
KNOCK
!
SHUT!
UH... COME IN!
HEY, WE'RE LEAVING FOR THE MOVIES SOON IF YOU'RE STILL COMING?
OH, UH, YEAH! I'LL BE DOWN IN A FEW.

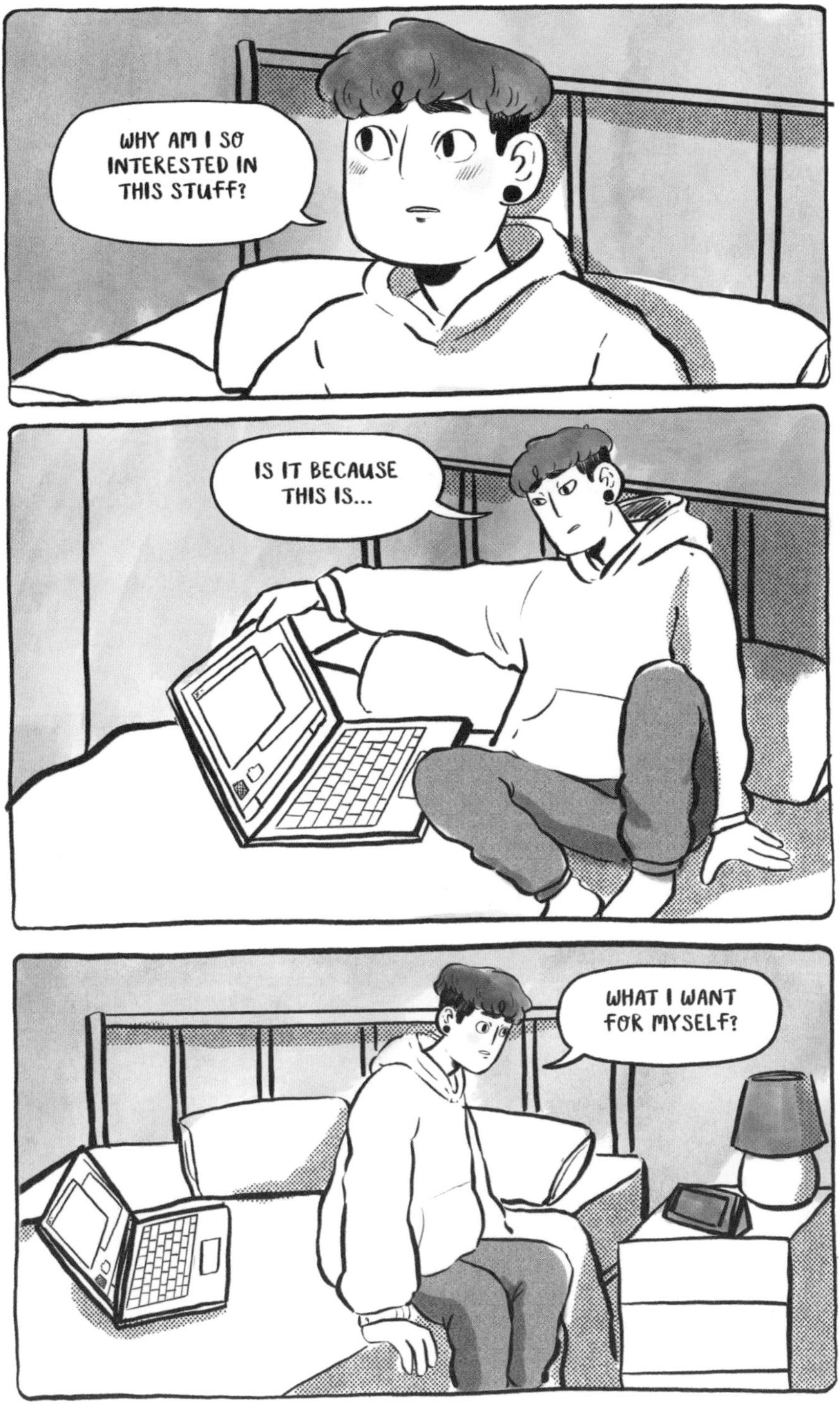
WHY AM I SO INTERESTED IN THIS STUFF?
IS IT BECAUSE THIS IS...
WHAT I WANT FOR MYSELF?

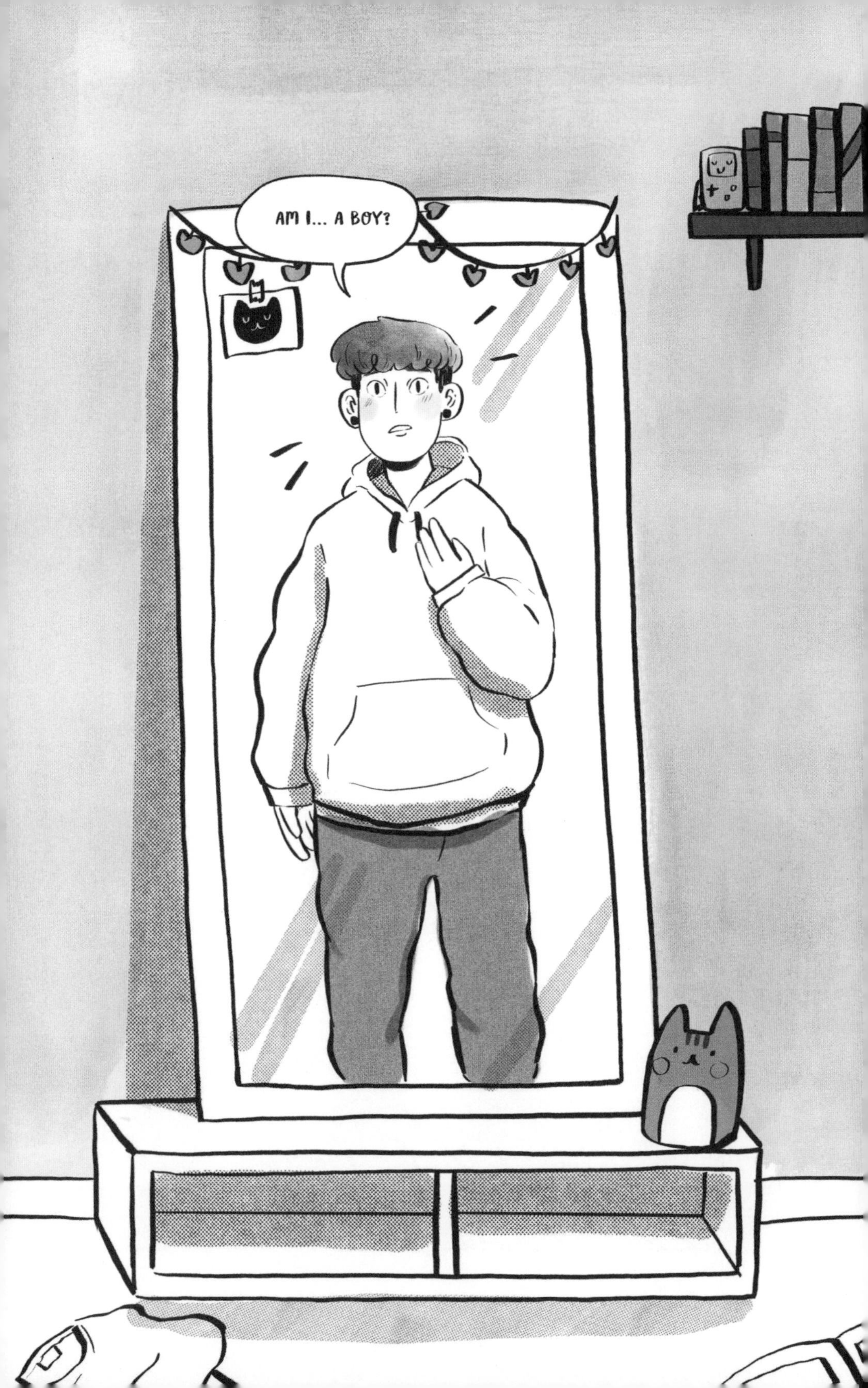
AM I... A BOY?

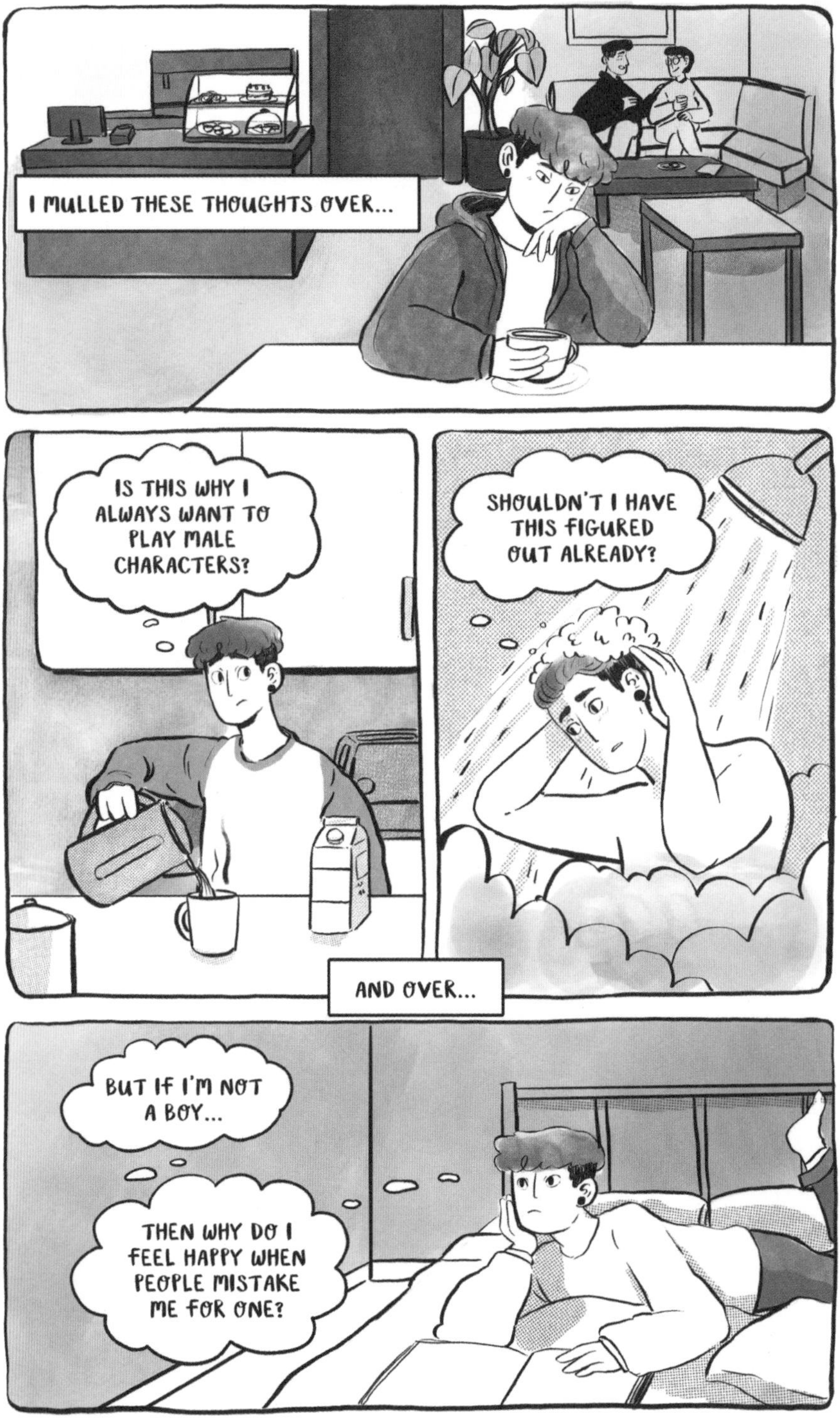
I MULLED THESE THOUGHTS OVER...
IS THIS WHY I ALWAYS WANT TO PLAY MALE CHARACTERS?
SHOULDN'T I HAVE THIS FIGURED OUT ALREADY?
AND OVER...
BUT IF I'M NOT A BOY...
THEN WHY DO I FEEL HAPPY WHEN PEOPLE MISTAKE ME FOR ONE?

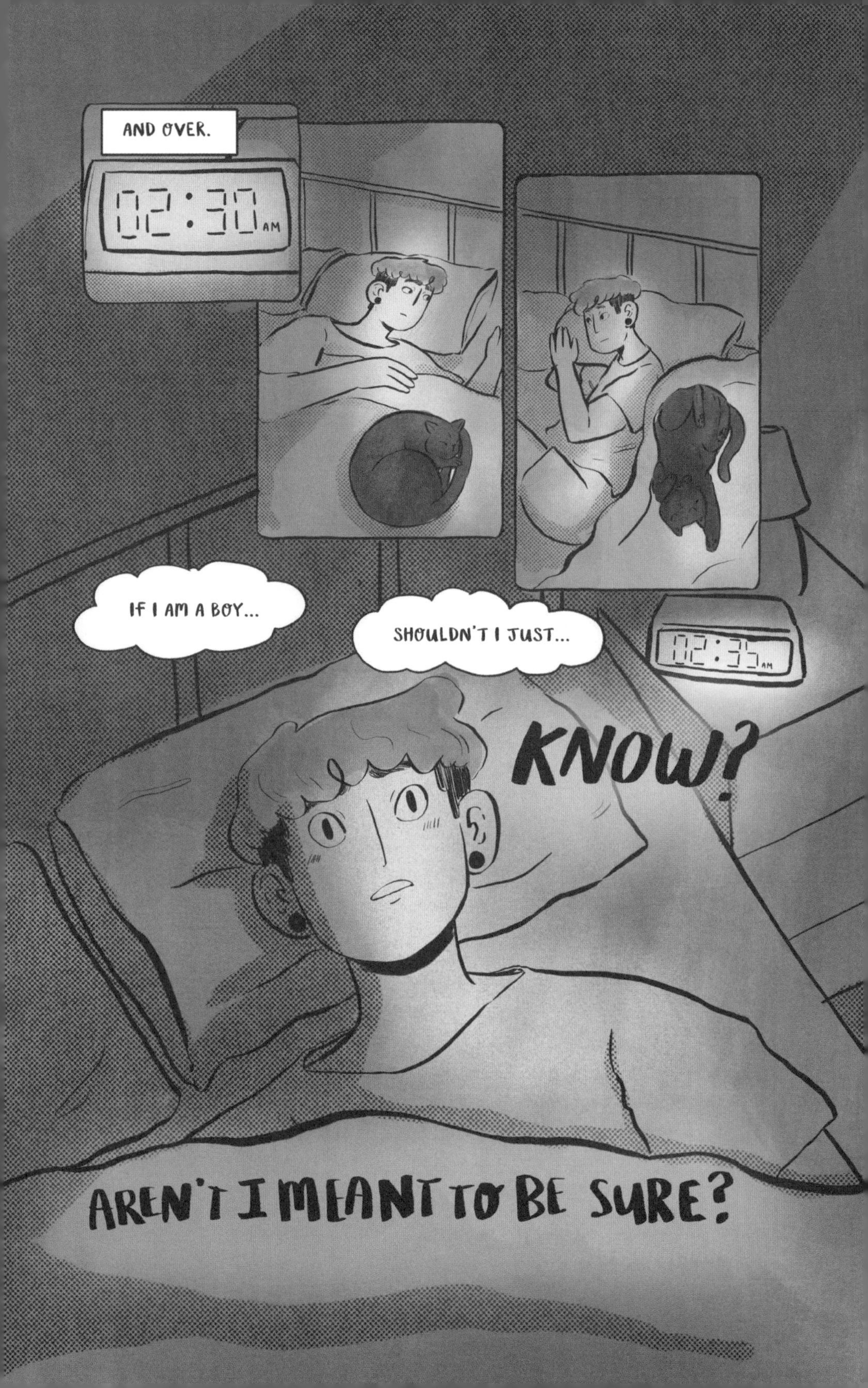
AND OVER.
02:30 AM
IF I AM A BOY...
SHOULDN'T I JUST...
02:35 AM
KNOW?
AREN'T I MEANT TO BE SURE?

THIS CIRCLE OF CONFUSION WENT ON FOR A WHILE. I KNEW THAT I WAS FEELING GROWING DISCOMFORT WITH BEING PERCEIVED AS A GIRL.

THIS WAS NOT AN ENTIRELY NEW FEELING...

GIRLS CAN'T PLAY CHESS!

IF YOU CARRY ON DRESSING LIKE THAT...

YOU'LL NEVER GET A BOYFRIEND.

CAN I HELP YOU, MISS?

LET'S KEEP IT SOFT AND FEMININE.

BUT THIS "DISCOMFORT" WAS TRULY PUT INTO PERSPECTIVE WHEN I BEGAN TO HAVE EXPERIENCES THAT AFFIRMED HOW I LONGED TO BE SEEN INSTEAD...

TO HAVE THOSE MOMENTS OF JOY AT BEING PERCEIVED BY OTHERS IN A WAY THAT FELT COMFORTABLE, TO SEE MYSELF IN A WAY THAT ALIGNED WITH HOW I FELT INSIDE...

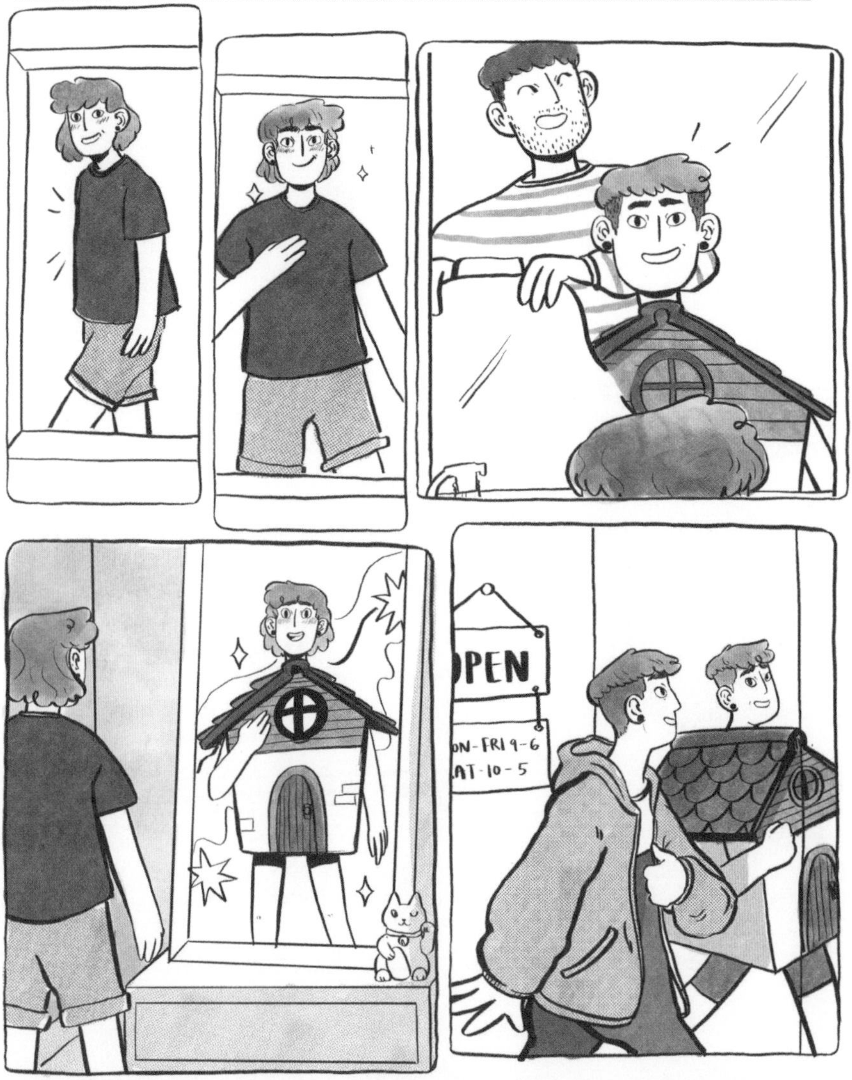
PEN
ON-FRI 9-6
AT-10-5

THESE MOMENTS OF GENDER EUPHORIA WERE WHAT ENCOURAGED ME TO ALLOW MYSELF TO HONOR THESE FEELINGS I WAS HAVING.

I FINALLY DECIDED THAT I DESERVED TO UNDERSTAND MYSELF AND

to find an answer.

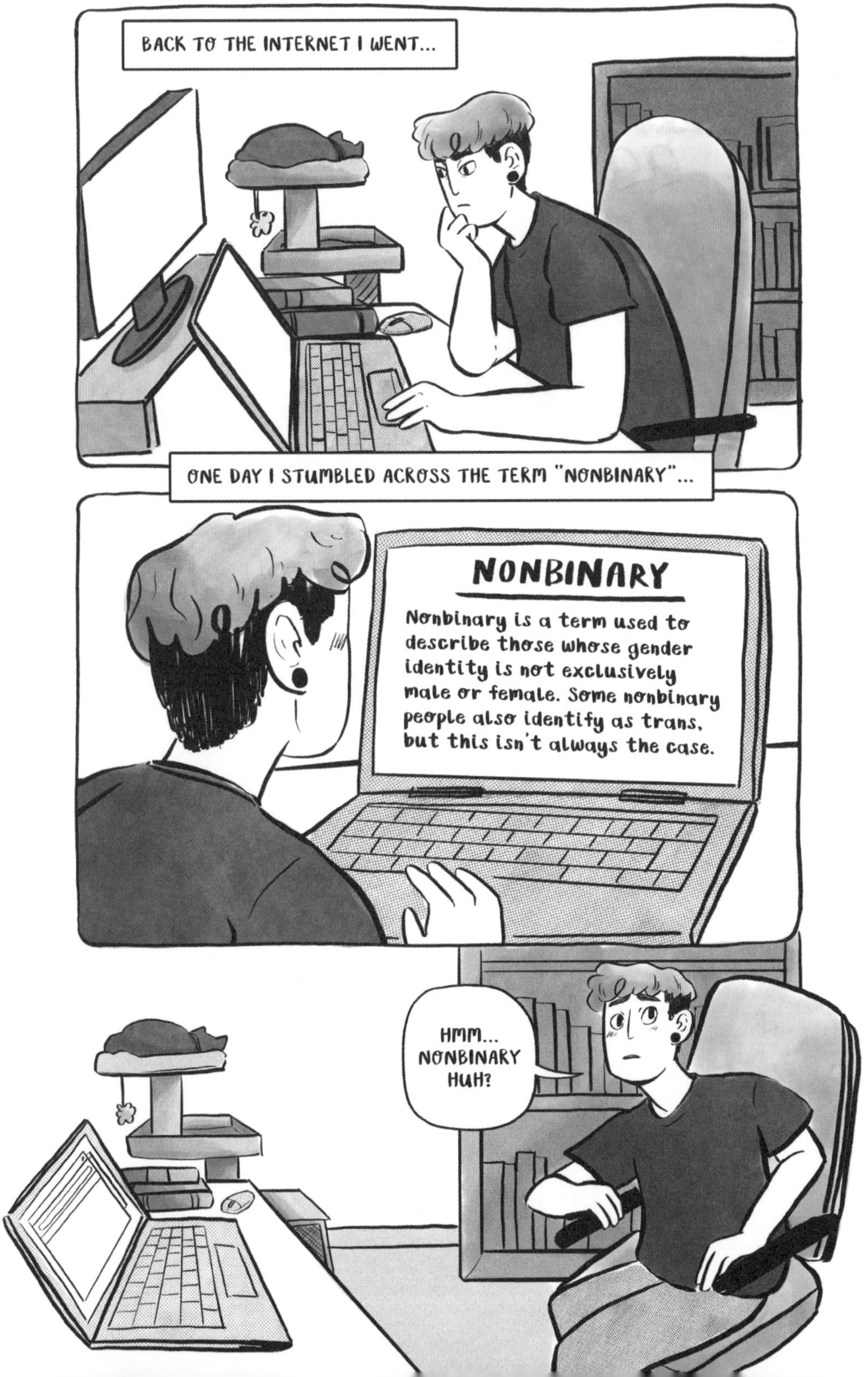
BACK TO THE INTERNET I WENT...
ONE DAY I STUMBLED ACROSS THE TERM "NONBINARY"...
NONBINARY
Nonbinary is a term used to describe those whose gender identity is not exclusively male or female. Some nonbinary people also identify as trans, but this isn't always the case.
HMM... NONBINARY HUH?

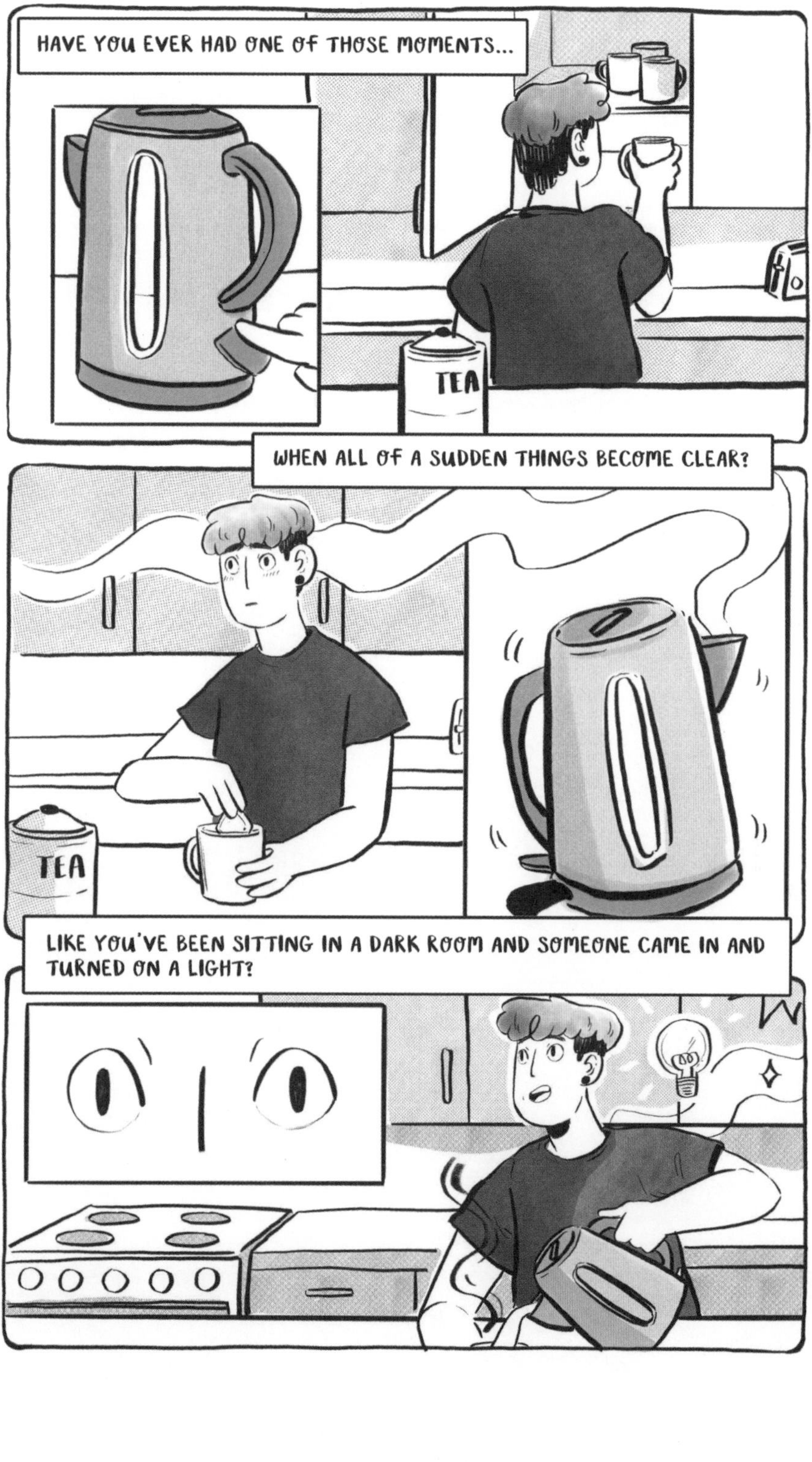
HAVE YOU EVER HAD ONE OF THOSE MOMENTS...
TEA
WHEN ALL OF A SUDDEN THINGS BECOME CLEAR?
TEA
LIKE YOU'VE BEEN SITTING IN A DARK ROOM AND SOMEONE CAME IN AND TURNED ON A LIGHT?

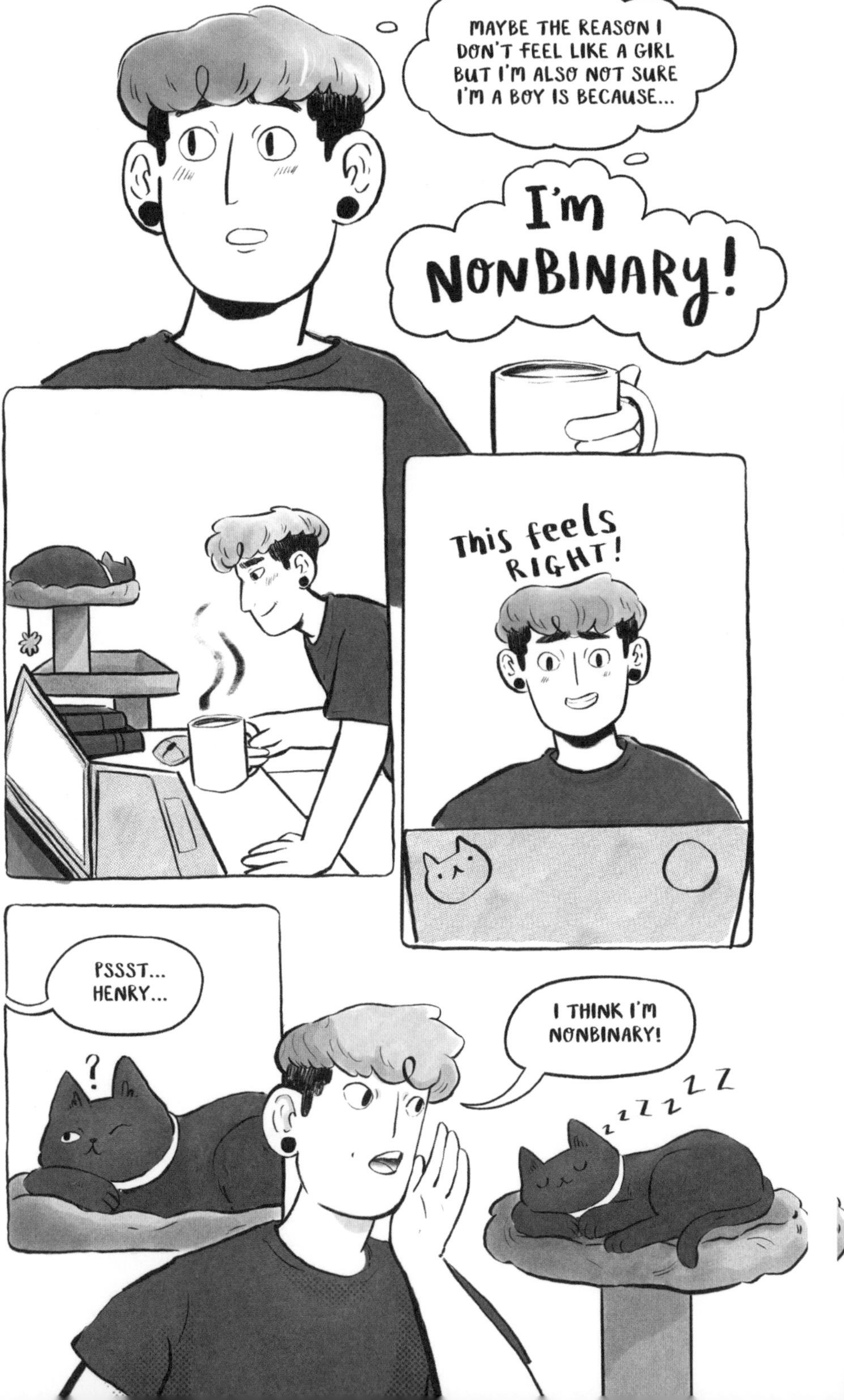
MAYBE THE REASON I DON'T FEEL LIKE A GIRL BUT I'M ALSO NOT SURE I'M A BOY IS BECAUSE...
I'M NONBINARY!
This feels RIGHT!
PSSST... HENRY...
I THINK I'M NONBINARY!
?
zzzzzZZ

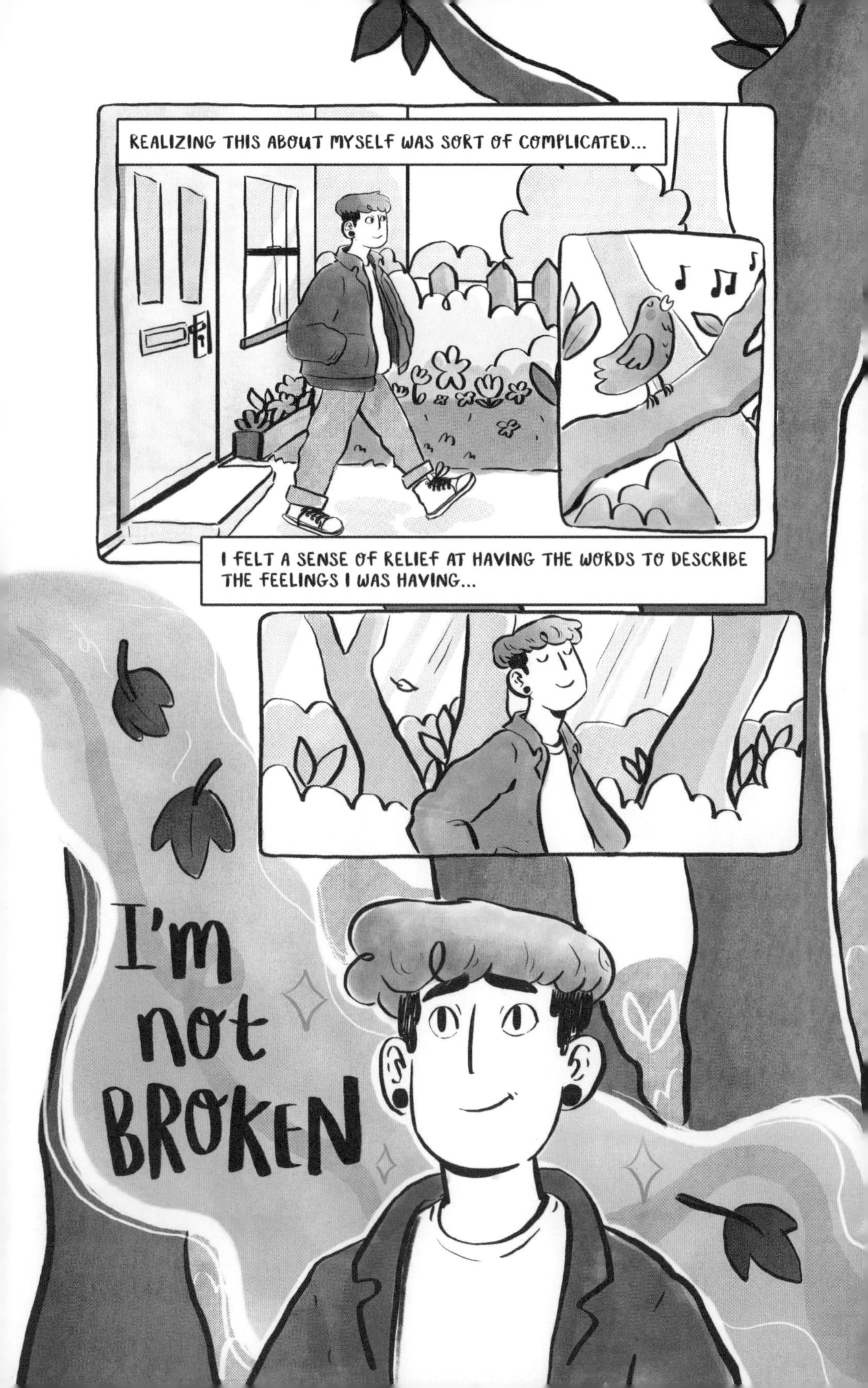
REALIZING THIS ABOUT MYSELF WAS SORT OF COMPLICATED...
I FELT A SENSE OF RELIEF AT HAVING THE WORDS TO DESCRIBE THE FEELINGS I WAS HAVING...
I'm not BROKEN

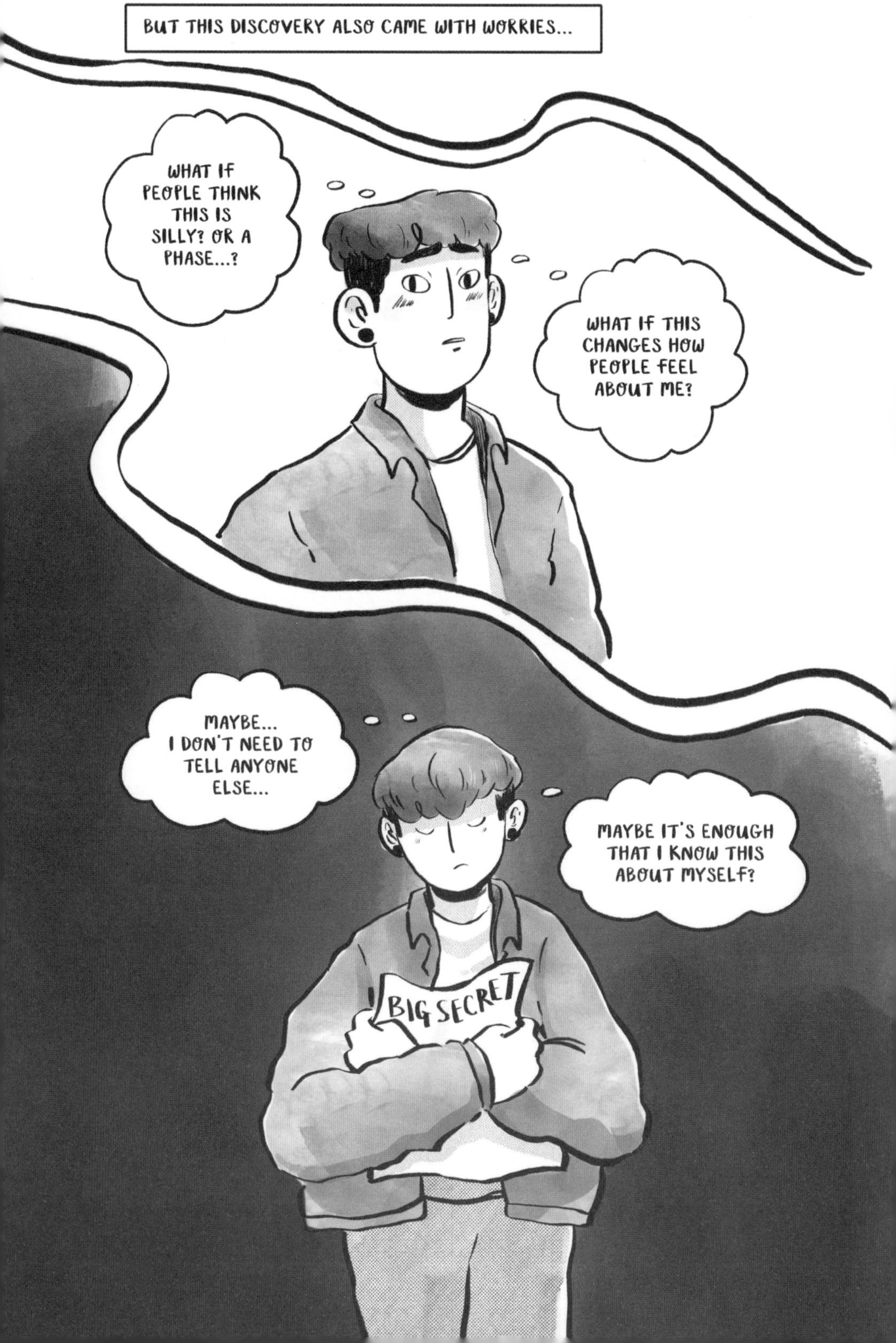
BUT THIS DISCOVERY ALSO CAME WITH WORRIES...
WHAT IF PEOPLE THINK THIS IS SILLY? OR A PHASE...?
WHAT IF THIS CHANGES HOW PEOPLE FEEL ABOUT ME?
MAYBE... I DON'T NEED TO TELL ANYONE ELSE...
MAYBE IT'S ENOUGH THAT I KNOW THIS ABOUT MYSELF?
BIG SECRET

KEEPING IT ALL INSIDE... THAT FELT LIKE I WAS HIDING PART OF WHO I WAS. LIKE I WAS WATCHING THE REST OF THE WORLD FROM THE SHADOWS, UNABLE TO LET MYSELF BE FULLY PART OF IT.

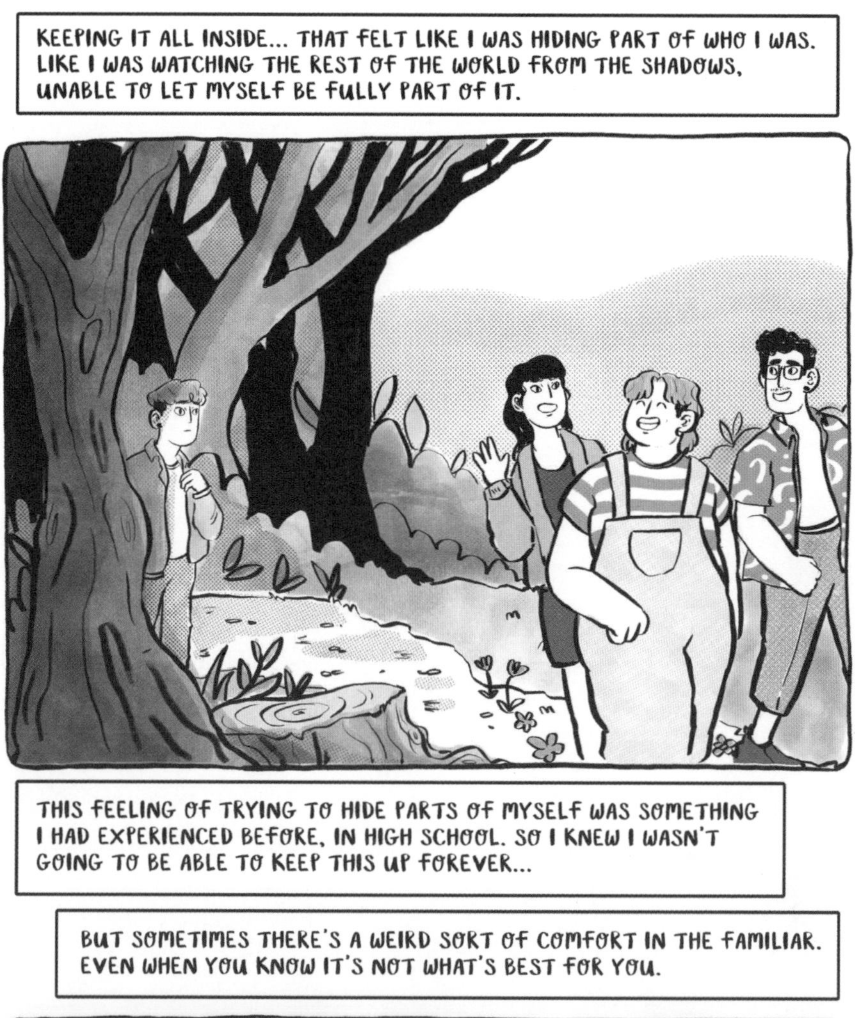

THIS FEELING OF TRYING TO HIDE PARTS OF MYSELF WAS SOMETHING I HAD EXPERIENCED BEFORE, IN HIGH SCHOOL. SO I KNEW I WASN'T GOING TO BE ABLE TO KEEP THIS UP FOREVER...

BUT SOMETIMES THERE'S A WEIRD SORT OF COMFORT IN THE FAMILIAR. EVEN WHEN YOU KNOW IT'S NOT WHAT'S BEST FOR YOU.

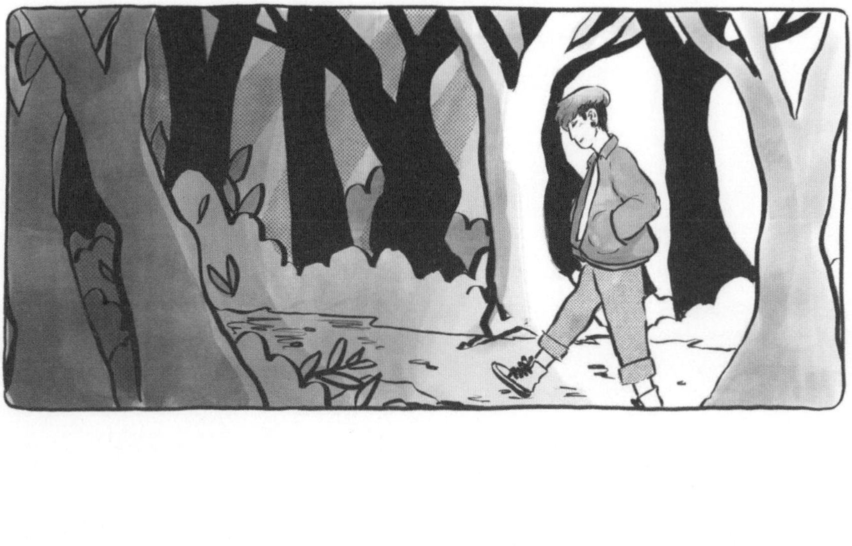

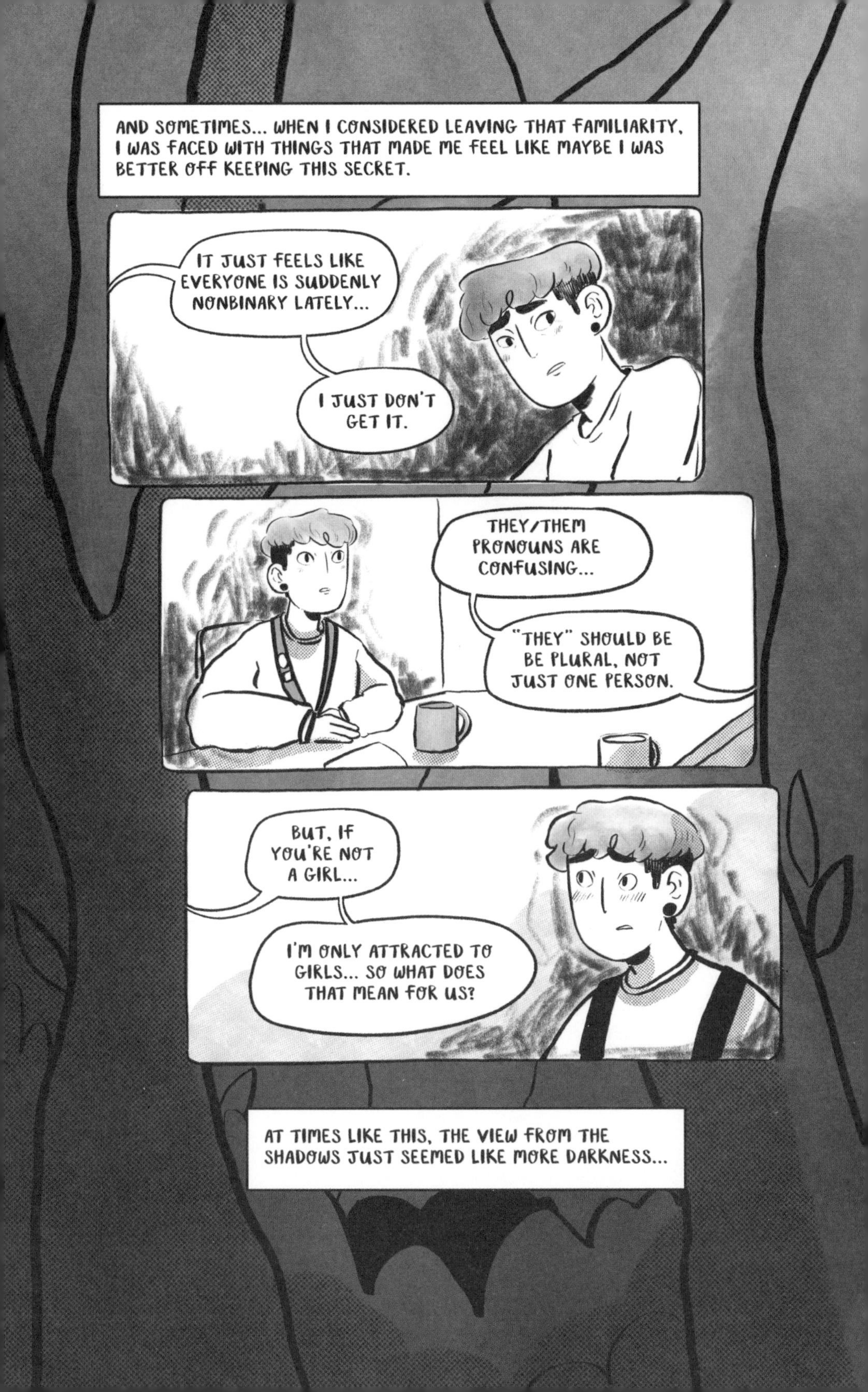
AND SOMETIMES... WHEN I CONSIDERED LEAVING THAT FAMILIARITY, I WAS FACED WITH THINGS THAT MADE ME FEEL LIKE MAYBE I WAS BETTER OFF KEEPING THIS SECRET.
IT JUST FEELS LIKE EVERYONE IS SUDDENLY NONBINARY LATELY...
I JUST DON'T GET IT.
THEY/THEM PRONOUNS ARE CONFUSING...
"THEY" SHOULD BE BE PLURAL, NOT JUST ONE PERSON.
BUT, IF YOU'RE NOT A GIRL...
I'M ONLY ATTRACTED TO GIRLS... SO WHAT DOES THAT MEAN FOR US?
AT TIMES LIKE THIS, THE VIEW FROM THE SHADOWS JUST SEEMED LIKE MORE DARKNESS...

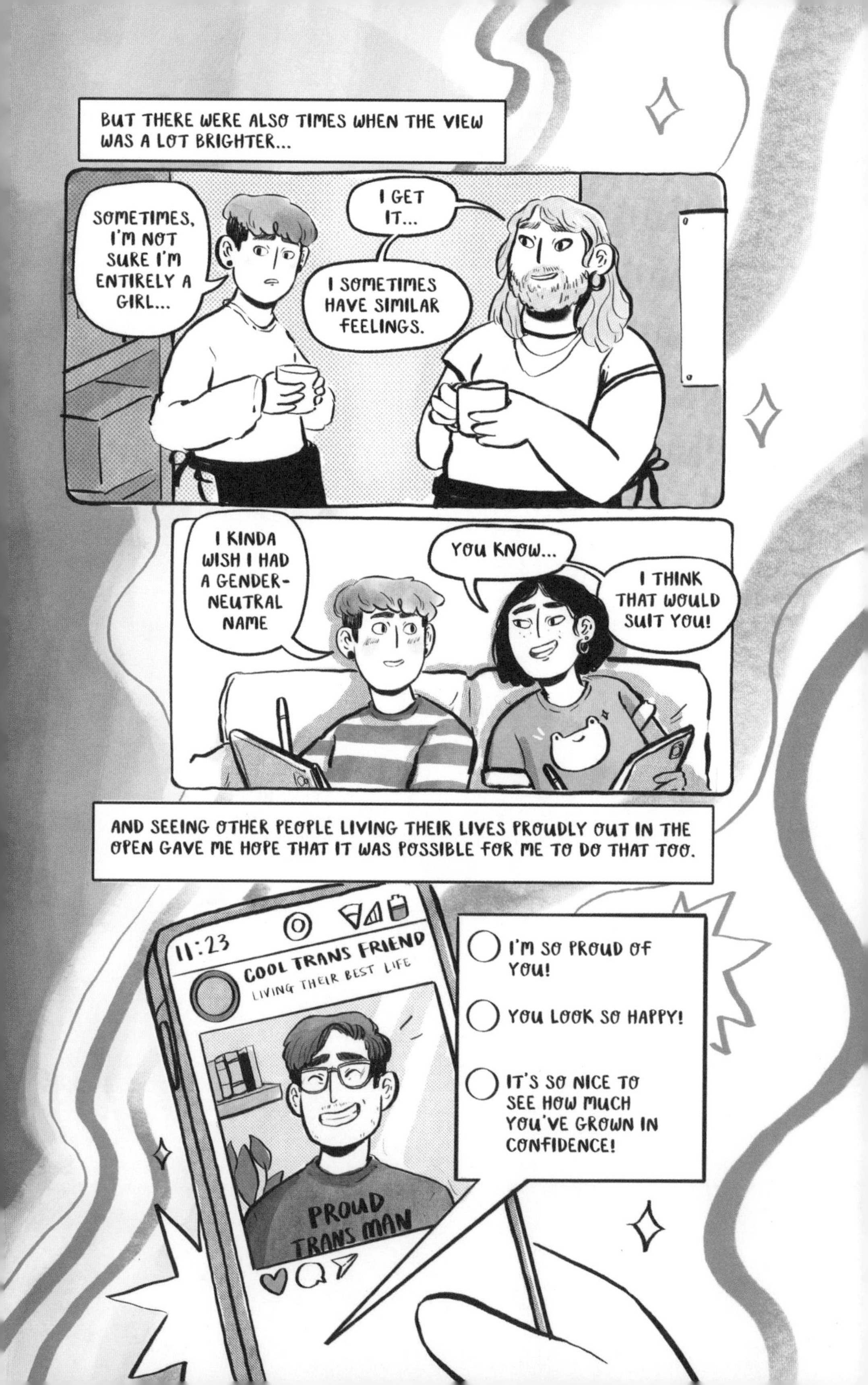
BUT THERE WERE ALSO TIMES WHEN THE VIEW WAS A LOT BRIGHTER...
SOMETIMES, I'M NOT SURE I'M ENTIRELY A GIRL...
I GET IT...
I SOMETIMES HAVE SIMILAR FEELINGS.
I KINDA WISH I HAD A GENDER-NEUTRAL NAME
YOU KNOW...
I THINK THAT WOULD SUIT YOU!
AND SEEING OTHER PEOPLE LIVING THEIR LIVES PROUDLY OUT IN THE OPEN GAVE ME HOPE THAT IT WAS POSSIBLE FOR ME TO DO THAT TOO.
11:23
COOL TRANS FRIEND
LIVING THEIR BEST LIFE
PROUD TRANS MAN
I'M SO PROUD OF YOU!
YOU LOOK SO HAPPY!
IT'S SO NICE TO SEE HOW MUCH YOU'VE GROWN IN CONFIDENCE!

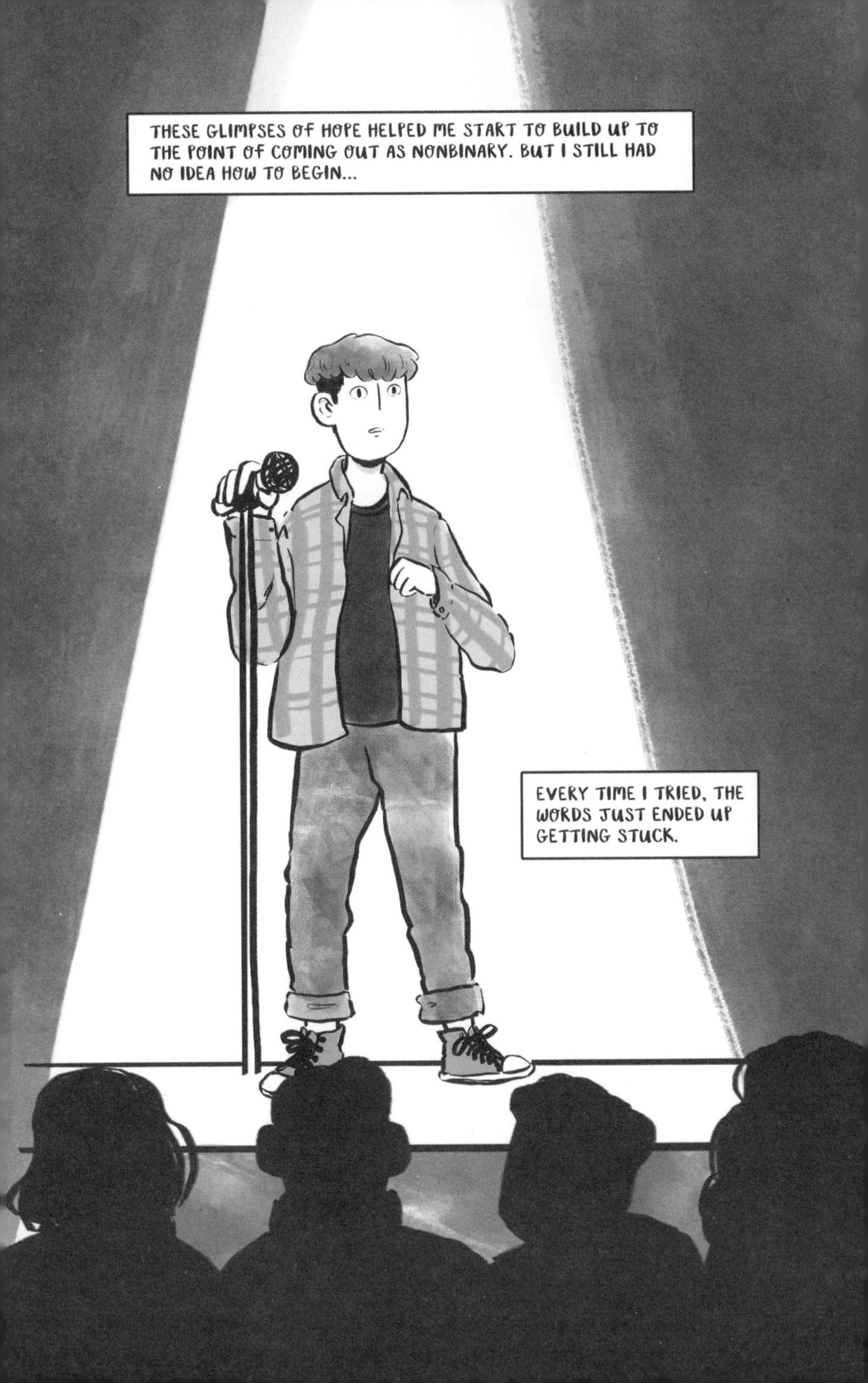
THESE GLIMPSES OF HOPE HELPED ME START TO BUILD UP TO THE POINT OF COMING OUT AS NONBINARY. BUT I STILL HAD NO IDEA HOW TO BEGIN...
EVERY TIME I TRIED, THE WORDS JUST ENDED UP GETTING STUCK.

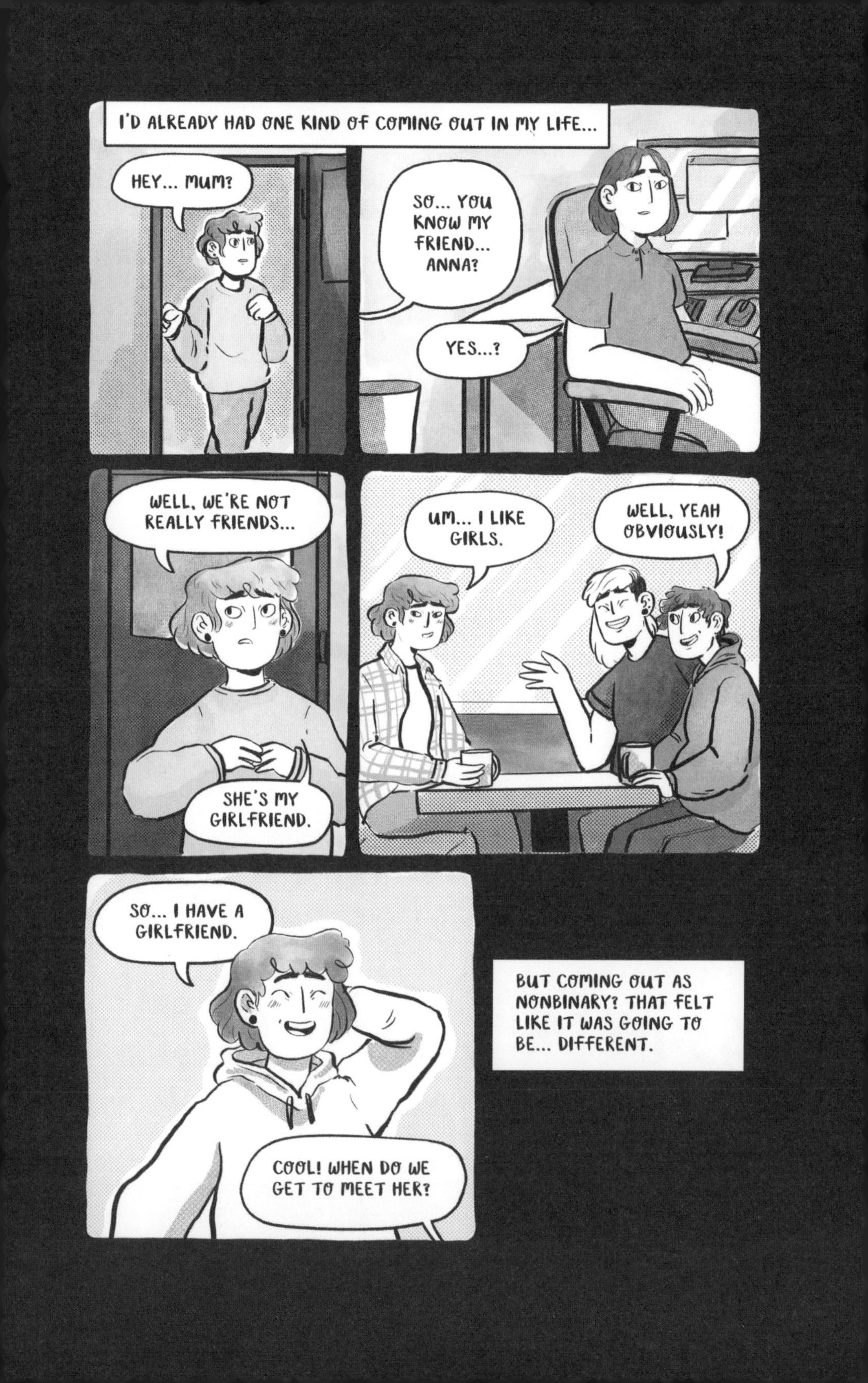
I'D ALREADY HAD ONE KIND OF COMING OUT IN MY LIFE...
HEY... MUM?
SO... YOU KNOW MY FRIEND... ANNA?
YES...?
WELL, WE'RE NOT REALLY FRIENDS...
SHE'S MY GIRLFRIEND.
UM... I LIKE GIRLS.
WELL, YEAH OBVIOUSLY!
SO... I HAVE A GIRLFRIEND.
COOL! WHEN DO WE GET TO MEET HER?
BUT COMING OUT AS NONBINARY? THAT FELT LIKE IT WAS GOING TO BE... DIFFERENT.

I WOULD BE ASKING PEOPLE TO CHANGE THE WAY THEY REFERRED TO ME...

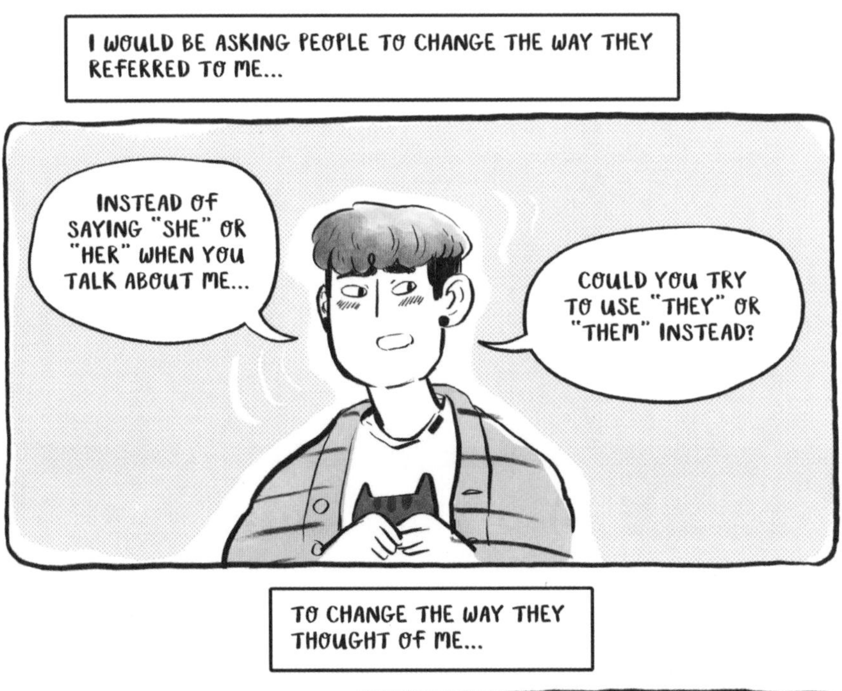
INSTEAD OF SAYING "SHE" OR "HER" WHEN YOU TALK ABOUT ME...
COULD YOU TRY TO USE "THEY" OR "THEM" INSTEAD?

TO CHANGE THE WAY THEY THOUGHT OF ME...

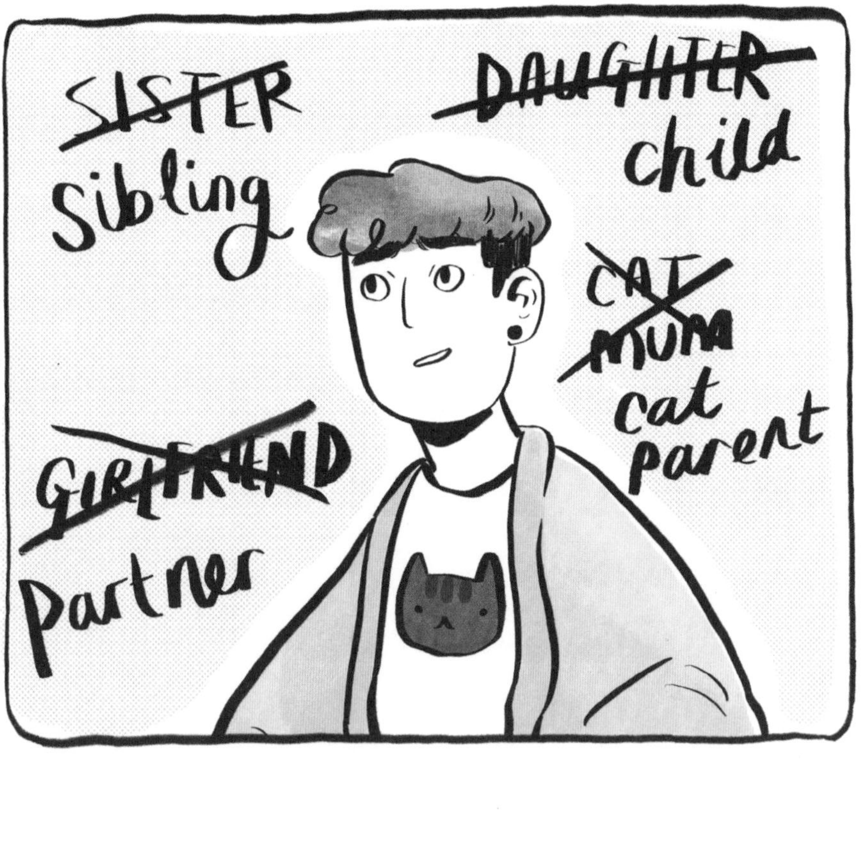
~~SISTER~~
Sibling
~~DAUGHTER~~
child
~~CAT MUM~~
cat parent
~~GIRLFRIEND~~
Partner

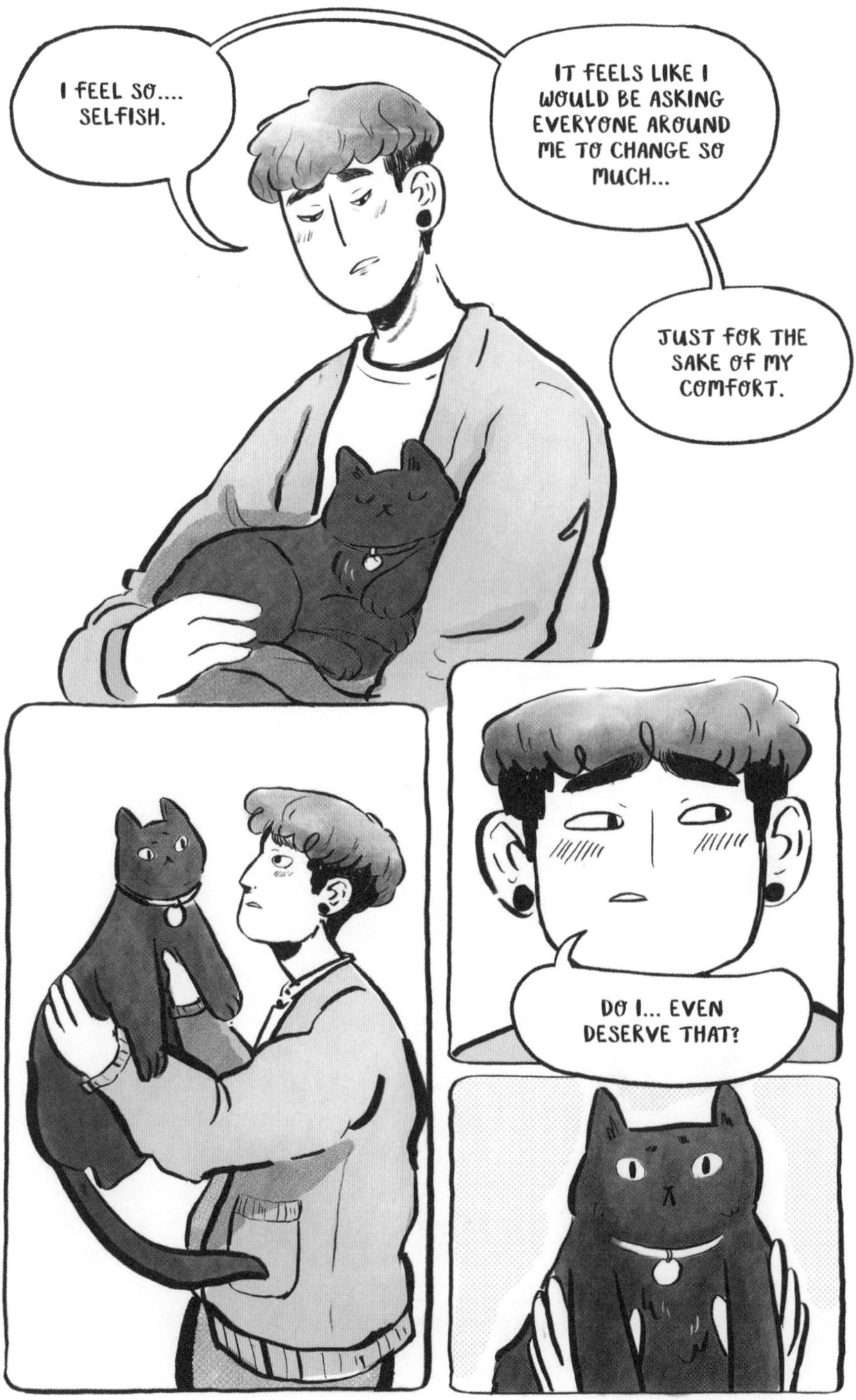
I FEEL SO.... SELFISH.
IT FEELS LIKE I WOULD BE ASKING EVERYONE AROUND ME TO CHANGE SO MUCH...
JUST FOR THE SAKE OF MY COMFORT.
DO I... EVEN DESERVE THAT?

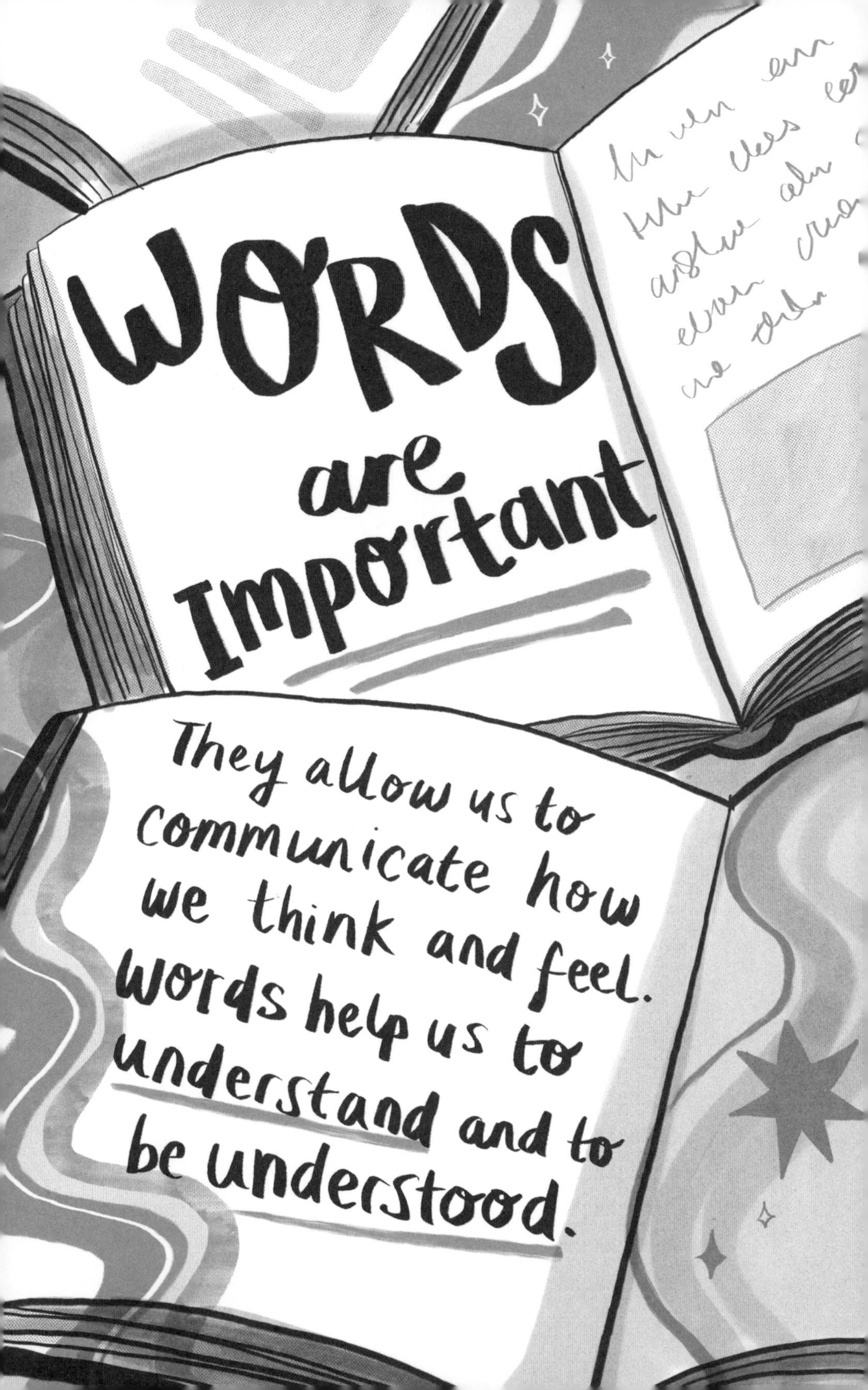
WORDS are Important
They allow us to communicate how we think and feel. Words help us to understand and to be understood.

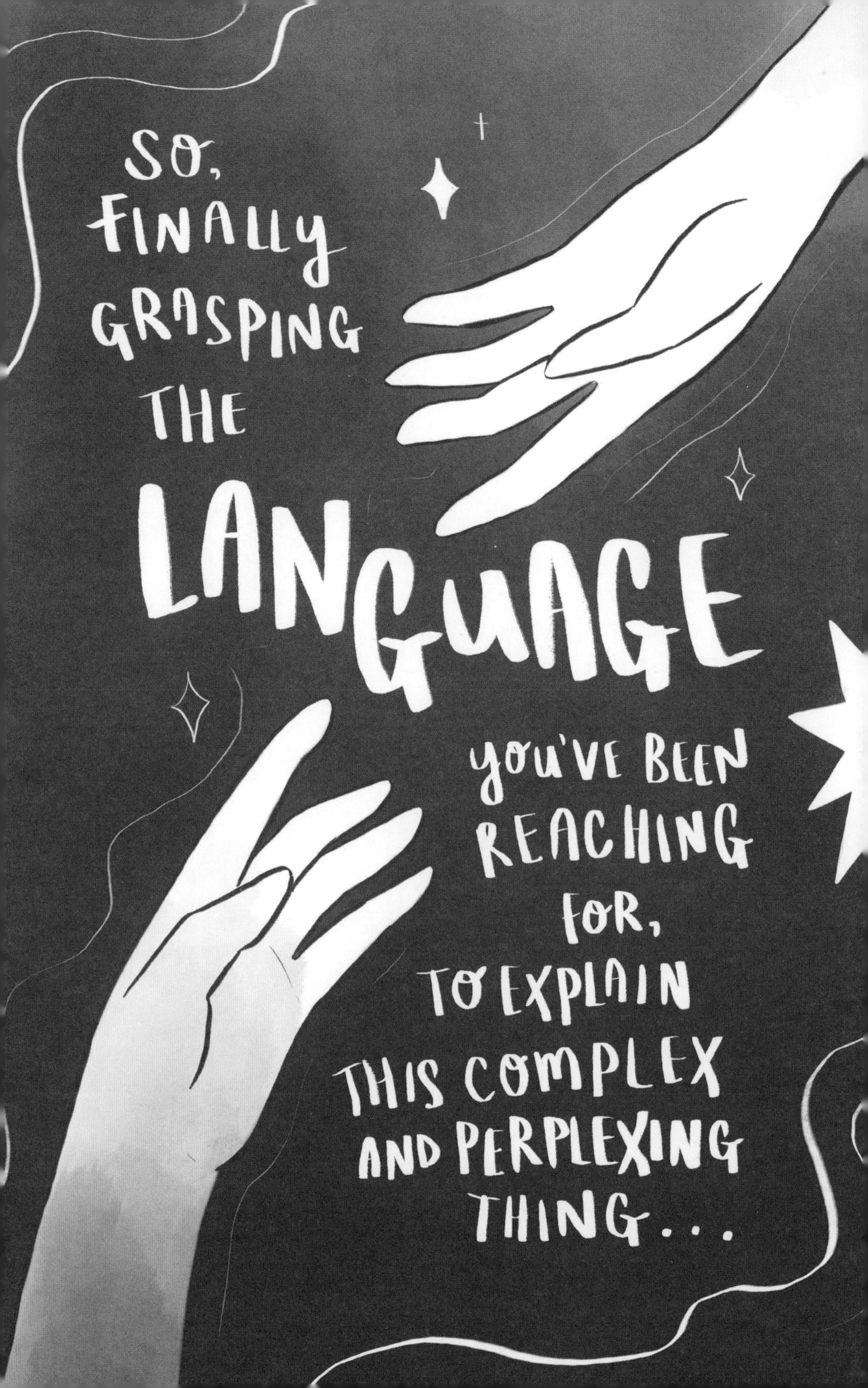
SO, FINALLY GRASPING THE
LANGUAGE
YOU'VE BEEN REACHING FOR, TO EXPLAIN THIS COMPLEX AND PERPLEXING THING...

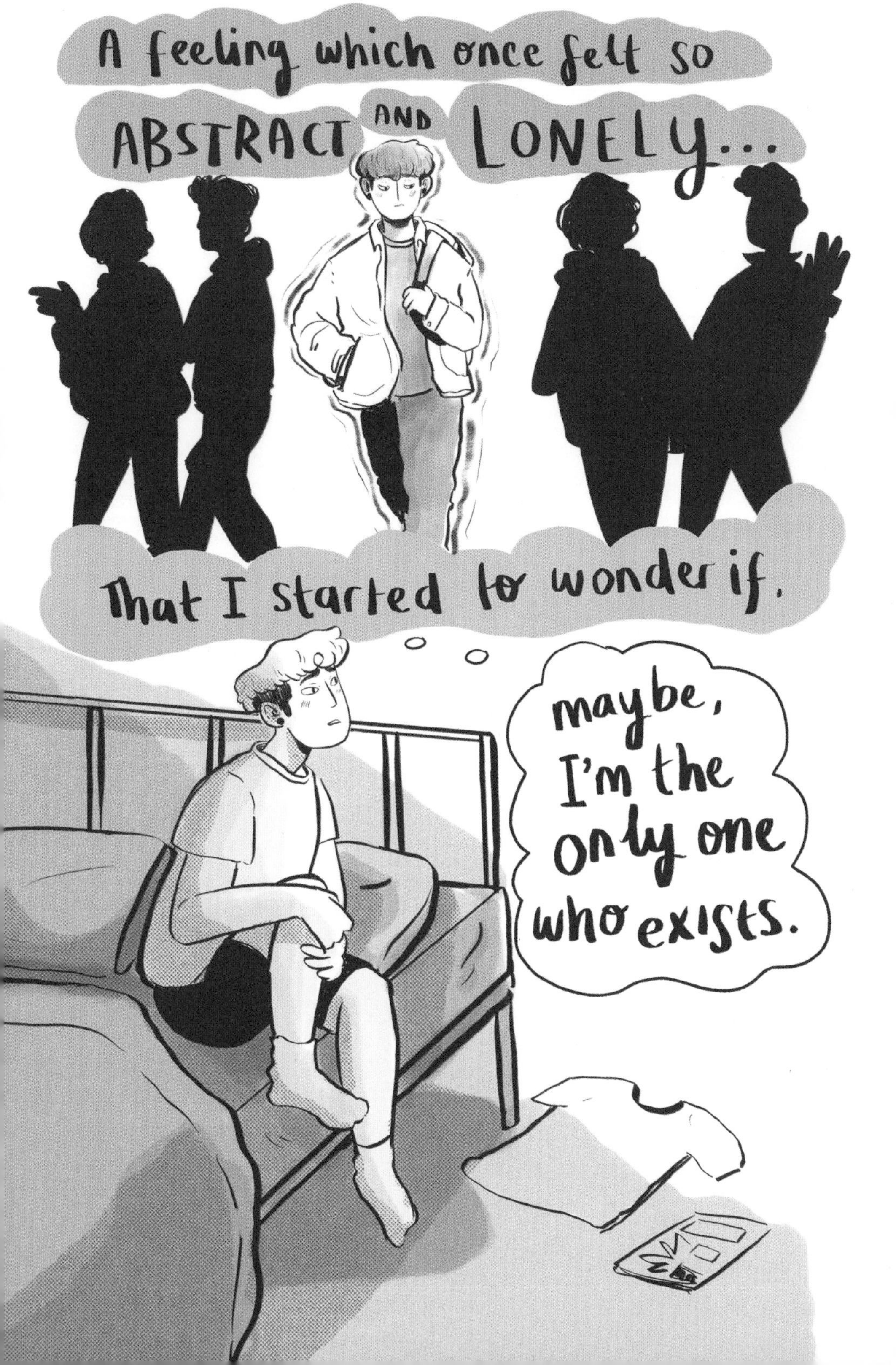
A feeling which once felt so
ABSTRACT AND LONELY...
That I started to wonder if.
maybe, I'm the only one who exists.

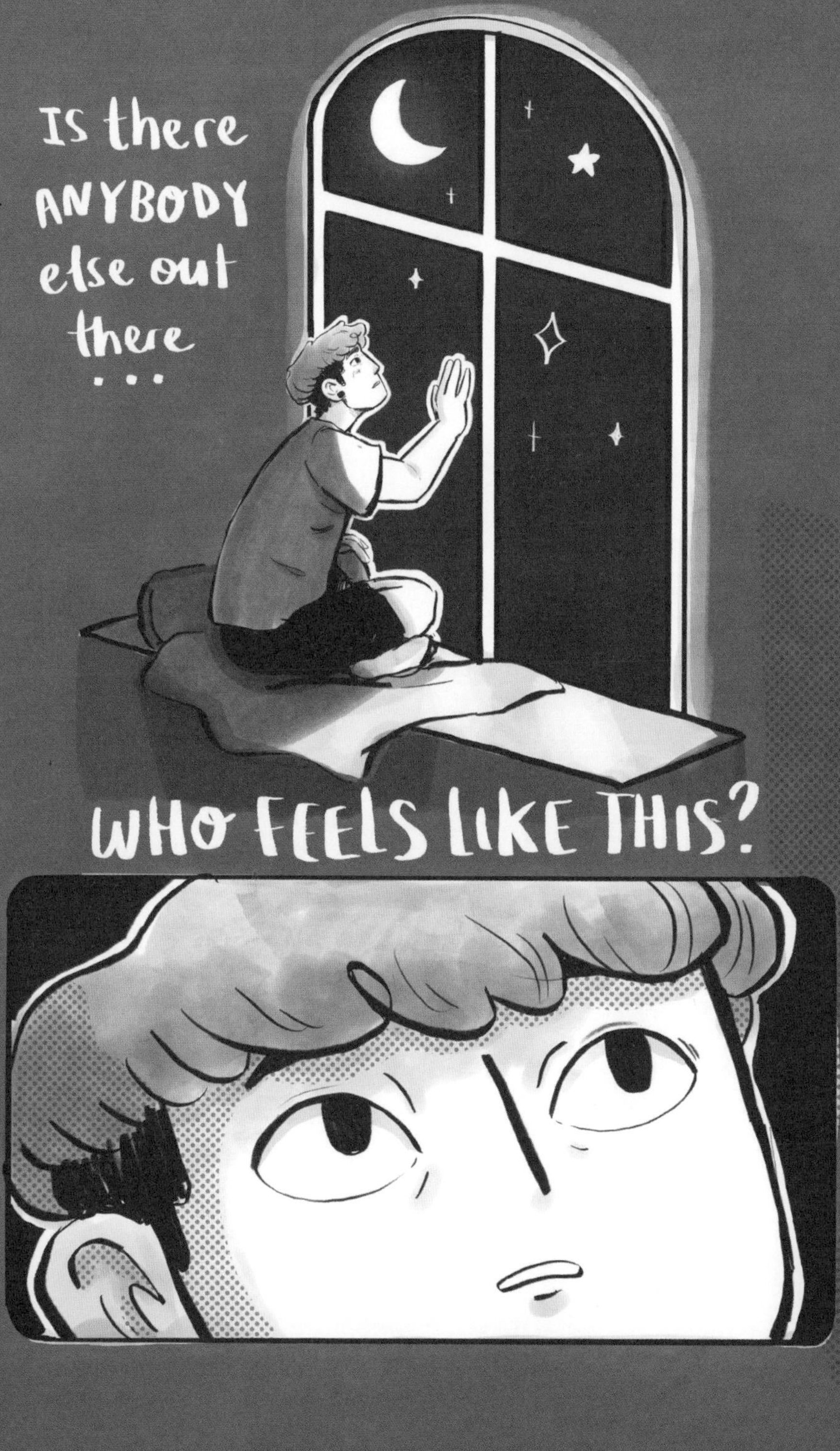
Is there ANYBODY else out there . . .
WHO FEELS LIKE THIS?

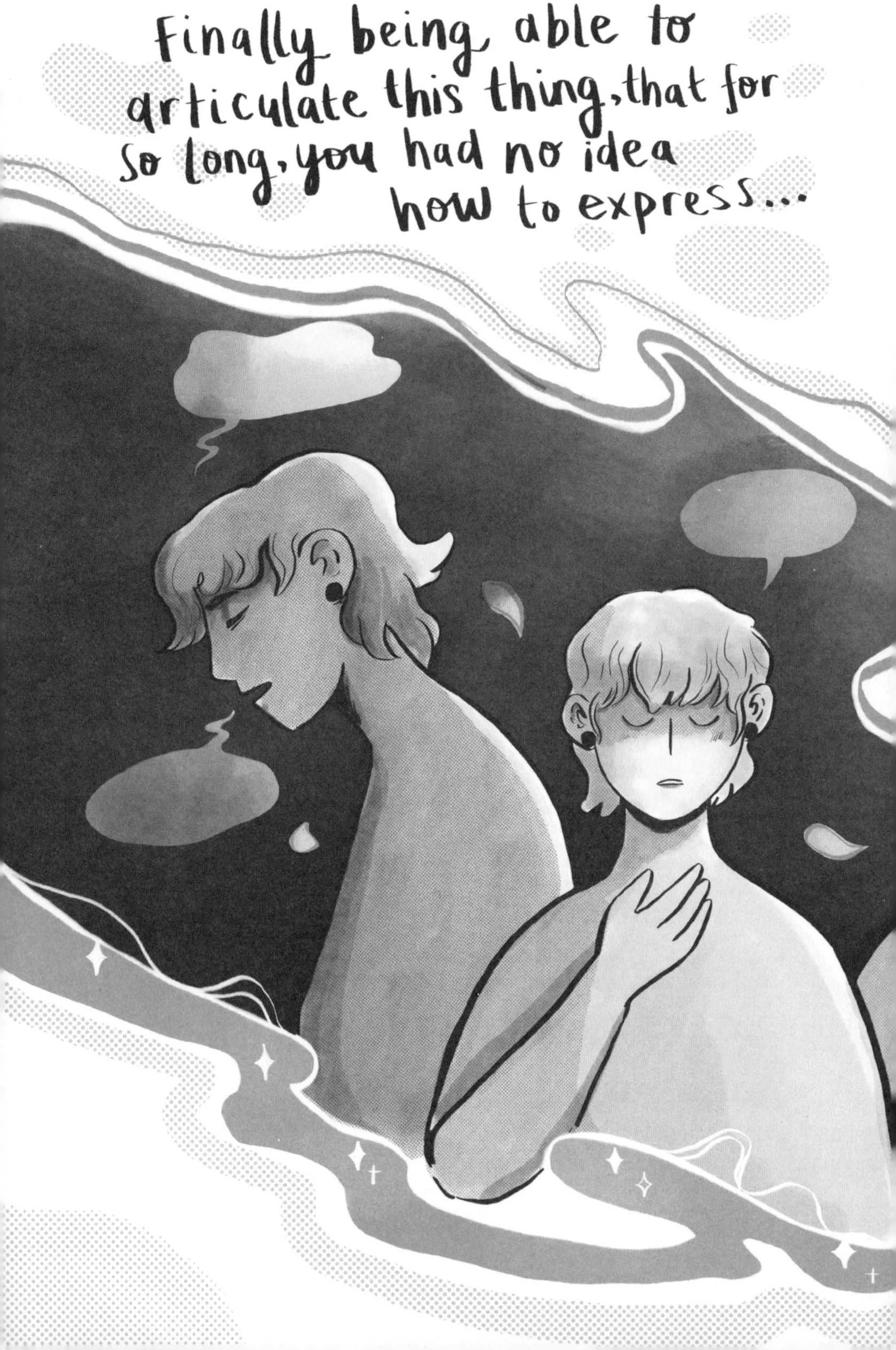
Finally being able to articulate this thing, that for so long, you had no idea how to express...

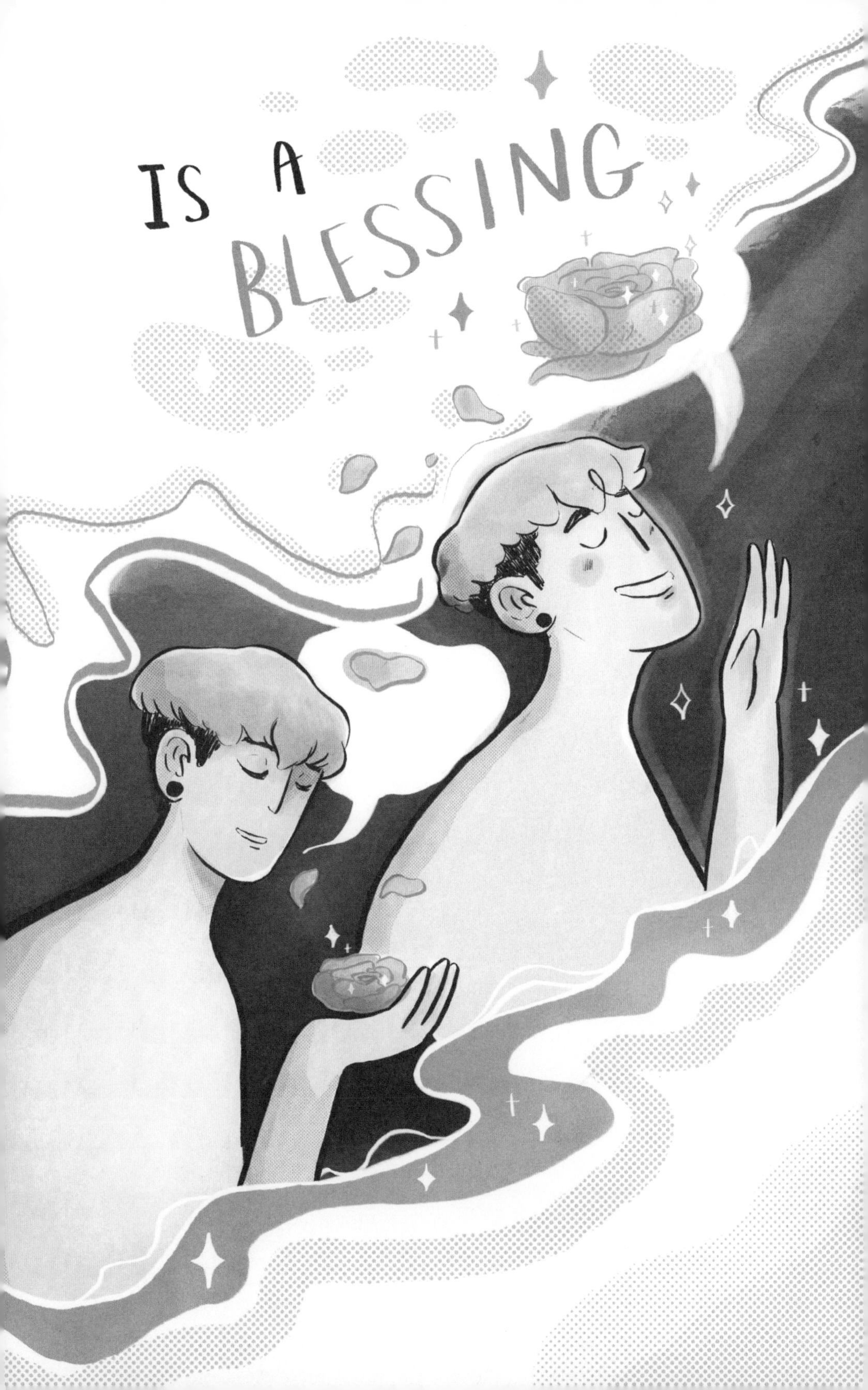
IS A BLESSING

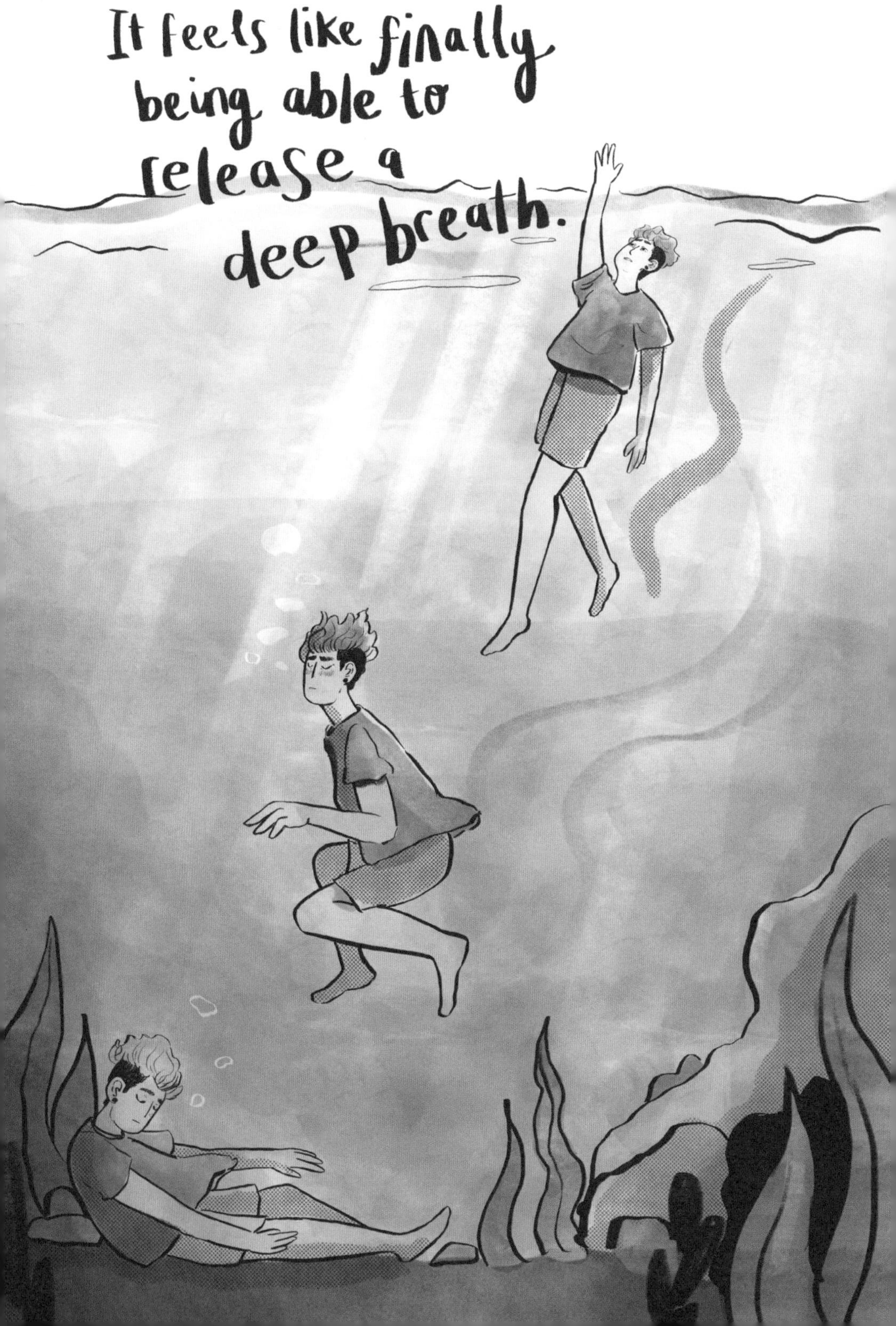
It feels like finally being able to release a deep breath.

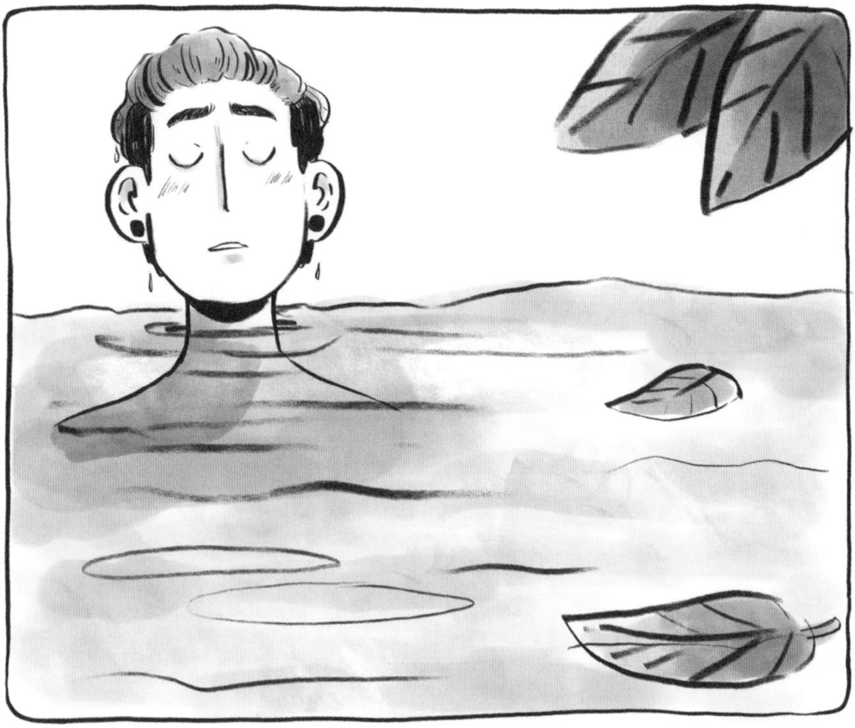

ONE YOU DIDN'T EVEN REALIZE YOU WERE HOLDING.

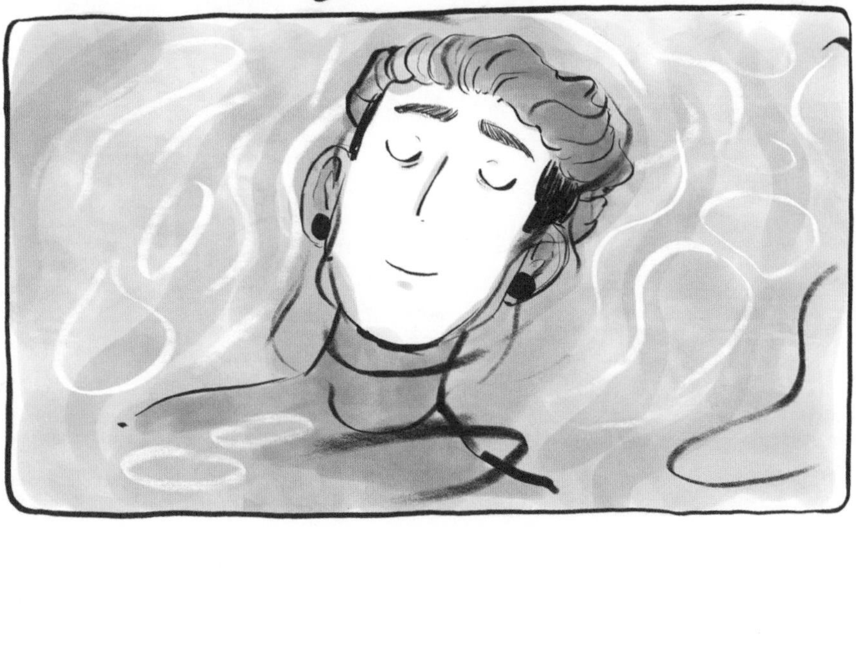

I AM SEEN

I EXIST

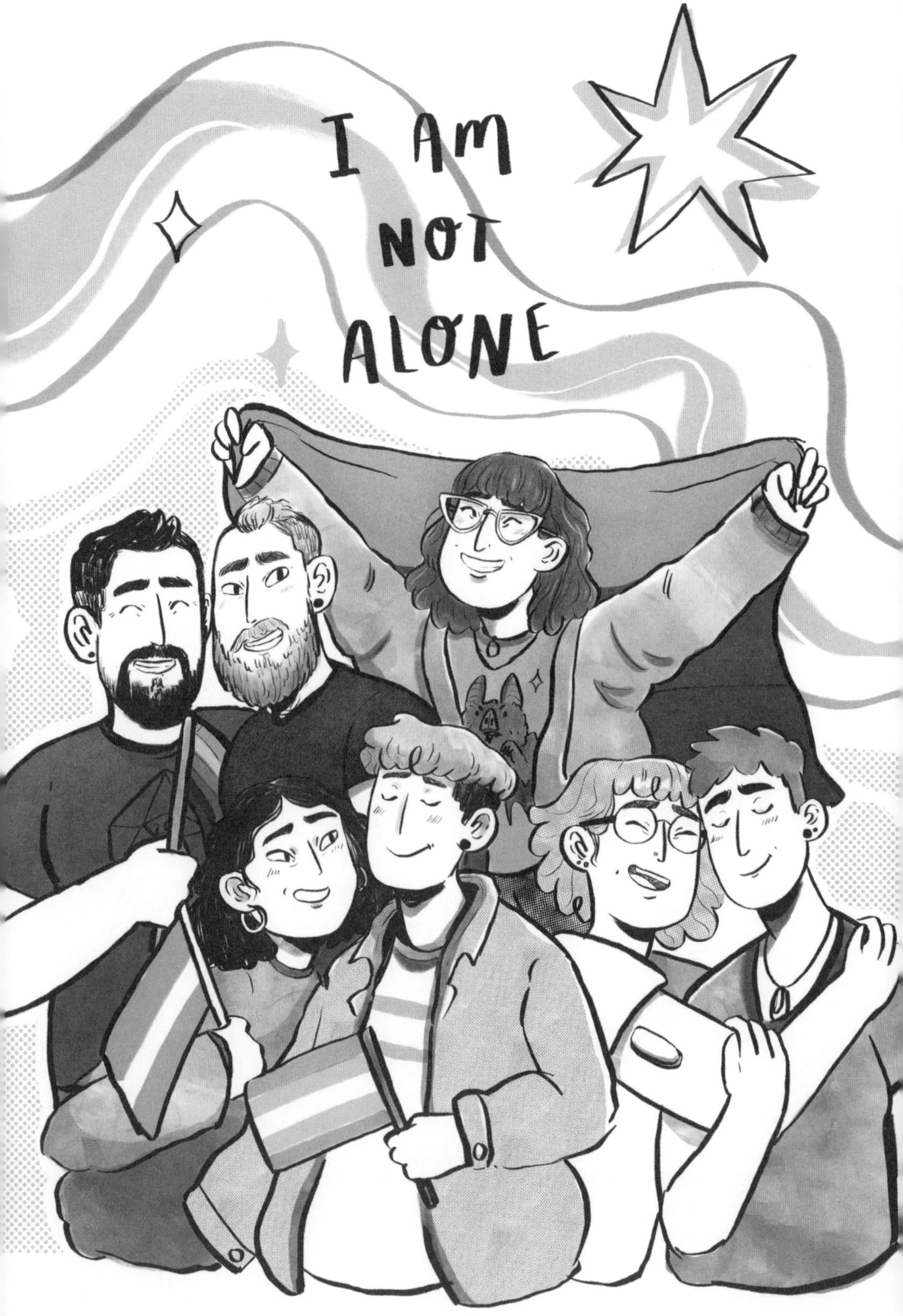
I AM NOT ALONE

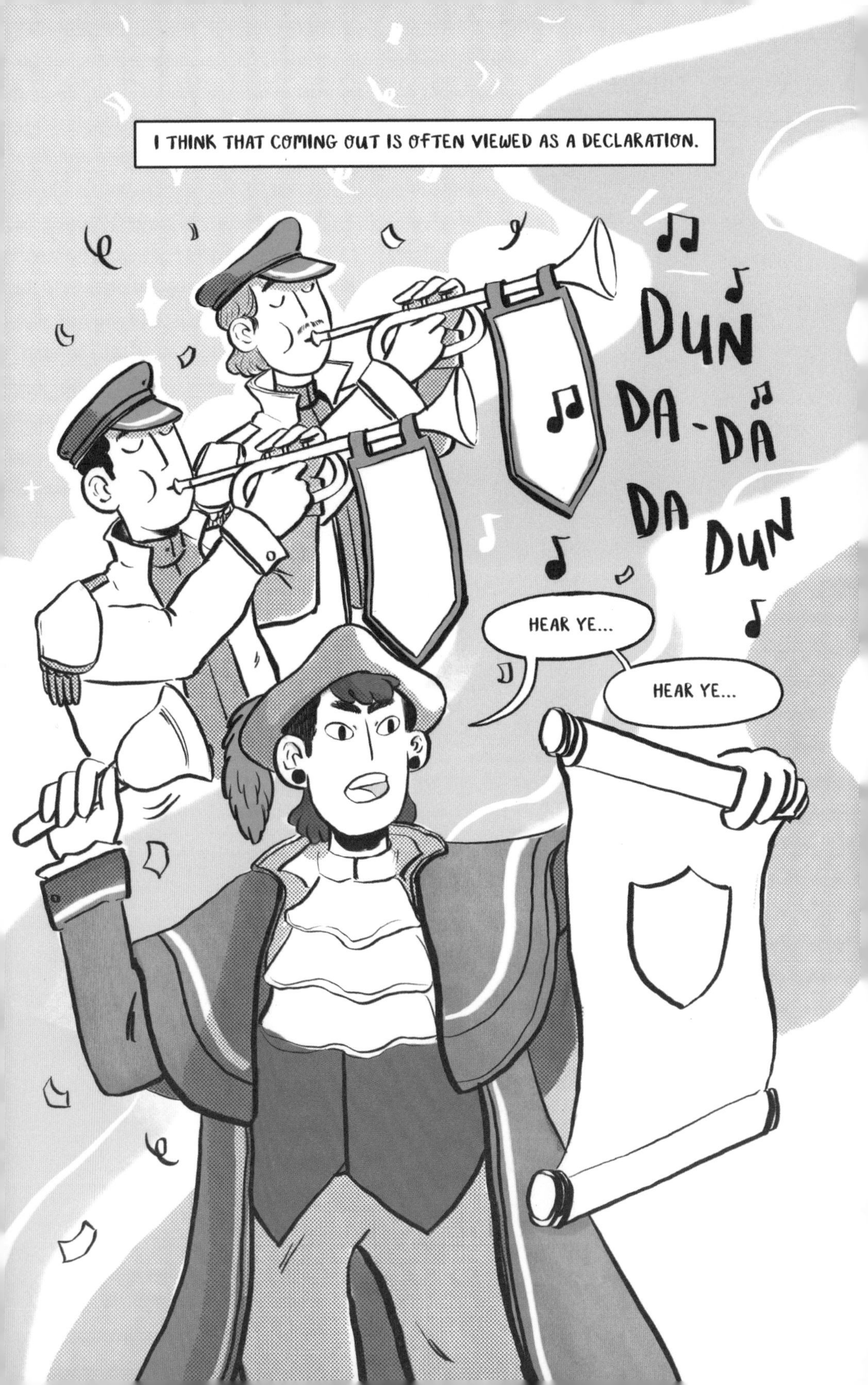
I THINK THAT COMING OUT IS OFTEN VIEWED AS A DECLARATION.
DUN DA-DA DA DUN
HEAR YE...
HEAR YE...

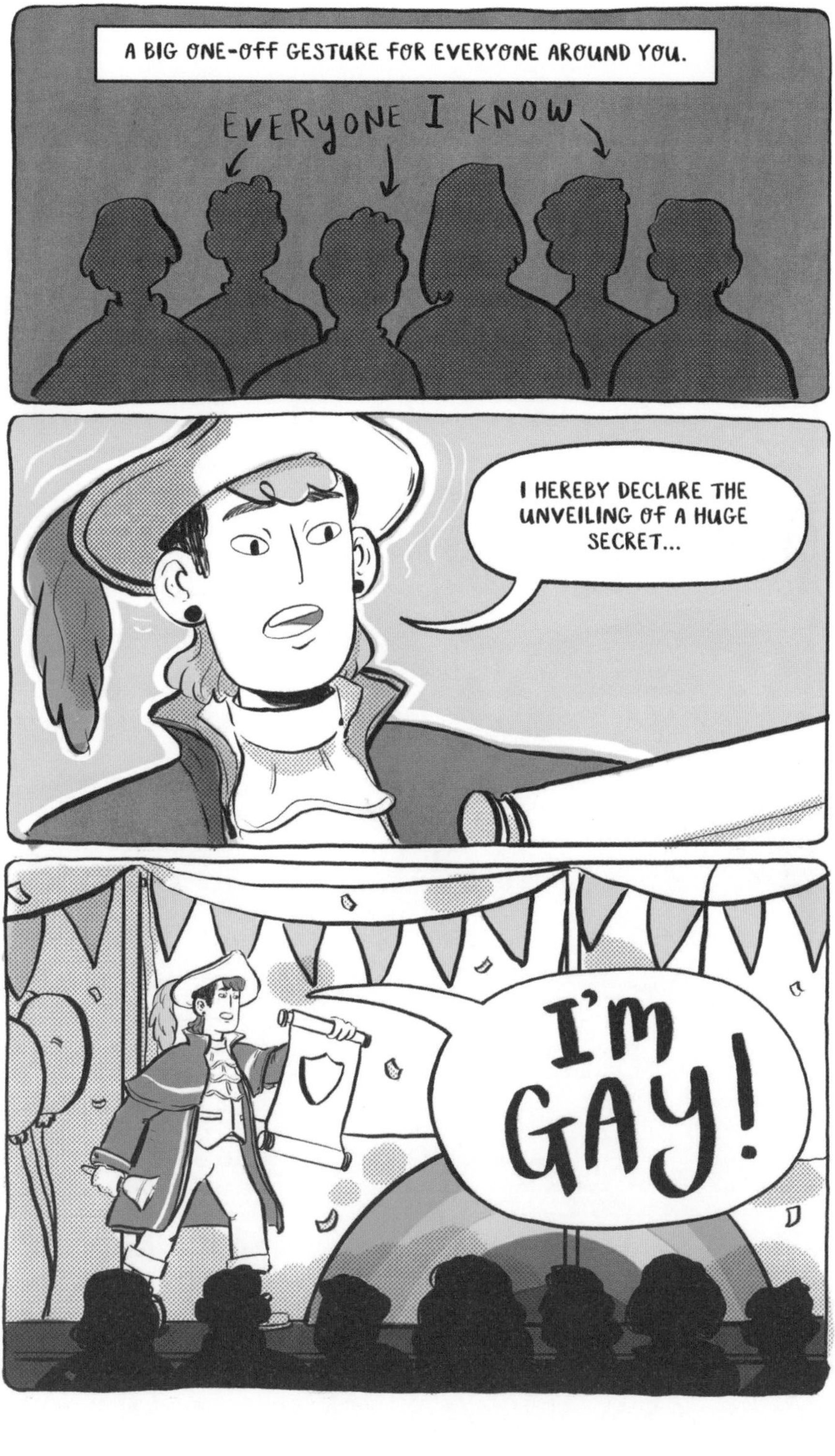
A BIG ONE-OFF GESTURE FOR EVERYONE AROUND YOU.
EVERYONE I KNOW
I HEREBY DECLARE THE UNVEILING OF A HUGE SECRET...
I'M GAY!

BUT IN REALITY THE PROCESS STARTS WITH COMING OUT TO YOURSELF...

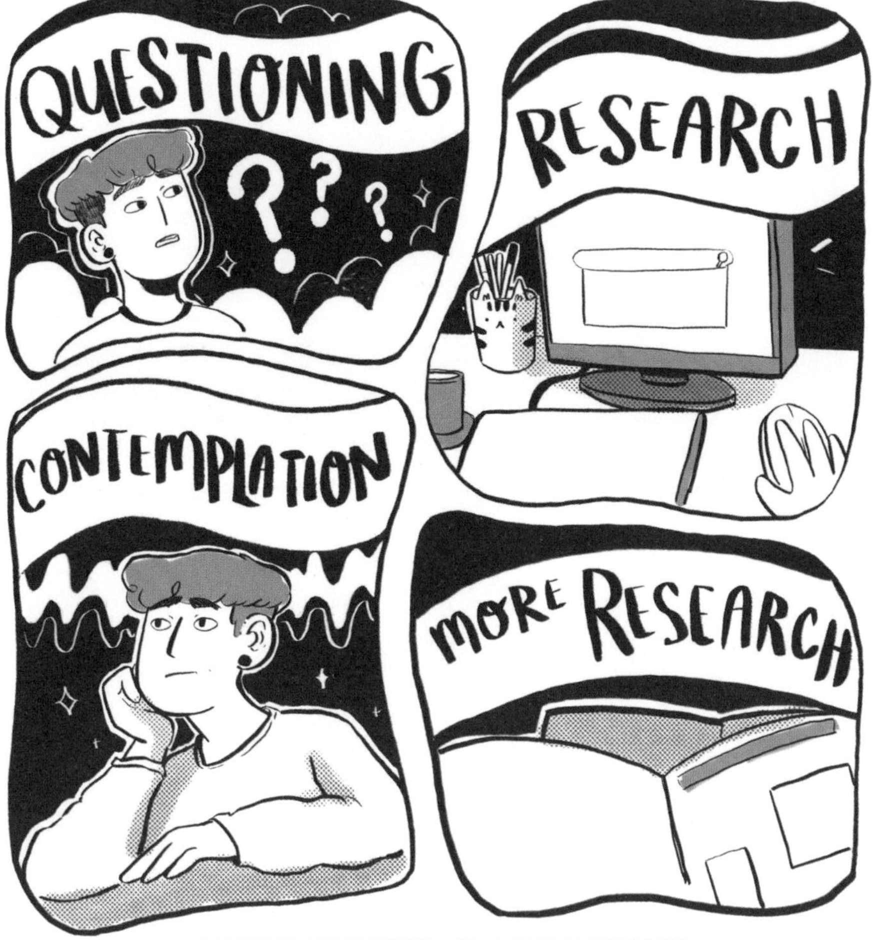
QUESTIONING
RESEARCH
CONTEMPLATION
MORE RESEARCH

BY FINDING AND ACCEPTING WHO YOU ARE.

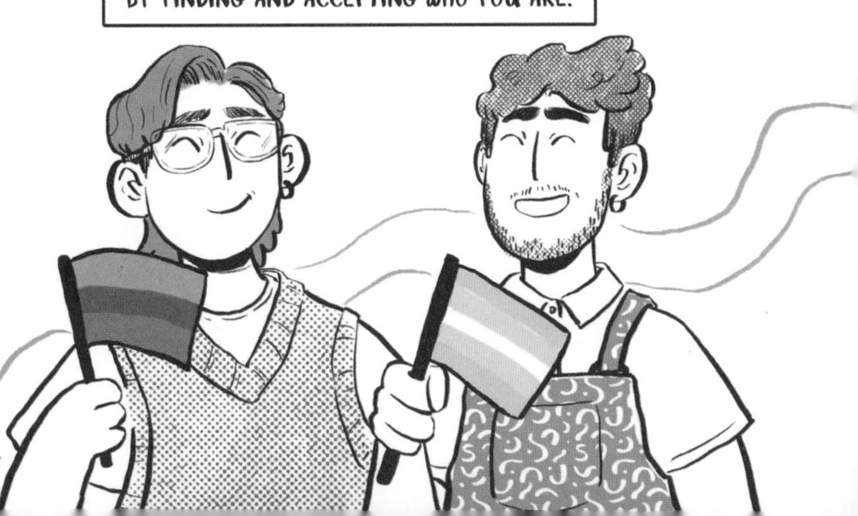

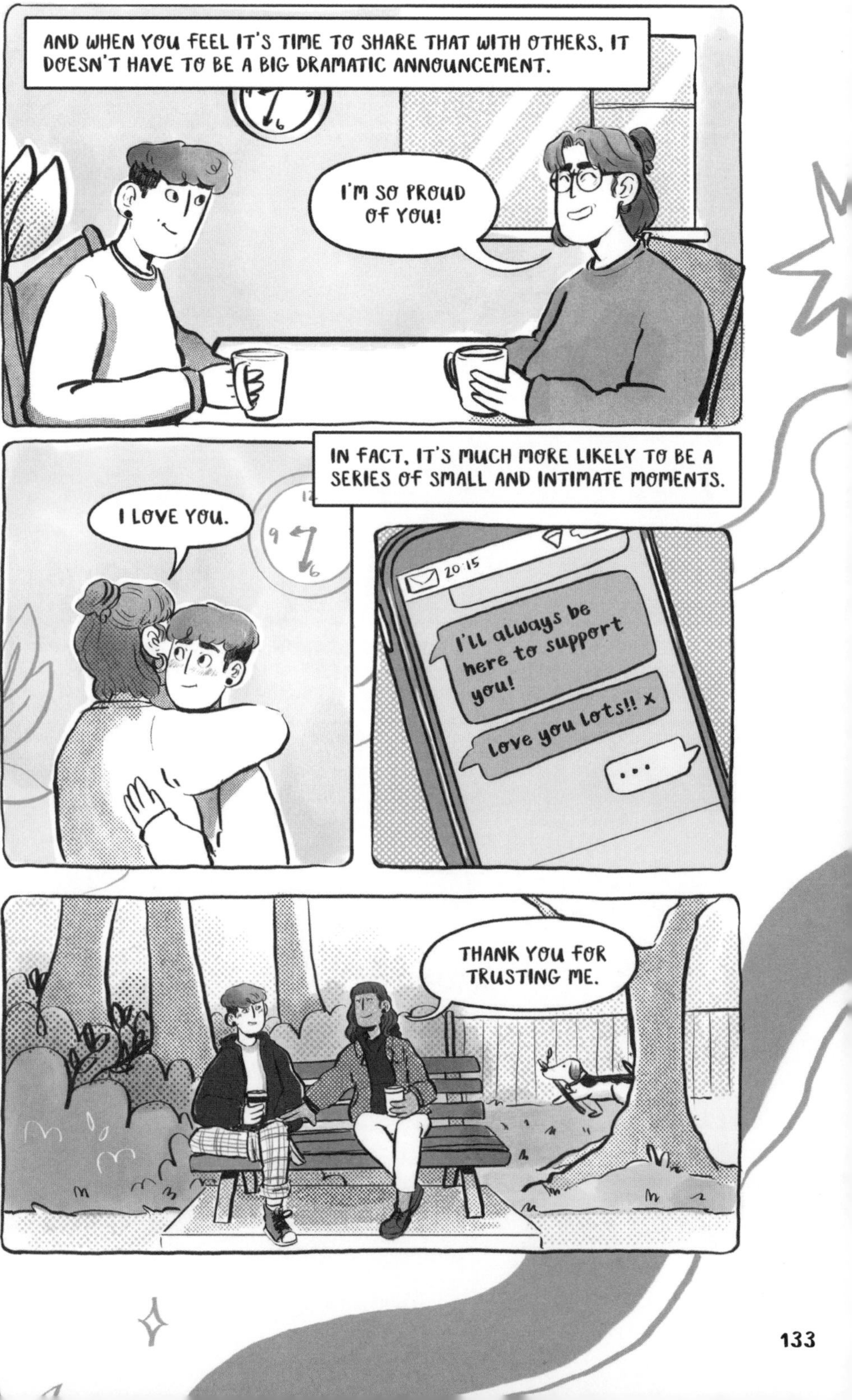
AND WHEN YOU FEEL IT'S TIME TO SHARE THAT WITH OTHERS, IT DOESN'T HAVE TO BE A BIG DRAMATIC ANNOUNCEMENT.
I'M SO PROUD OF YOU!
IN FACT, IT'S MUCH MORE LIKELY TO BE A SERIES OF SMALL AND INTIMATE MOMENTS.
I LOVE YOU.
20:15
I'll always be here to support you!
Love you lots!! x
...
THANK YOU FOR TRUSTING ME.

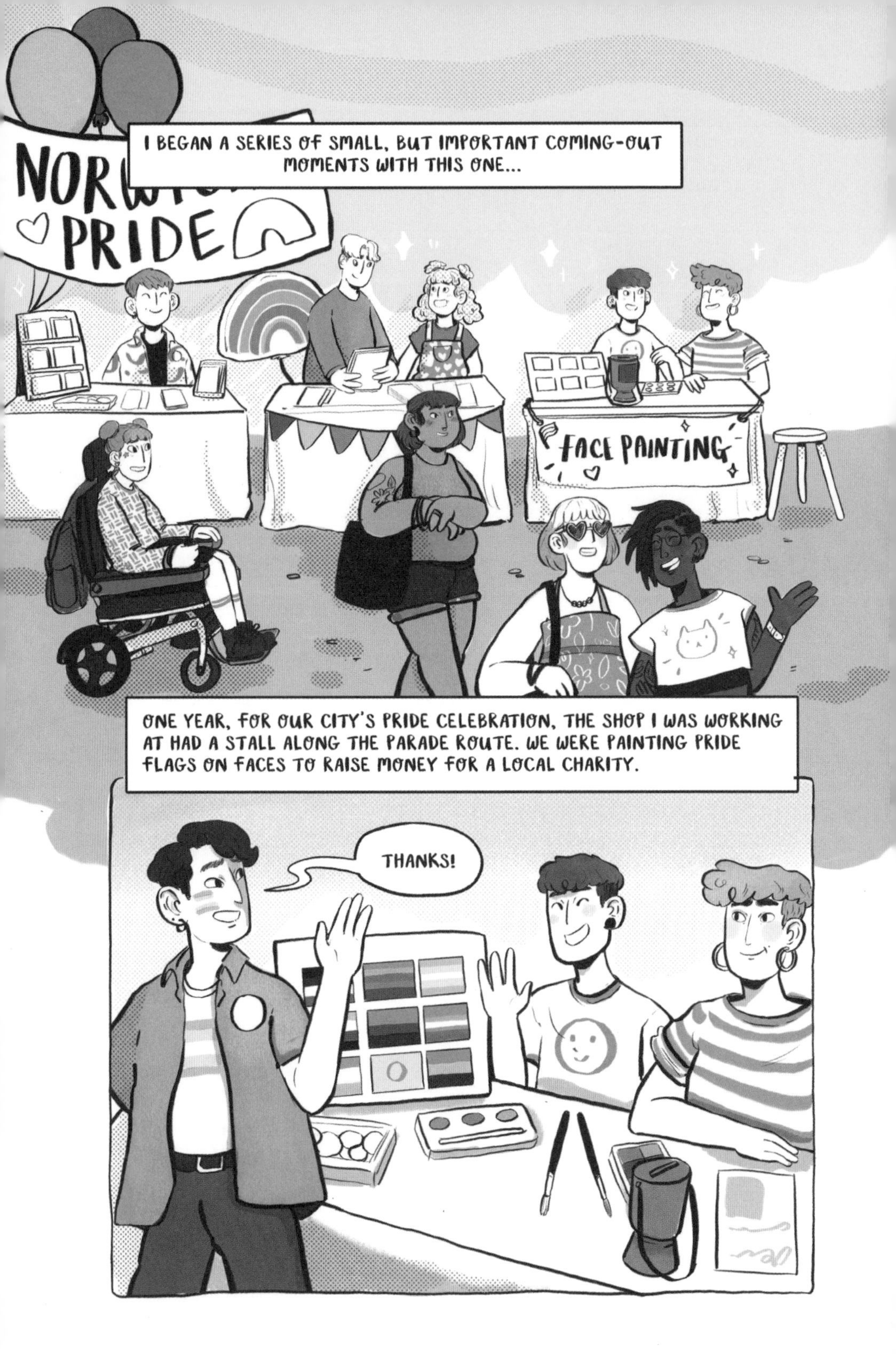
I BEGAN A SERIES OF SMALL, BUT IMPORTANT COMING-OUT MOMENTS WITH THIS ONE...
PRIDE
FACE PAINTING
ONE YEAR, FOR OUR CITY'S PRIDE CELEBRATION, THE SHOP I WAS WORKING AT HAD A STALL ALONG THE PARADE ROUTE. WE WERE PAINTING PRIDE FLAGS ON FACES TO RAISE MONEY FOR A LOCAL CHARITY.
THANKS!

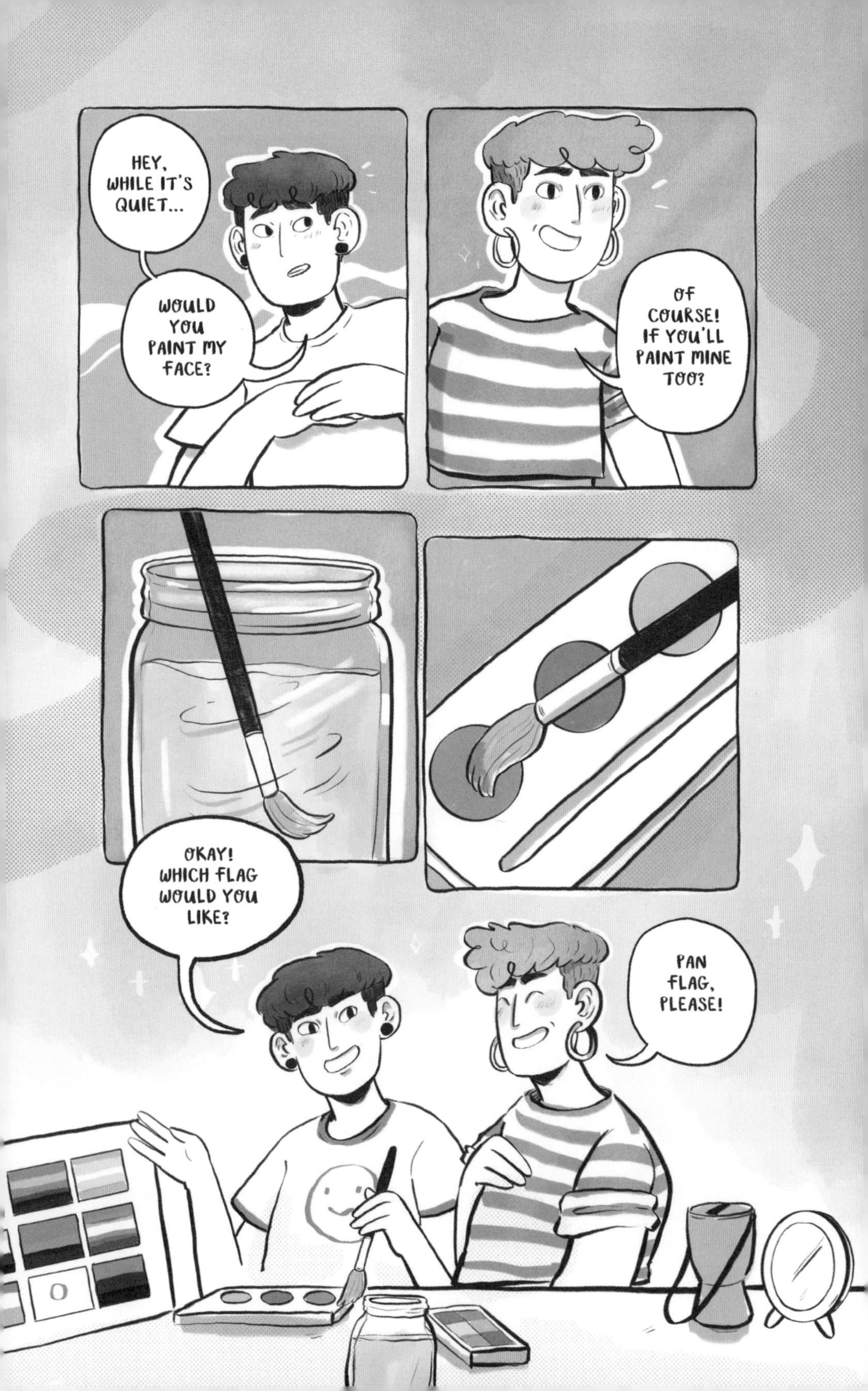
HEY, WHILE IT'S QUIET...
WOULD YOU PAINT MY FACE?
OF COURSE! IF YOU'LL PAINT MINE TOO?
OKAY! WHICH FLAG WOULD YOU LIKE?
PAN FLAG, PLEASE!

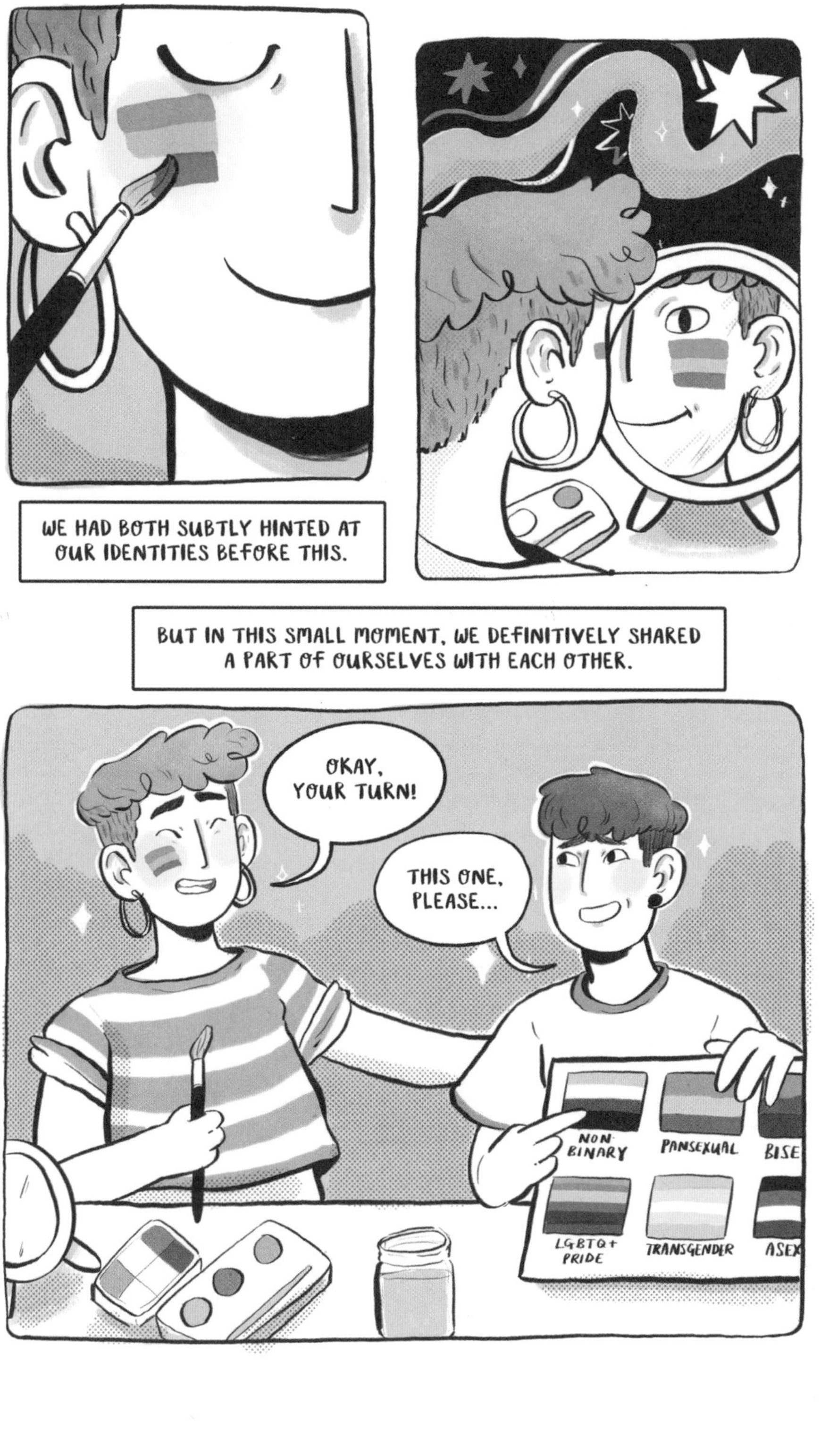
WE HAD BOTH SUBTLY HINTED AT OUR IDENTITIES BEFORE THIS.
BUT IN THIS SMALL MOMENT, WE DEFINITIVELY SHARED A PART OF OURSELVES WITH EACH OTHER.
OKAY, YOUR TURN!
THIS ONE, PLEASE...
NON-BINARY
PANSEXUAL
LGBTQ+ PRIDE
TRANSGENDER

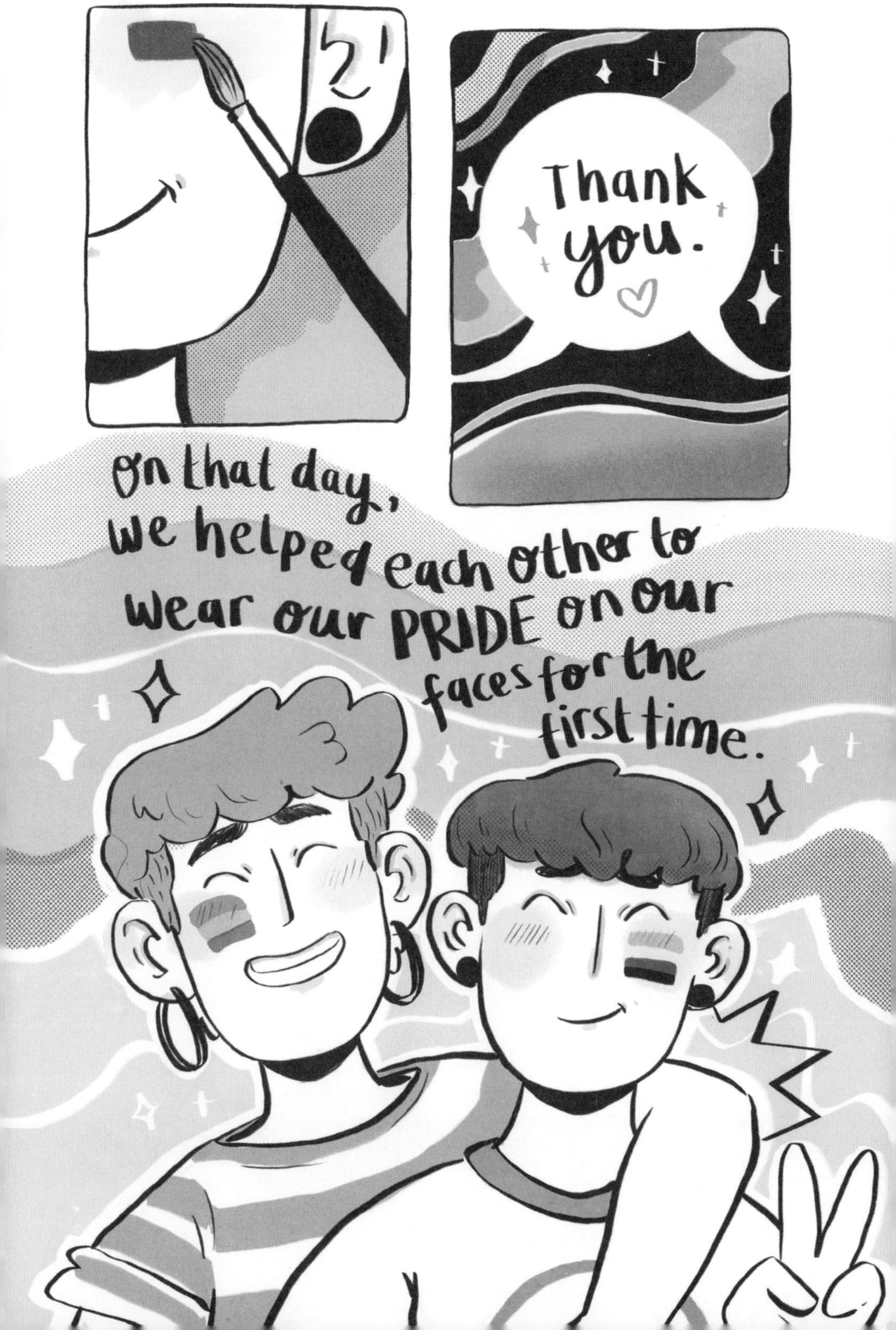
Thank you.
On that day, we helped each other to wear our PRIDE on our faces for the first time.

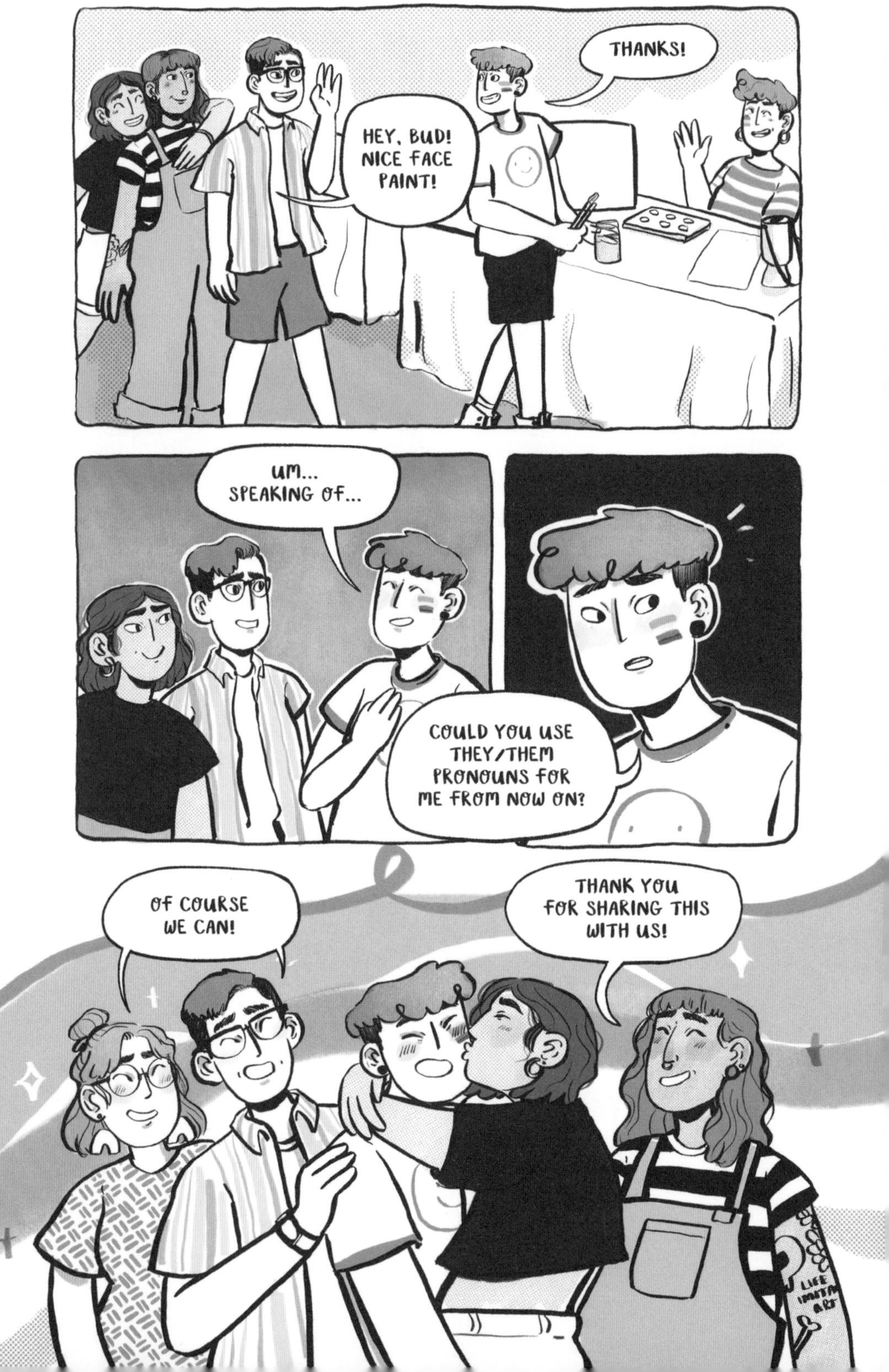
HEY, BUD! NICE FACE PAINT!
THANKS!
UM... SPEAKING OF...
COULD YOU USE THEY/THEM PRONOUNS FOR ME FROM NOW ON?
OF COURSE WE CAN!
THANK YOU FOR SHARING THIS WITH US!
LIFE IMITATES ART

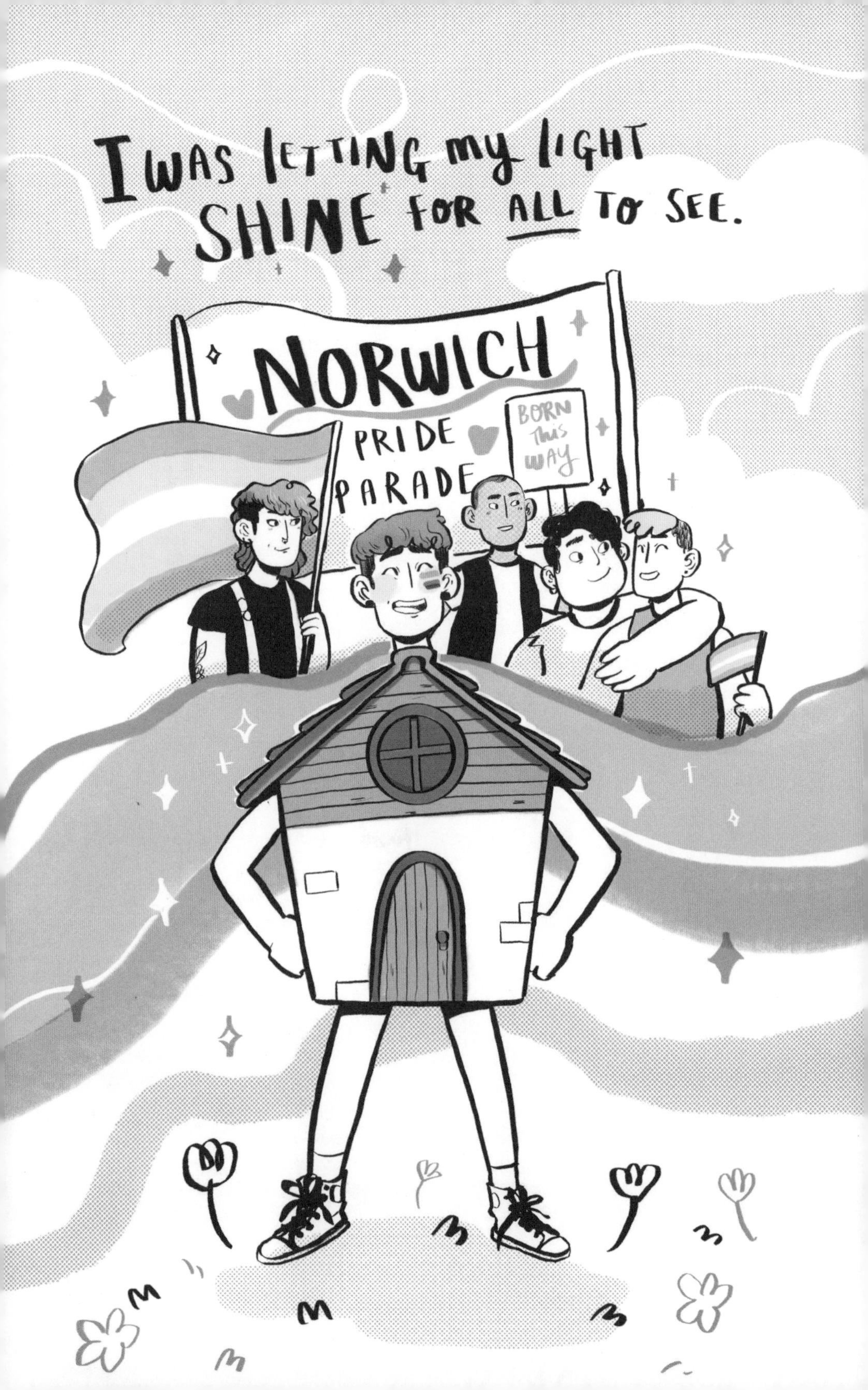
I WAS LETTING MY LIGHT SHINE FOR ALL TO SEE.
NORWICH PRIDE PARADE
BORN THIS WAY

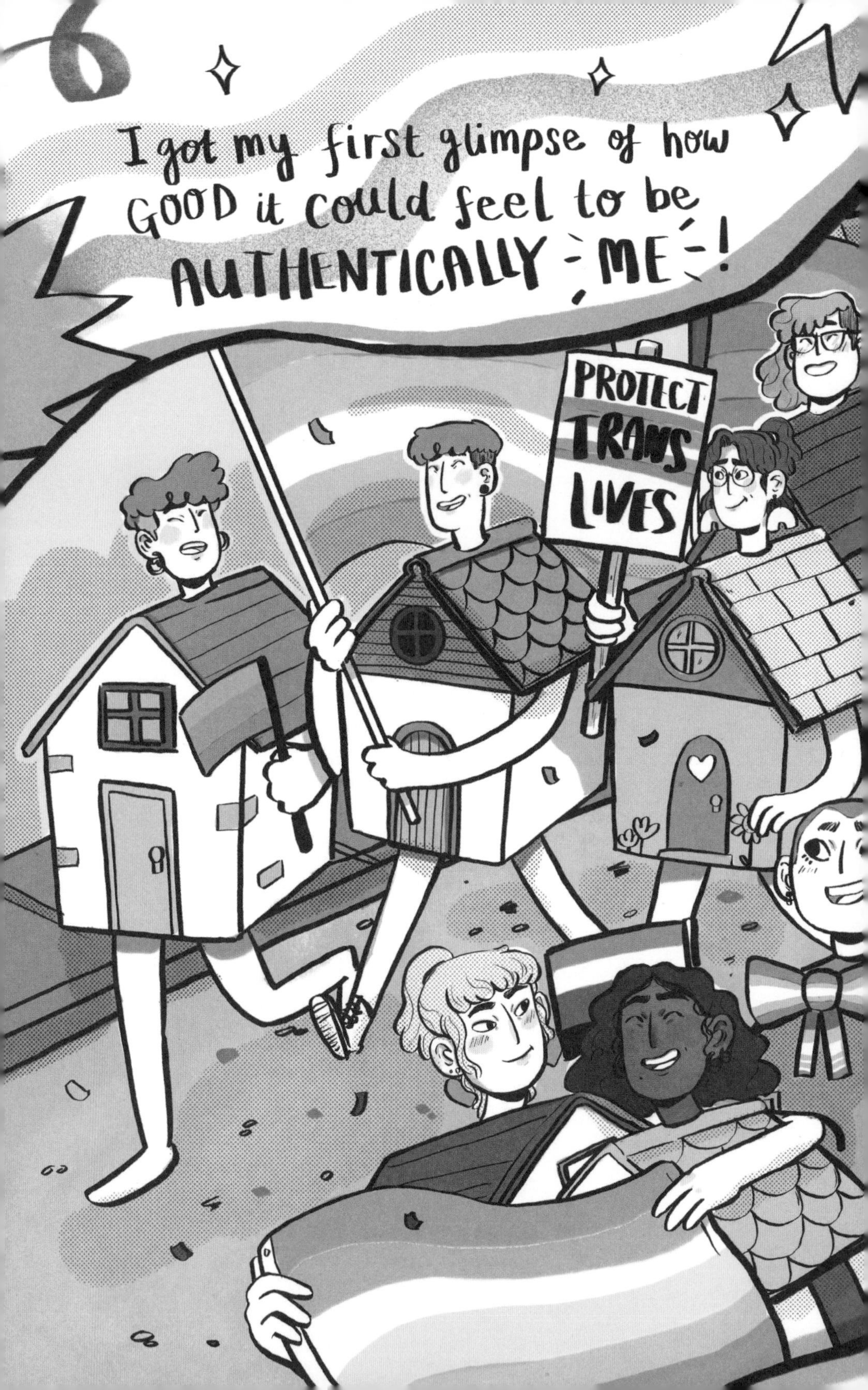
6
I got my first glimpse of how GOOD it could feel to be AUTHENTICALLY ME!
PROTECT TRANS LIVES

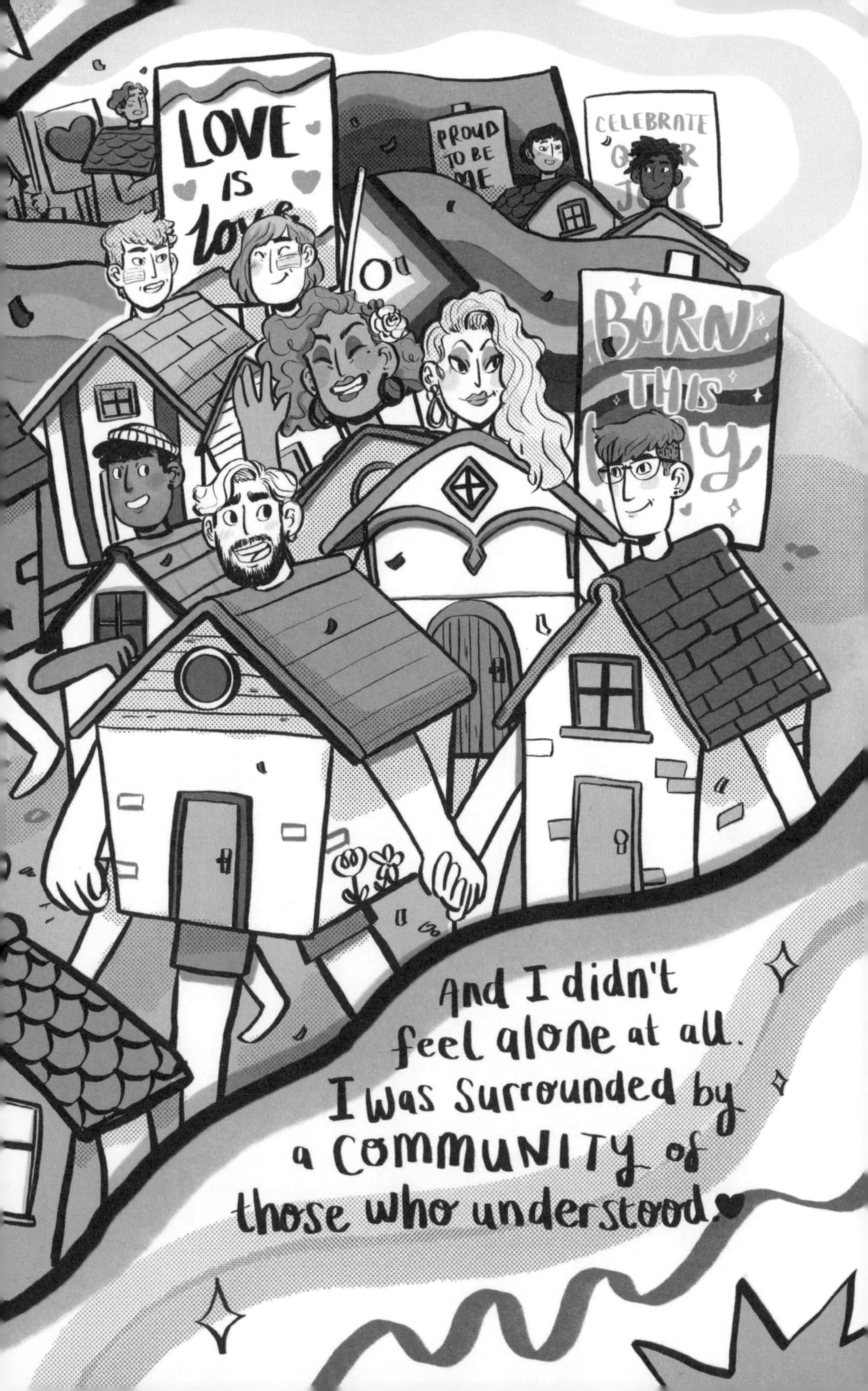
LOVE IS
PROUD TO BE ME
CELEBRATE
BORN THIS
And I didn't feel alone at all. I was surrounded by a COMMUNITY of those who understood.

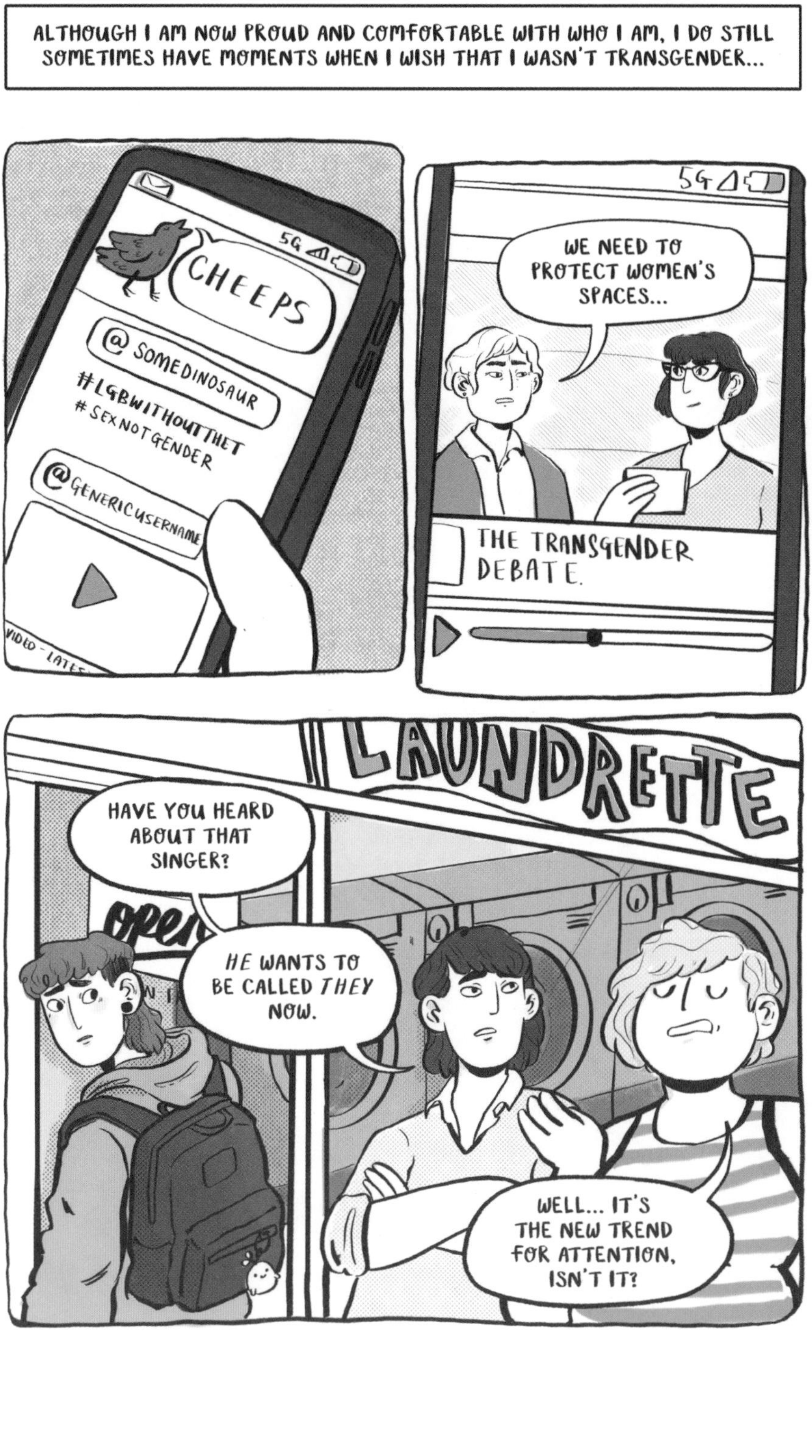
ALTHOUGH I AM NOW PROUD AND COMFORTABLE WITH WHO I AM, I DO STILL SOMETIMES HAVE MOMENTS WHEN I WISH THAT I WASN'T TRANSGENDER...
5G
CHEEPS
@SOMEDINOSAUR
#LGBWITHOUTTHET
#SEXNOTGENDER
@GENERICUSERNAME
5G
WE NEED TO PROTECT WOMEN'S SPACES...
THE TRANSGENDER DEBATE.
LAUNDRETTE
HAVE YOU HEARD ABOUT THAT SINGER?
HE WANTS TO BE CALLED *THEY* NOW.
WELL... IT'S THE NEW TREND FOR ATTENTION, ISN'T IT?

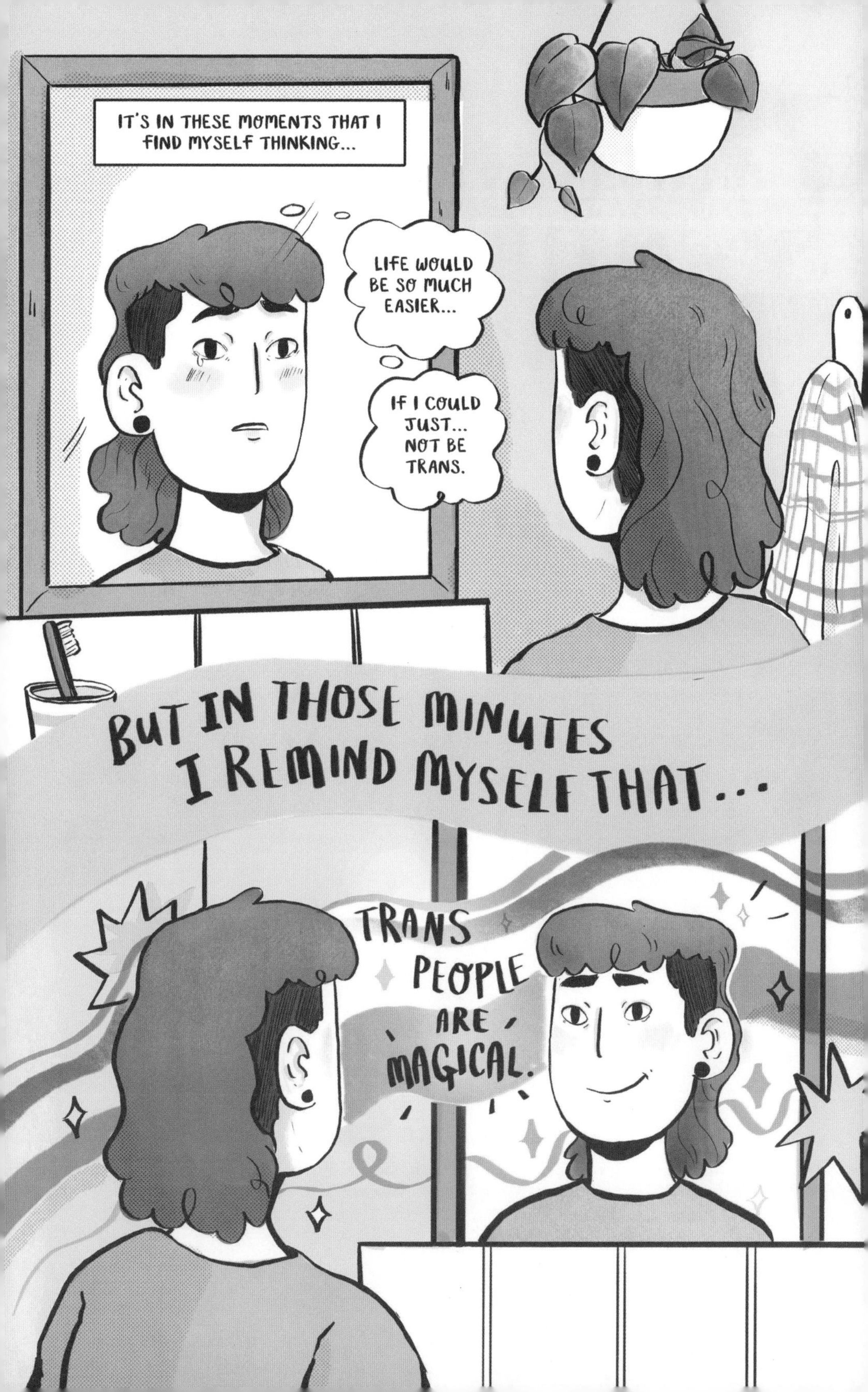
IT'S IN THESE MOMENTS THAT I FIND MYSELF THINKING...
LIFE WOULD BE SO MUCH EASIER...
IF I COULD JUST... NOT BE TRANS.
BUT IN THOSE MINUTES I REMIND MYSELF THAT...
TRANS PEOPLE ARE MAGICAL.

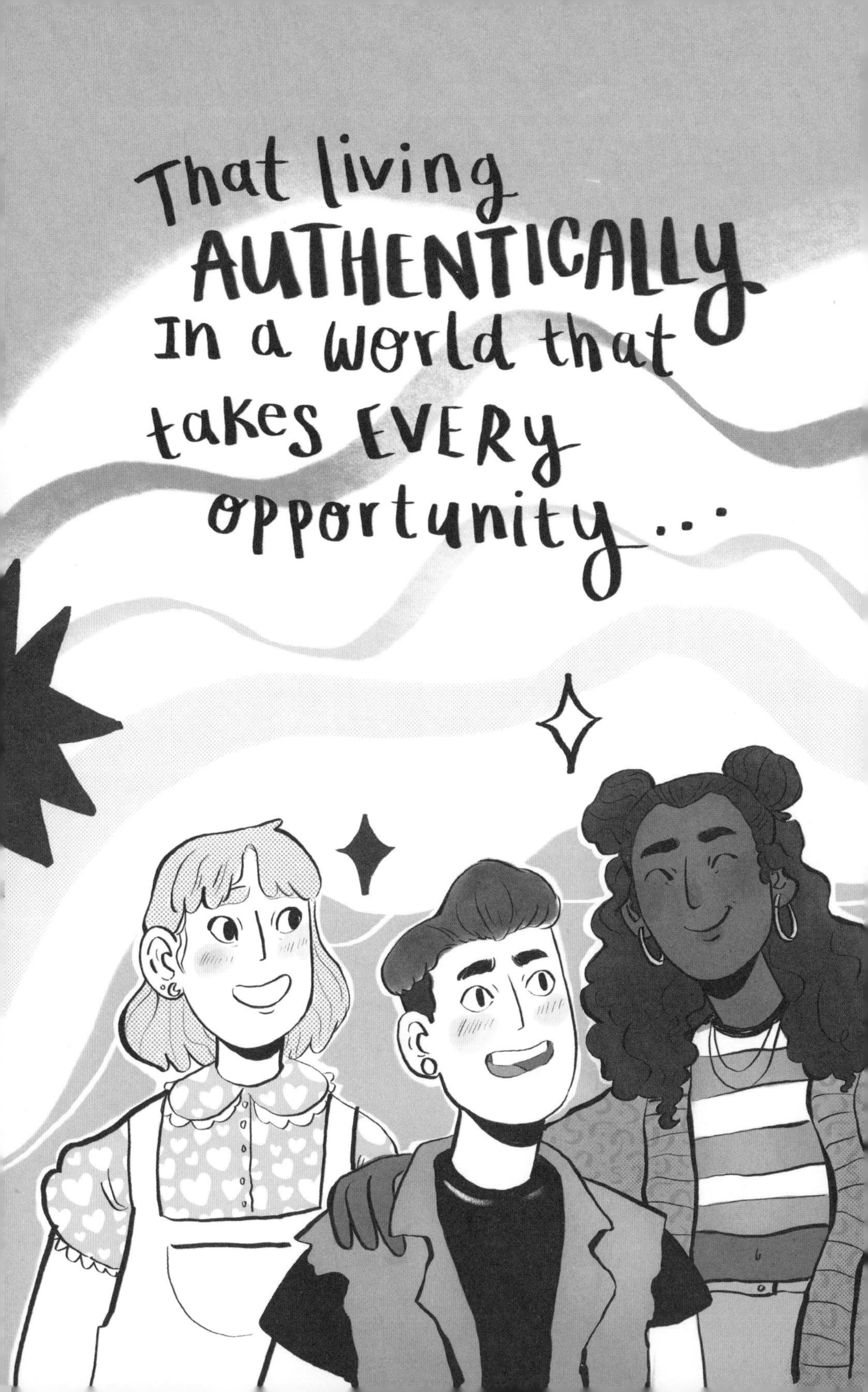
That living AUTHENTICALLY In a world that takes EVERY opportunity . . .

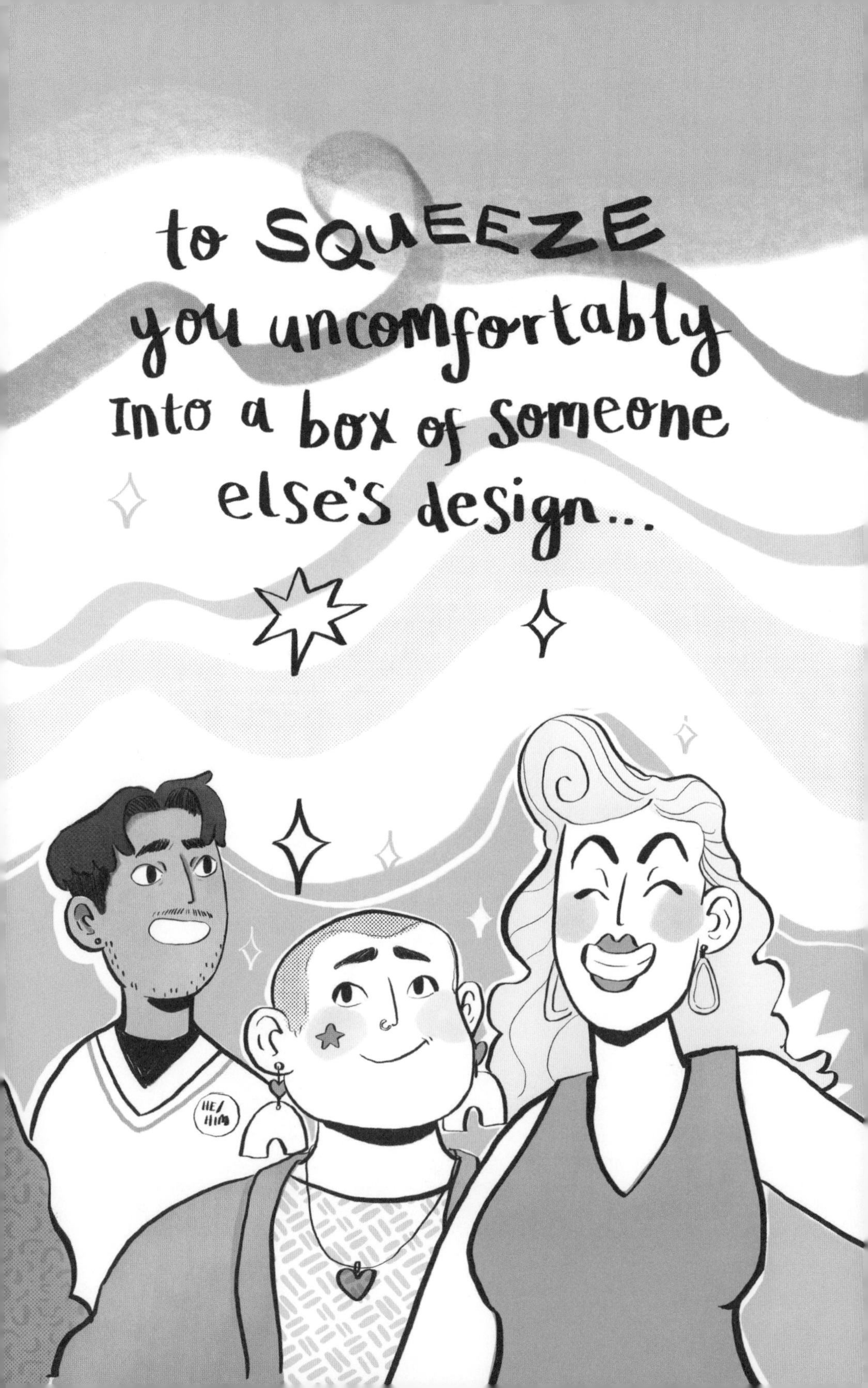
to SQUEEZE
you uncomfortably
Into a box of Someone
else's design...
HE/HIM

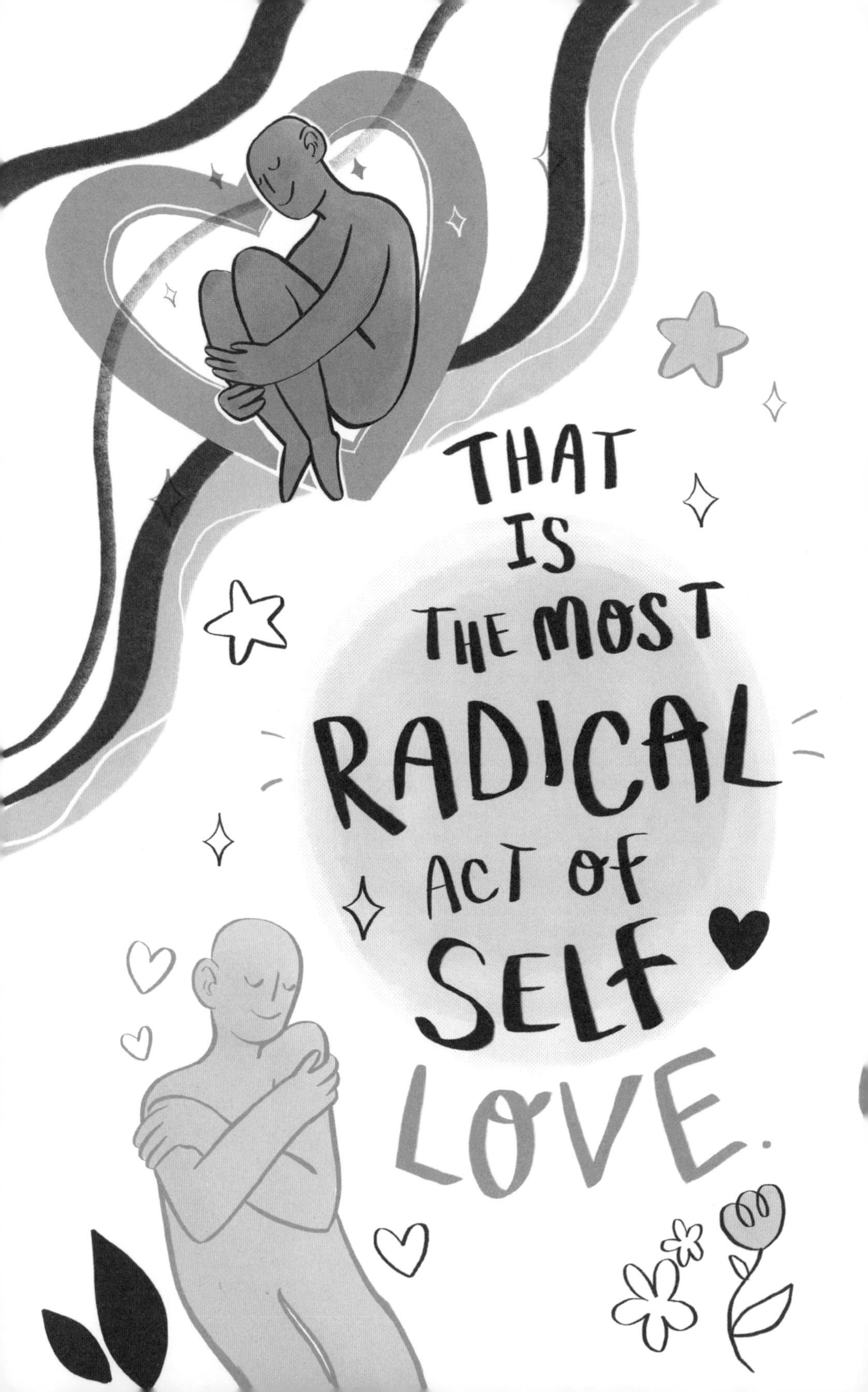
THAT IS THE MOST RADICAL ACT OF SELF LOVE.

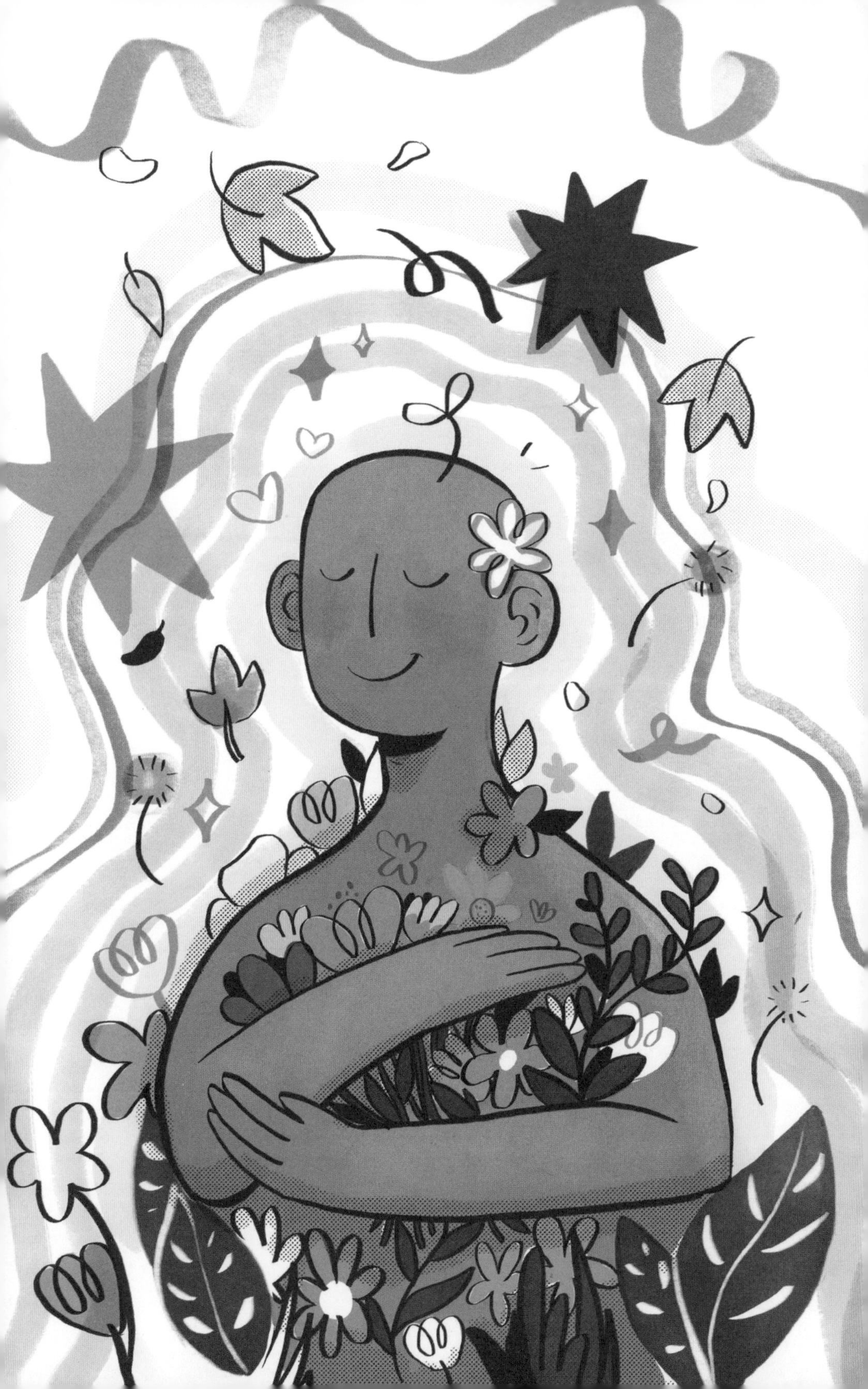

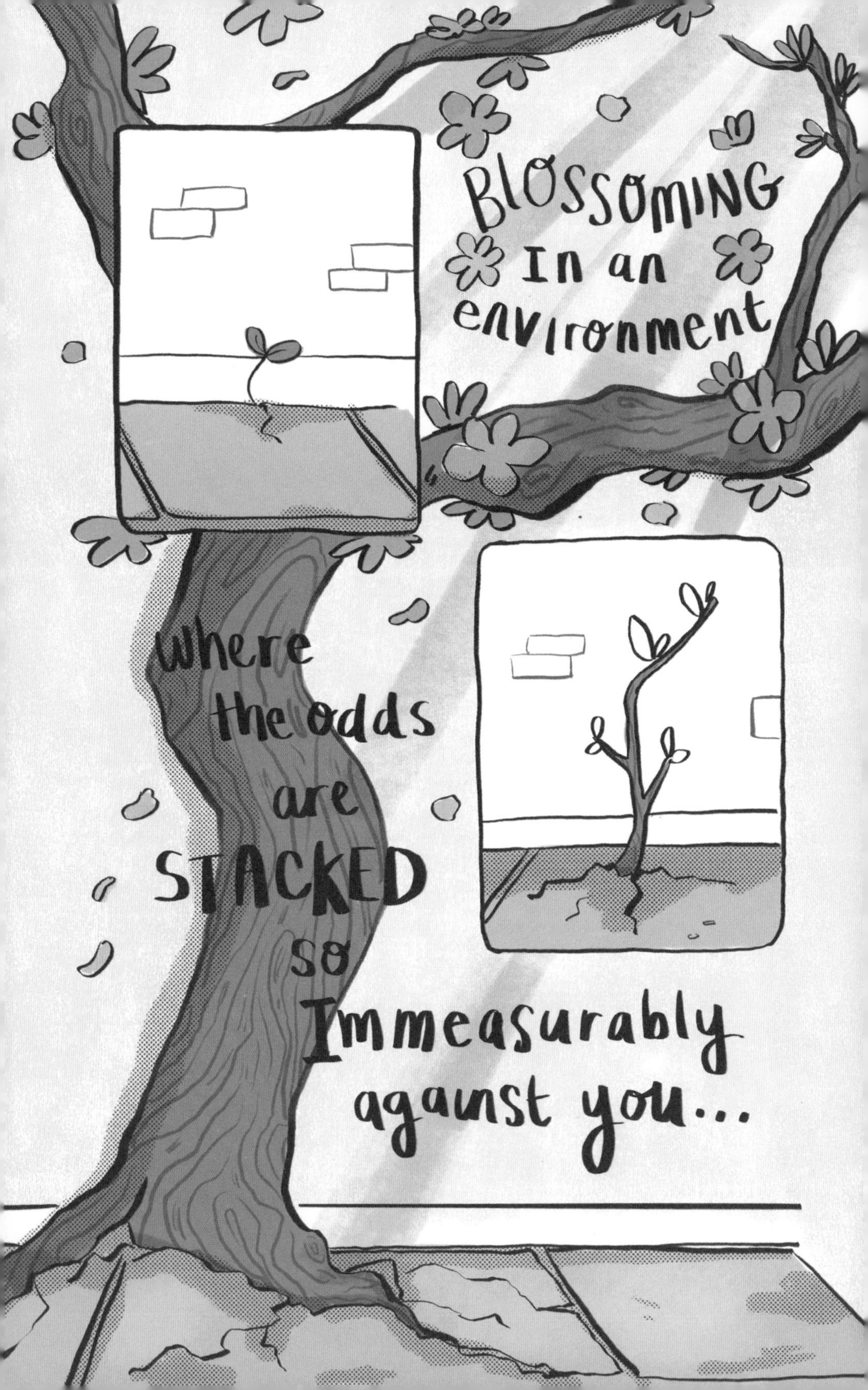
BLOSSOMING In an environment
Where the odds are STACKED so Immeasurably against you...

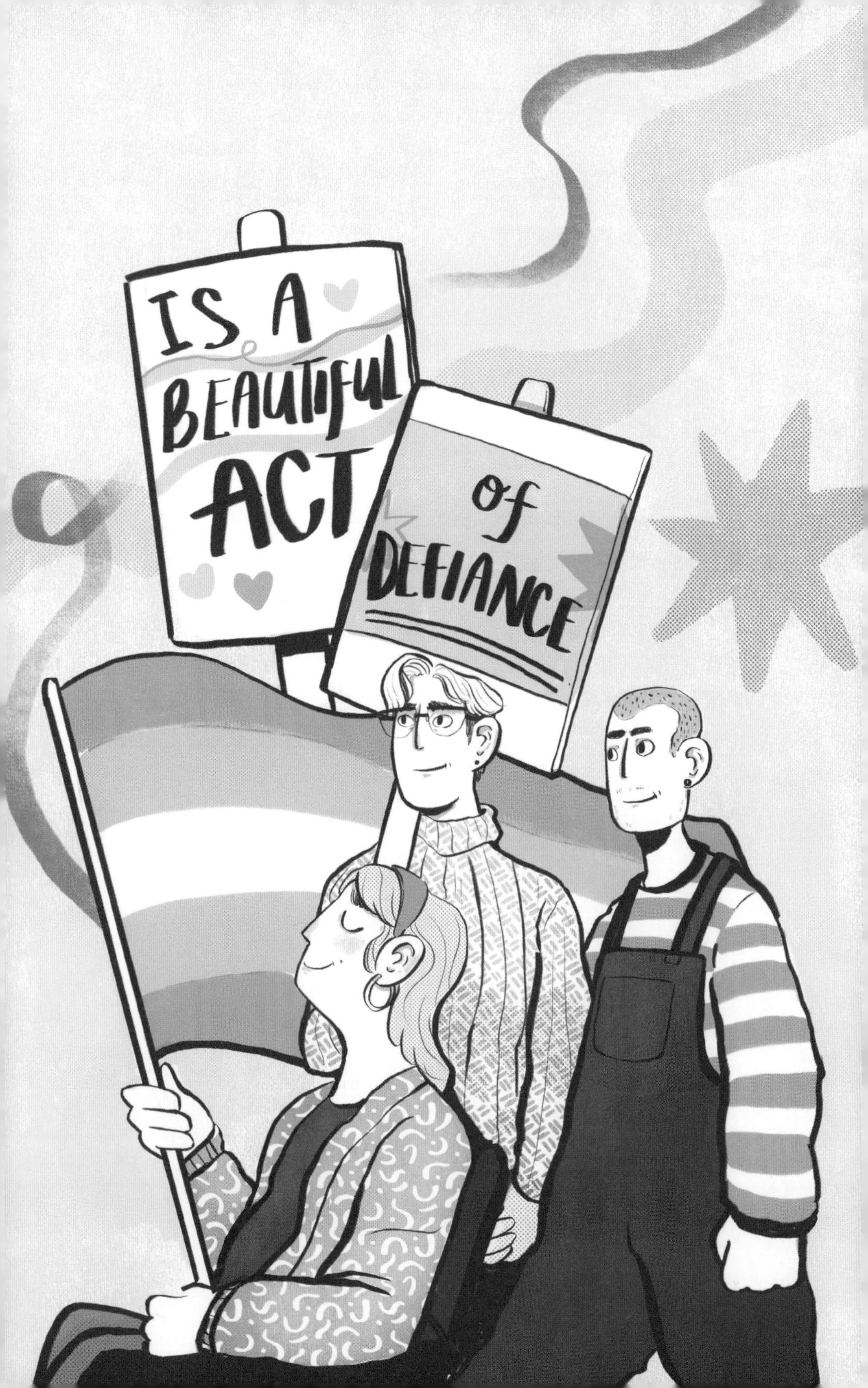
IS A
BEAUTIFUL
ACT
of
DEFIANCE

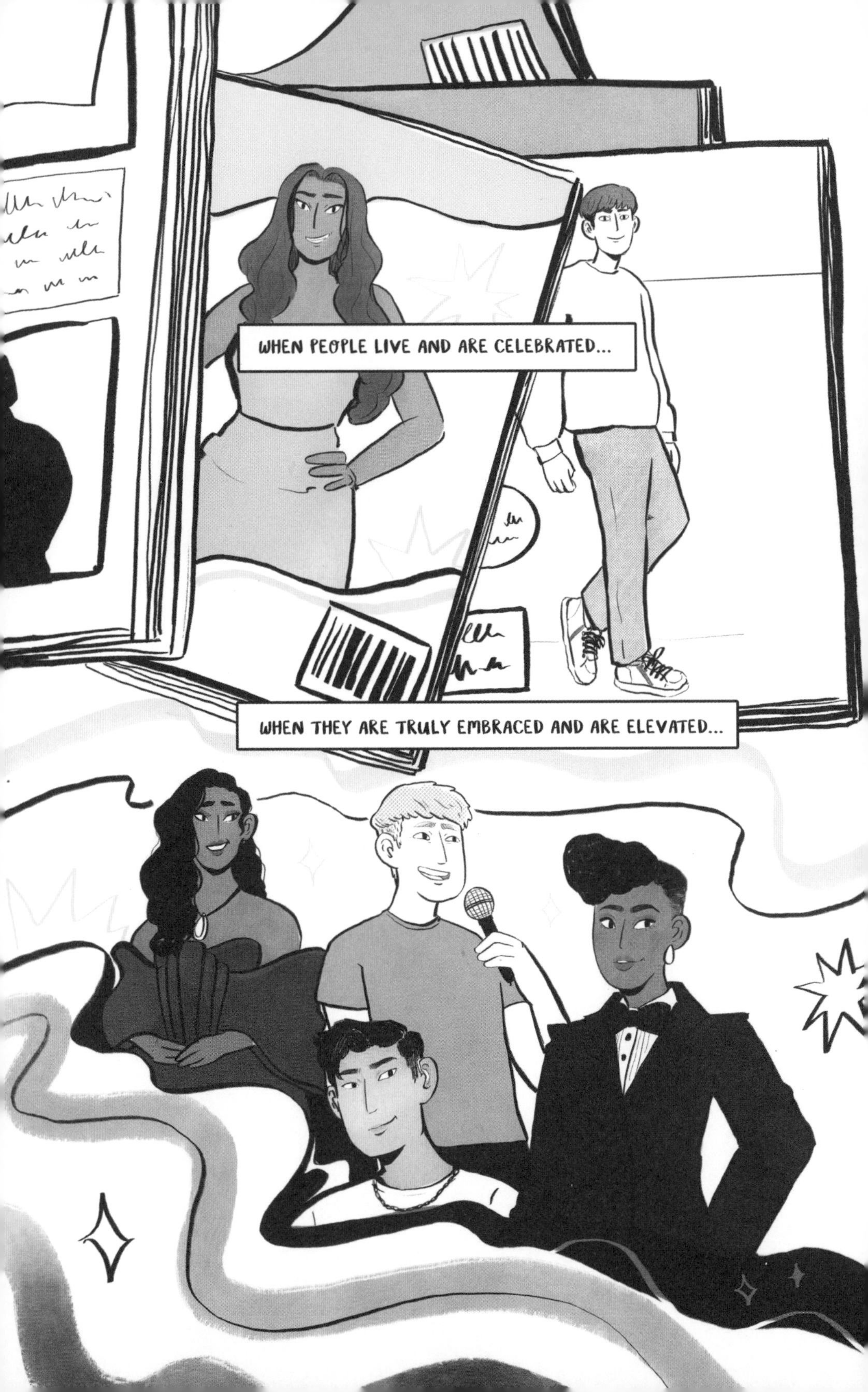
WHEN PEOPLE LIVE AND ARE CELEBRATED...
WHEN THEY ARE TRULY EMBRACED AND ARE ELEVATED...

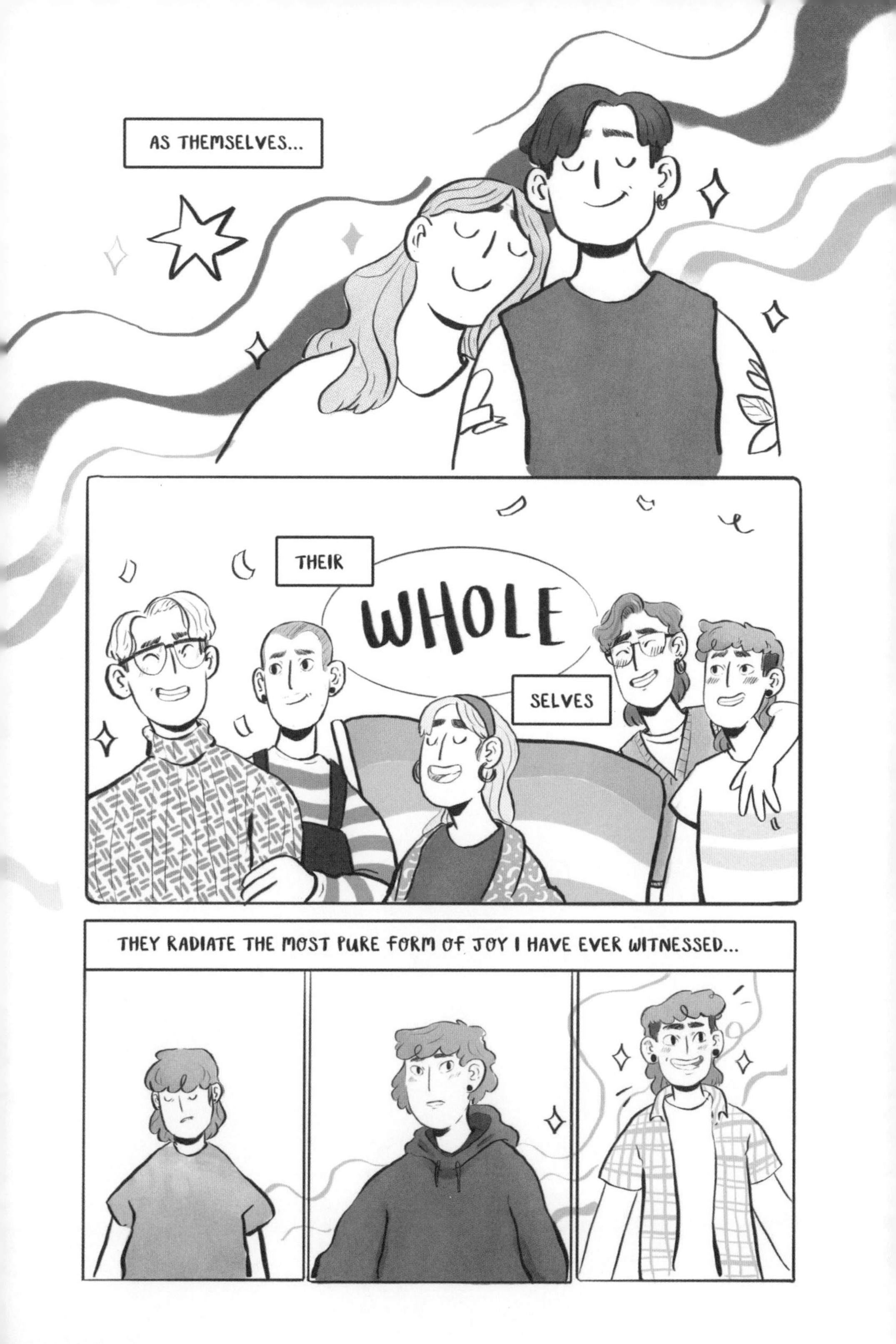
AS THEMSELVES...
THEIR
WHOLE
SELVES
THEY RADIATE THE MOST PURE FORM OF JOY I HAVE EVER WITNESSED...

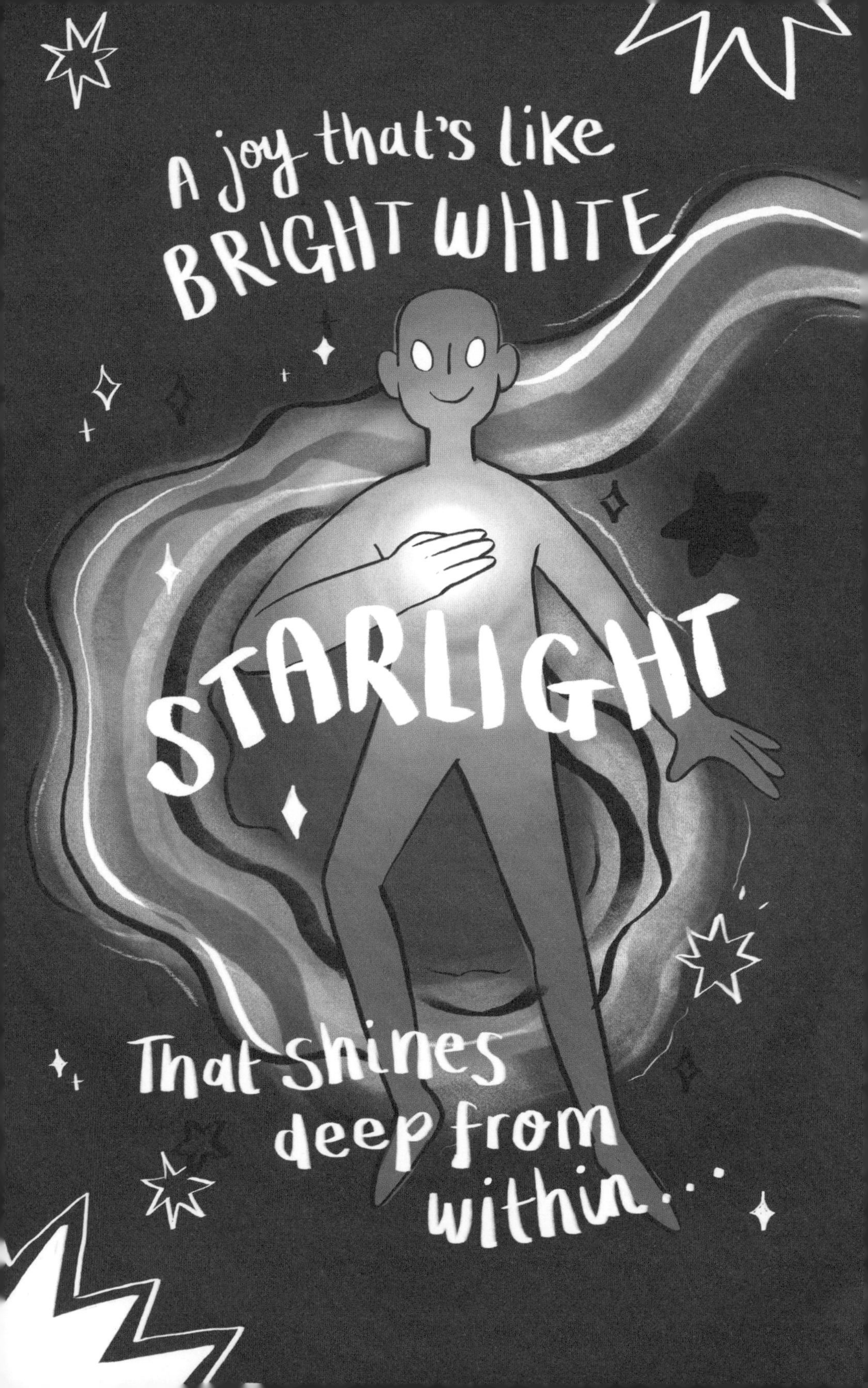
A joy that's like
BRIGHT WHITE
STARLIGHT
That shines
deep from
within . . .

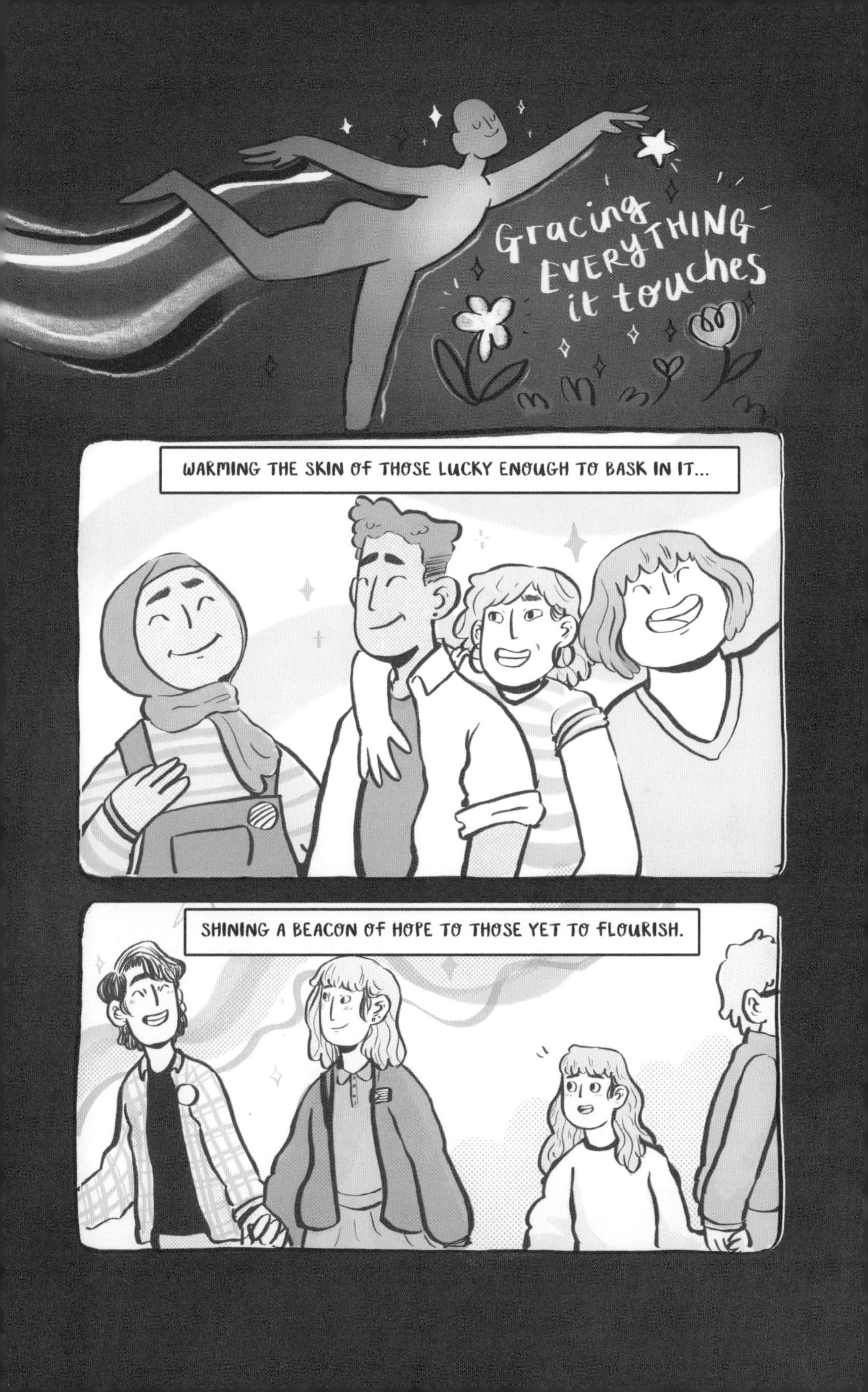
Gracing EVERYTHING it touches
WARMING THE SKIN OF THOSE LUCKY ENOUGH TO BASK IN IT...
SHINING A BEACON OF HOPE TO THOSE YET TO FLOURISH.

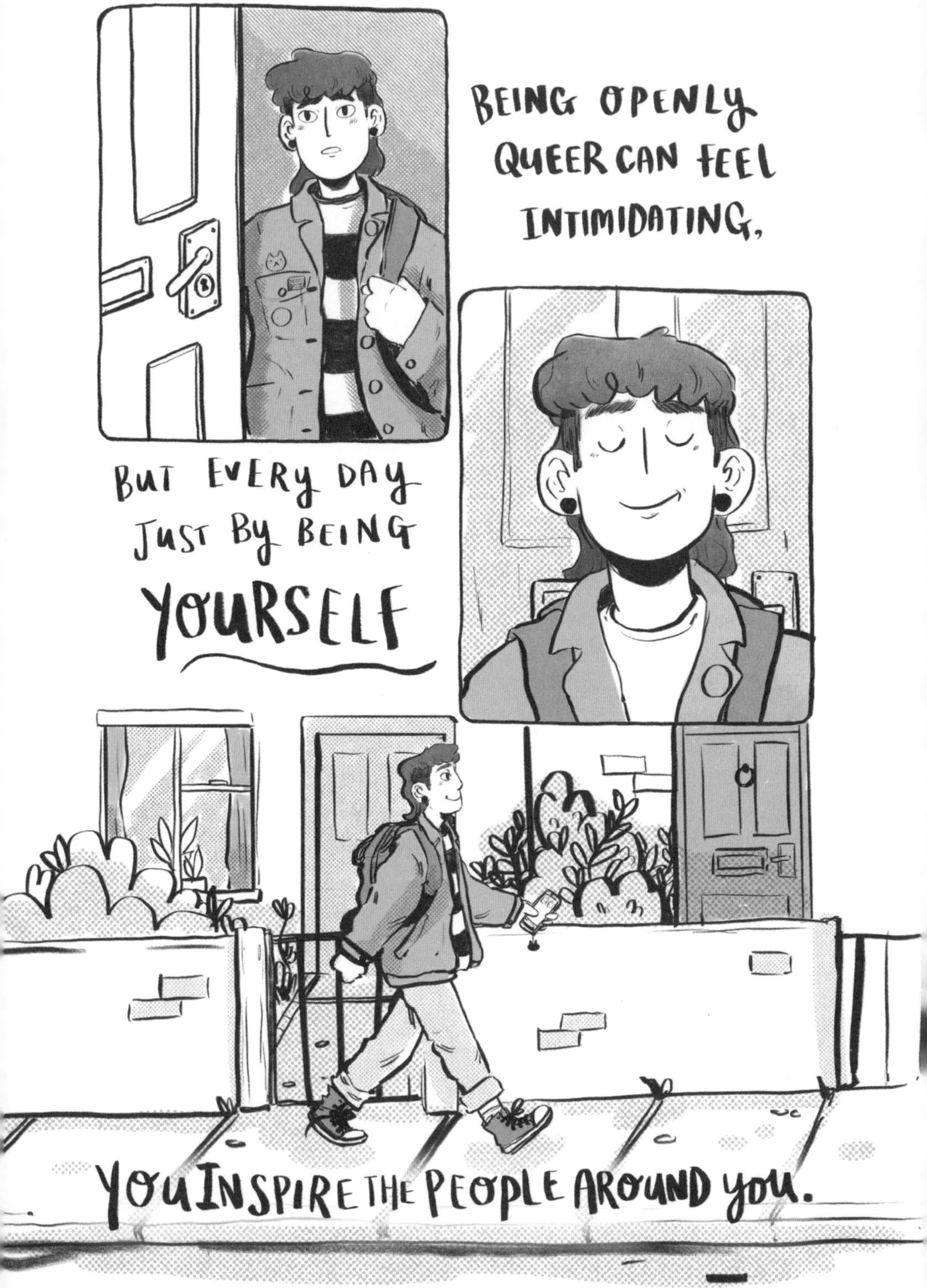
BEING OPENLY QUEER CAN FEEL INTIMIDATING,
BUT EVERY DAY JUST BY BEING YOURSELF
YOU INSPIRE THE PEOPLE AROUND YOU.

YOU DON'T HAVE TO BE AN INFLUENCER TO INFLUENCE!

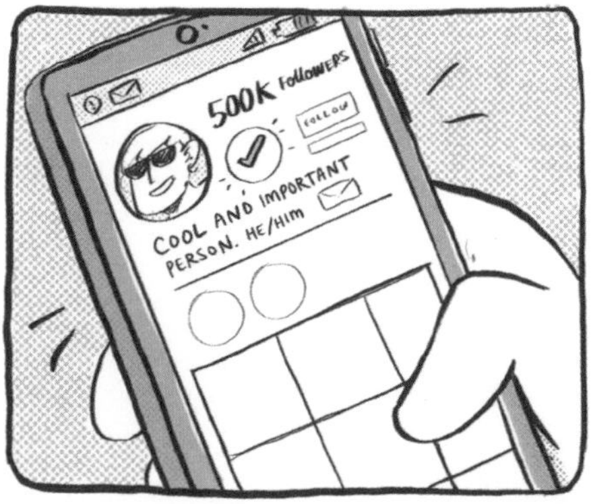
500K FOLLOWERS
FOLLOW
COOL AND IMPORTANT PERSON. HE/HIM

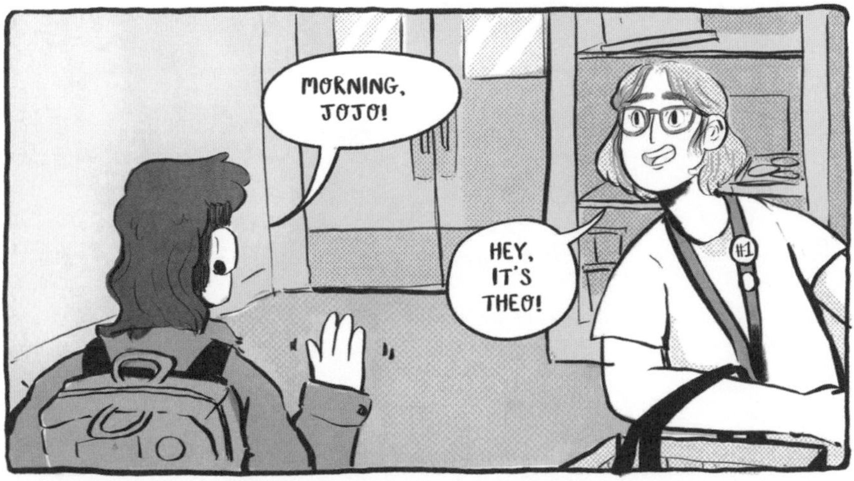
MORNING, JOJO!
HEY, IT'S THEO!
#1

WHOEVER YOU ARE AND WHATEVER YOU DO...

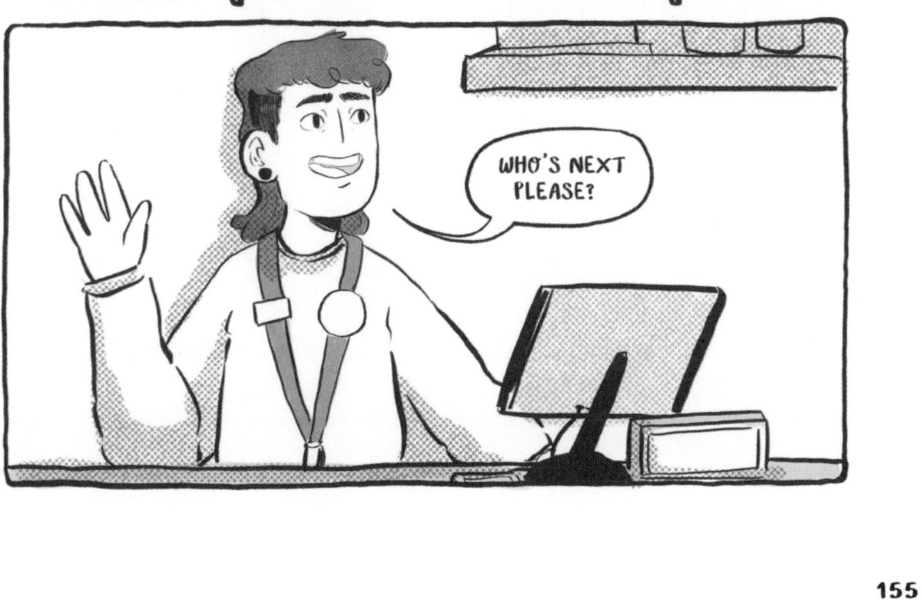
WHO'S NEXT PLEASE?

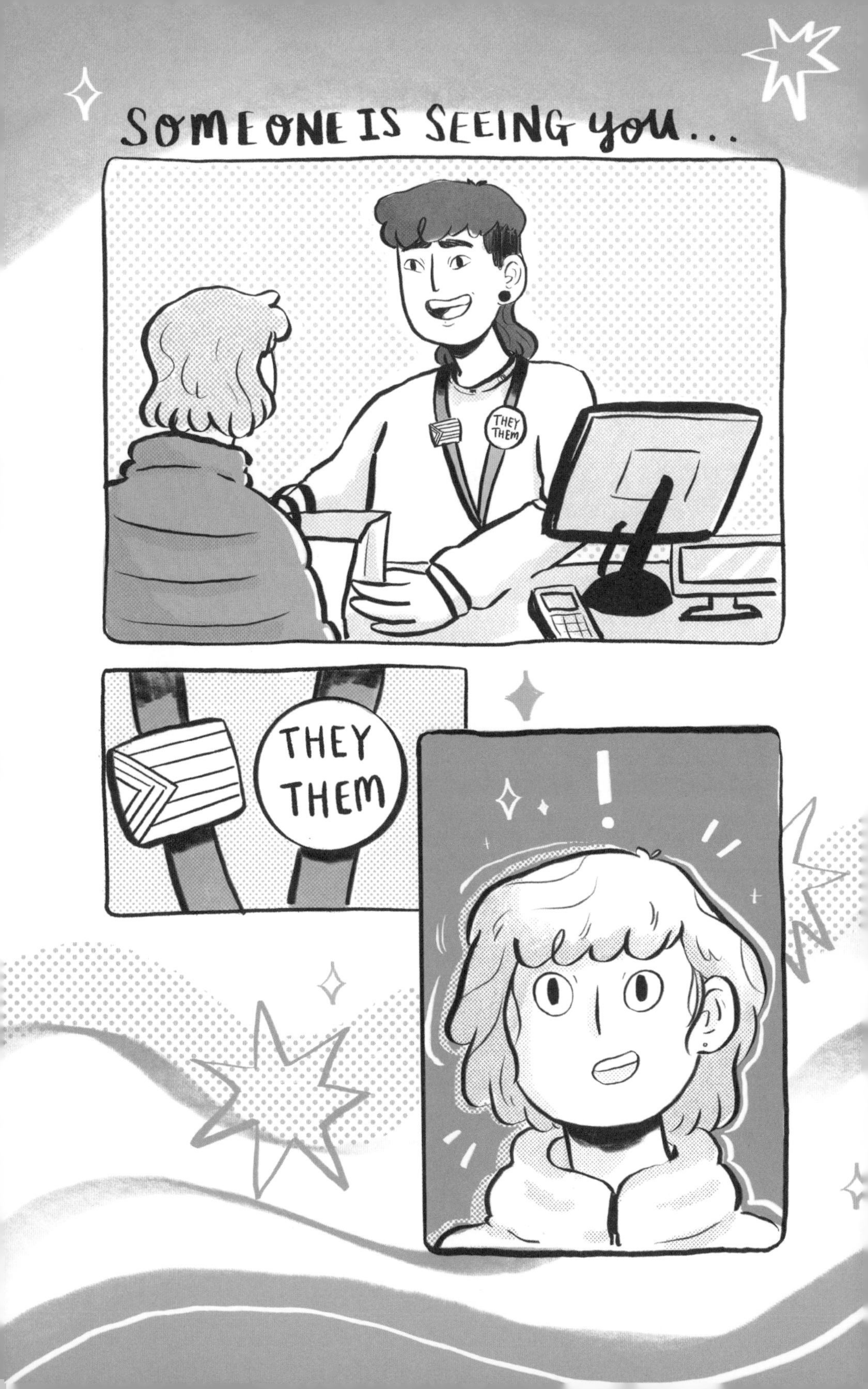
SOMEONE IS SEEING you...
THEY THEM
THEY THEM
!

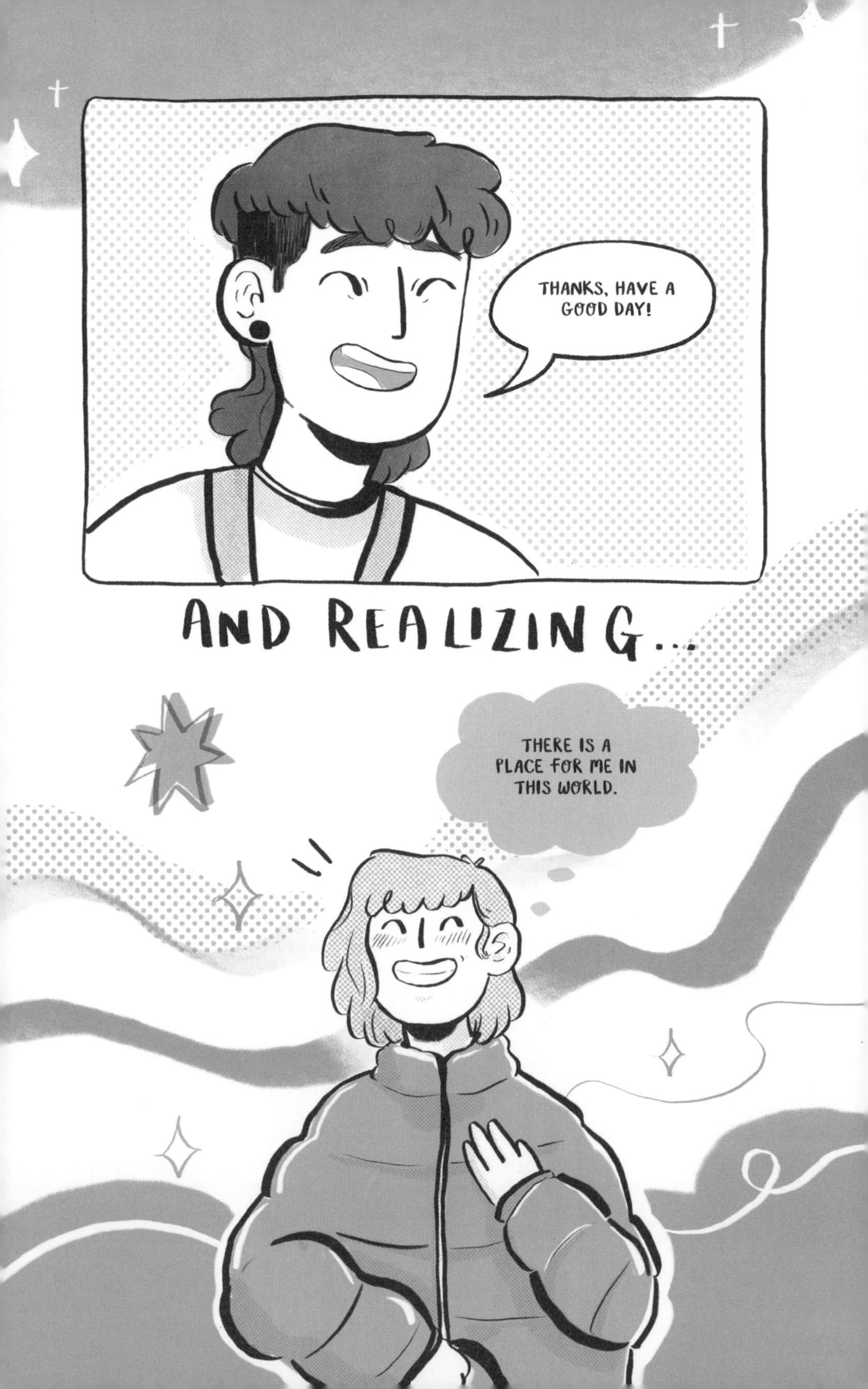
THANKS, HAVE A GOOD DAY!
AND REALIZING...
THERE IS A PLACE FOR ME IN THIS WORLD.

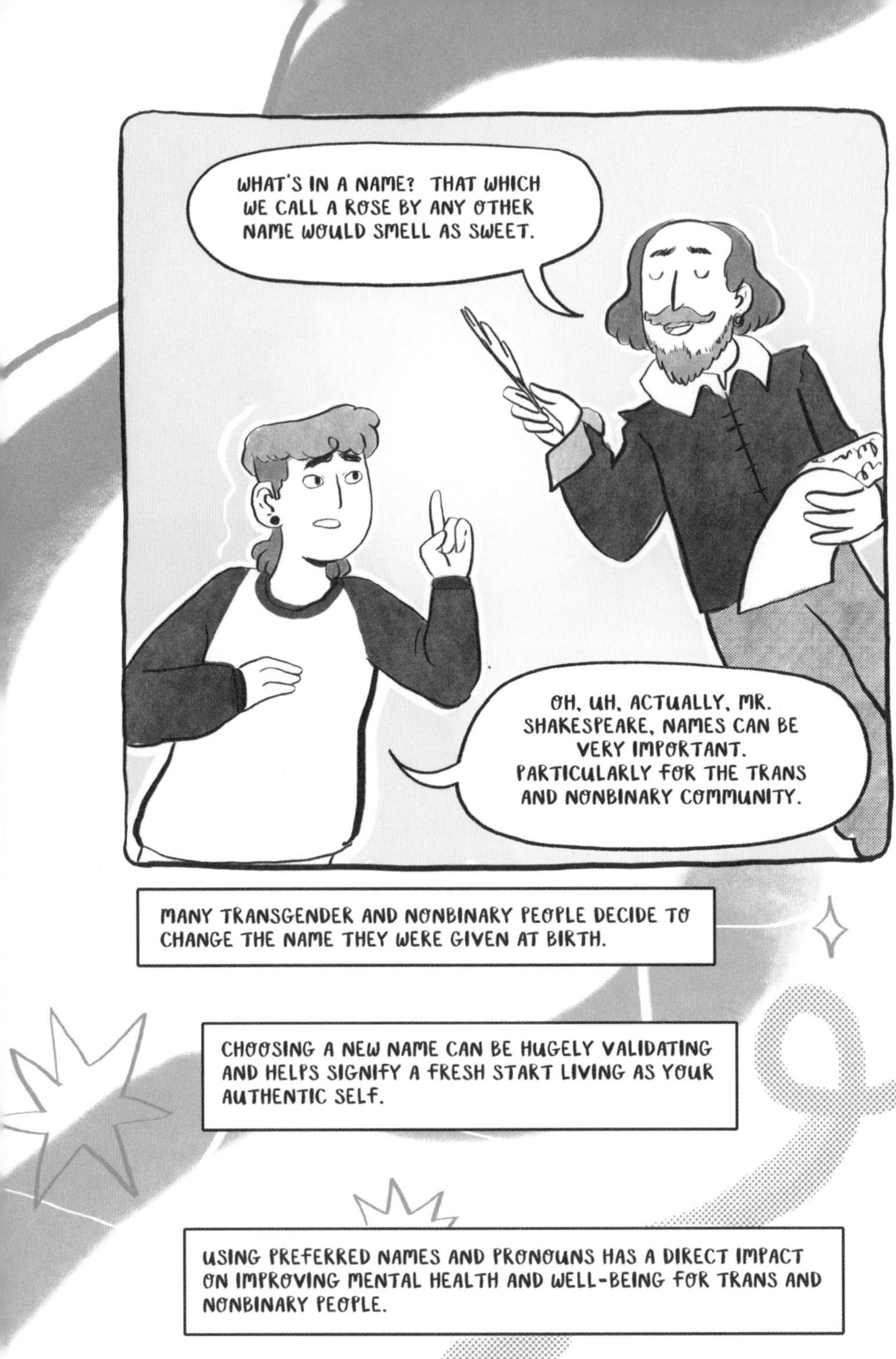
WHAT'S IN A NAME? THAT WHICH WE CALL A ROSE BY ANY OTHER NAME WOULD SMELL AS SWEET.
OH, UH, ACTUALLY, MR. SHAKESPEARE, NAMES CAN BE VERY IMPORTANT. PARTICULARLY FOR THE TRANS AND NONBINARY COMMUNITY.

MANY TRANSGENDER AND NONBINARY PEOPLE DECIDE TO CHANGE THE NAME THEY WERE GIVEN AT BIRTH.

CHOOSING A NEW NAME CAN BE HUGELY VALIDATING AND HELPS SIGNIFY A FRESH START LIVING AS YOUR AUTHENTIC SELF.

USING PREFERRED NAMES AND PRONOUNS HAS A DIRECT IMPACT ON IMPROVING MENTAL HEALTH AND WELL-BEING FOR TRANS AND NONBINARY PEOPLE.

WHAT IS A DEADNAME?

DEADNAMING IS WHEN SOMEONE USES THE BIRTH NAME (ALSO REFERRED TO AS DEADNAME) OF A TRANS PERSON AFTER BEING TOLD THEIR PREFERRED NAME.

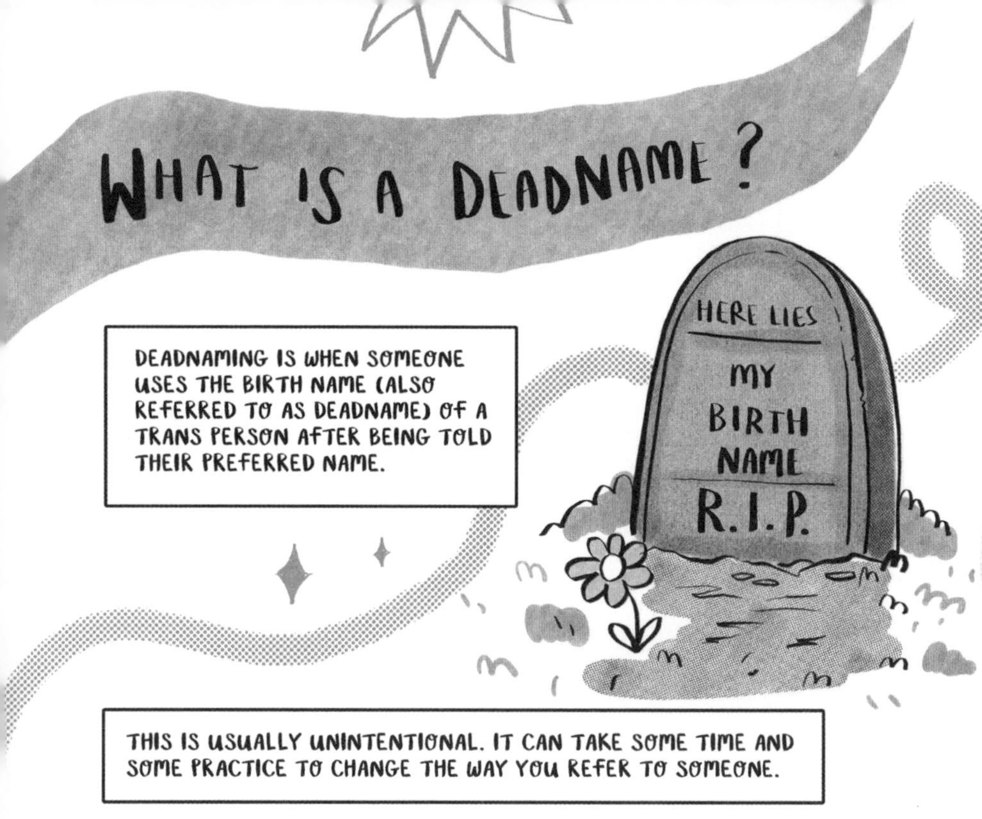
HERE LIES
MY BIRTH NAME
R.I.P.

THIS IS USUALLY UNINTENTIONAL. IT CAN TAKE SOME TIME AND SOME PRACTICE TO CHANGE THE WAY YOU REFER TO SOMEONE.

HEARING OR SEEING YOUR DEADNAME CAN BE VERY UNCOMFORTABLE. IT CAN FEEL LIKE YOUR IDENTITY IS BEING INVALIDATED OR REMIND YOU OF TIMES IN THE PAST WHERE YOU WEREN'T ABLE TO BE YOURSELF.

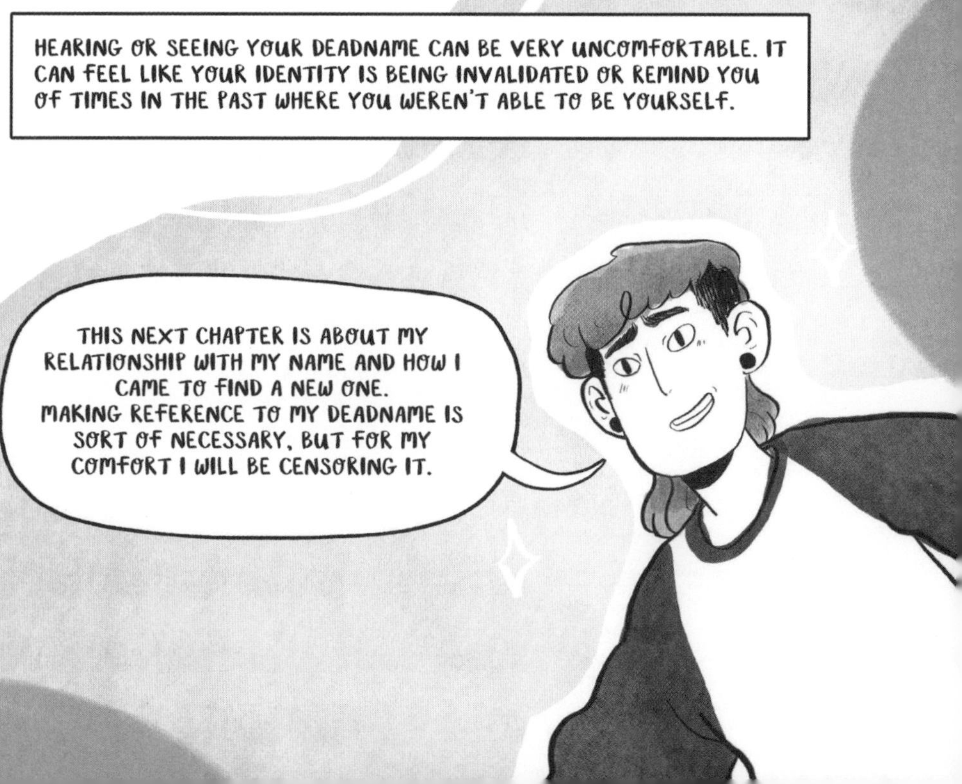
THIS NEXT CHAPTER IS ABOUT MY RELATIONSHIP WITH MY NAME AND HOW I CAME TO FIND A NEW ONE. MAKING REFERENCE TO MY DEADNAME IS SORT OF NECESSARY, BUT FOR MY COMFORT I WILL BE CENSORING IT.

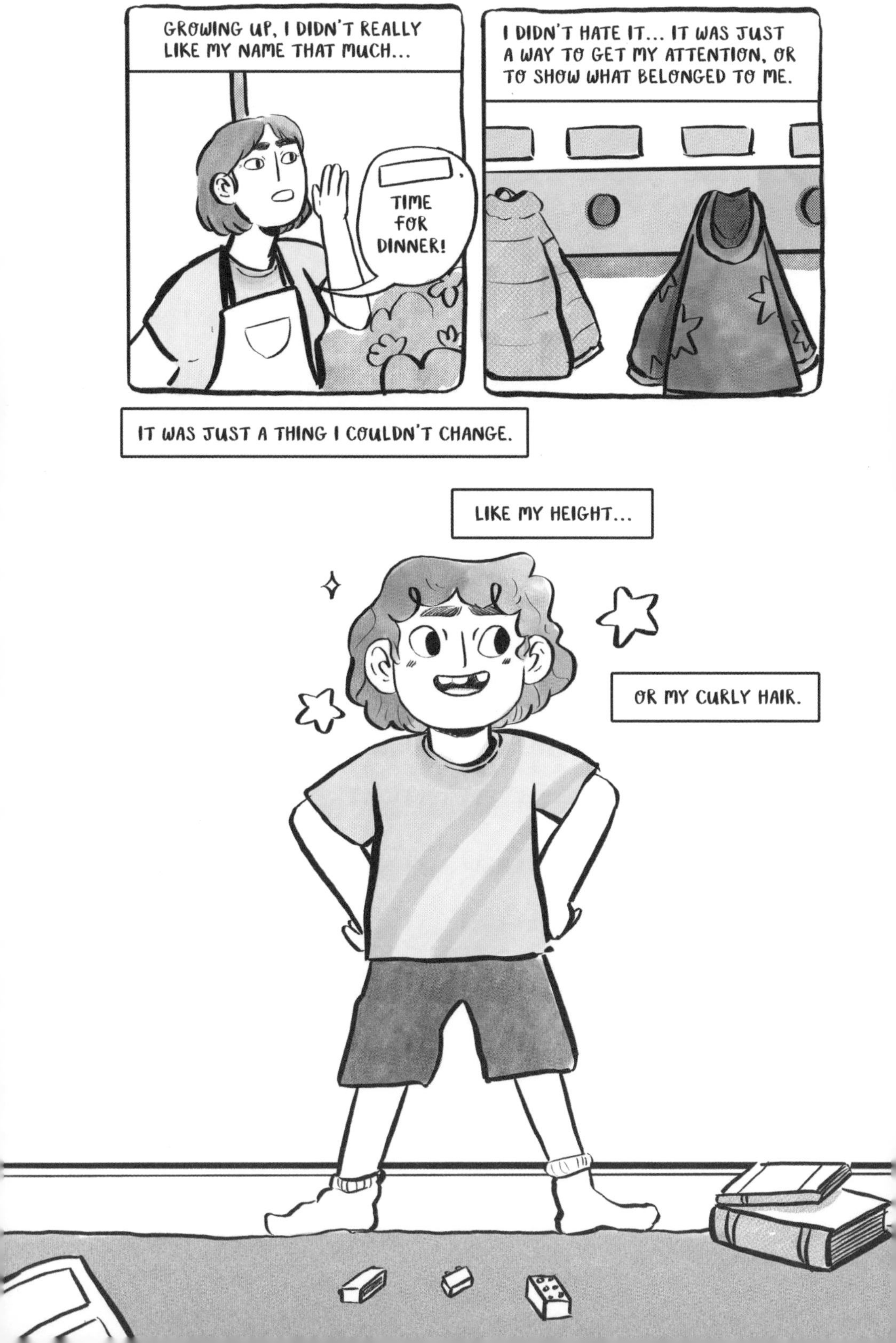
GROWING UP, I DIDN'T REALLY LIKE MY NAME THAT MUCH...
TIME FOR DINNER!
I DIDN'T HATE IT... IT WAS JUST A WAY TO GET MY ATTENTION, OR TO SHOW WHAT BELONGED TO ME.
IT WAS JUST A THING I COULDN'T CHANGE.
LIKE MY HEIGHT...
OR MY CURLY HAIR.

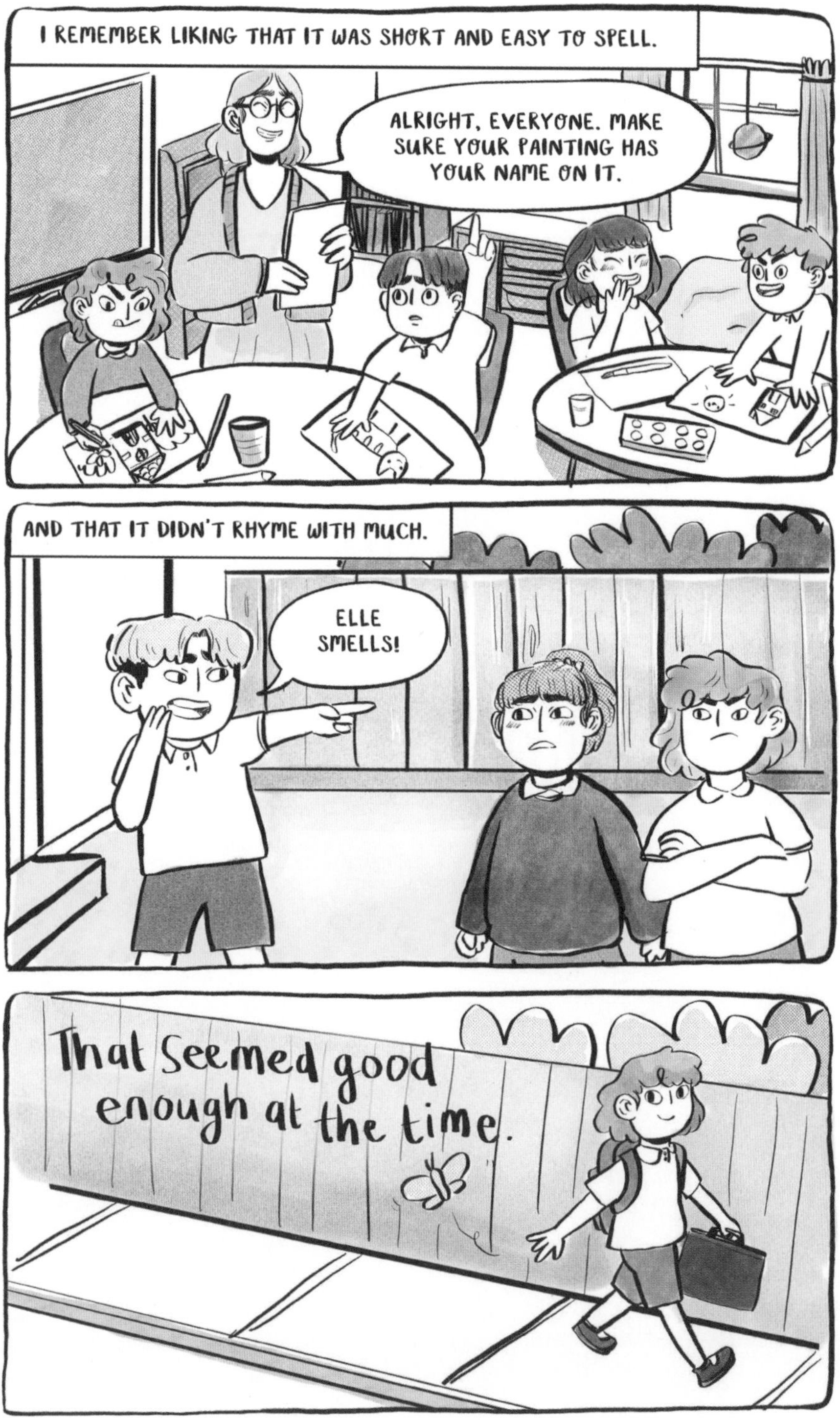
I REMEMBER LIKING THAT IT WAS SHORT AND EASY TO SPELL.
ALRIGHT, EVERYONE. MAKE SURE YOUR PAINTING HAS YOUR NAME ON IT.
AND THAT IT DIDN'T RHYME WITH MUCH.
ELLE SMELLS!
That seemed good enough at the time.

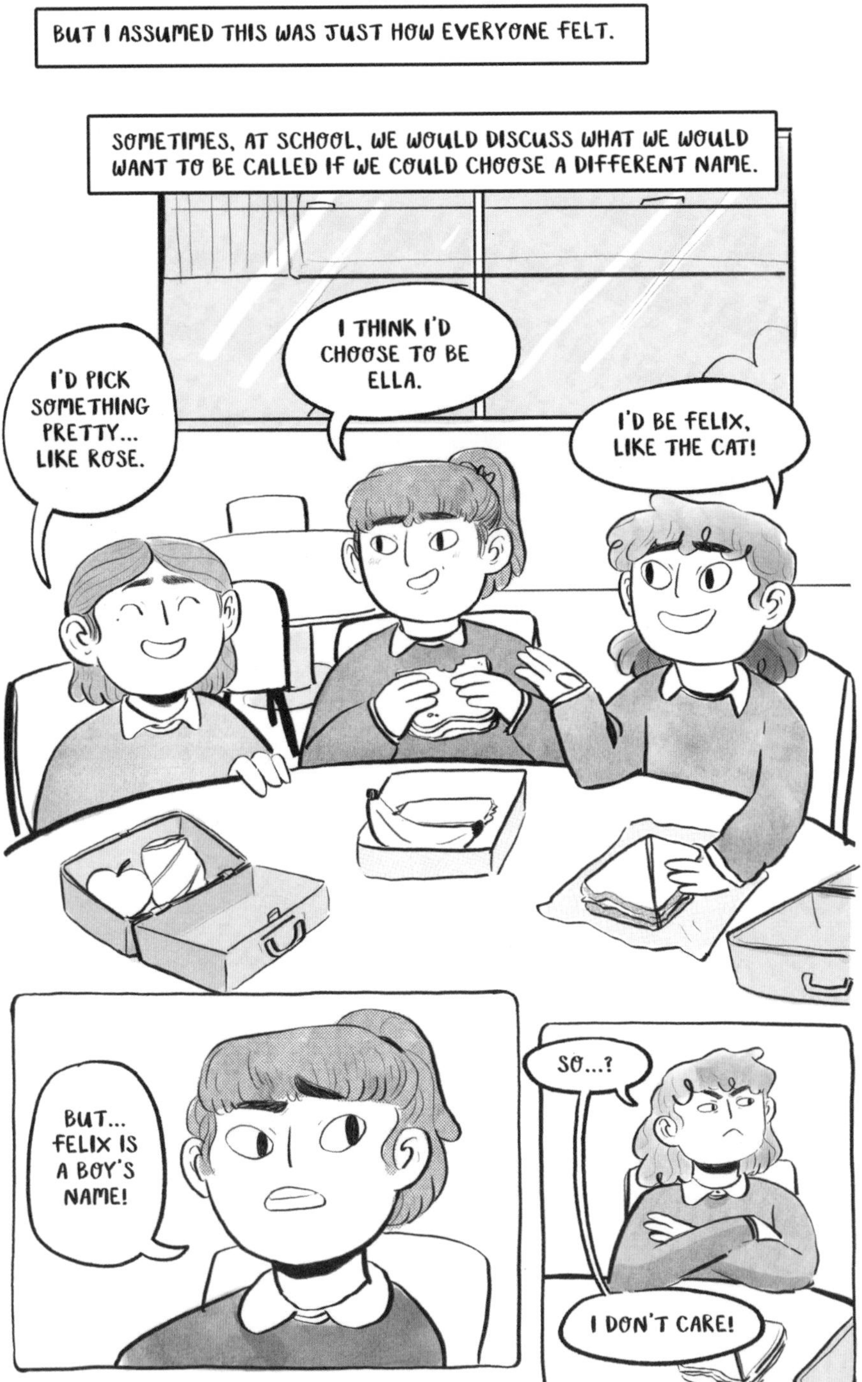
BUT I ASSUMED THIS WAS JUST HOW EVERYONE FELT.
SOMETIMES, AT SCHOOL, WE WOULD DISCUSS WHAT WE WOULD WANT TO BE CALLED IF WE COULD CHOOSE A DIFFERENT NAME.
I'D PICK SOMETHING PRETTY... LIKE ROSE.
I THINK I'D CHOOSE TO BE ELLA.
I'D BE FELIX, LIKE THE CAT!
BUT... FELIX IS A BOY'S NAME!
SO...?
I DON'T CARE!

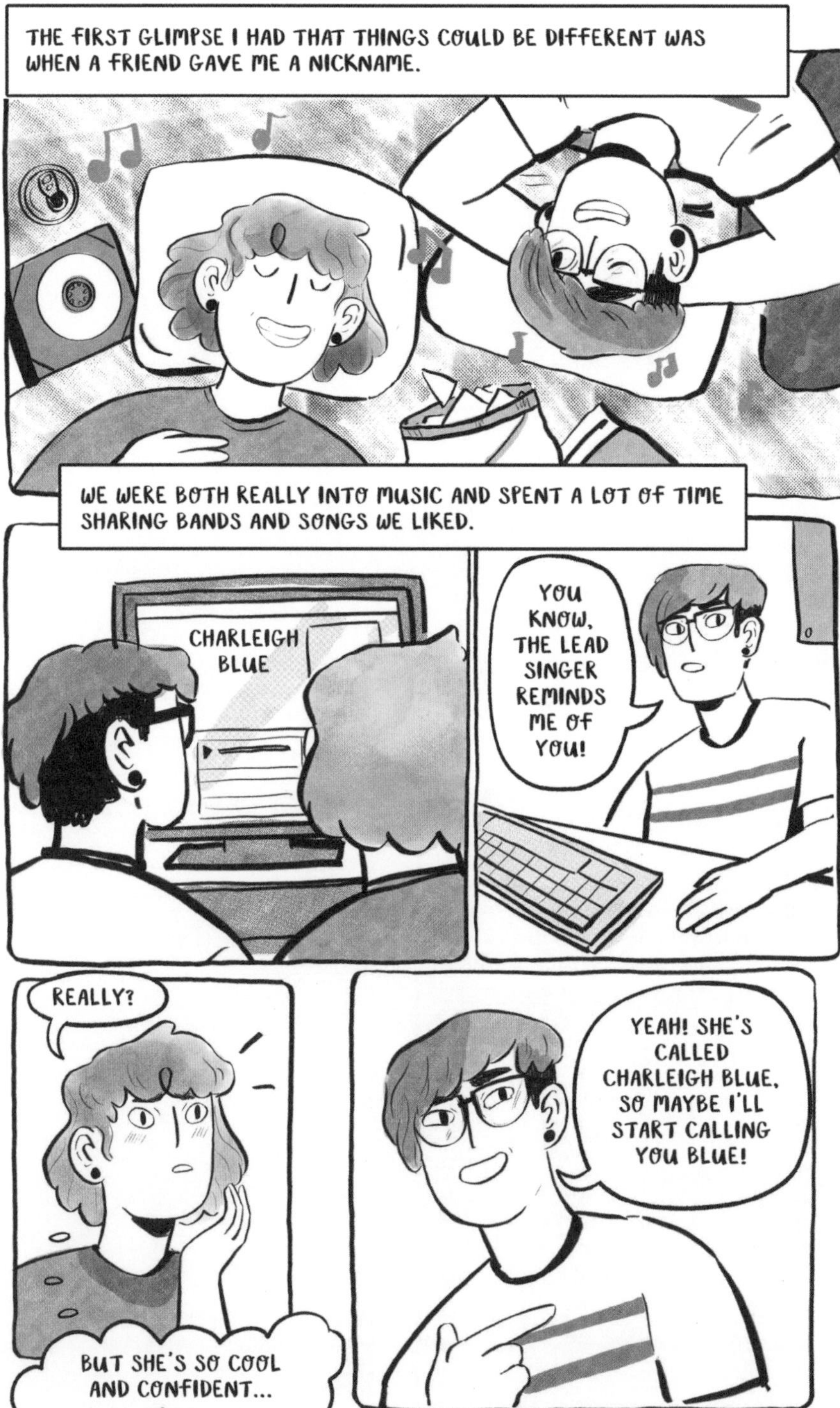
THE FIRST GLIMPSE I HAD THAT THINGS COULD BE DIFFERENT WAS WHEN A FRIEND GAVE ME A NICKNAME.
WE WERE BOTH REALLY INTO MUSIC AND SPENT A LOT OF TIME SHARING BANDS AND SONGS WE LIKED.
CHARLEIGH BLUE
YOU KNOW, THE LEAD SINGER REMINDS ME OF YOU!
REALLY?
BUT SHE'S SO COOL AND CONFIDENT...
YEAH! SHE'S CALLED CHARLEIGH BLUE, SO MAYBE I'LL START CALLING YOU BLUE!

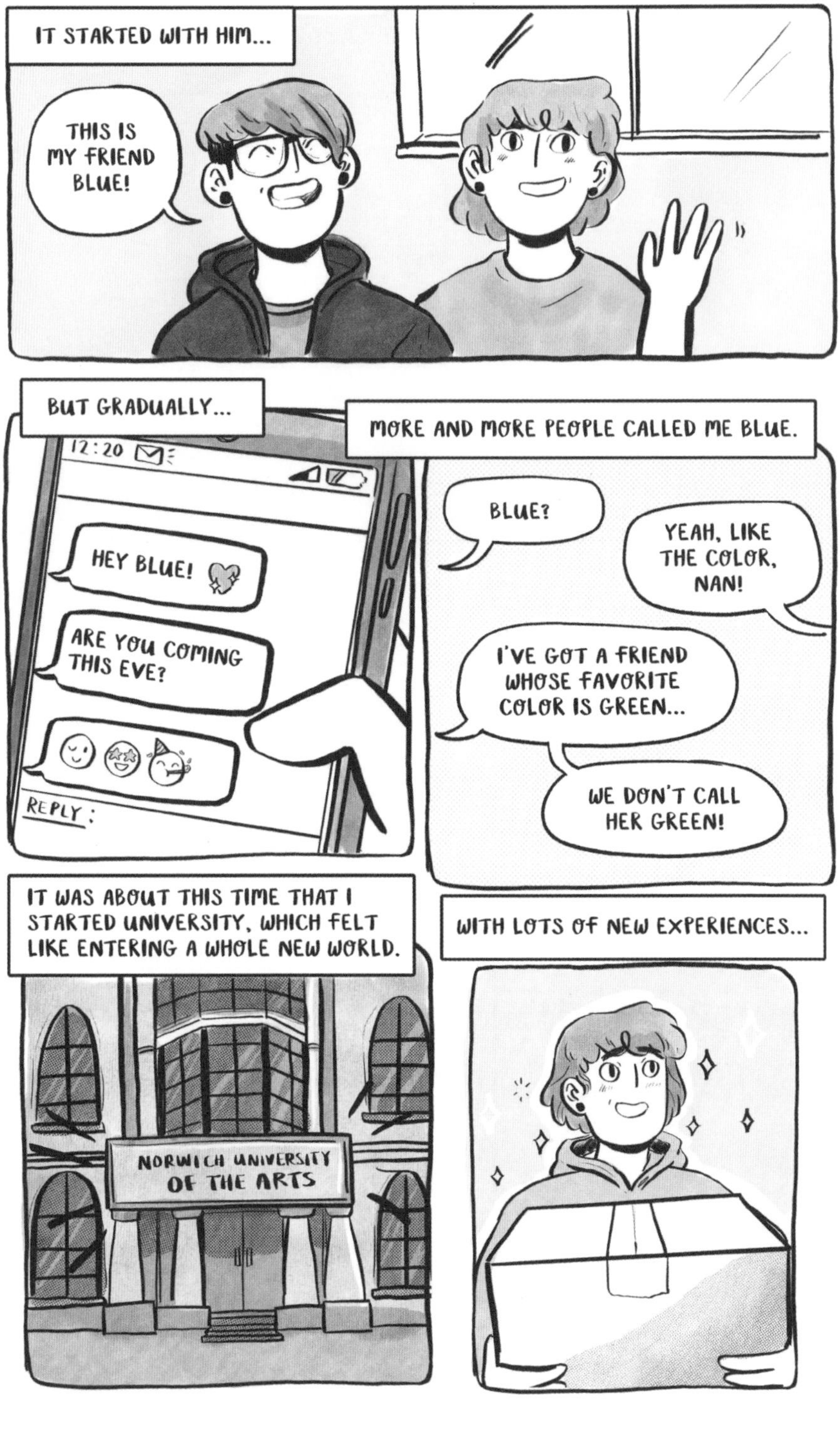
IT STARTED WITH HIM...
THIS IS MY FRIEND BLUE!
BUT GRADUALLY...
12:20
HEY BLUE!
ARE YOU COMING THIS EVE?
REPLY :
MORE AND MORE PEOPLE CALLED ME BLUE.
BLUE?
YEAH, LIKE THE COLOR, NAN!
I'VE GOT A FRIEND WHOSE FAVORITE COLOR IS GREEN...
WE DON'T CALL HER GREEN!
IT WAS ABOUT THIS TIME THAT I STARTED UNIVERSITY, WHICH FELT LIKE ENTERING A WHOLE NEW WORLD.
NORWICH UNIVERSITY OF THE ARTS
WITH LOTS OF NEW EXPERIENCES...

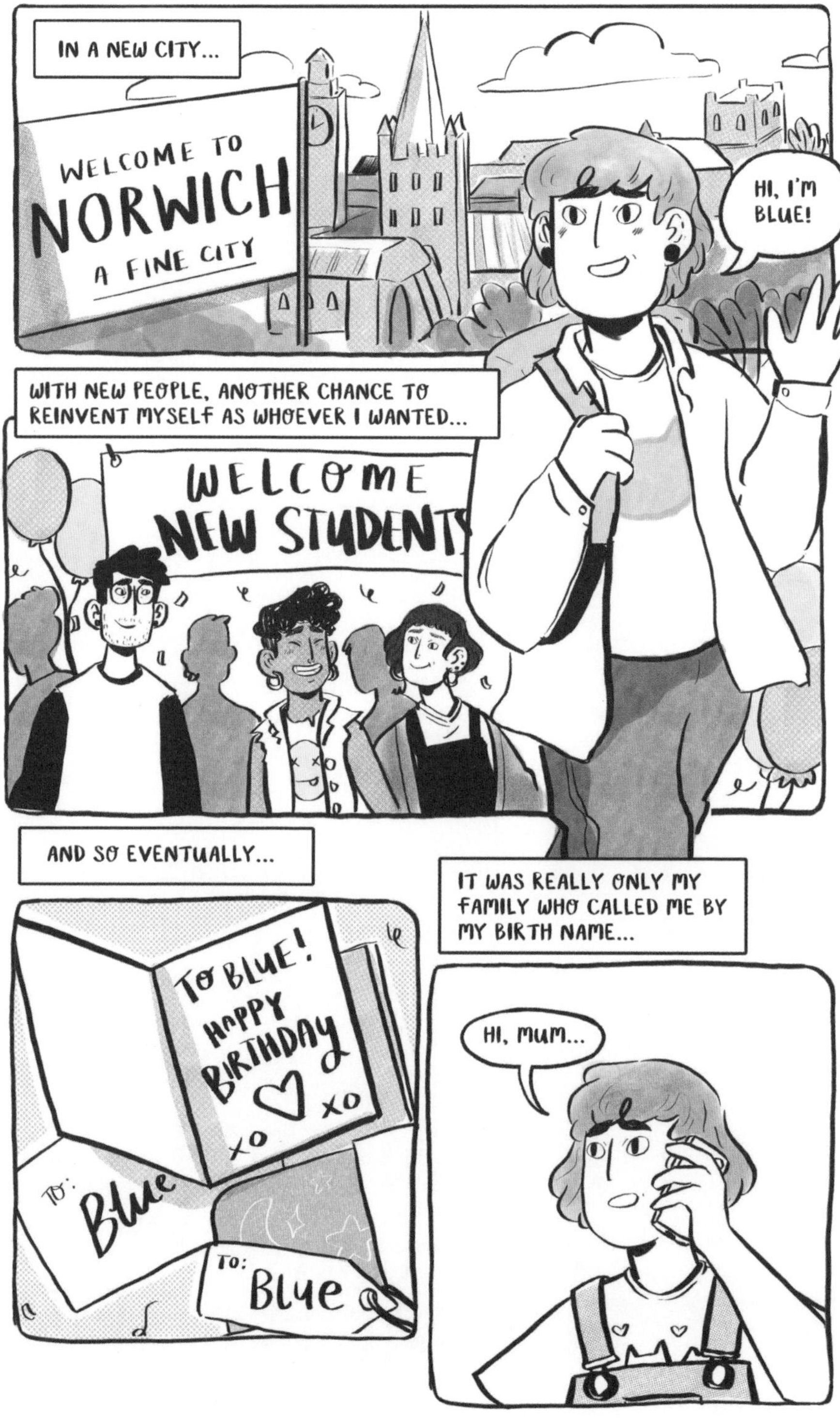

IN A NEW CITY...
WELCOME TO NORWICH A FINE CITY
HI, I'M BLUE!
WITH NEW PEOPLE, ANOTHER CHANCE TO REINVENT MYSELF AS WHOEVER I WANTED...
WELCOME NEW STUDENTS
AND SO EVENTUALLY...
IT WAS REALLY ONLY MY FAMILY WHO CALLED ME BY MY BIRTH NAME...
TO BLUE! HAPPY BIRTHDAY XO XO
TO: Blue
TO: Blue
HI, MUM...

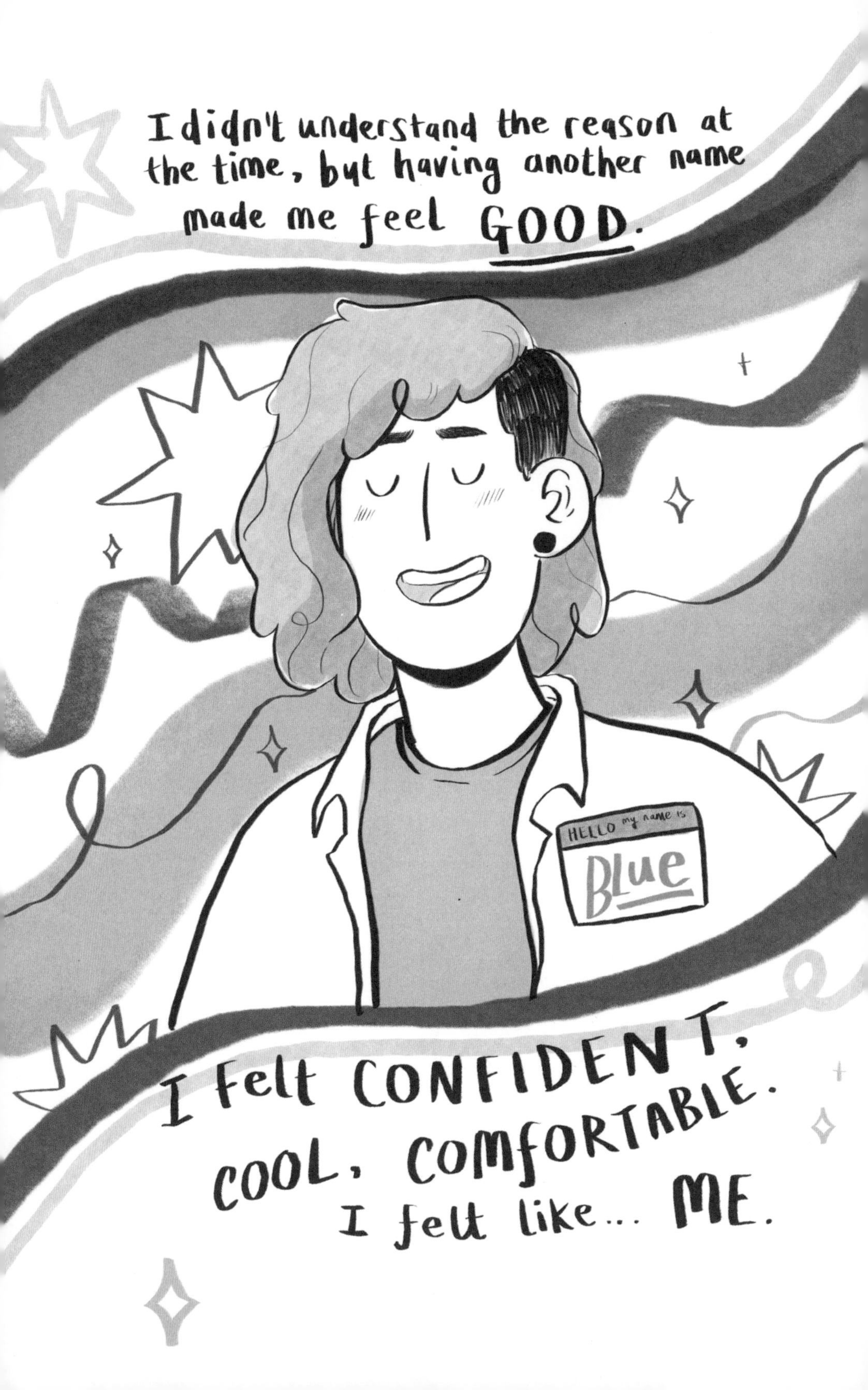
I didn't understand the reason at the time, but having another name made me feel GOOD.
HELLO my name is
BLue
I felt CONFIDENT, COOL, COMFORTABLE.
I felt like... ME.

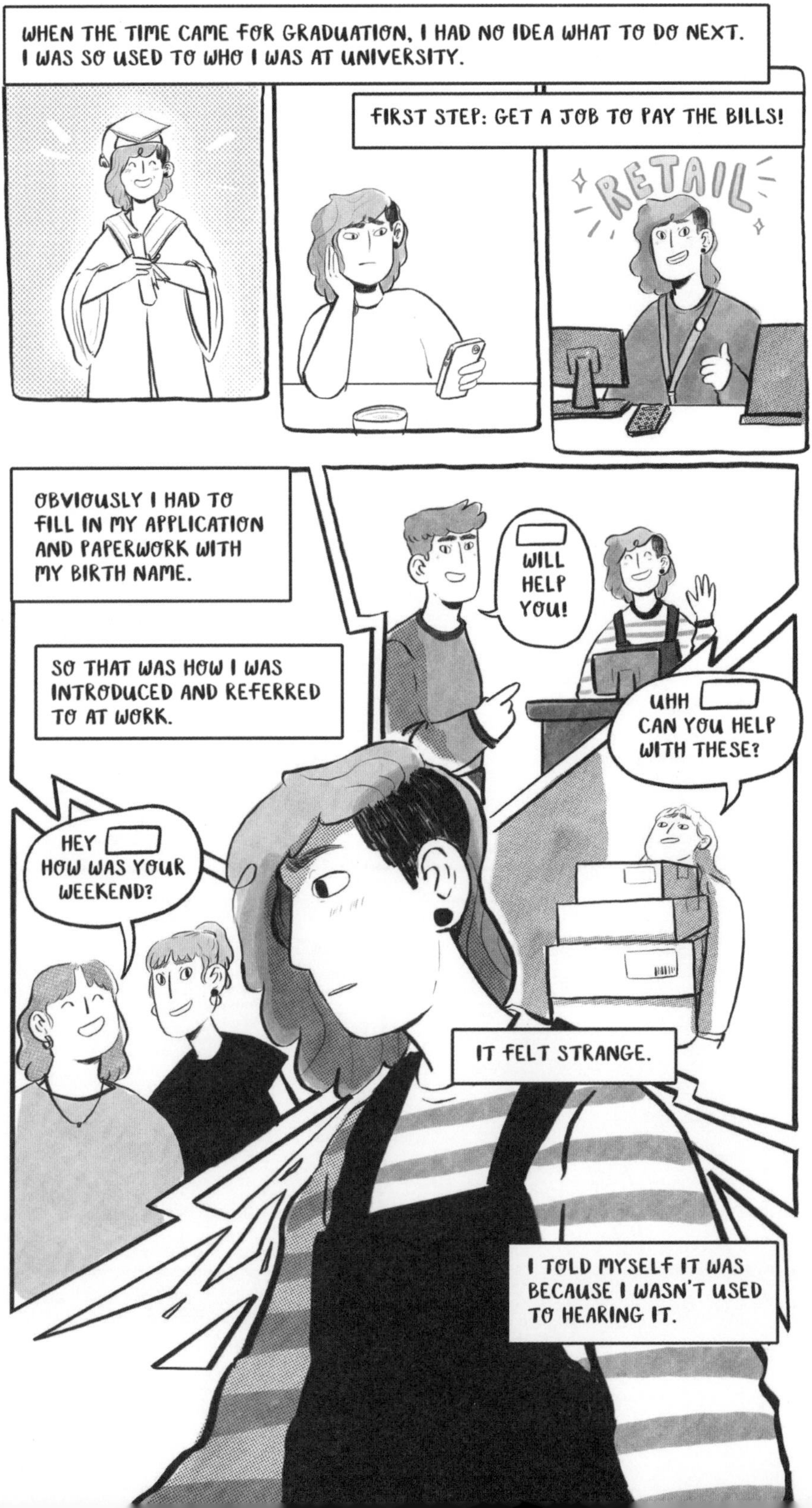
WHEN THE TIME CAME FOR GRADUATION, I HAD NO IDEA WHAT TO DO NEXT. I WAS SO USED TO WHO I WAS AT UNIVERSITY.
FIRST STEP: GET A JOB TO PAY THE BILLS!
RETAIL
OBVIOUSLY I HAD TO FILL IN MY APPLICATION AND PAPERWORK WITH MY BIRTH NAME.
WILL HELP YOU!
SO THAT WAS HOW I WAS INTRODUCED AND REFERRED TO AT WORK.
UHH CAN YOU HELP WITH THESE?
HEY HOW WAS YOUR WEEKEND?
IT FELT STRANGE.
I TOLD MYSELF IT WAS BECAUSE I WASN'T USED TO HEARING IT.

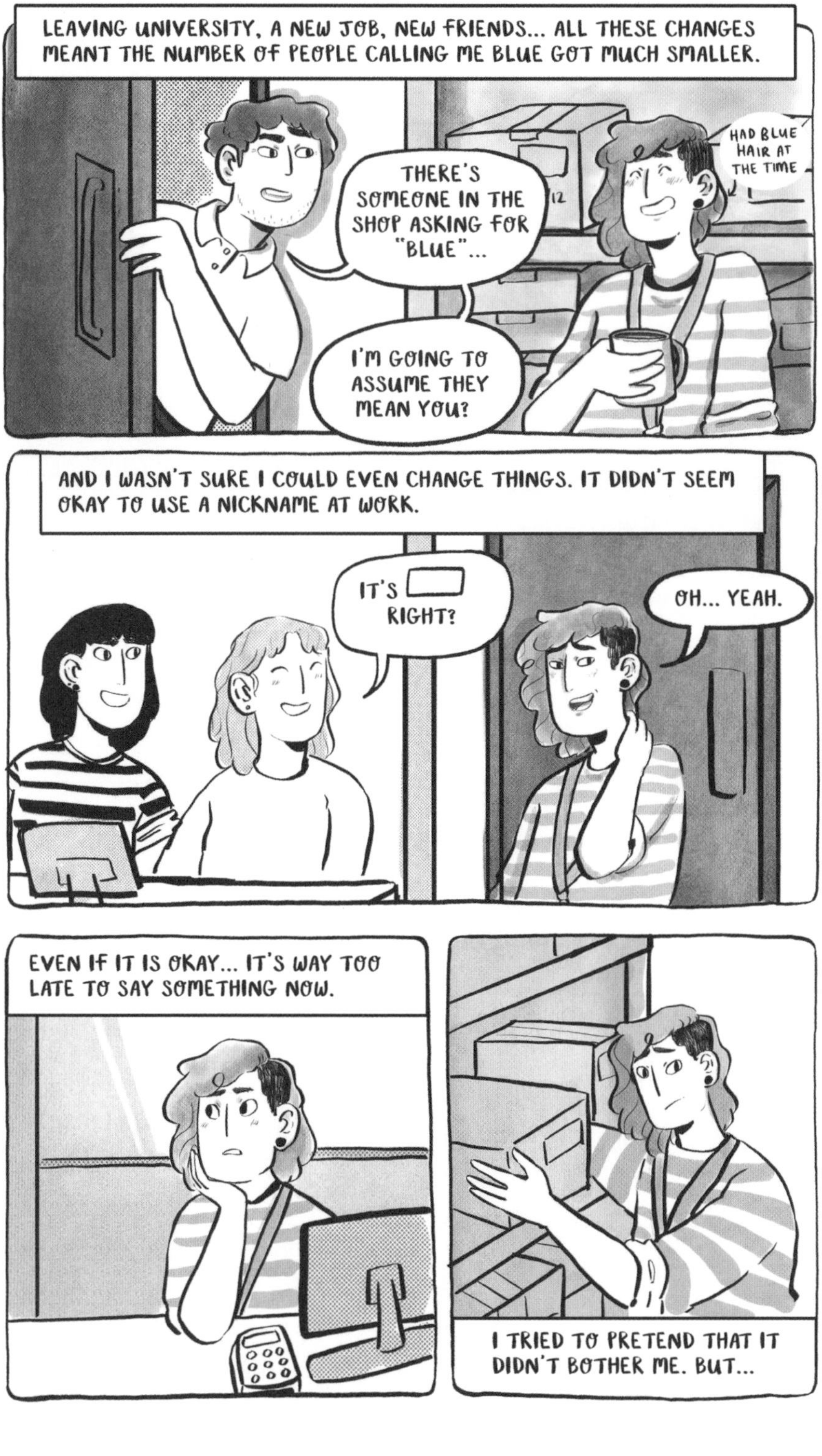
LEAVING UNIVERSITY, A NEW JOB, NEW FRIENDS... ALL THESE CHANGES MEANT THE NUMBER OF PEOPLE CALLING ME BLUE GOT MUCH SMALLER.
THERE'S SOMEONE IN THE SHOP ASKING FOR "BLUE"...
I'M GOING TO ASSUME THEY MEAN YOU?
HAD BLUE HAIR AT THE TIME
AND I WASN'T SURE I COULD EVEN CHANGE THINGS. IT DIDN'T SEEM OKAY TO USE A NICKNAME AT WORK.
IT'S RIGHT?
OH... YEAH.
EVEN IF IT IS OKAY... IT'S WAY TOO LATE TO SAY SOMETHING NOW.
I TRIED TO PRETEND THAT IT DIDN'T BOTHER ME. BUT...

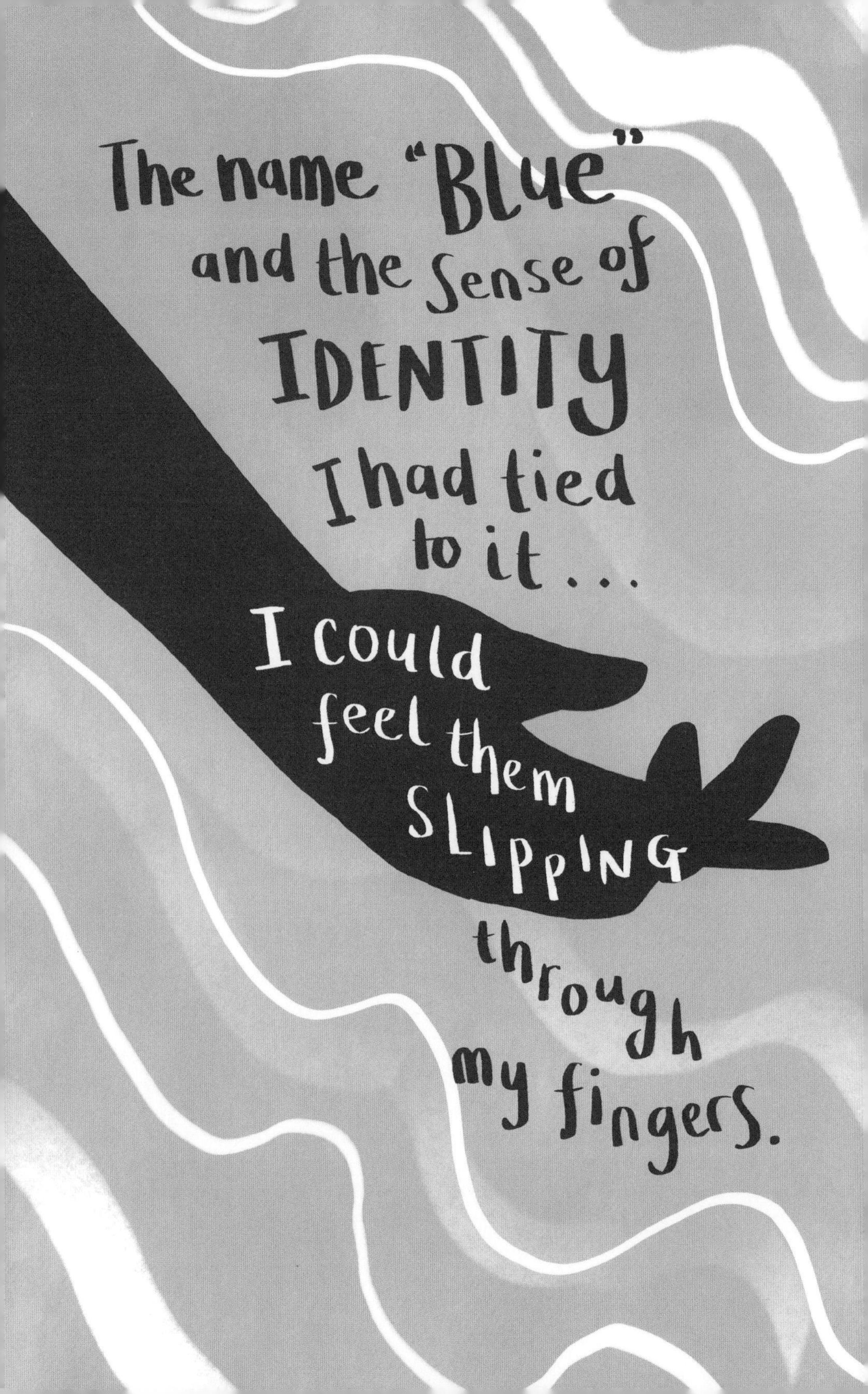
The name "Blue" and the sense of IDENTITY I had tied to it . . .
I could feel them SLIPPING through my fingers.

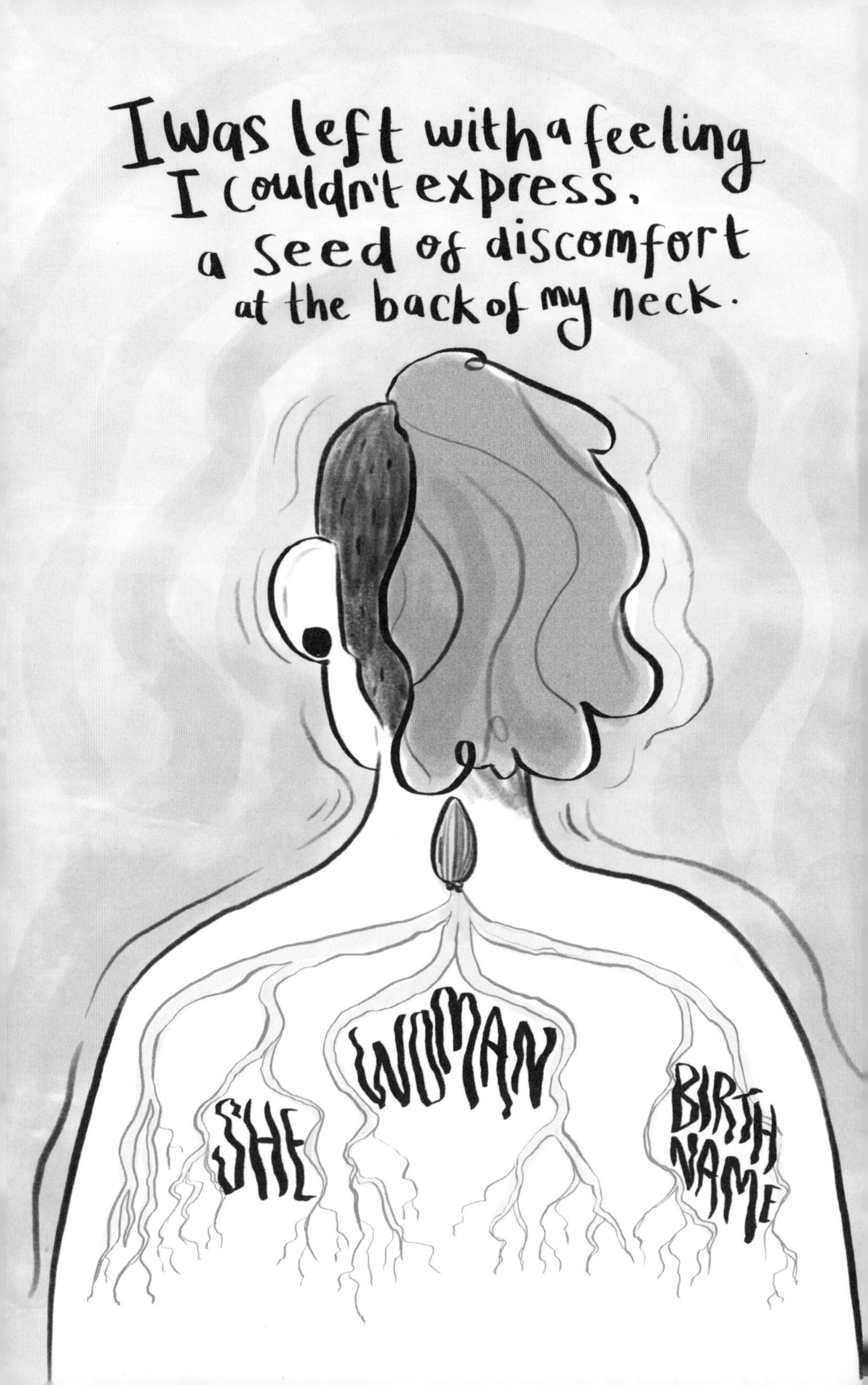
I was left with a feeling I couldn't express,
a seed of discomfort at the back of my neck.
SHE
WOMAN
BIRTH NAME

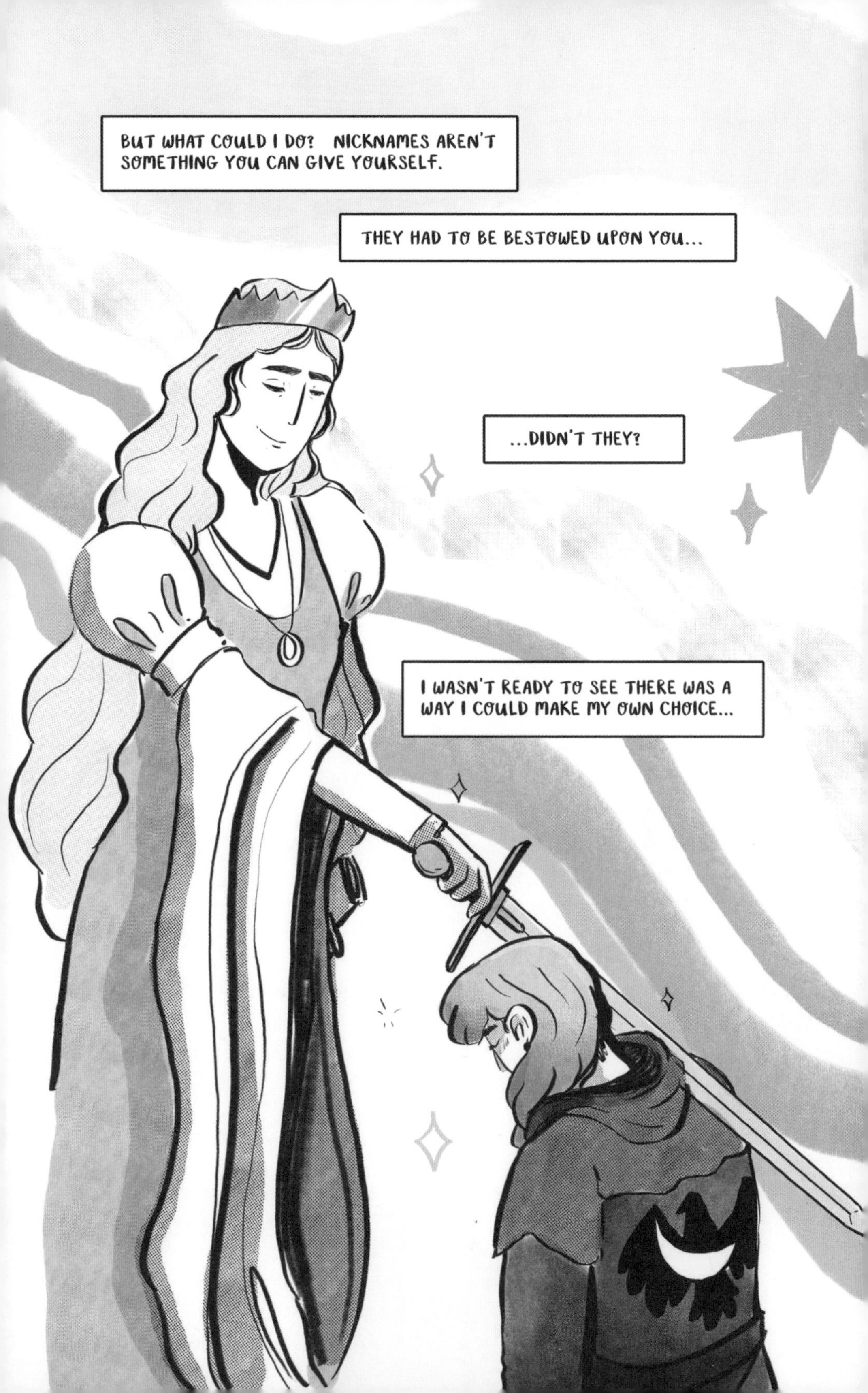
BUT WHAT COULD I DO? NICKNAMES AREN'T SOMETHING YOU CAN GIVE YOURSELF.
THEY HAD TO BE BESTOWED UPON YOU...
...DIDN'T THEY?
I WASN'T READY TO SEE THERE WAS A WAY I COULD MAKE MY OWN CHOICE...

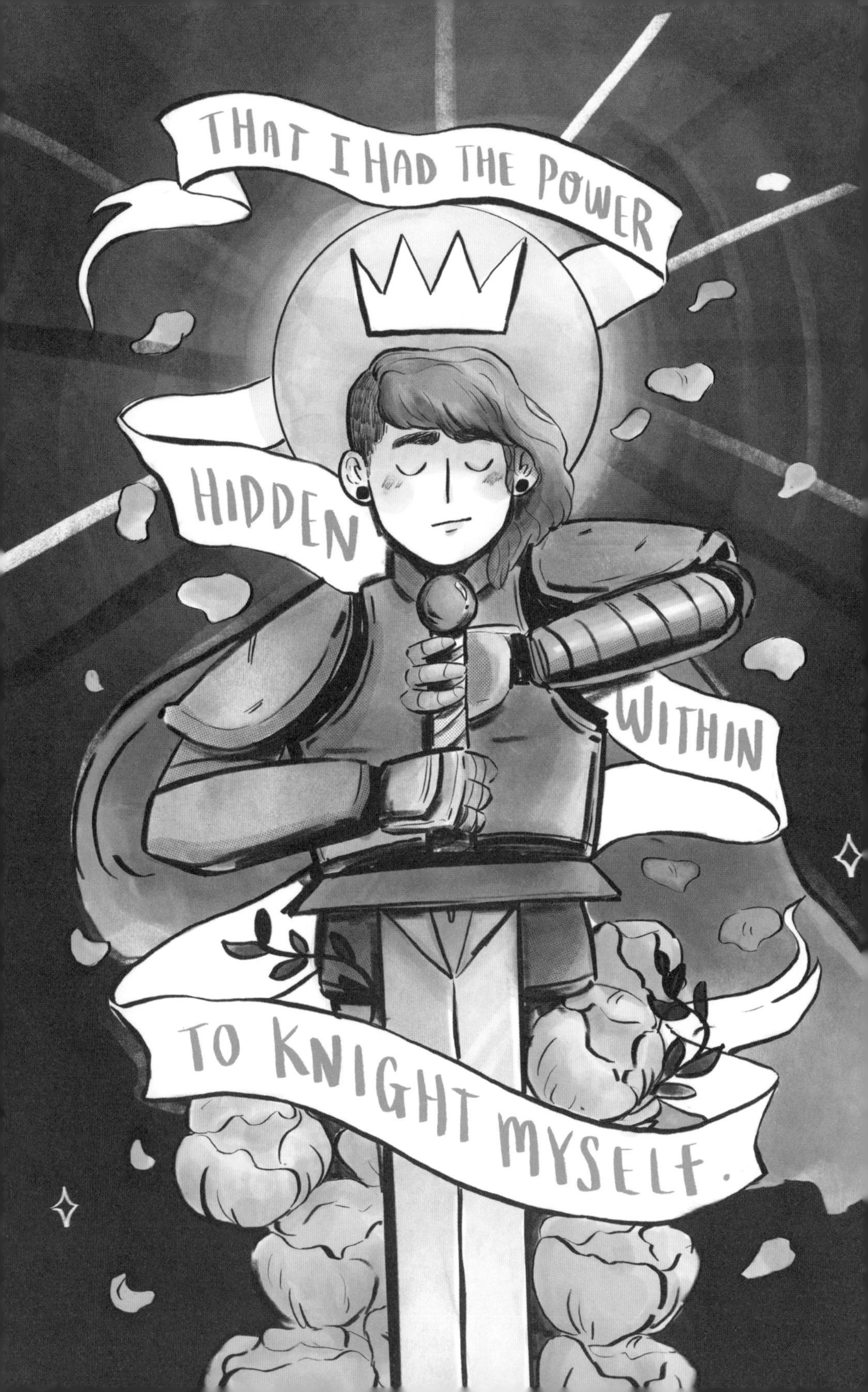
THAT I HAD THE POWER
HIDDEN
WITHIN
TO KNIGHT MYSELF.

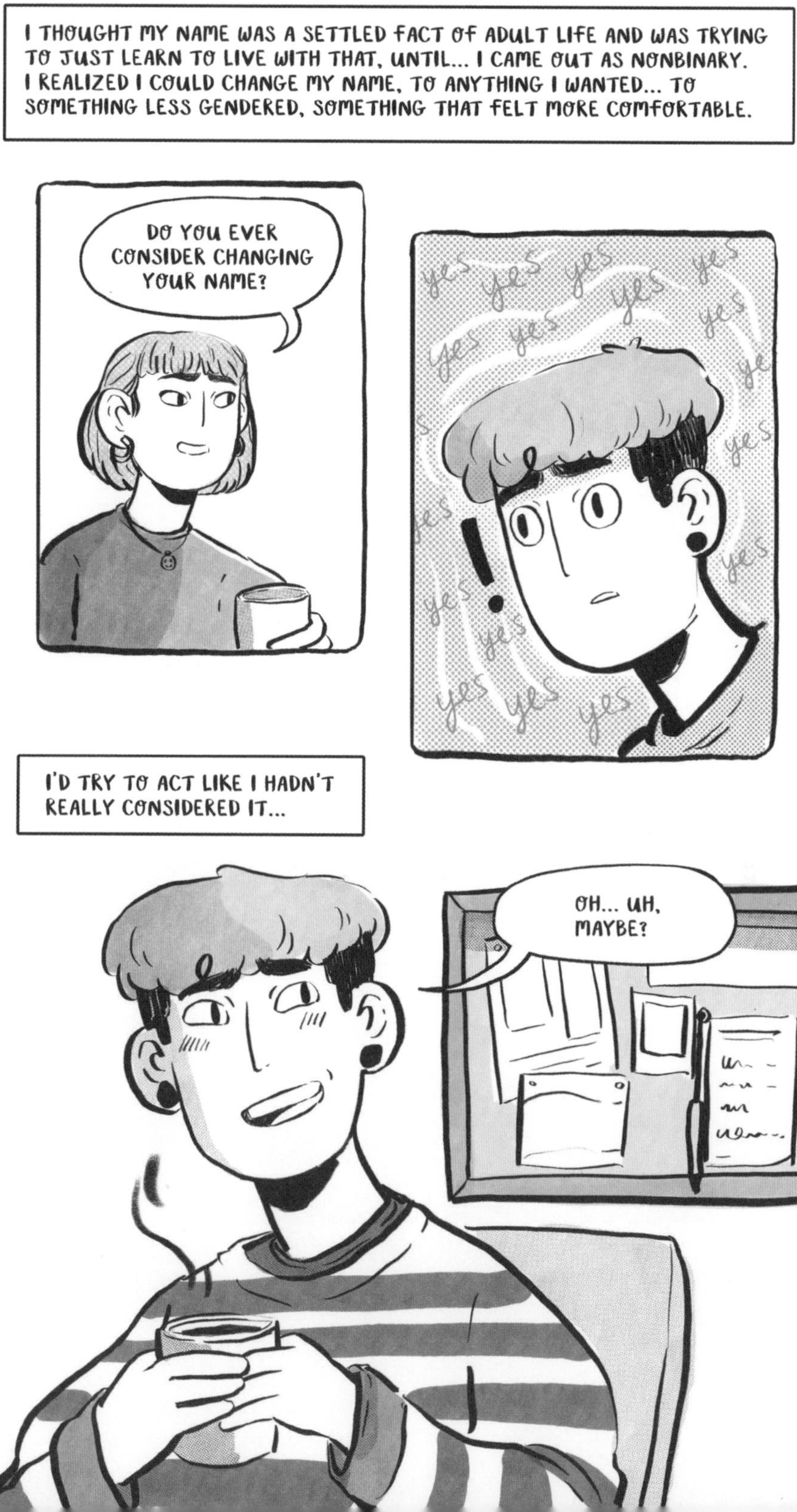
I THOUGHT MY NAME WAS A SETTLED FACT OF ADULT LIFE AND WAS TRYING TO JUST LEARN TO LIVE WITH THAT, UNTIL... I CAME OUT AS NONBINARY. I REALIZED I COULD CHANGE MY NAME, TO ANYTHING I WANTED... TO SOMETHING LESS GENDERED, SOMETHING THAT FELT MORE COMFORTABLE.
DO YOU EVER CONSIDER CHANGING YOUR NAME?
I'D TRY TO ACT LIKE I HADN'T REALLY CONSIDERED IT...
OH... UH, MAYBE?

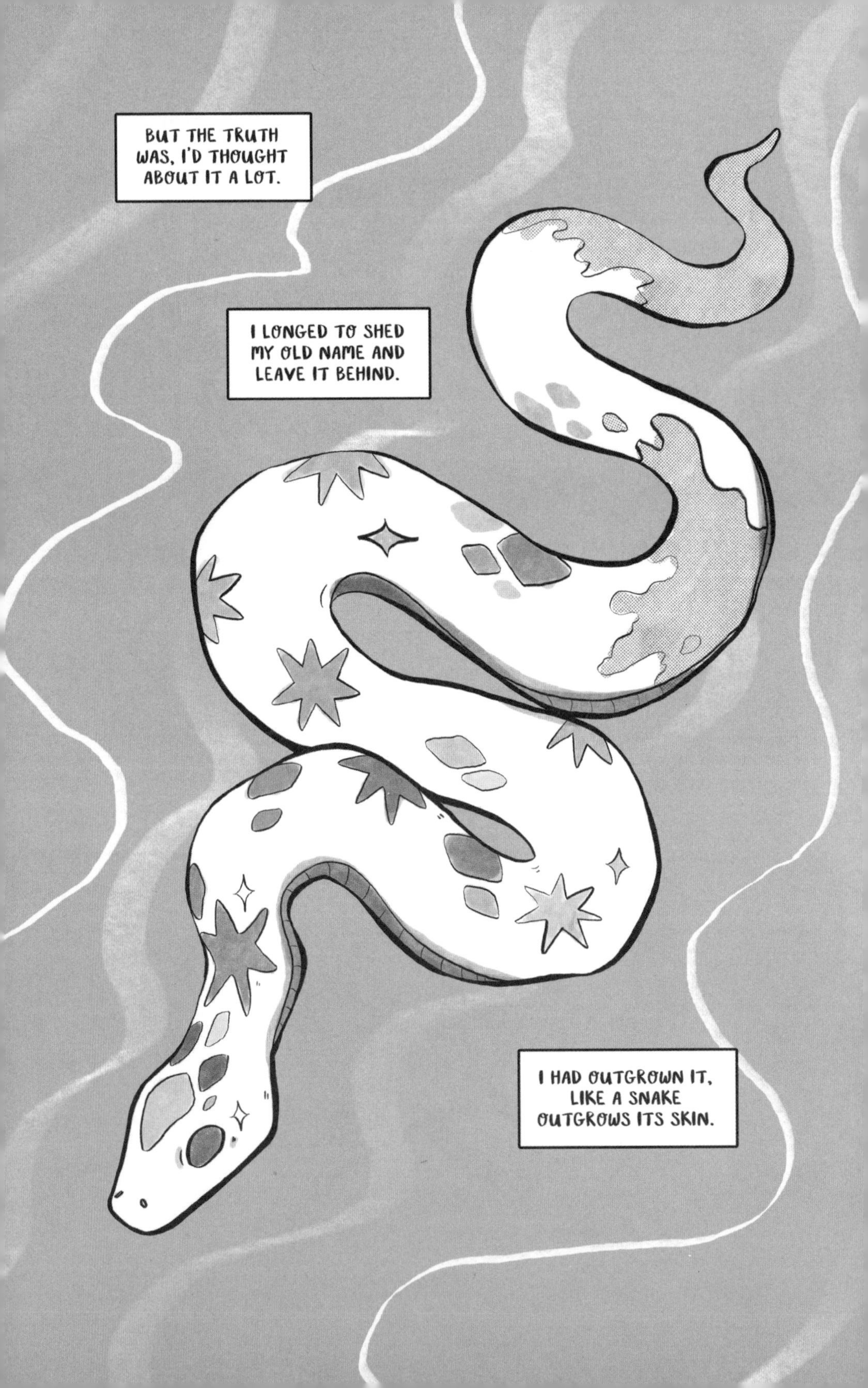
BUT THE TRUTH WAS, I'D THOUGHT ABOUT IT A LOT.
I LONGED TO SHED MY OLD NAME AND LEAVE IT BEHIND.
I HAD OUTGROWN IT, LIKE A SNAKE OUTGROWS ITS SKIN.

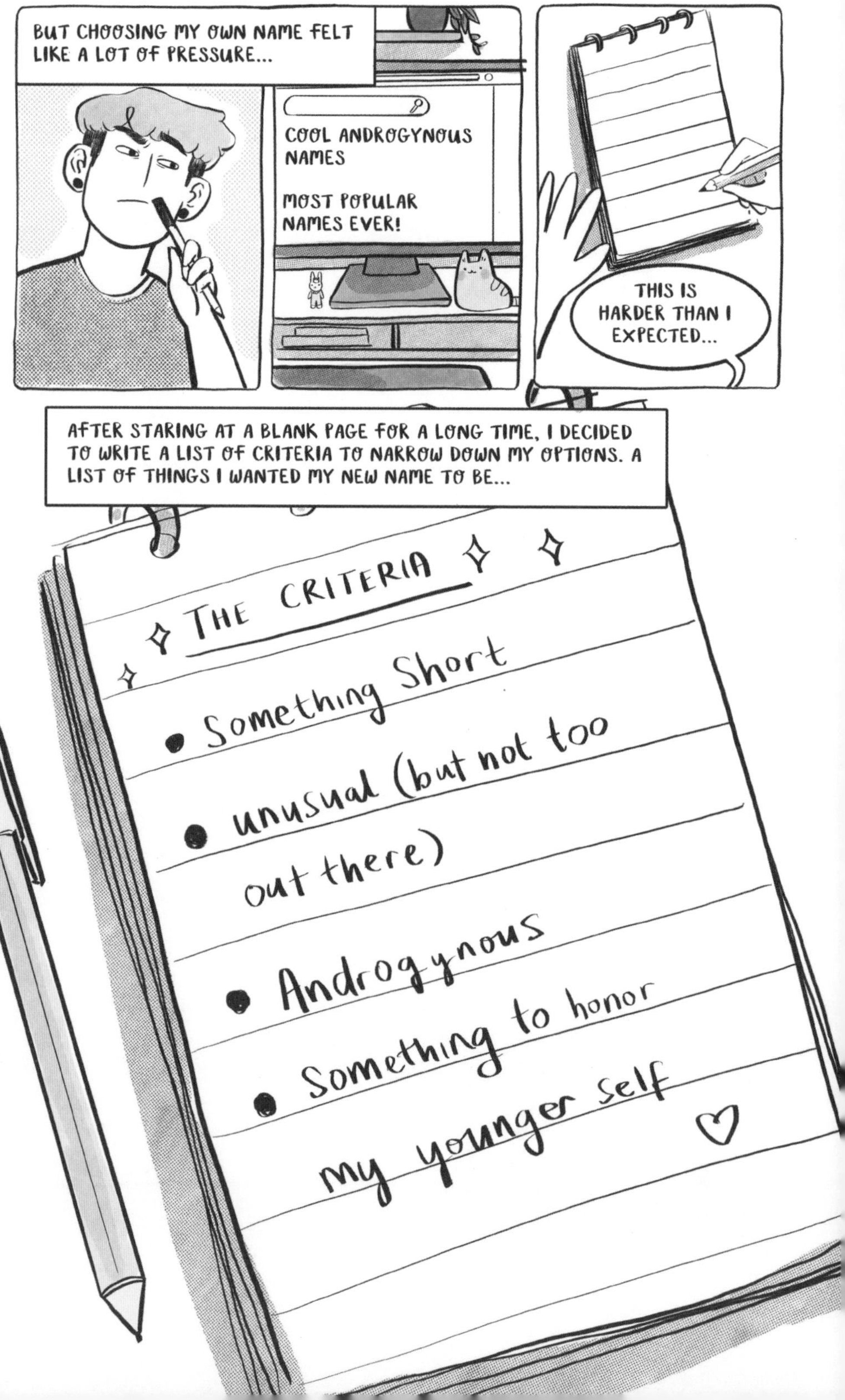
BUT CHOOSING MY OWN NAME FELT LIKE A LOT OF PRESSURE...
COOL ANDROGYNOUS NAMES
MOST POPULAR NAMES EVER!
THIS IS HARDER THAN I EXPECTED...
AFTER STARING AT A BLANK PAGE FOR A LONG TIME, I DECIDED TO WRITE A LIST OF CRITERIA TO NARROW DOWN MY OPTIONS. A LIST OF THINGS I WANTED MY NEW NAME TO BE...
THE CRITERIA
• Something Short
• unusual (but not too out there)
• Androgynous
• Something to honor my younger self

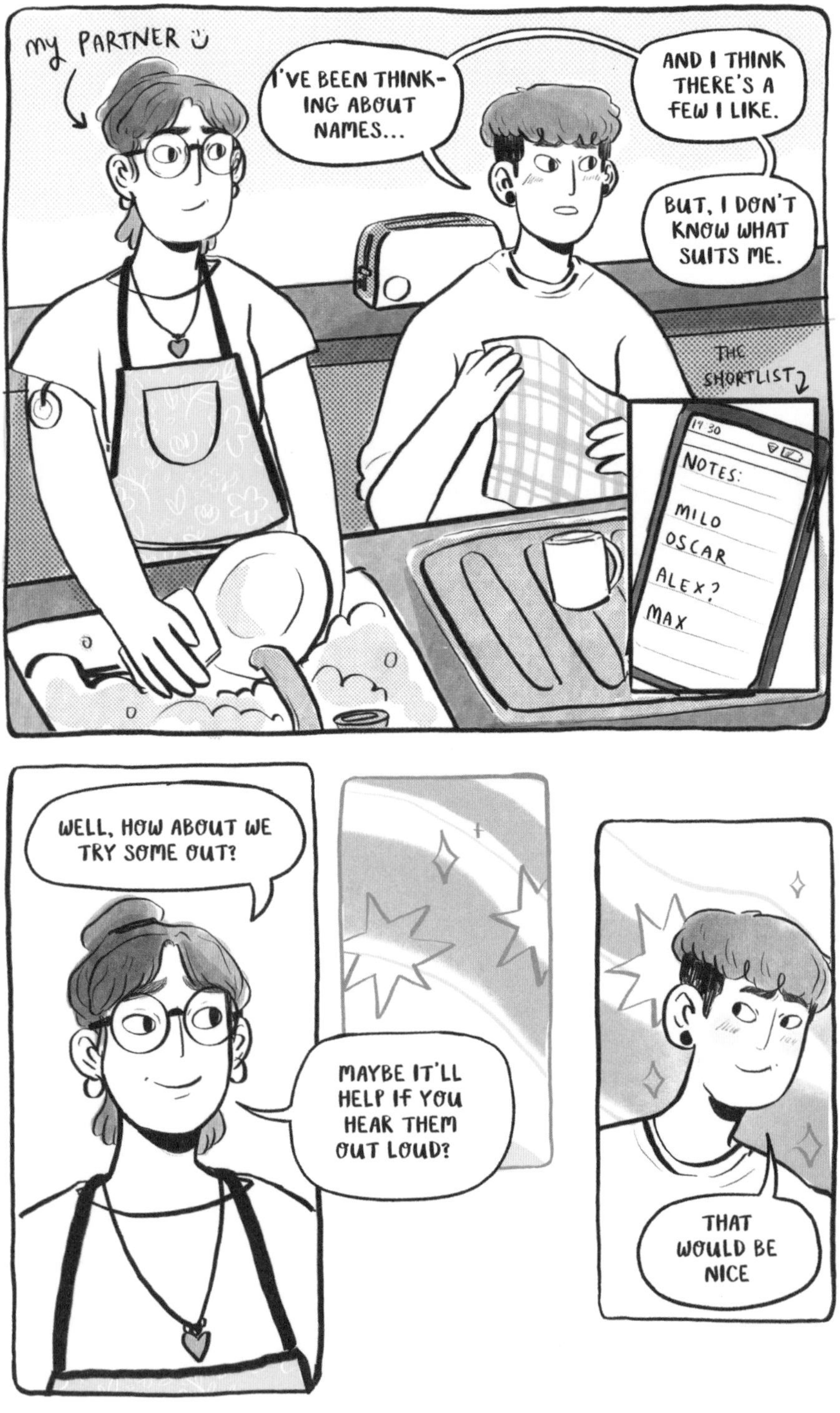

MY PARTNER
I'VE BEEN THINKING ABOUT NAMES...
AND I THINK THERE'S A FEW I LIKE.
BUT, I DON'T KNOW WHAT SUITS ME.
THE SHORTLIST
17:30
NOTES:
MILO
OSCAR
ALEX?
MAX
WELL, HOW ABOUT WE TRY SOME OUT?
MAYBE IT'LL HELP IF YOU HEAR THEM OUT LOUD?
THAT WOULD BE NICE

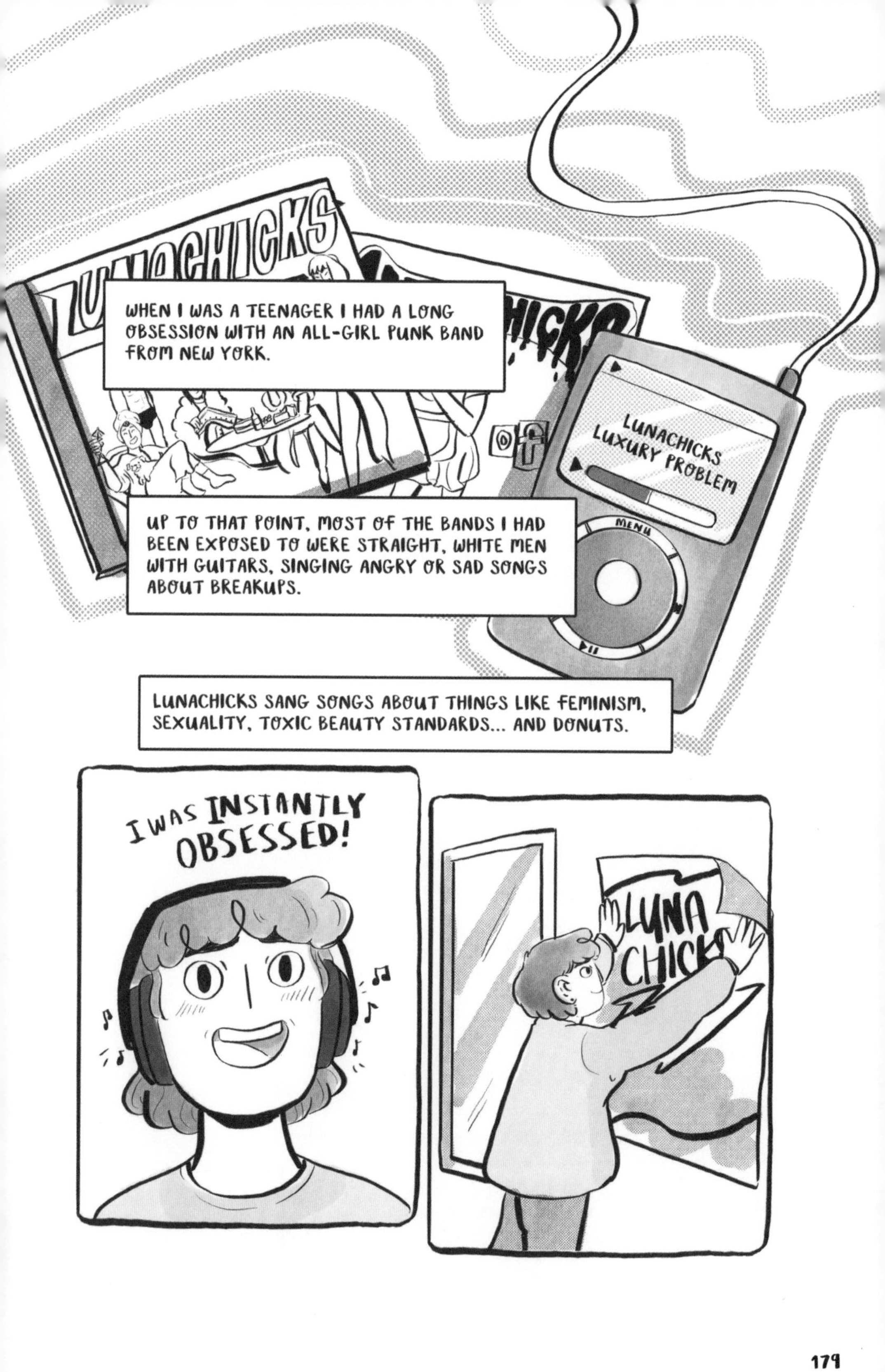
LUNACHICKS
WHEN I WAS A TEENAGER I HAD A LONG OBSESSION WITH AN ALL-GIRL PUNK BAND FROM NEW YORK.
LUNACHICKS
LUXURY PROBLEM
MENU
UP TO THAT POINT, MOST OF THE BANDS I HAD BEEN EXPOSED TO WERE STRAIGHT, WHITE MEN WITH GUITARS, SINGING ANGRY OR SAD SONGS ABOUT BREAKUPS.
LUNACHICKS SANG SONGS ABOUT THINGS LIKE FEMINISM, SEXUALITY, TOXIC BEAUTY STANDARDS... AND DONUTS.
I WAS INSTANTLY OBSESSED!
LUNA CHICKS

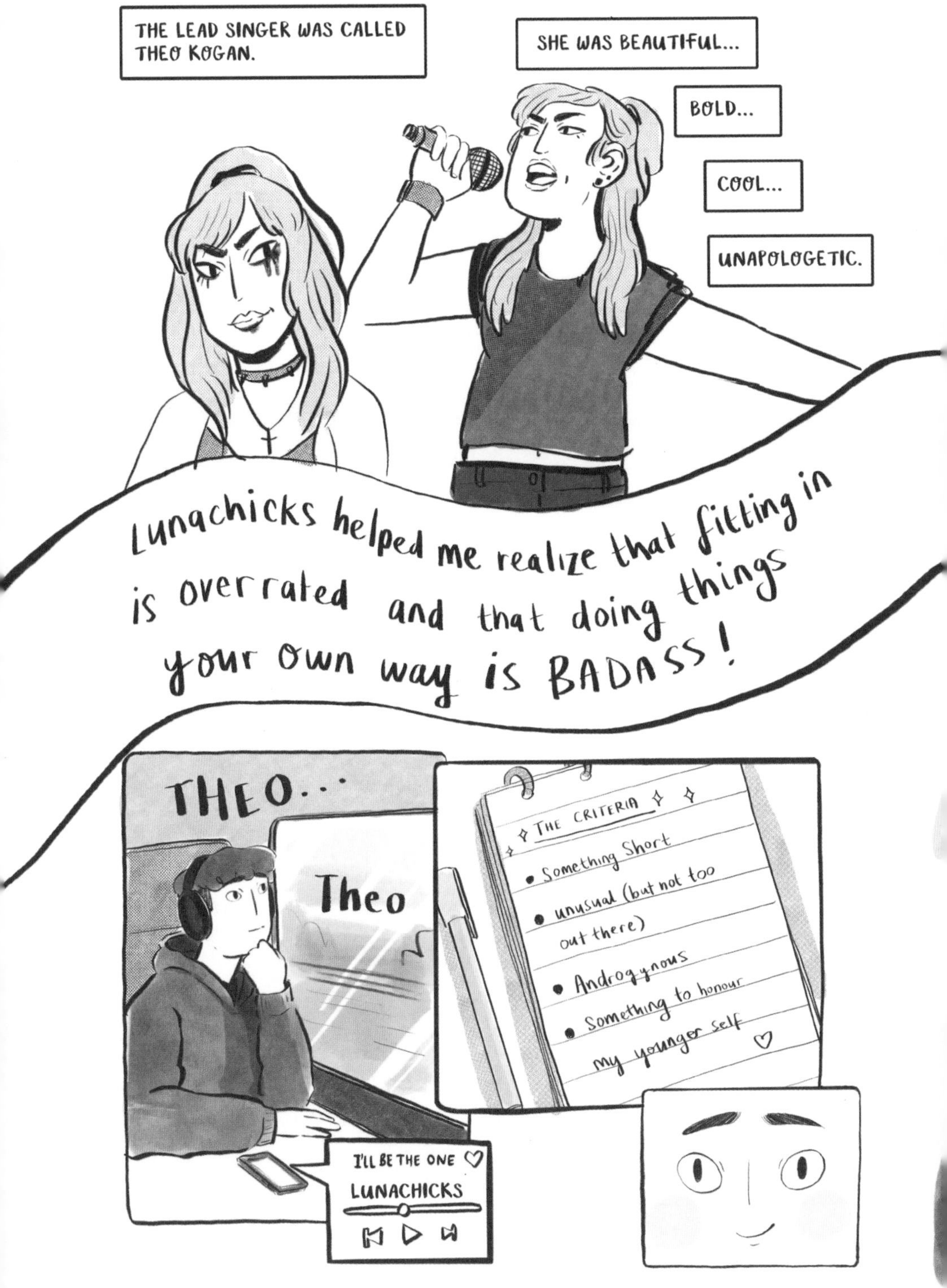
THE LEAD SINGER WAS CALLED THEO KOGAN.
SHE WAS BEAUTIFUL...
BOLD...
COOL...
UNAPOLOGETIC.
Lunachicks helped me realize that fitting in is overrated and that doing things your own way is BADASS!
THEO...
Theo
THE CRITERIA
• Something Short
• unusual (but not too out there)
• Androgynous
• Something to honour my younger self
I'LL BE THE ONE
LUNACHICKS

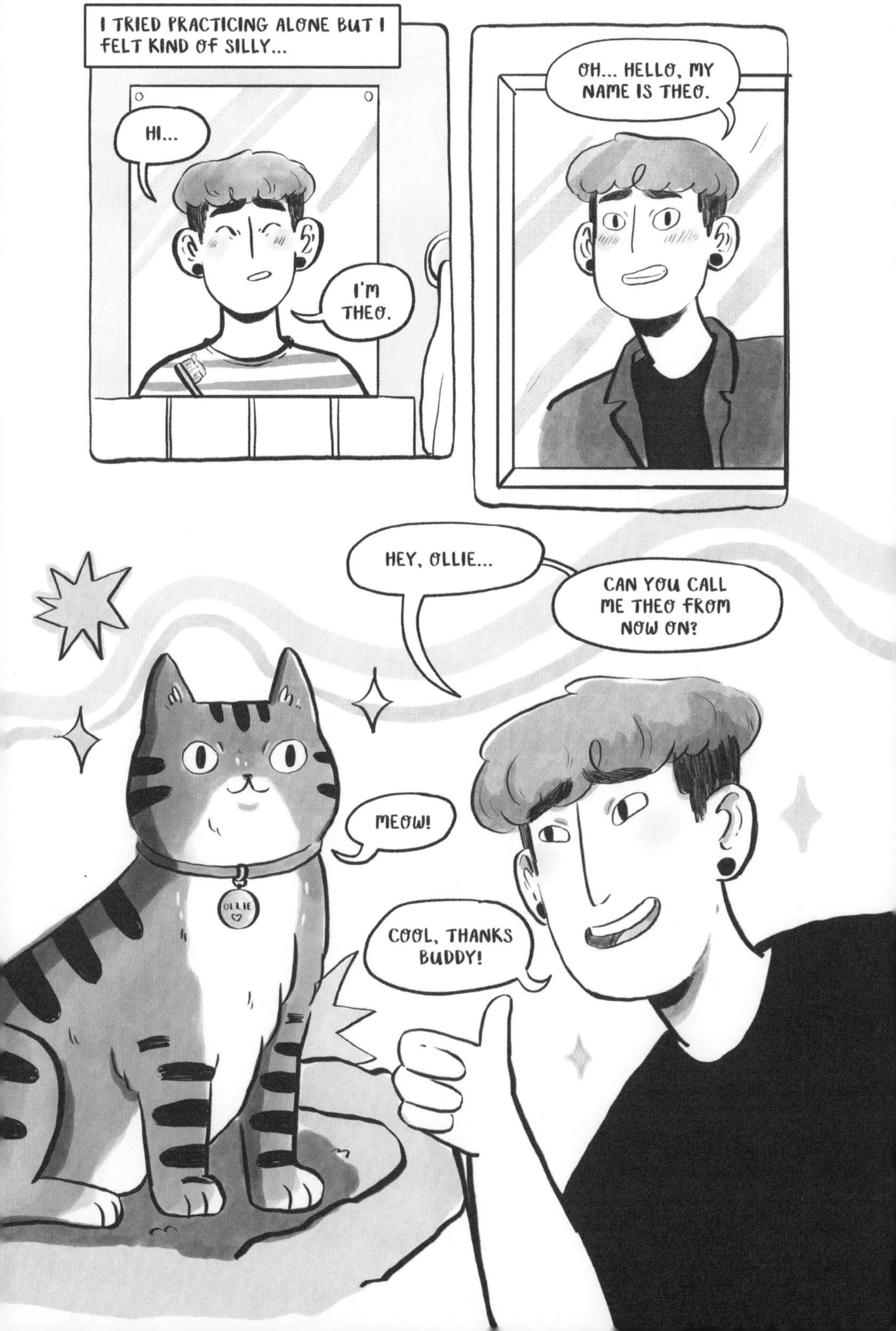
I TRIED PRACTICING ALONE BUT I FELT KIND OF SILLY...
HI...
I'M THEO.
OH... HELLO, MY NAME IS THEO.
HEY, OLLIE...
CAN YOU CALL ME THEO FROM NOW ON?
MEOW!
OLLIE
COOL, THANKS BUDDY!

THE CATS DIDN'T TURN OUT TO BE THAT USEFUL, SO I WENT TO MY PARTNER FOR HELP.

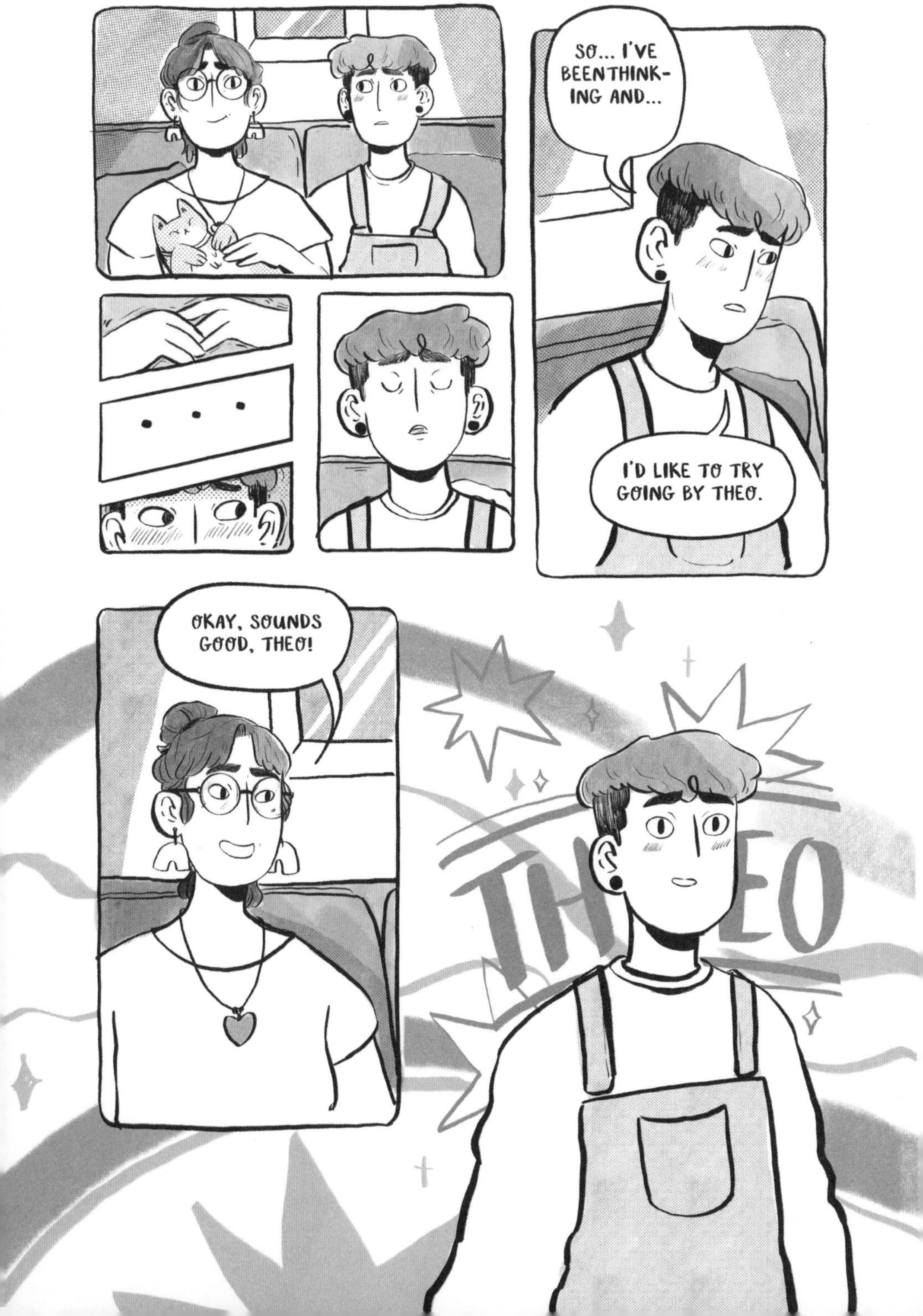

SO... I'VE BEENTHINK-ING AND...
I'D LIKE TO TRY GOING BY THEO.
OKAY, SOUNDS GOOD, THEO!
THEO

I REALLY DIDN'T EXPECT TO BE SO SURE SO SOON. I THOUGHT IT MIGHT TAKE TIME TO GET USED TO, TO BE SURE THIS WAS THE RIGHT NAME FOR ME. BUT AS SOON AS I HEARD IT, I KNEW...

It felt RIGHT.

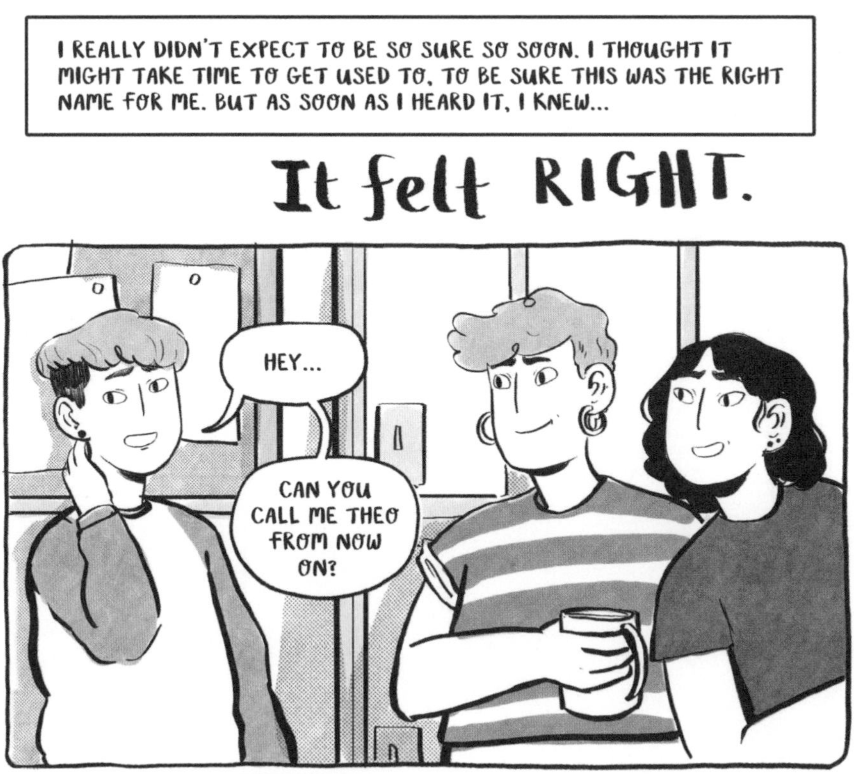
HEY...
CAN YOU CALL ME THEO FROM NOW ON?

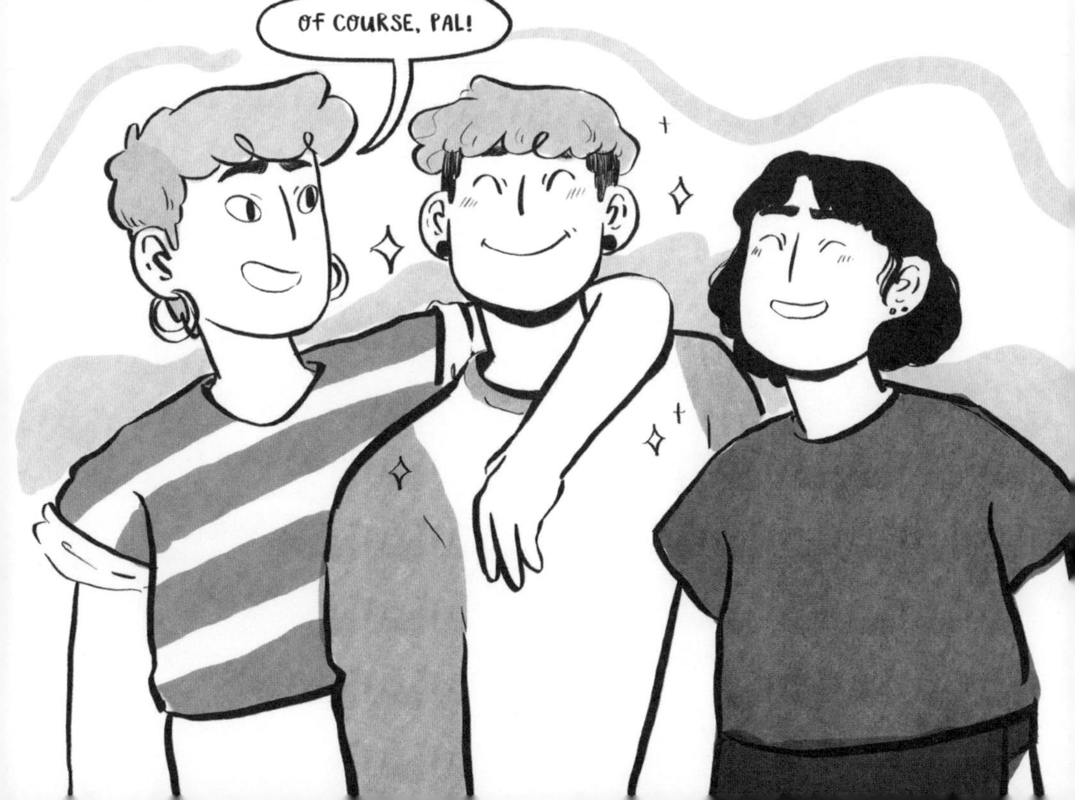
OF COURSE, PAL!

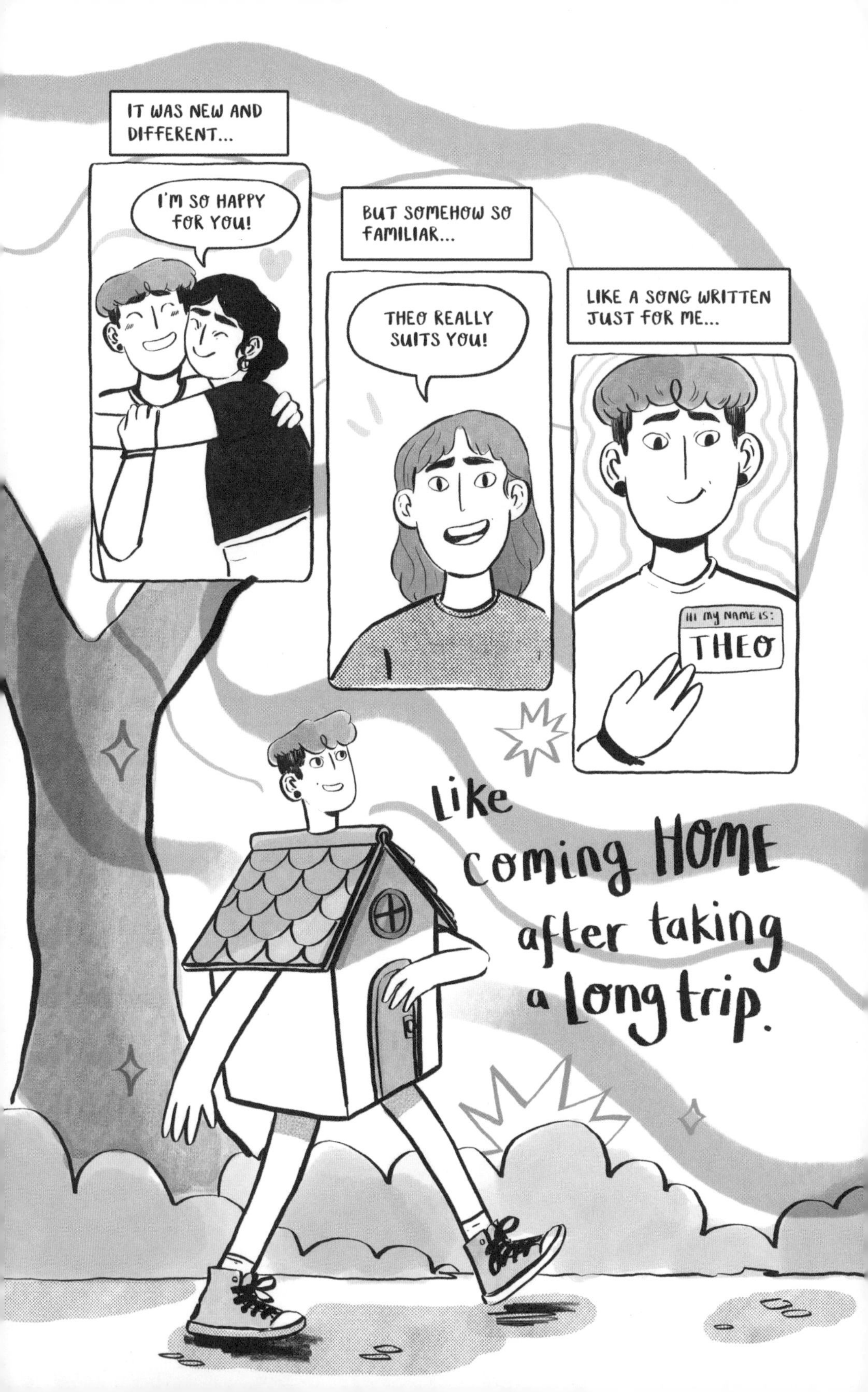
IT WAS NEW AND DIFFERENT...
I'M SO HAPPY FOR YOU!
BUT SOMEHOW SO FAMILIAR...
THEO REALLY SUITS YOU!
LIKE A SONG WRITTEN JUST FOR ME...
HI MY NAME IS:
THEO
Like coming HOME after taking a Long trip.

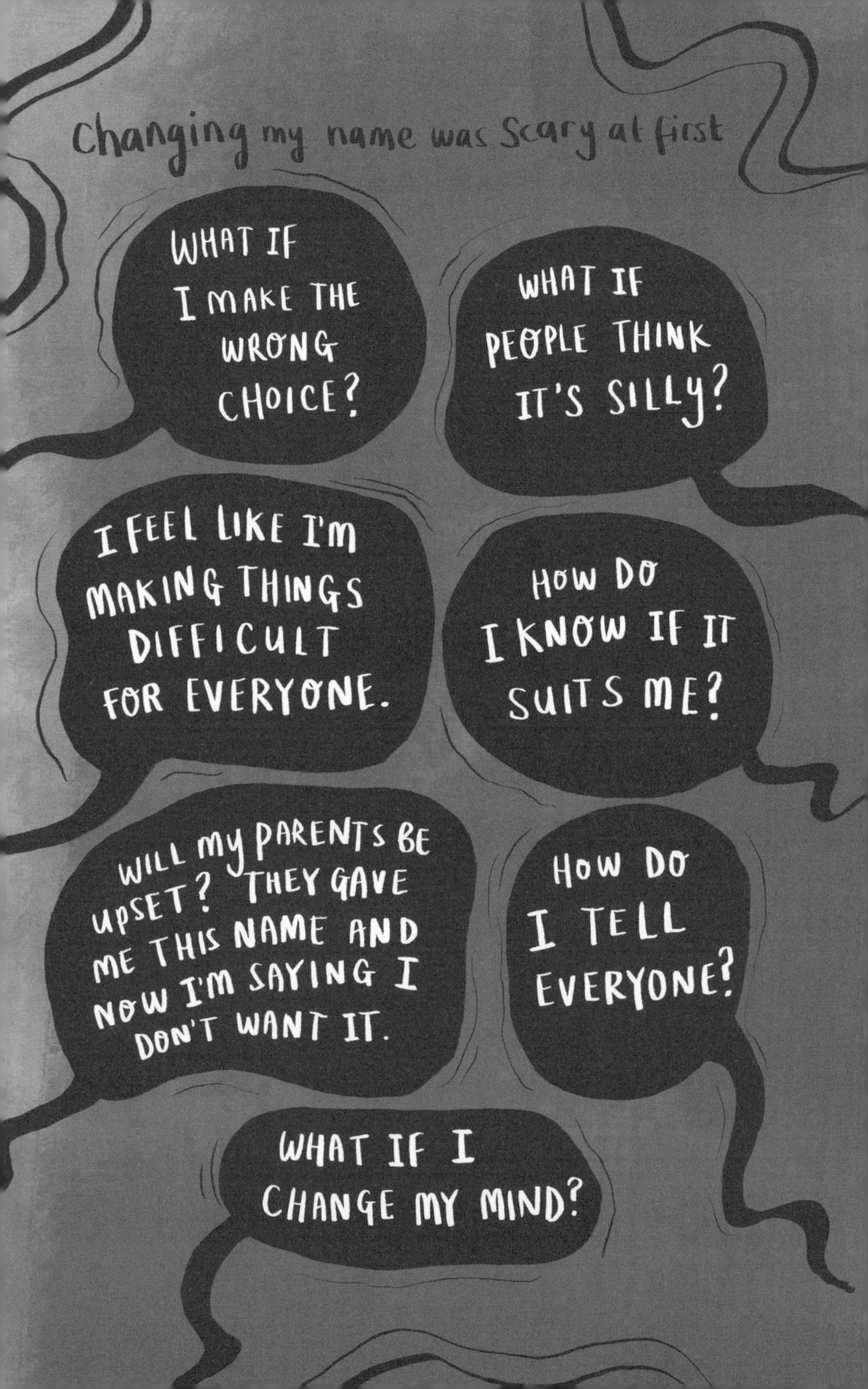
Changing my name was scary at first
WHAT IF I MAKE THE WRONG CHOICE?
WHAT IF PEOPLE THINK IT'S SILLY?
I FEEL LIKE I'M MAKING THINGS DIFFICULT FOR EVERYONE.
HOW DO I KNOW IF IT SUITS ME?
WILL MY PARENTS BE UPSET? THEY GAVE ME THIS NAME AND NOW I'M SAYING I DON'T WANT IT.
HOW DO I TELL EVERYONE?
WHAT IF I CHANGE MY MIND?

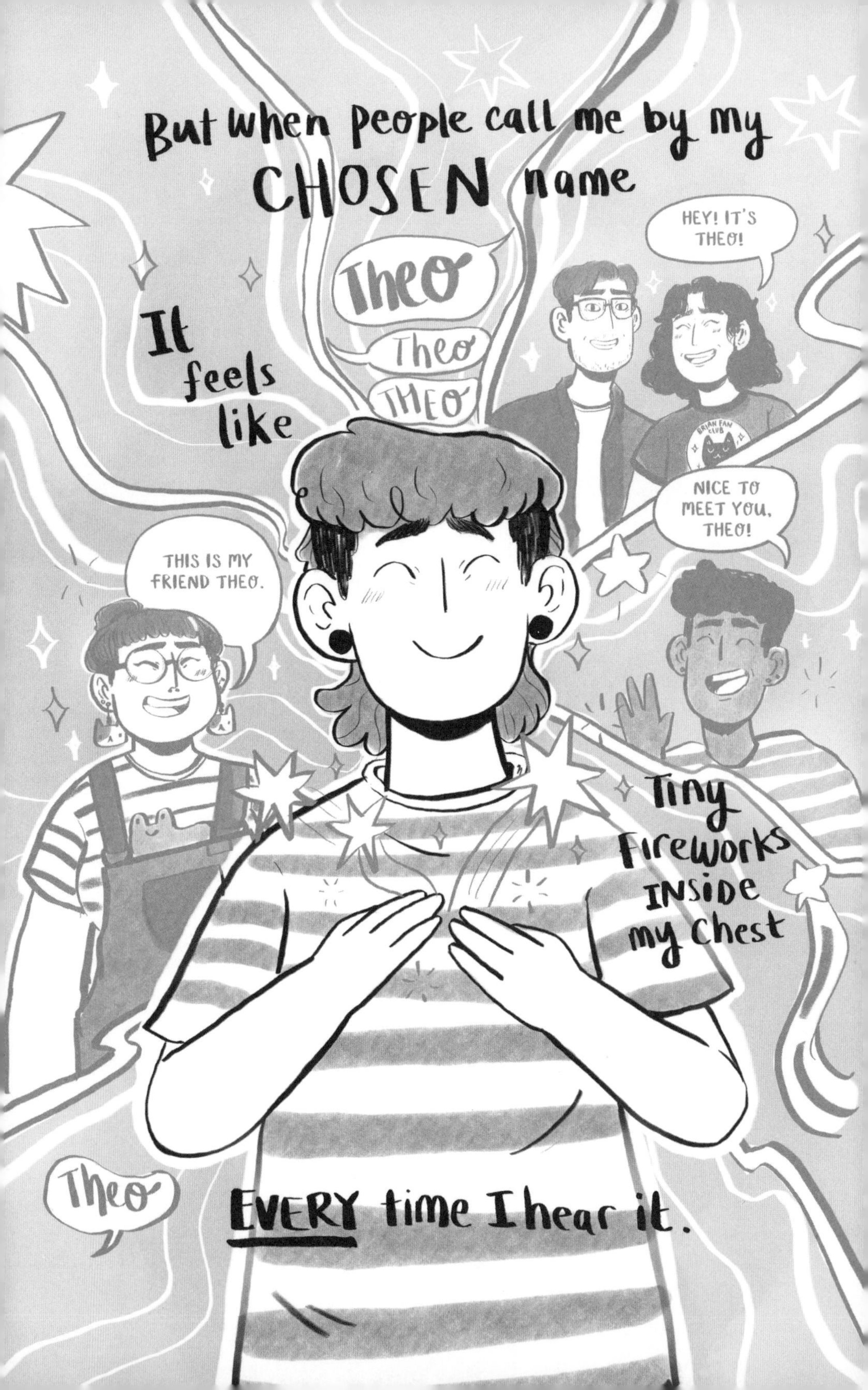
But when people call me by my
CHOSEN name
HEY! IT'S THEO!
Theo
Theo
THEO
It feels like
BRIAN FAN CLUB
NICE TO MEET YOU, THEO!
THIS IS MY FRIEND THEO.
Tiny Fireworks INSIDE my Chest
Theo
EVERY time I hear it.

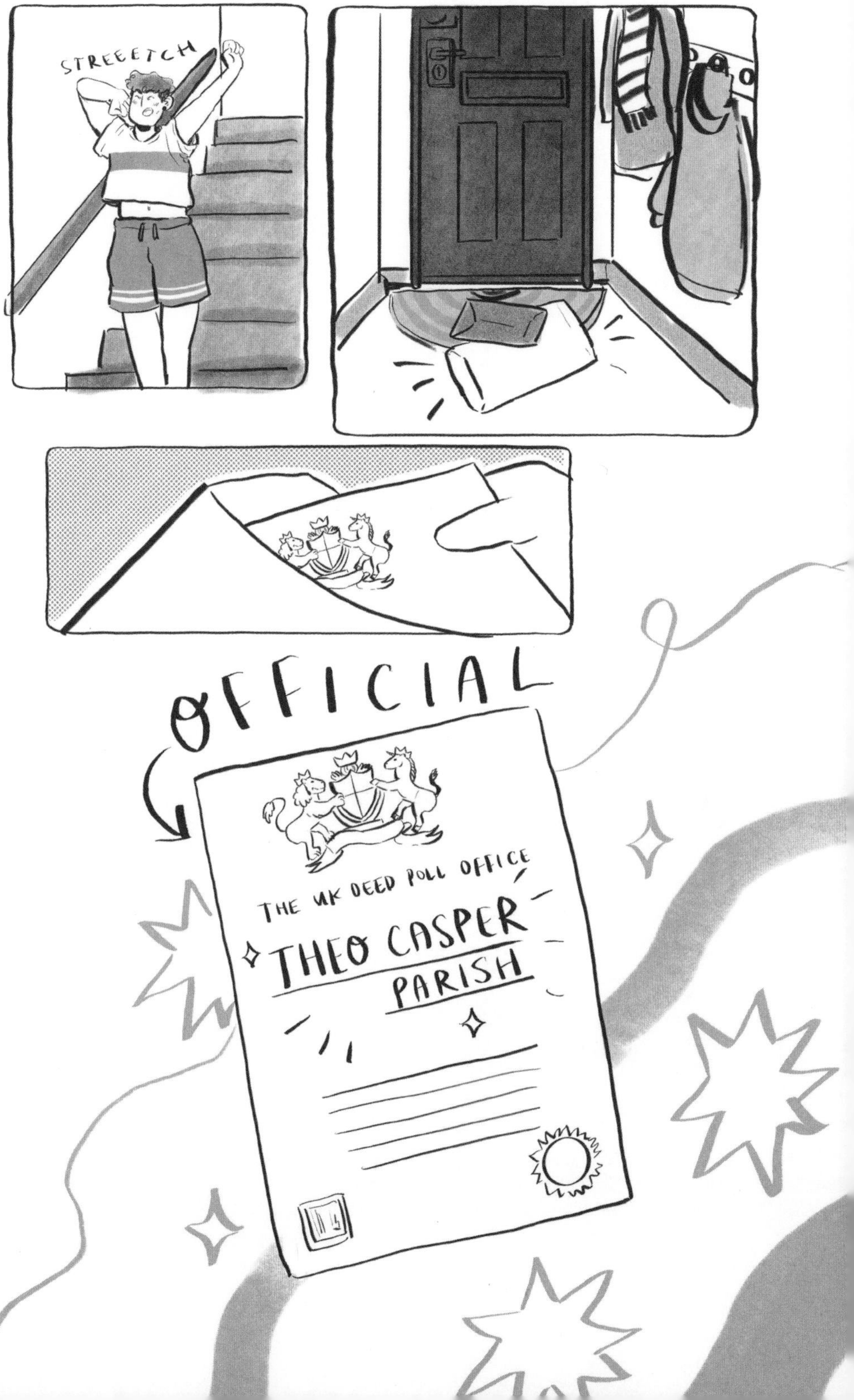
STREEETCH
OFFICIAL
THE UK DEED POLL OFFICE
THEO CASPER
PARISH

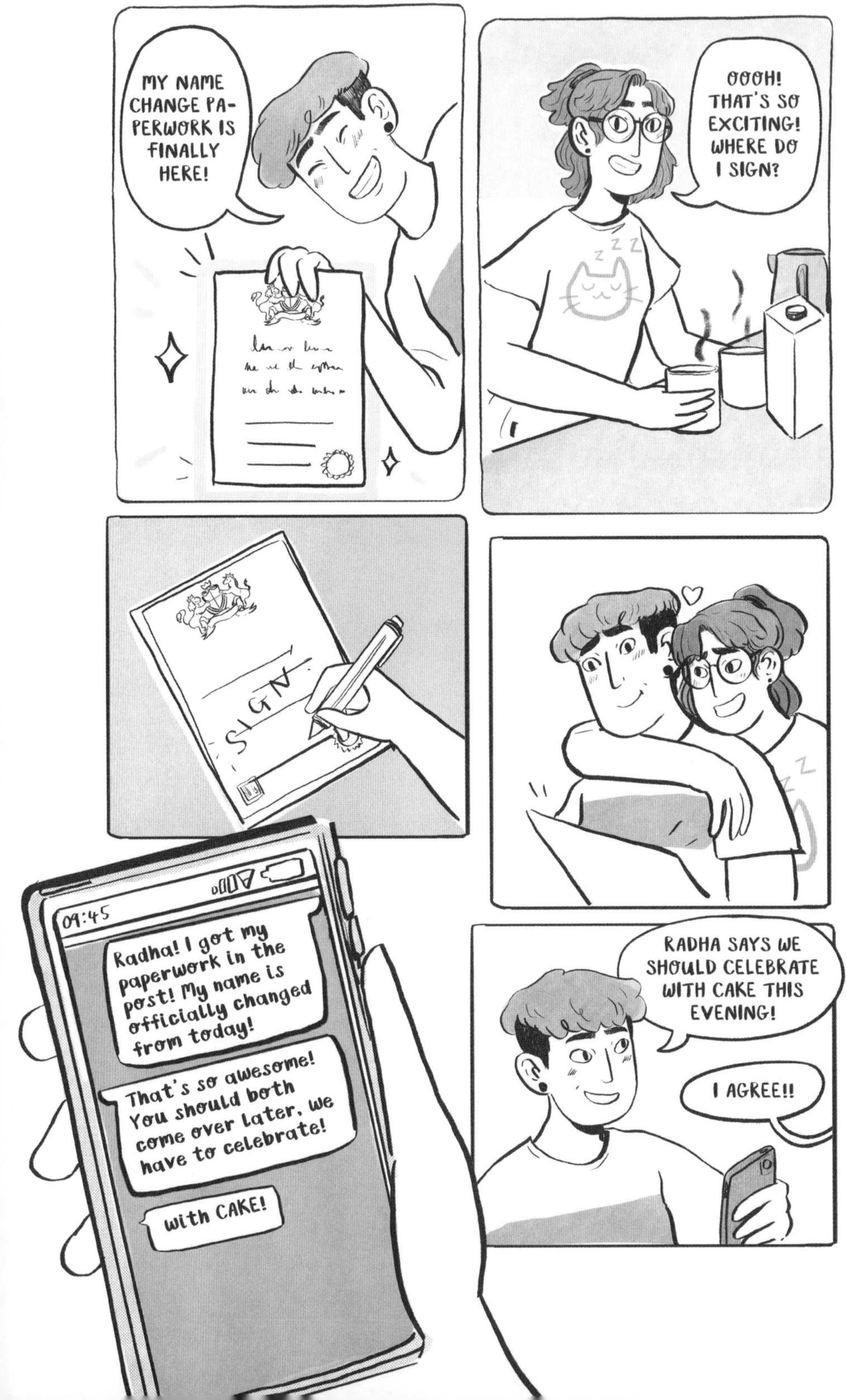
MY NAME CHANGE PA-PERWORK IS FINALLY HERE!
OOOH! THAT'S SO EXCITING! WHERE DO I SIGN?
SIGN
09:45
Radha! I got my paperwork in the post! My name is officially changed from today!
That's so awesome! You should both come over later, we have to celebrate!
with CAKE!
RADHA SAYS WE SHOULD CELEBRATE WITH CAKE THIS EVENING!
I AGREE!!

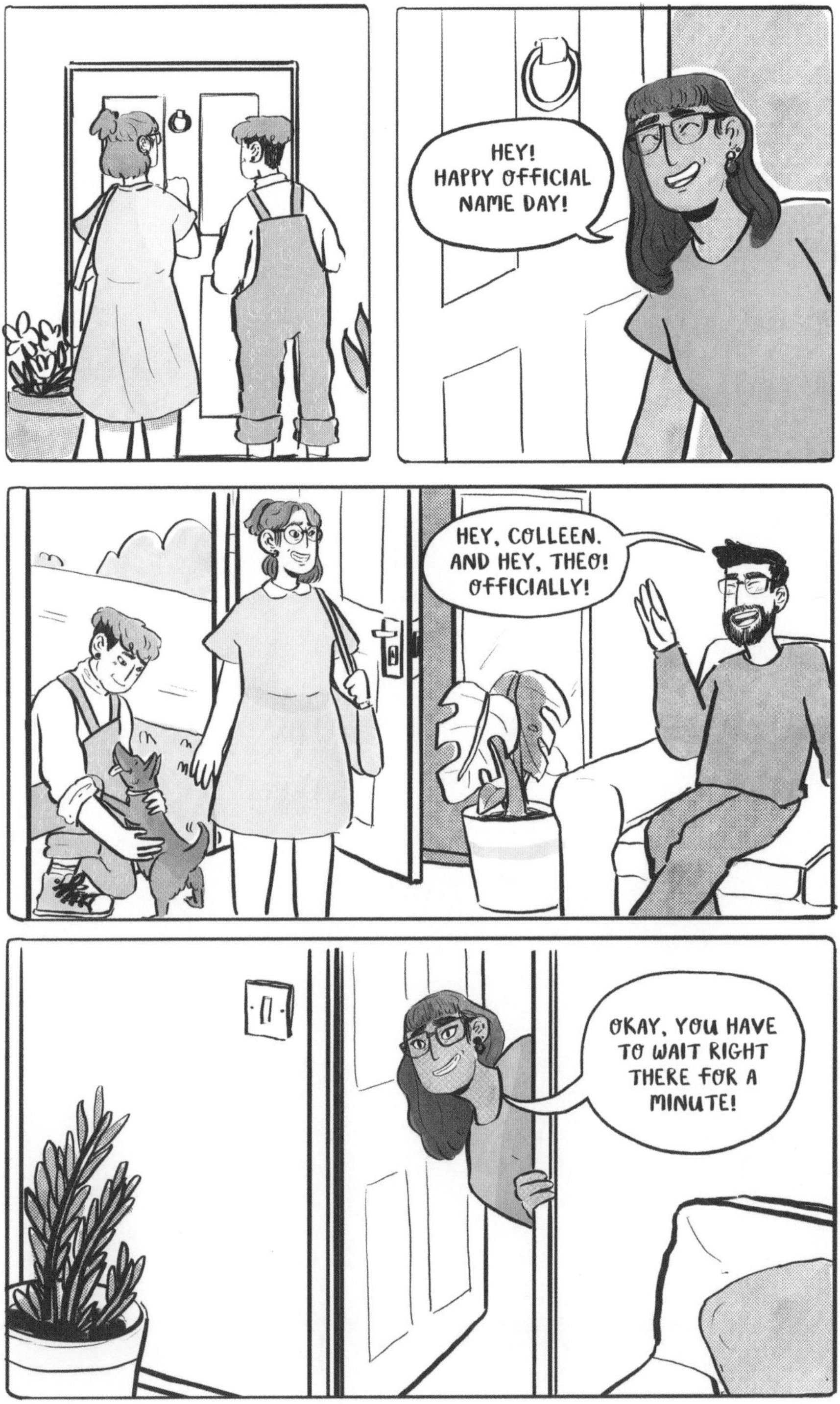
HEY! HAPPY OFFICIAL NAME DAY!
HEY, COLLEEN. AND HEY, THEO! OFFICIALLY!
OKAY, YOU HAVE TO WAIT RIGHT THERE FOR A MINUTE!

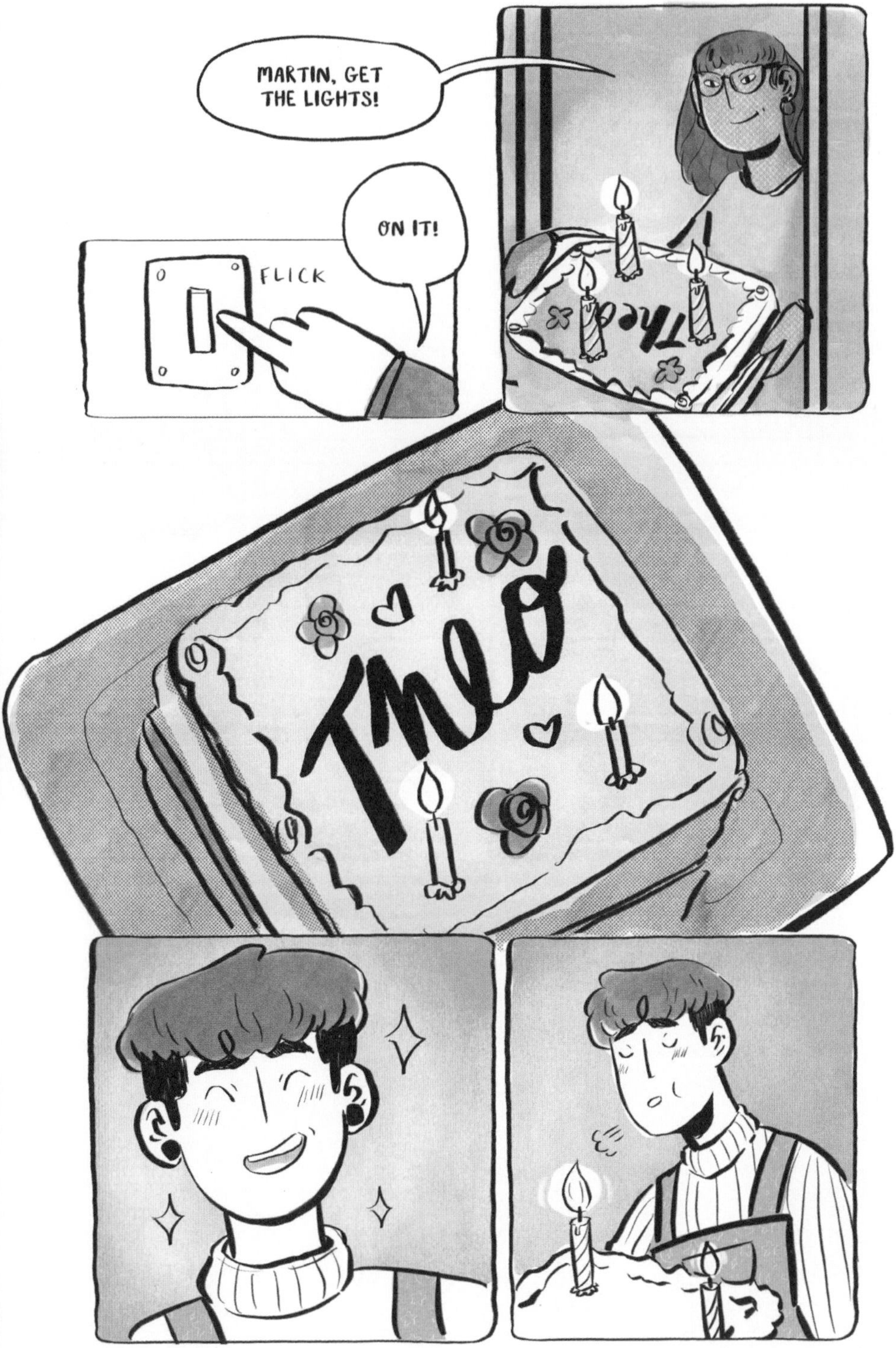
MARTIN, GET THE LIGHTS!
ON IT!
FLICK
Theo
Theo

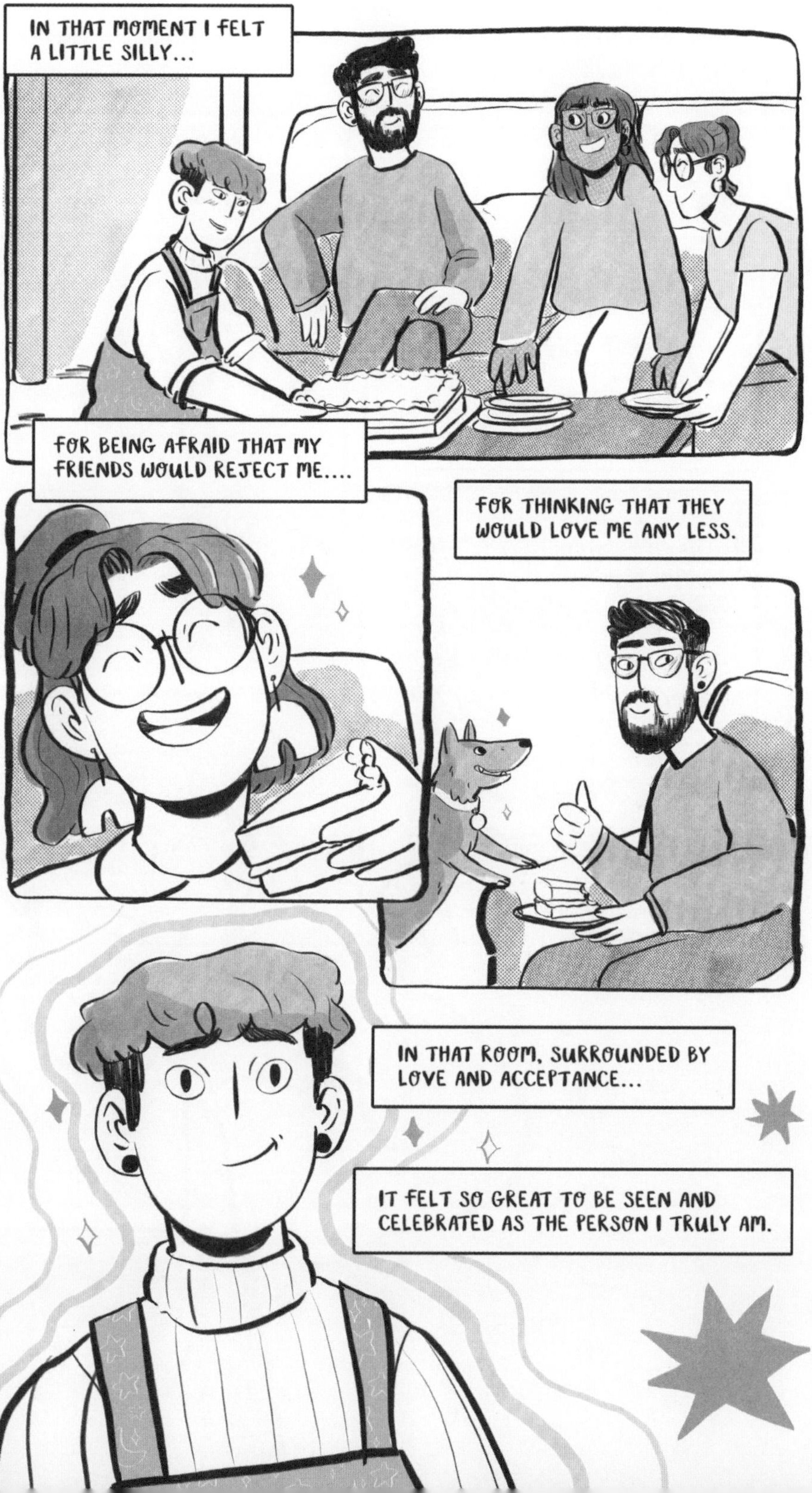
IN THAT MOMENT I FELT A LITTLE SILLY...
FOR BEING AFRAID THAT MY FRIENDS WOULD REJECT ME....
FOR THINKING THAT THEY WOULD LOVE ME ANY LESS.
IN THAT ROOM, SURROUNDED BY LOVE AND ACCEPTANCE...
IT FELT SO GREAT TO BE SEEN AND CELEBRATED AS THE PERSON I TRULY AM.

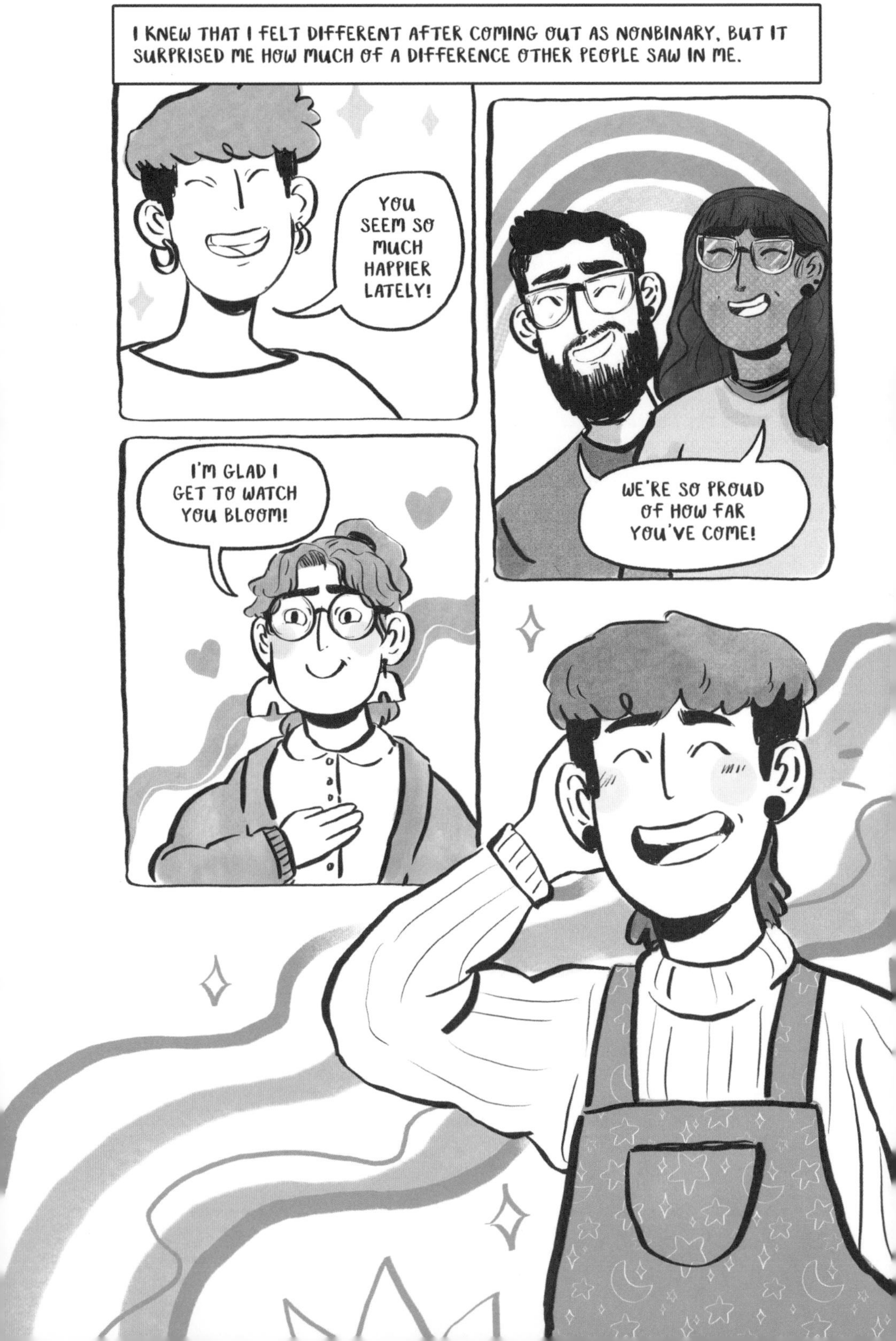
I KNEW THAT I FELT DIFFERENT AFTER COMING OUT AS NONBINARY, BUT IT SURPRISED ME HOW MUCH OF A DIFFERENCE OTHER PEOPLE SAW IN ME.
YOU SEEM SO MUCH HAPPIER LATELY!
WE'RE SO PROUD OF HOW FAR YOU'VE COME!
I'M GLAD I GET TO WATCH YOU BLOOM!

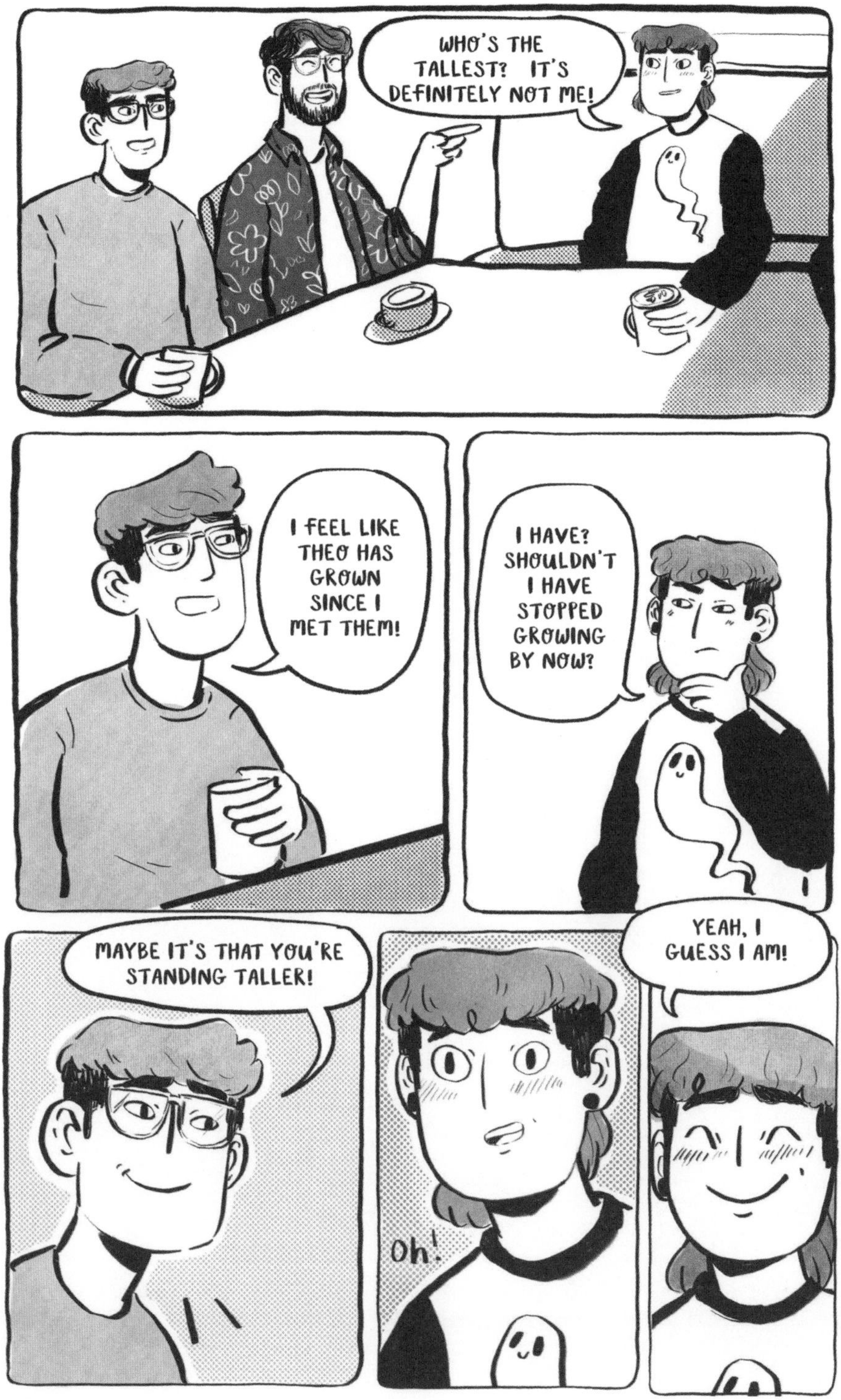
WHO'S THE TALLEST? IT'S DEFINITELY NOT ME!
I FEEL LIKE THEO HAS GROWN SINCE I MET THEM!
I HAVE? SHOULDN'T I HAVE STOPPED GROWING BY NOW?
MAYBE IT'S THAT YOU'RE STANDING TALLER!
Oh!
YEAH, I GUESS I AM!

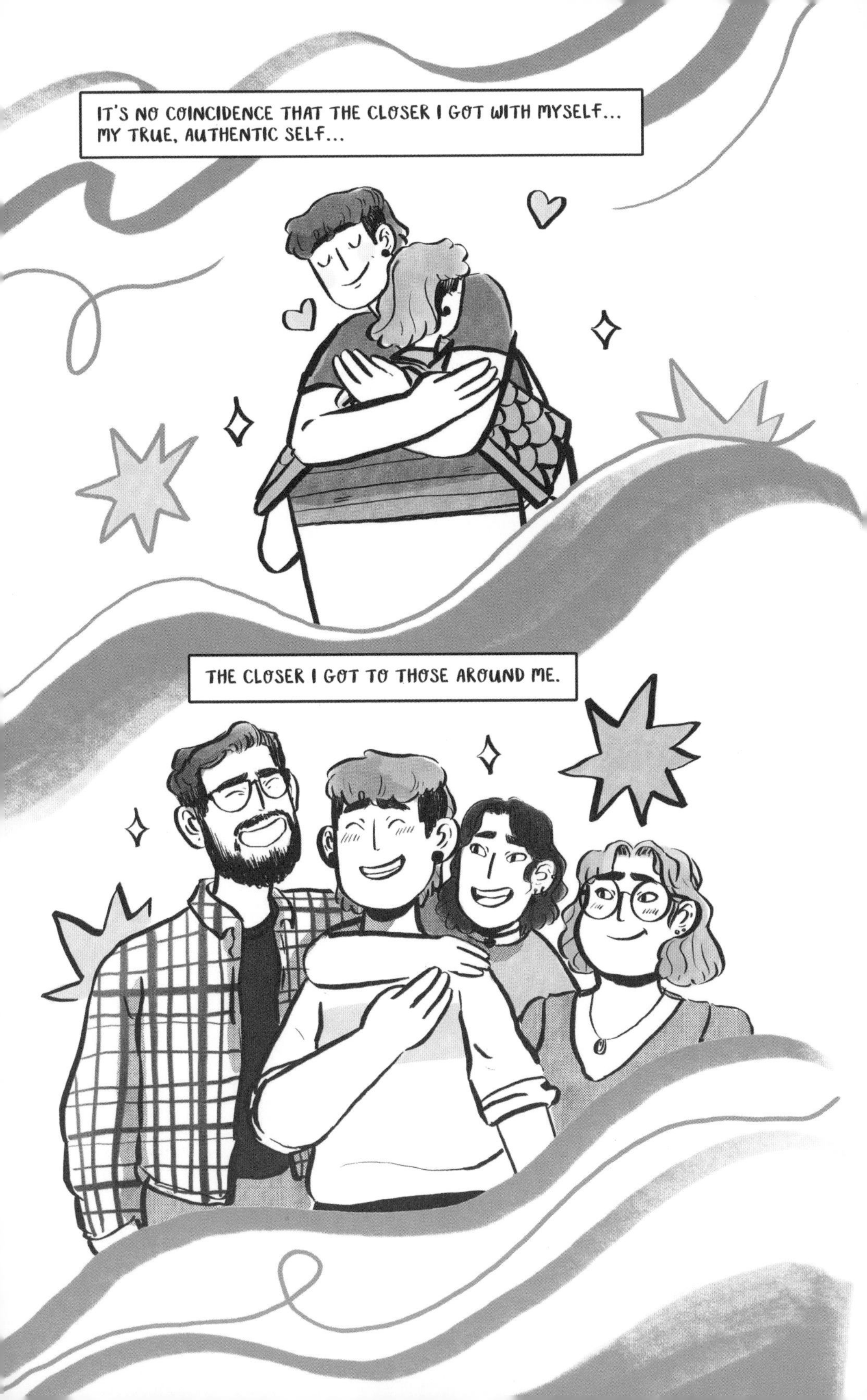
IT'S NO COINCIDENCE THAT THE CLOSER I GOT WITH MYSELF... MY TRUE, AUTHENTIC SELF...
THE CLOSER I GOT TO THOSE AROUND ME.

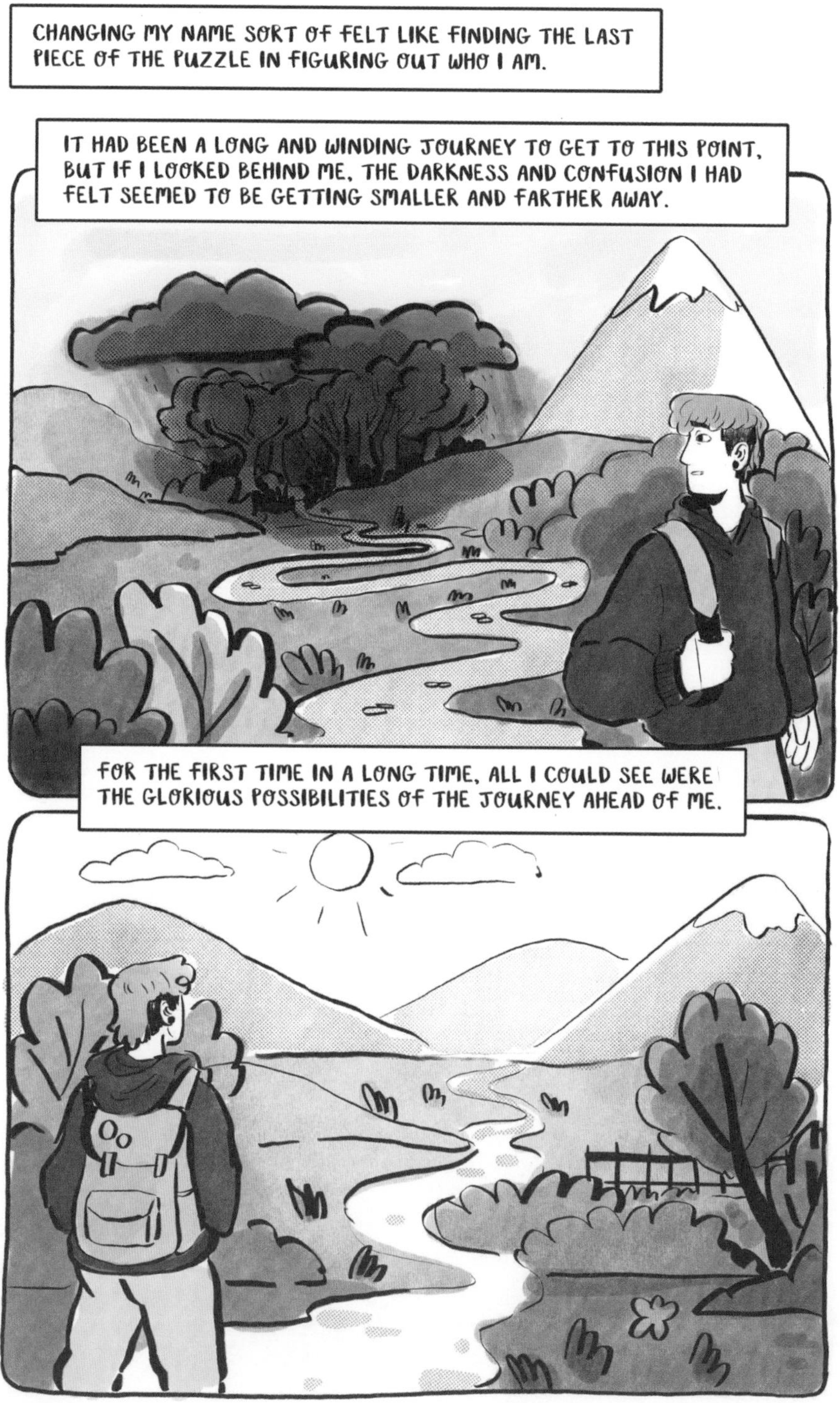
CHANGING MY NAME SORT OF FELT LIKE FINDING THE LAST PIECE OF THE PUZZLE IN FIGURING OUT WHO I AM.
IT HAD BEEN A LONG AND WINDING JOURNEY TO GET TO THIS POINT, BUT IF I LOOKED BEHIND ME, THE DARKNESS AND CONFUSION I HAD FELT SEEMED TO BE GETTING SMALLER AND FARTHER AWAY.
FOR THE FIRST TIME IN A LONG TIME, ALL I COULD SEE WERE THE GLORIOUS POSSIBILITIES OF THE JOURNEY AHEAD OF ME.
Oo

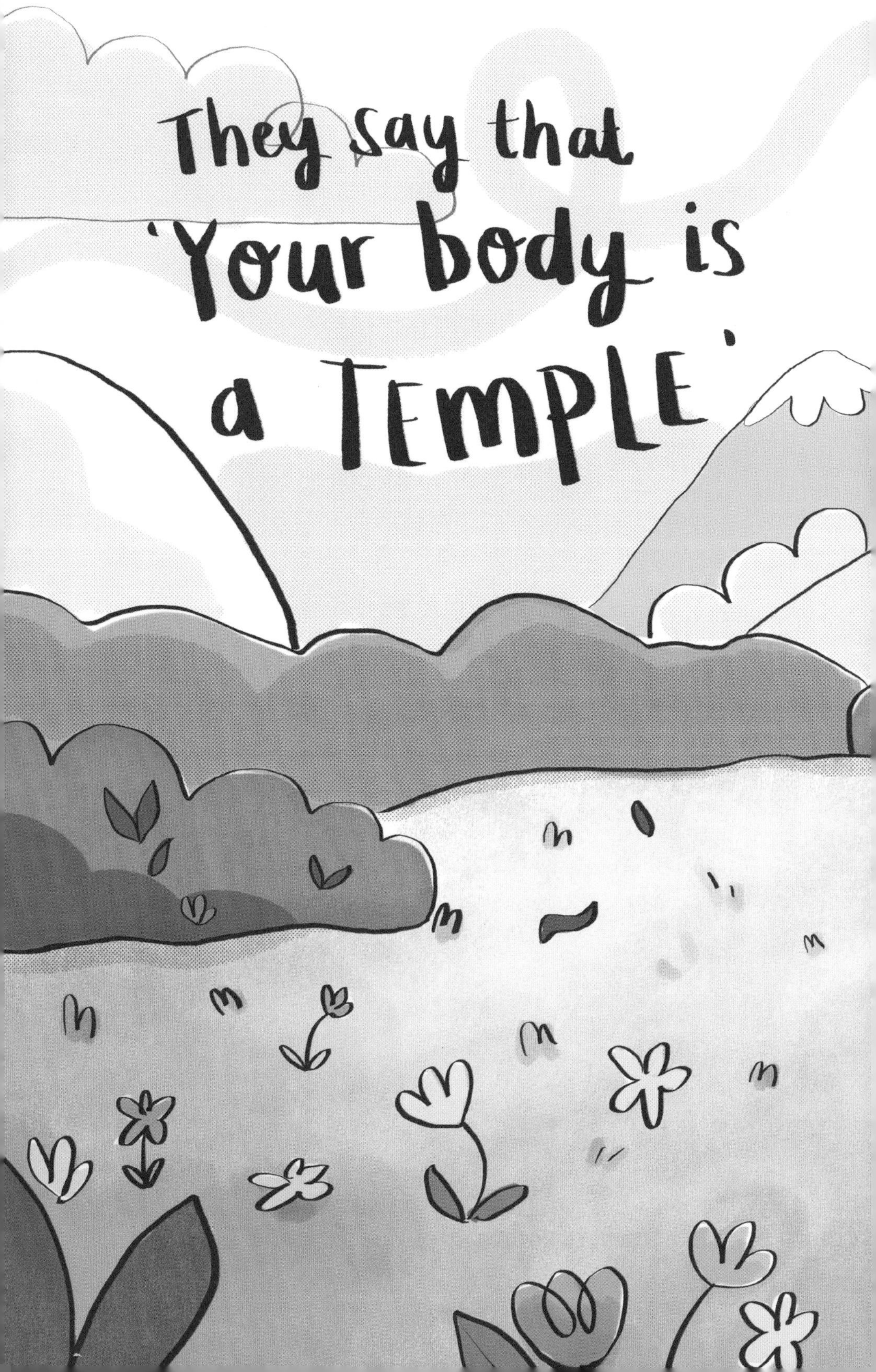
They say that
'Your body is
a TEMPLE'

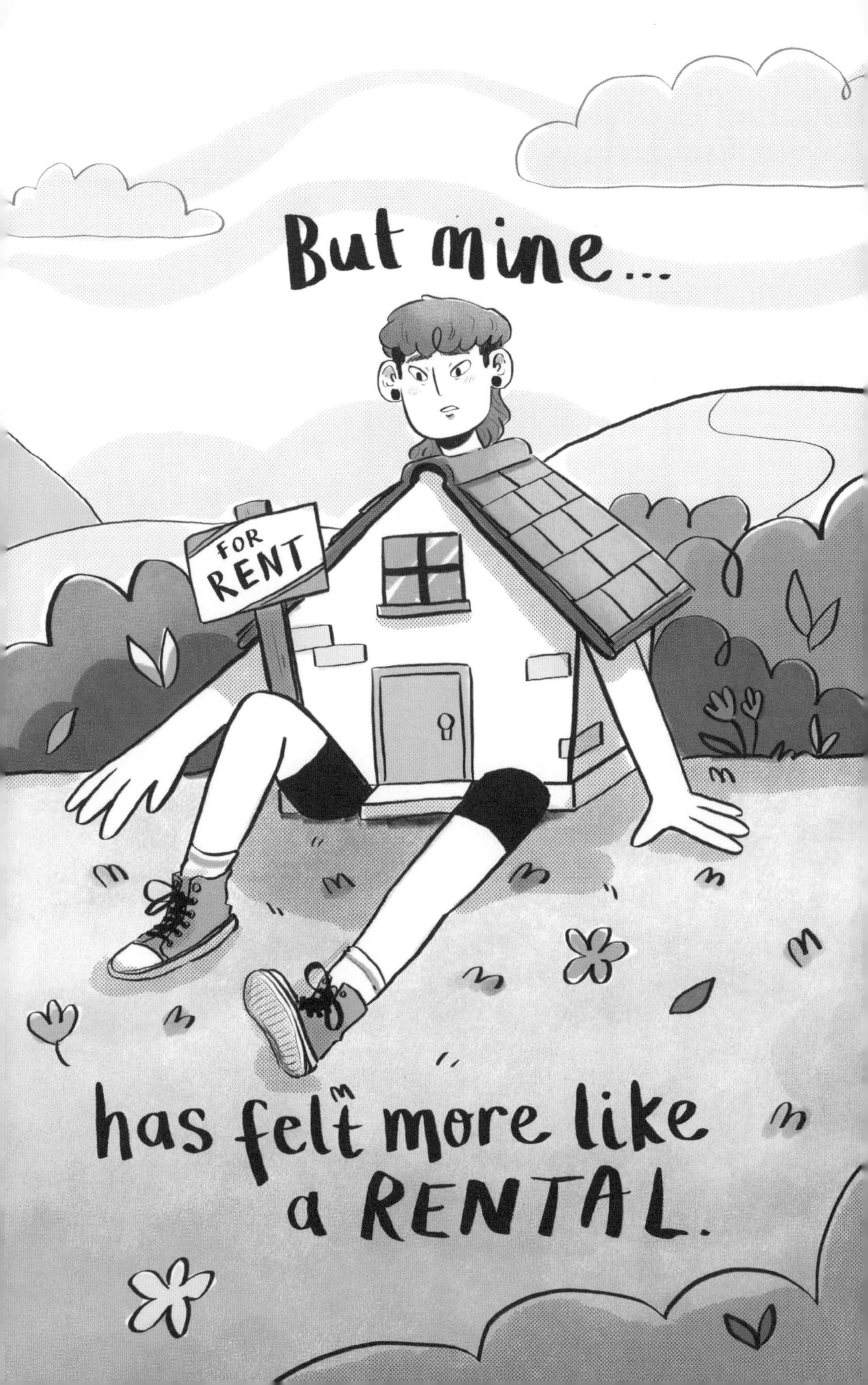
But mine...
FOR RENT
has felt more like a RENTAL.

A place to EXIST,

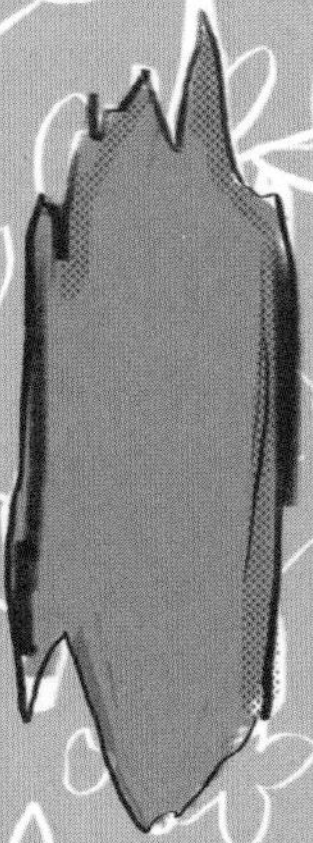

not to FLOURISH.

One that came already FURNISHED

with that wallpaper you just learn to live with.

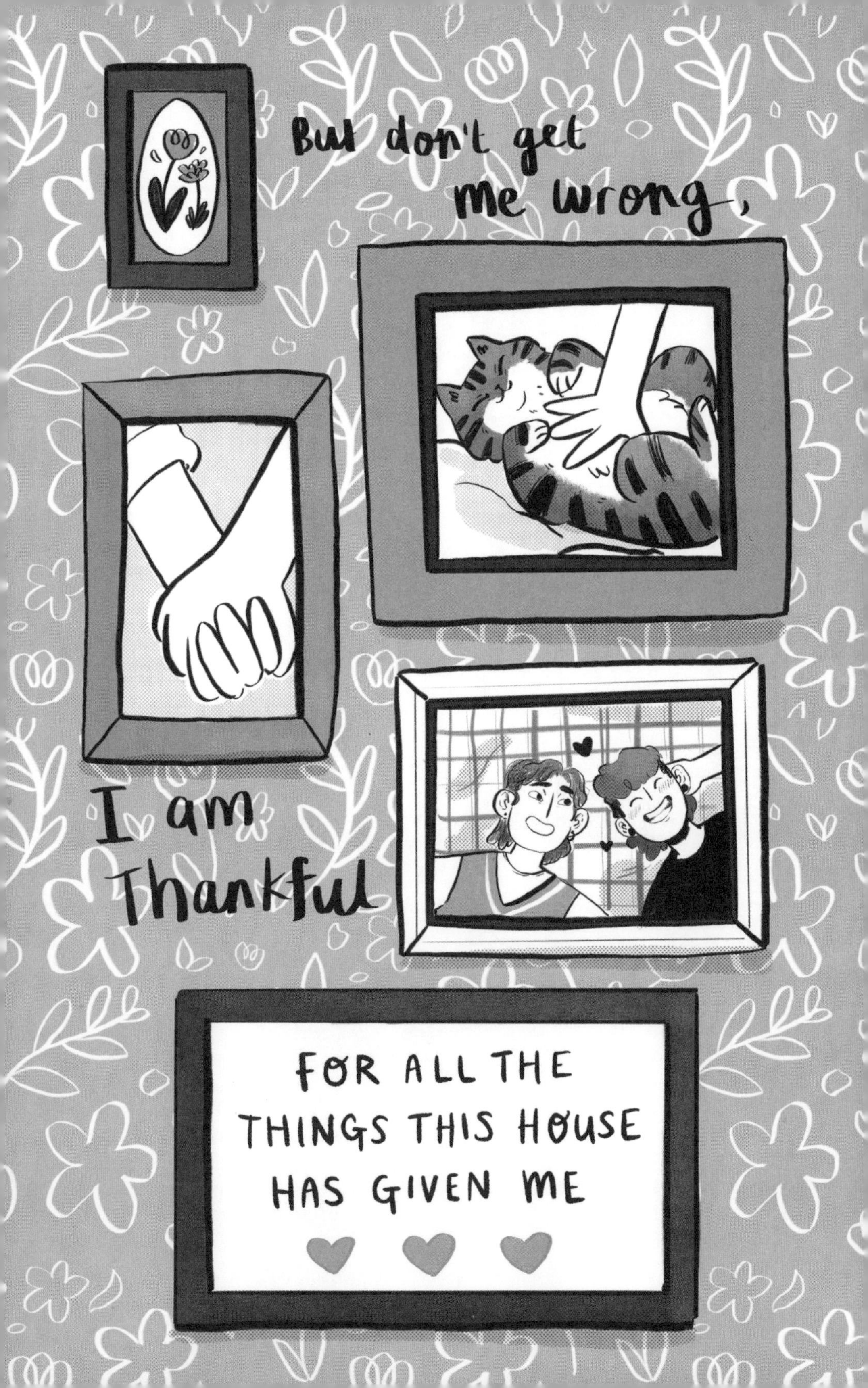
But don't get me wrong,
I am Thankful
FOR ALL THE THINGS THIS HOUSE HAS GIVEN ME

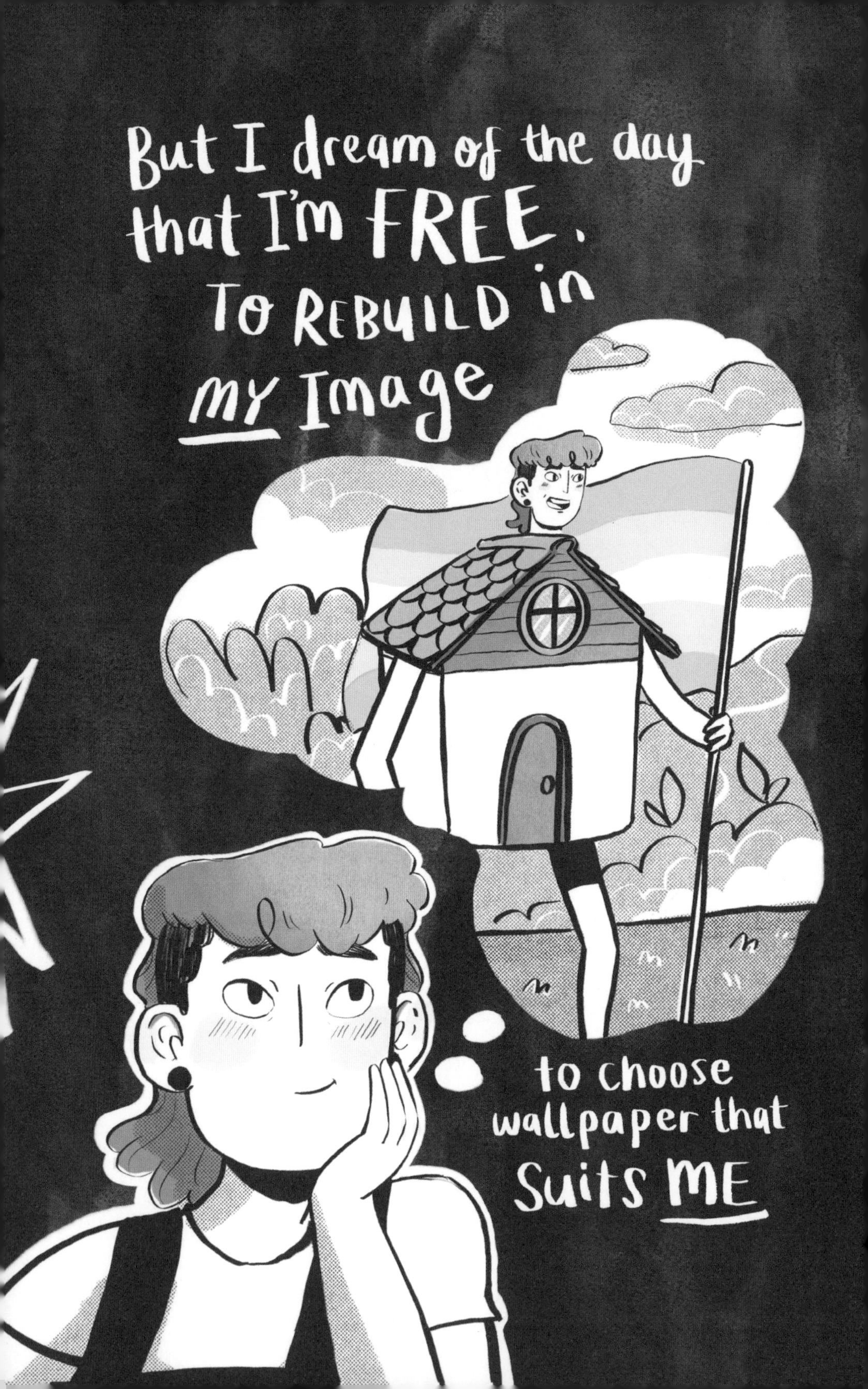
But I dream of the day that I'm FREE.
TO REBUILD in MY Image
to choose wallpaper that suits ME

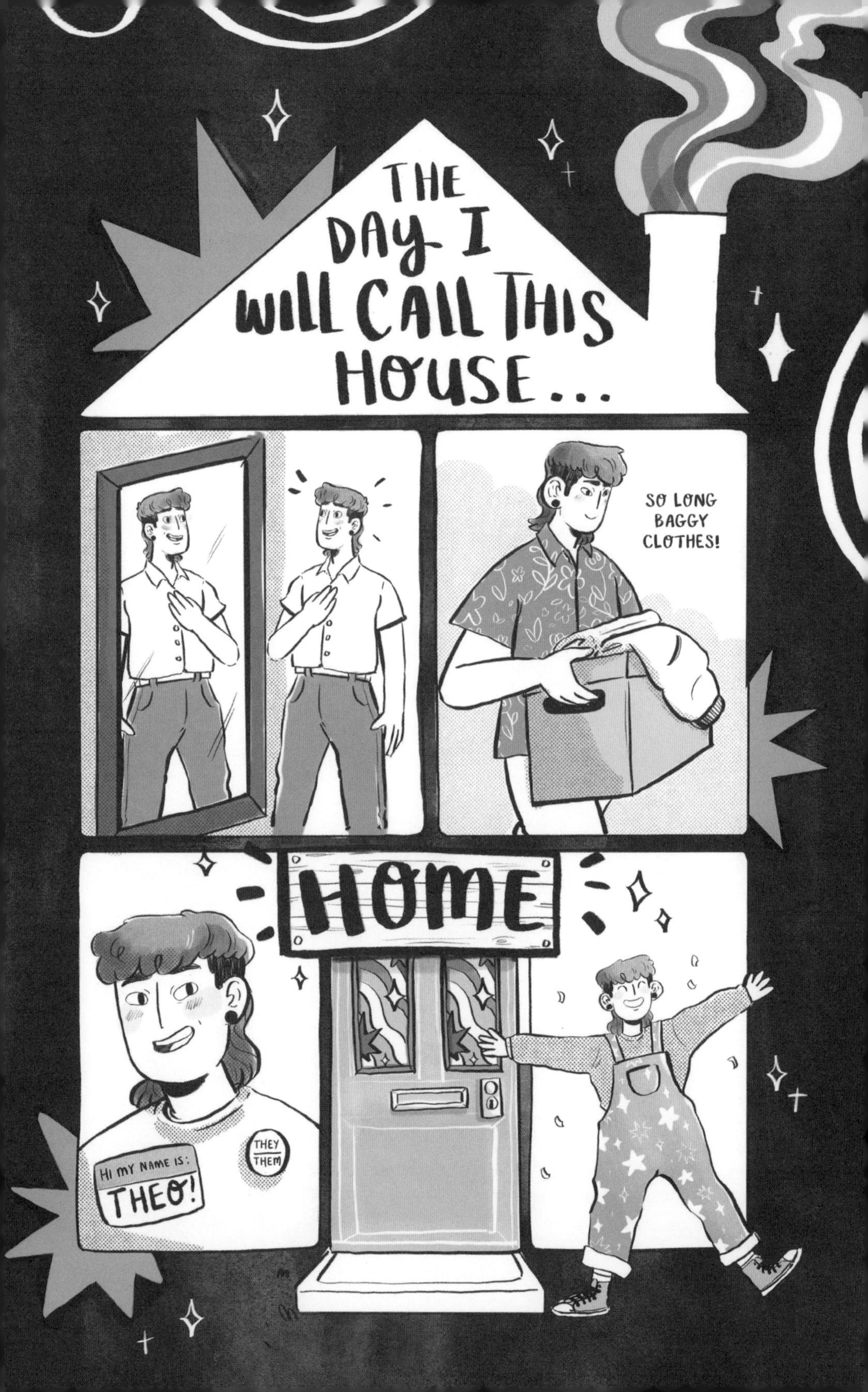
THE DAY I WILL CALL THIS HOUSE...
SO LONG BAGGY CLOTHES!
HOME
HI MY NAME IS: THEO!
THEY THEM

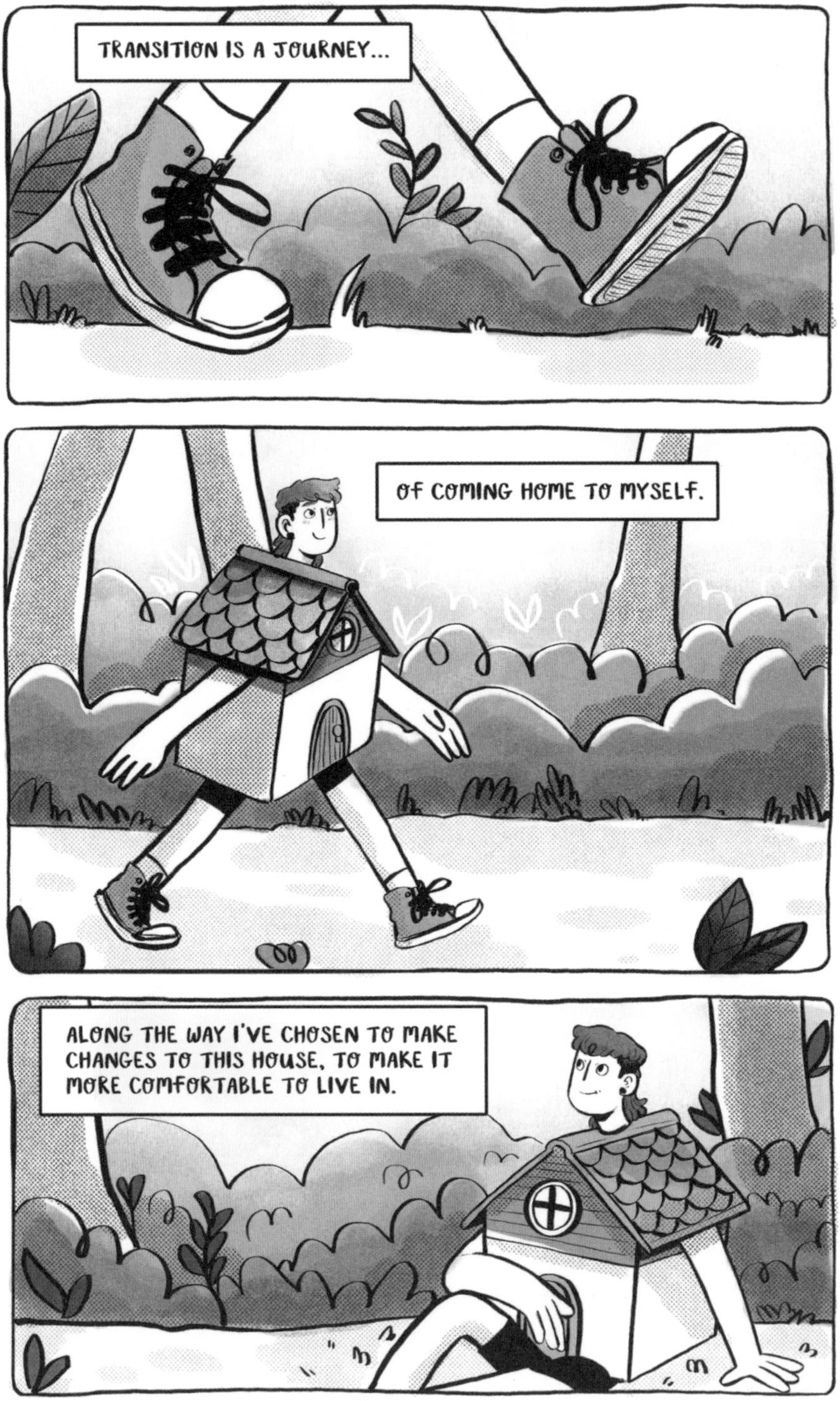
TRANSITION IS A JOURNEY...
OF COMING HOME TO MYSELF.
ALONG THE WAY I'VE CHOSEN TO MAKE CHANGES TO THIS HOUSE, TO MAKE IT MORE COMFORTABLE TO LIVE IN.

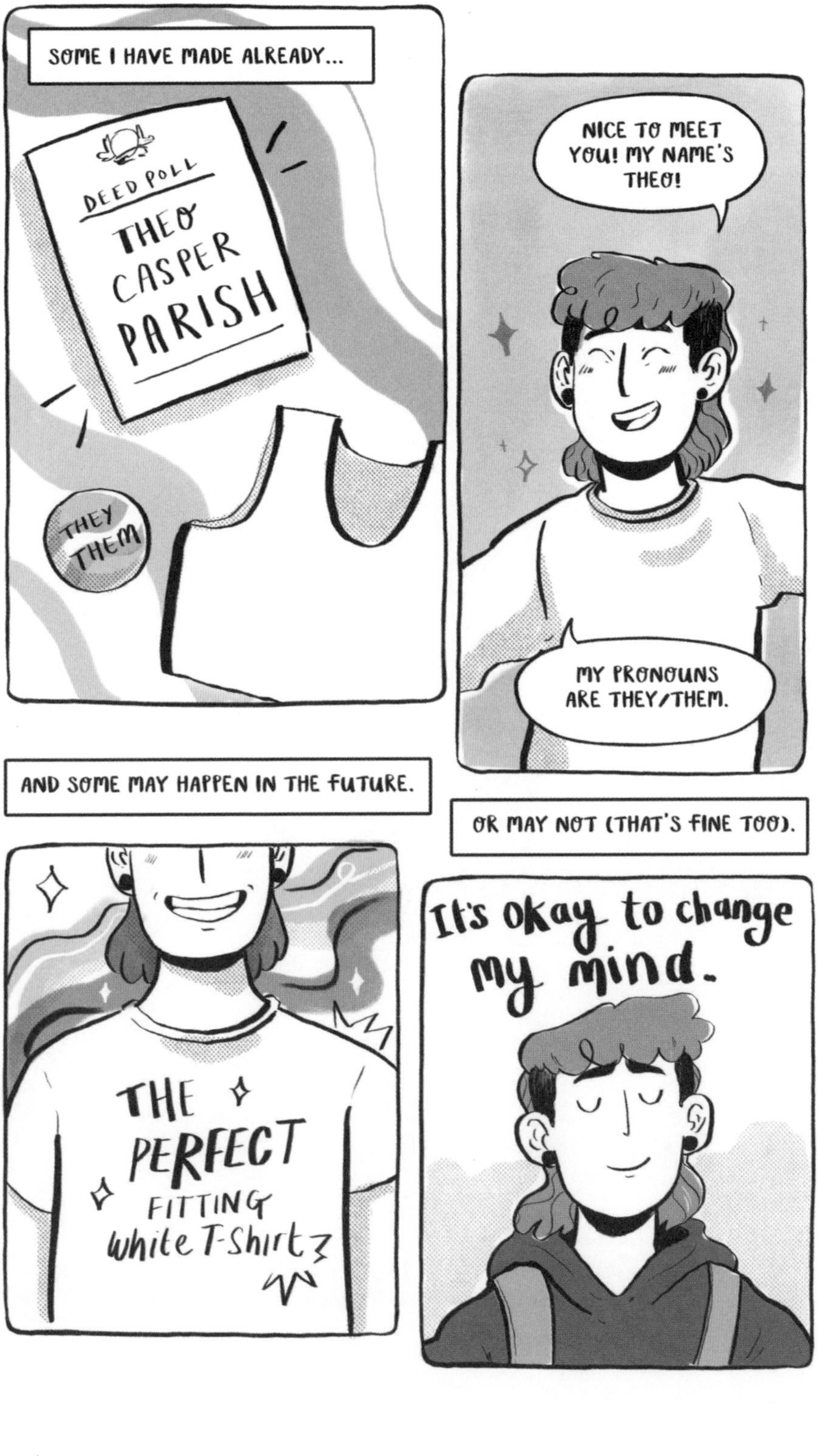
SOME I HAVE MADE ALREADY...
DEED POLL
THEO CASPER PARISH
THEY THEM
NICE TO MEET YOU! MY NAME'S THEO!
MY PRONOUNS ARE THEY/THEM.
AND SOME MAY HAPPEN IN THE FUTURE.
OR MAY NOT (THAT'S FINE TOO).
THE PERFECT FITTING White T-Shirt
It's okay to change my mind.

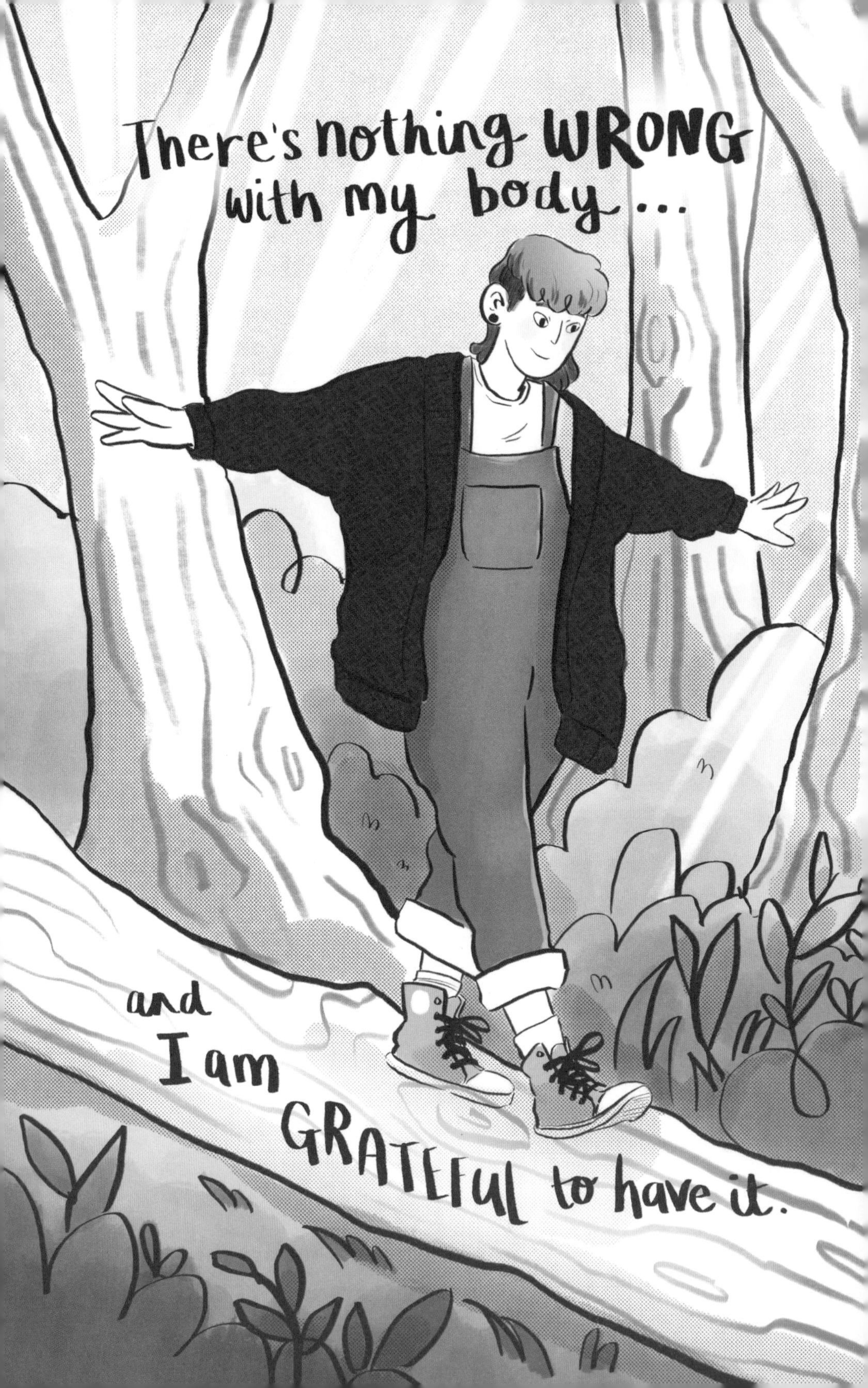
There's nothing WRONG with my body...
and I am GRATEFUL to have it.

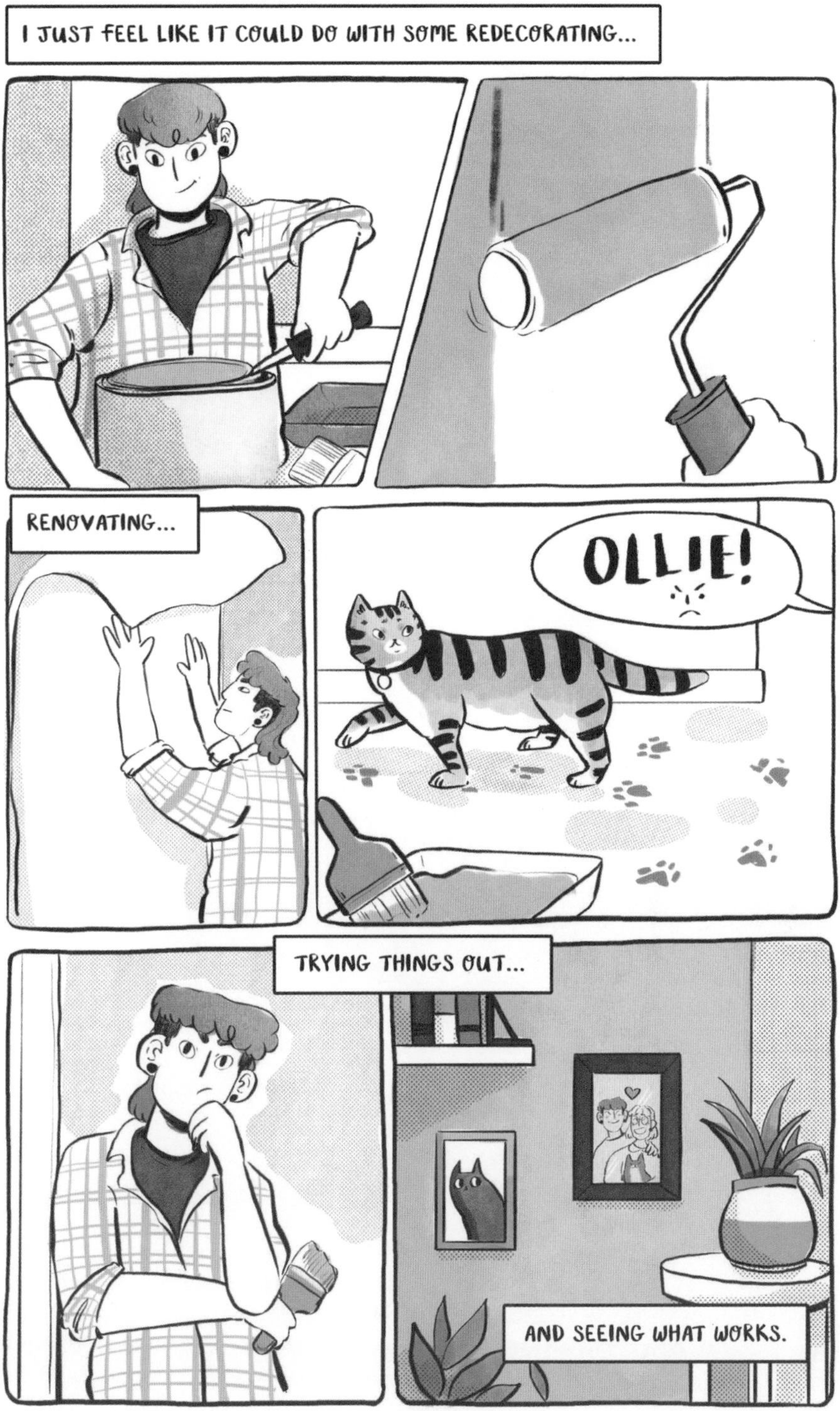
I JUST FEEL LIKE IT COULD DO WITH SOME REDECORATING...
RENOVATING...
OLLIE!
TRYING THINGS OUT...
AND SEEING WHAT WORKS.

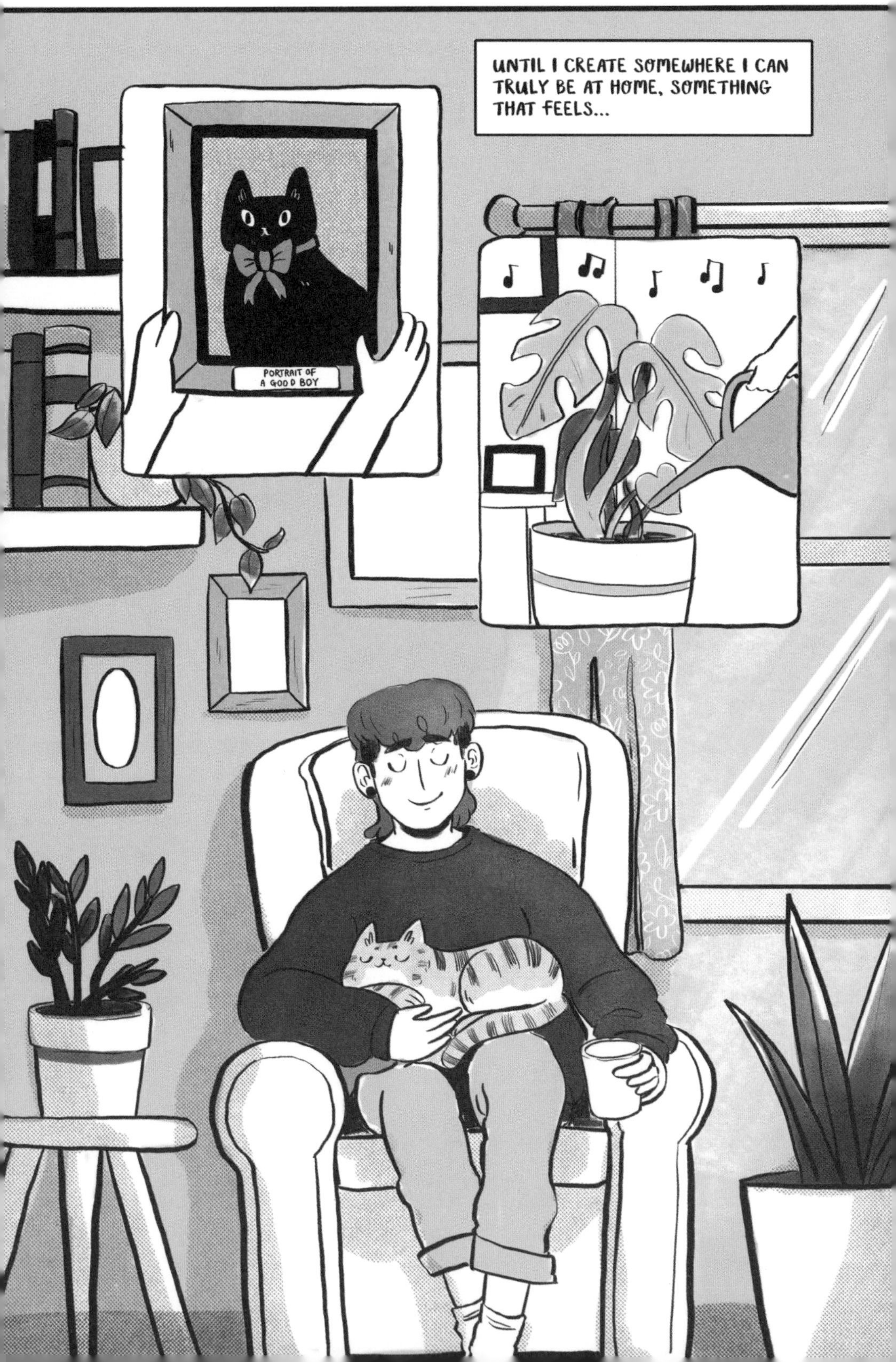
UNTIL I CREATE SOMEWHERE I CAN TRULY BE AT HOME, SOMETHING THAT FEELS...
PORTRAIT OF A GOOD BOY

MORE LIKE ME

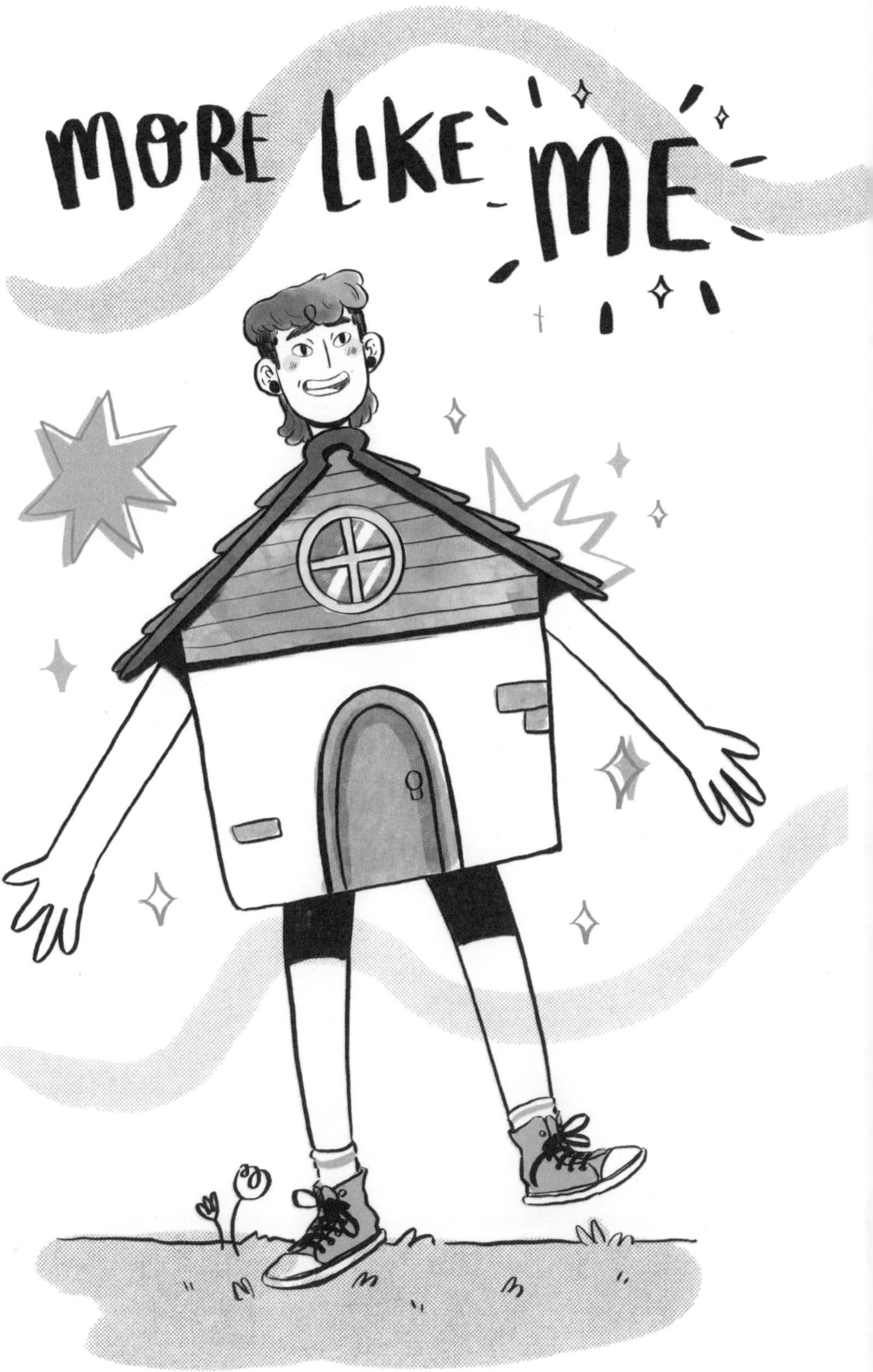

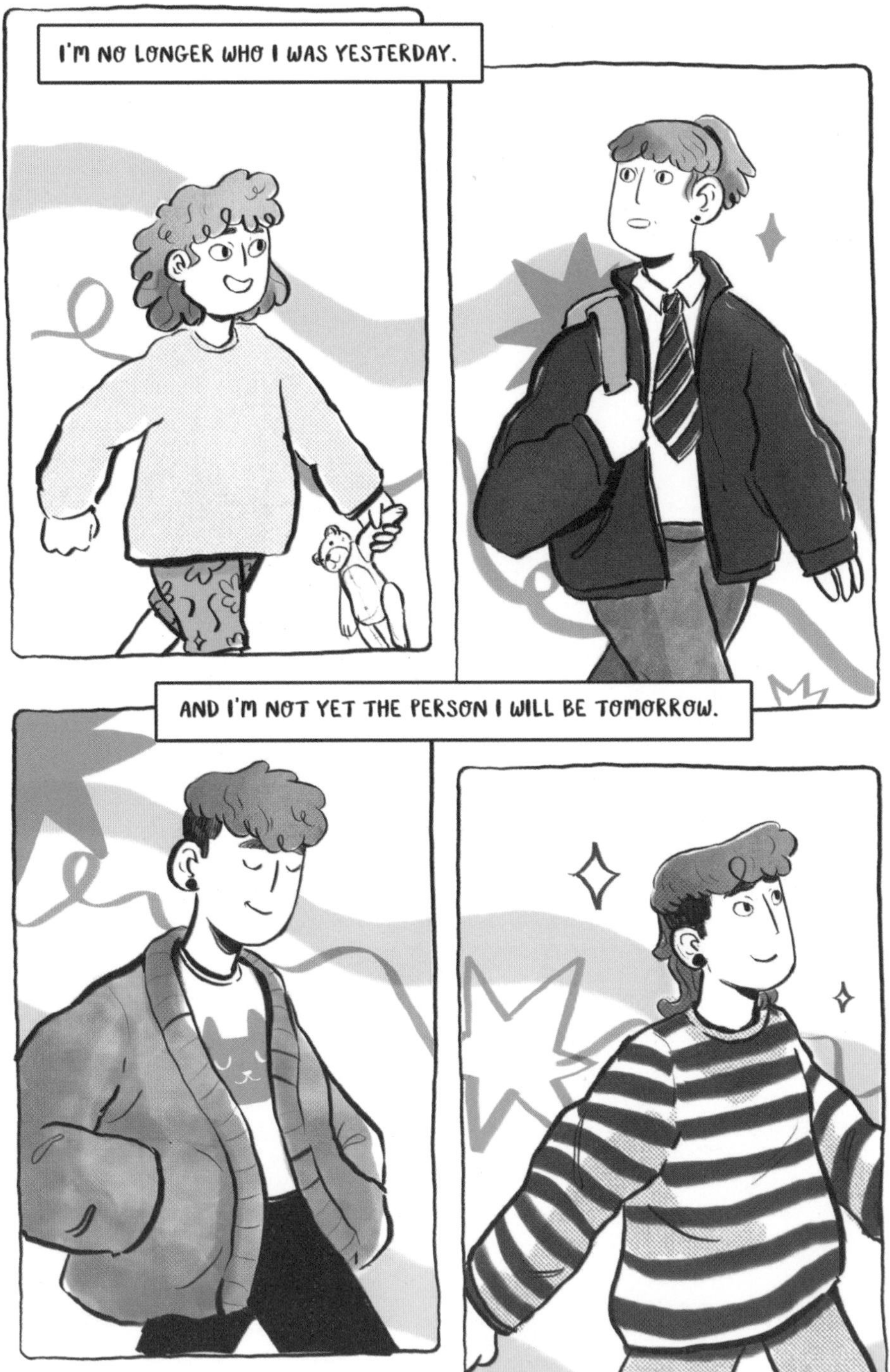
I'M NO LONGER WHO I WAS YESTERDAY.
AND I'M NOT YET THE PERSON I WILL BE TOMORROW.

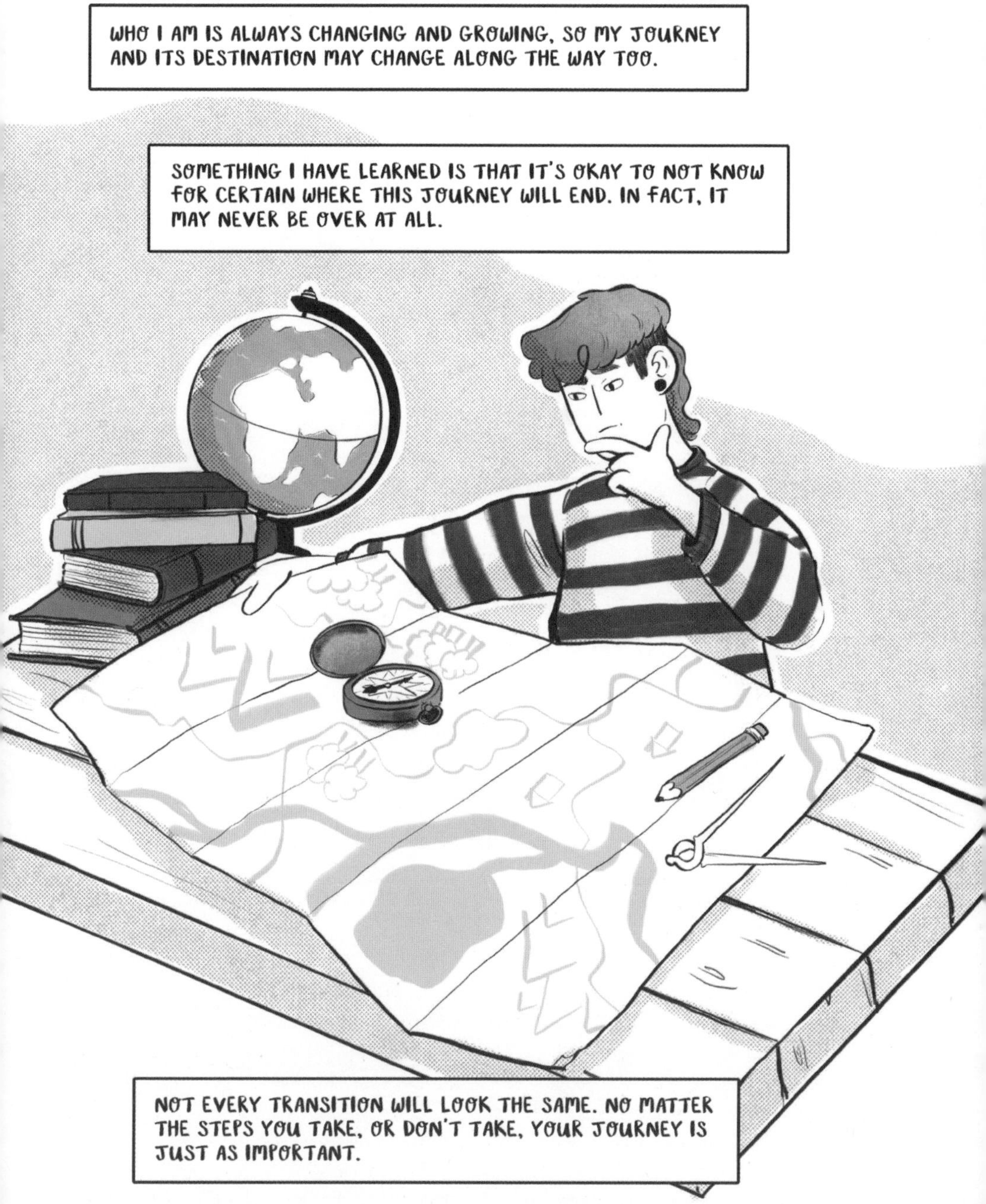
WHO I AM IS ALWAYS CHANGING AND GROWING, SO MY JOURNEY AND ITS DESTINATION MAY CHANGE ALONG THE WAY TOO.
SOMETHING I HAVE LEARNED IS THAT IT'S OKAY TO NOT KNOW FOR CERTAIN WHERE THIS JOURNEY WILL END. IN FACT, IT MAY NEVER BE OVER AT ALL.
NOT EVERY TRANSITION WILL LOOK THE SAME. NO MATTER THE STEPS YOU TAKE, OR DON'T TAKE, YOUR JOURNEY IS JUST AS IMPORTANT.

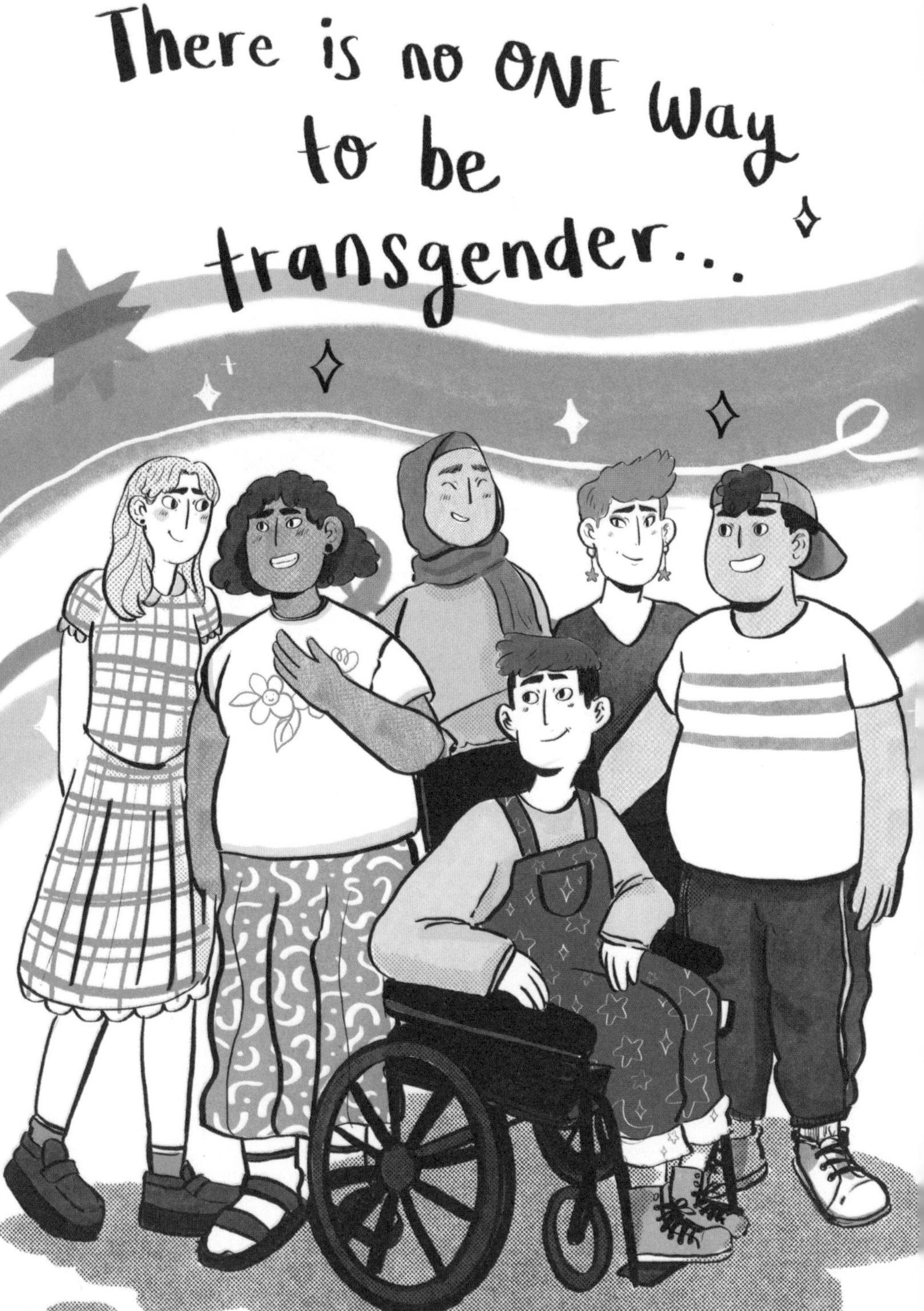
There is no ONE way to be transgender...

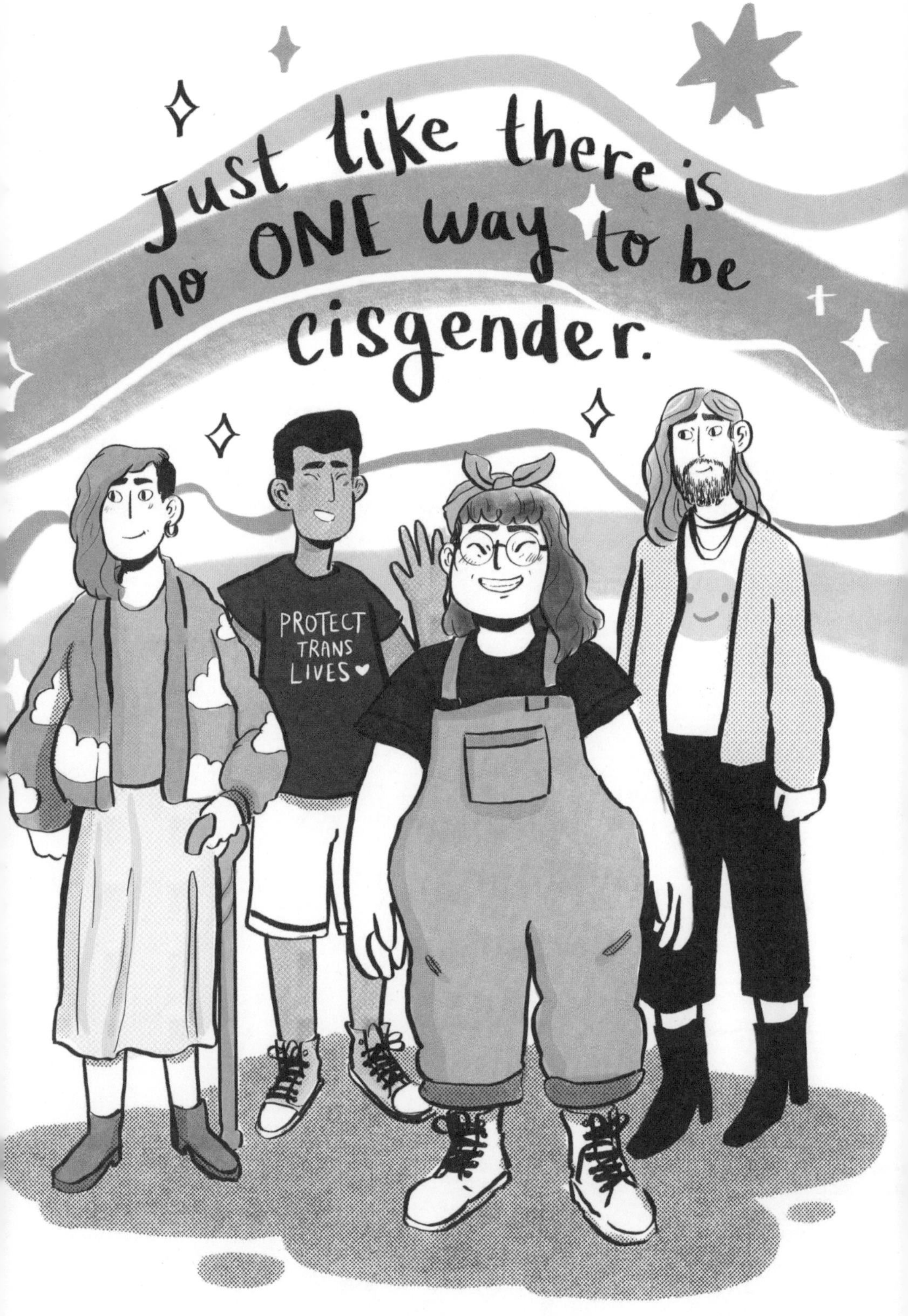
Just like there is no ONE way to be cisgender.
PROTECT TRANS LIVES

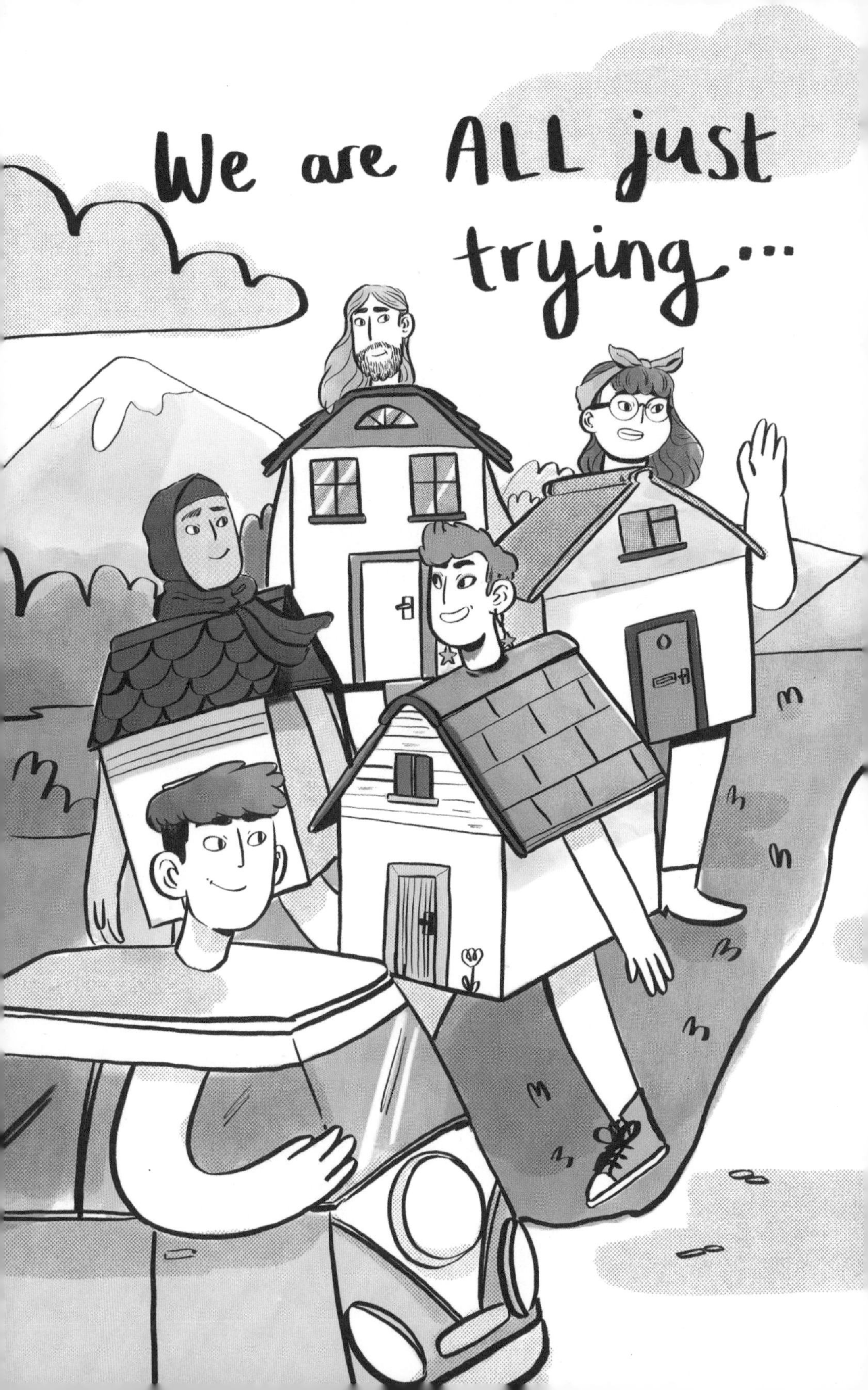
We are ALL just trying...

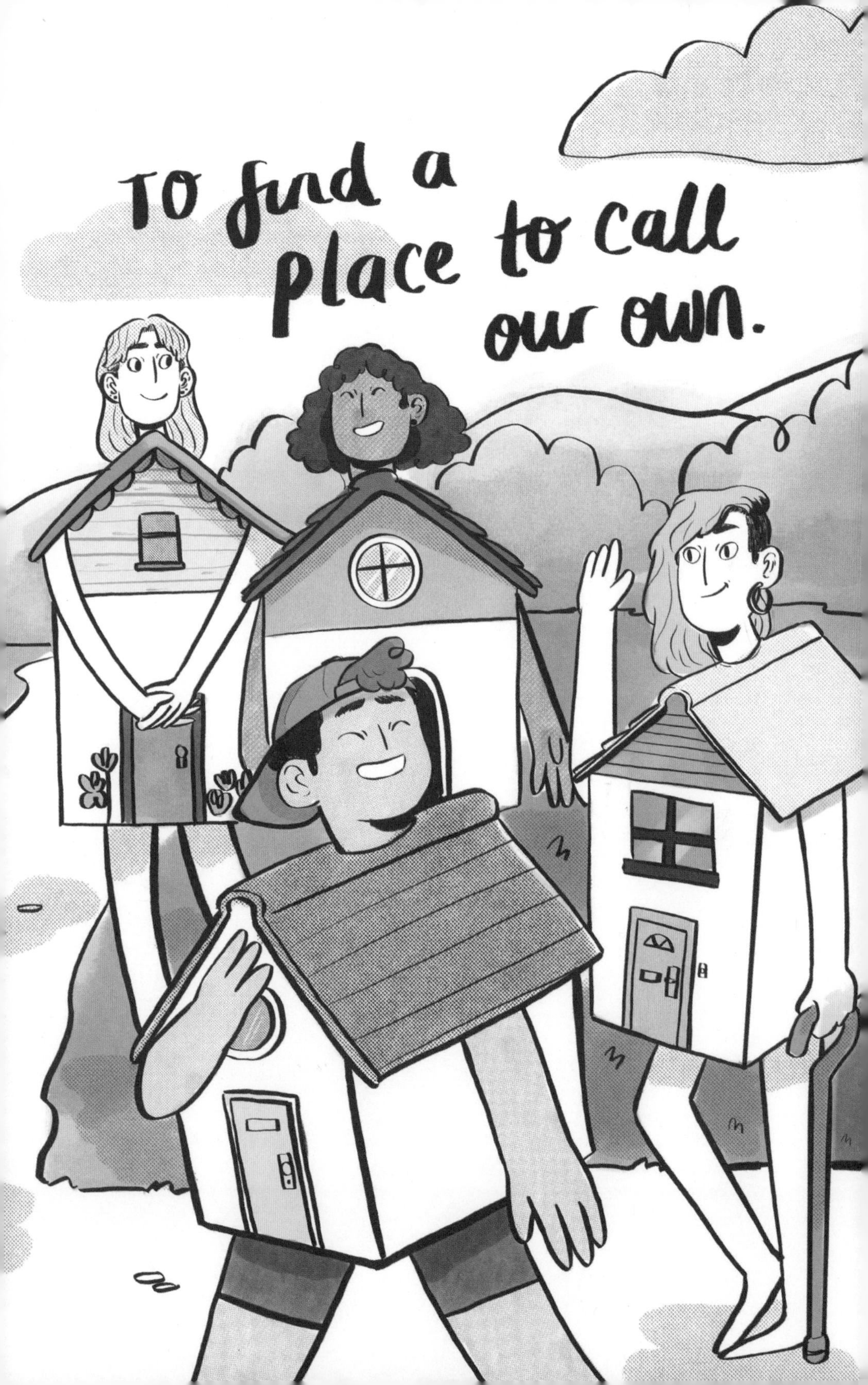
TO find a place to call our own.

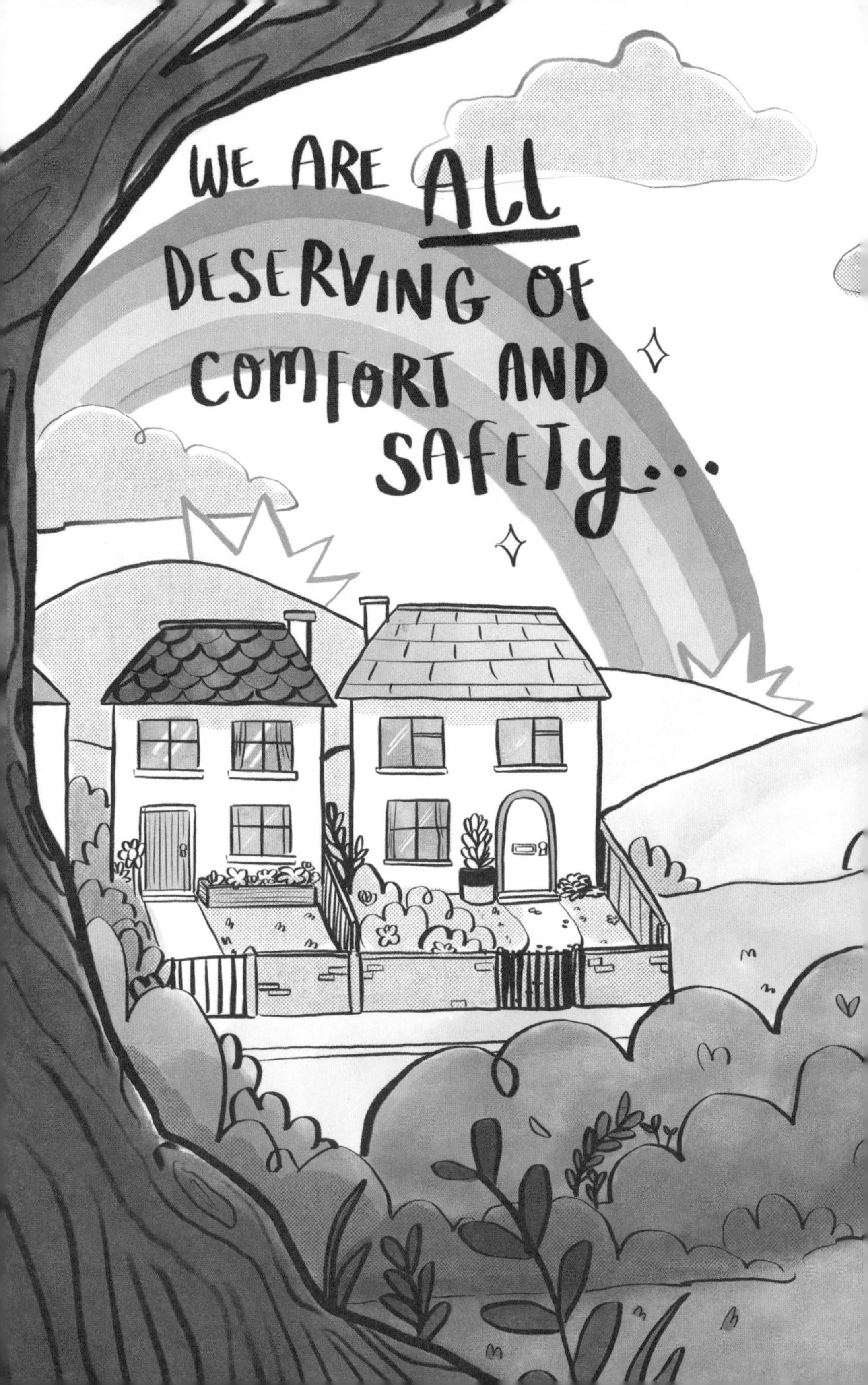
WE ARE ALL
DESERVING OF
COMFORT AND
SAFETY...

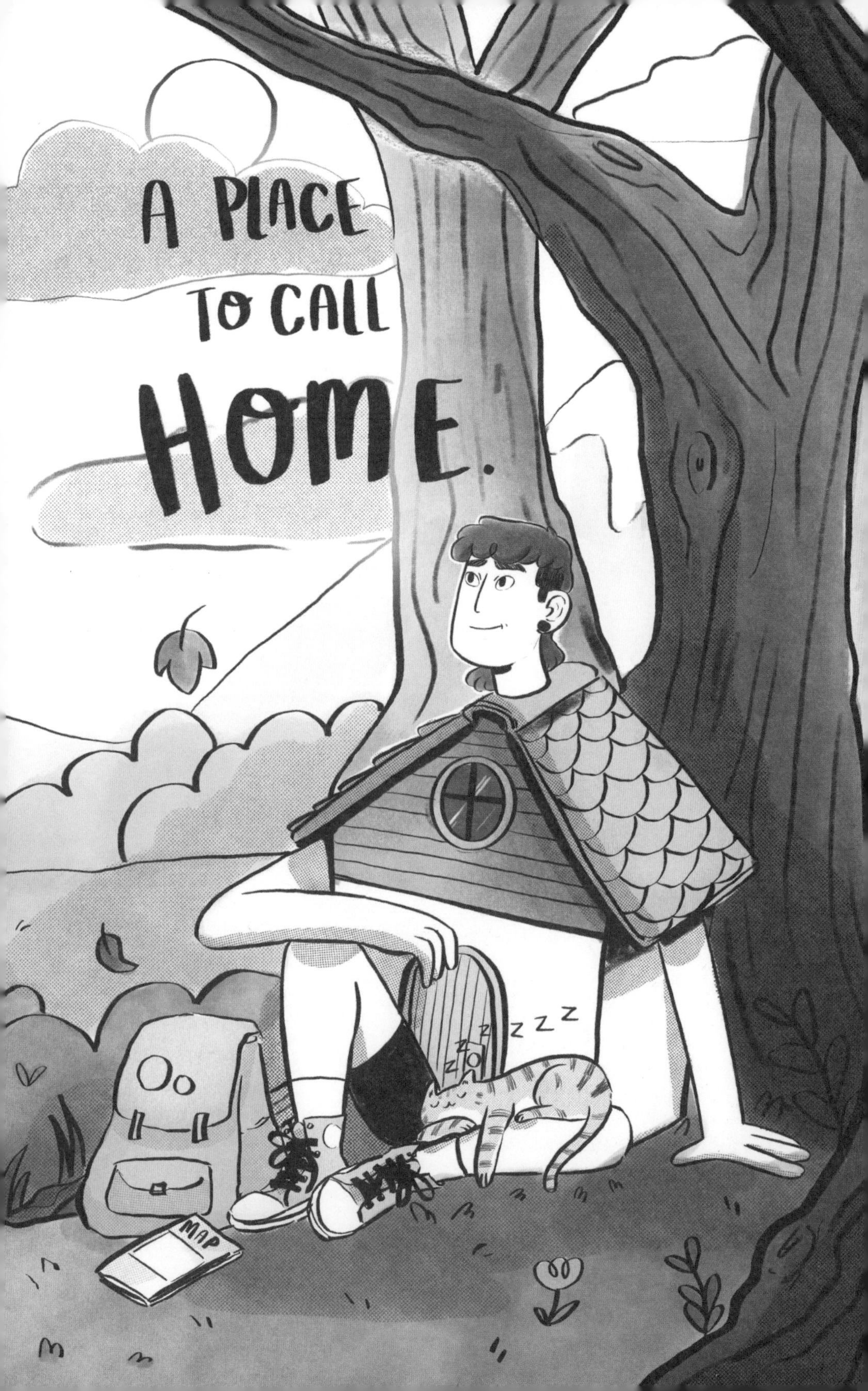
A PLACE TO CALL HOME.
MAP
Z Z Z Z
Oo

HomeBody

SKETCHBOOK PROCESS

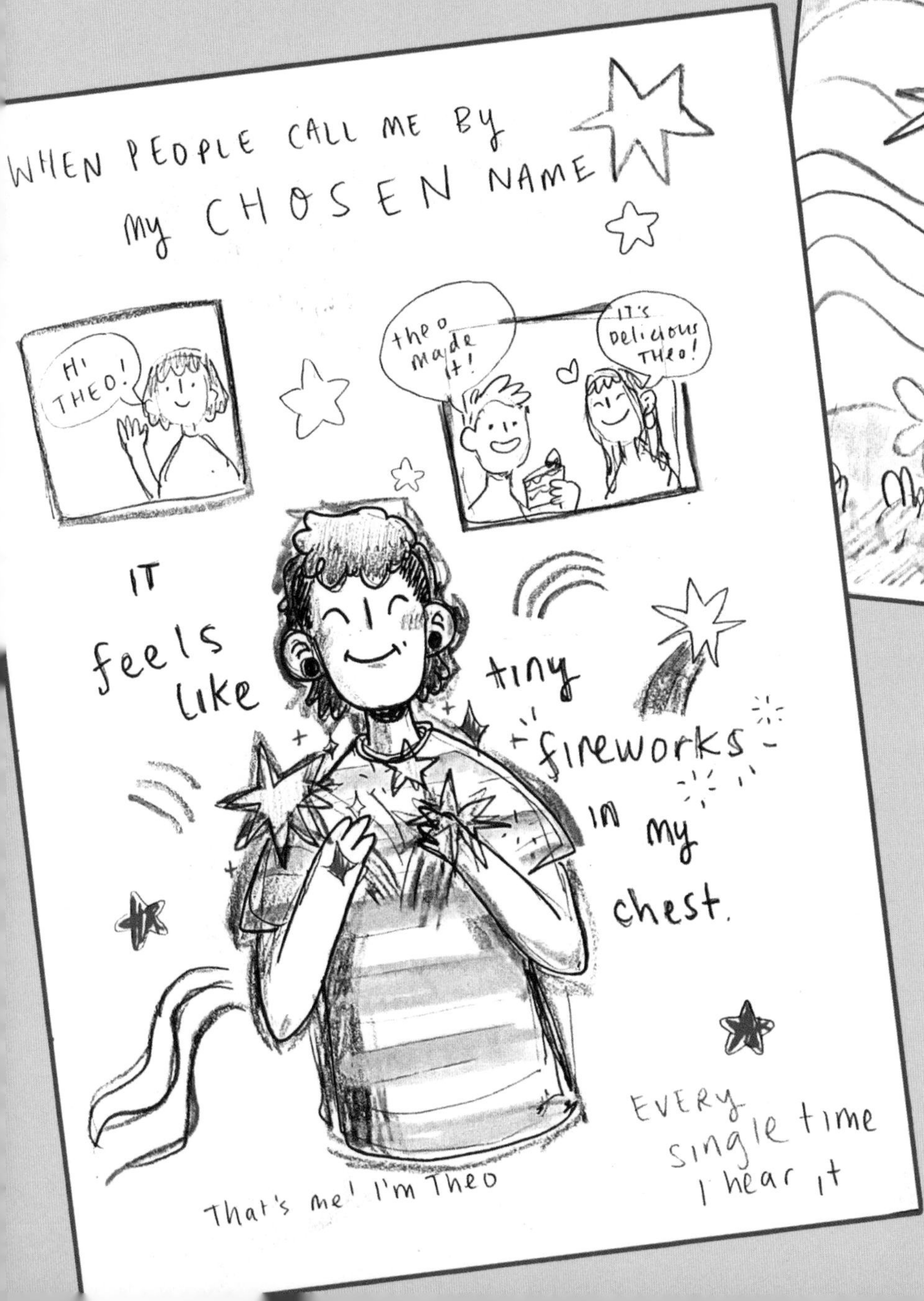
WHEN PEOPLE CALL ME BY
my CHOSEN NAME
HI THEO!
theo made it!
It's Delicious THEO!
IT feels like tiny fireworks in my chest.
That's me! I'm Theo
EVERY single time I hear it

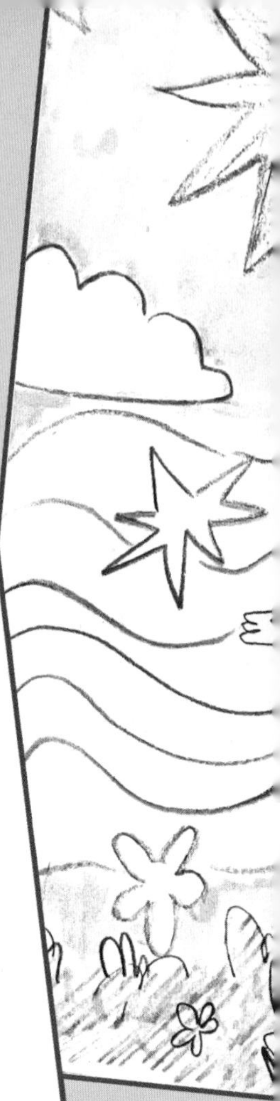

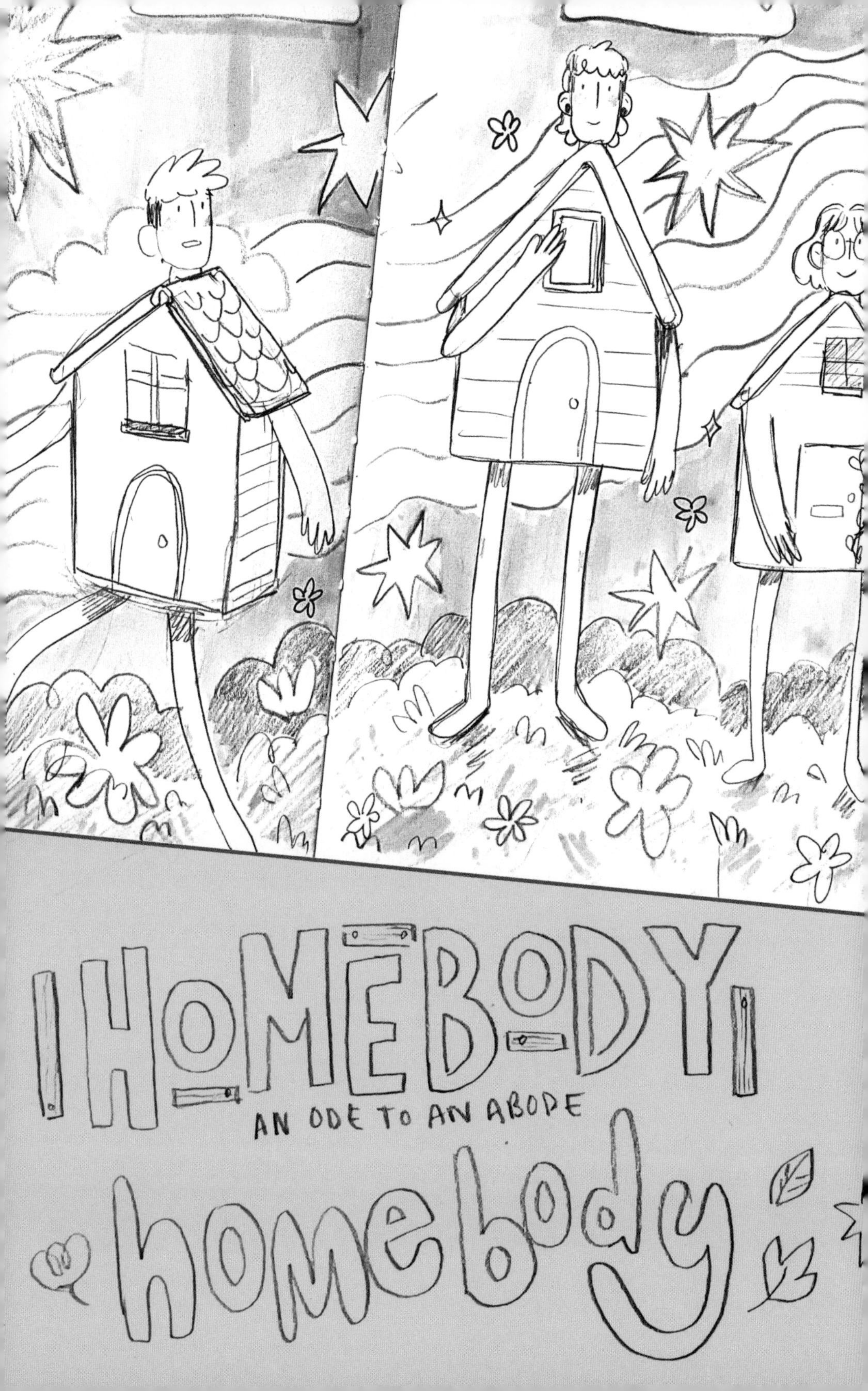
HOMEBODY
AN ODE TO AN ABODE
homebody

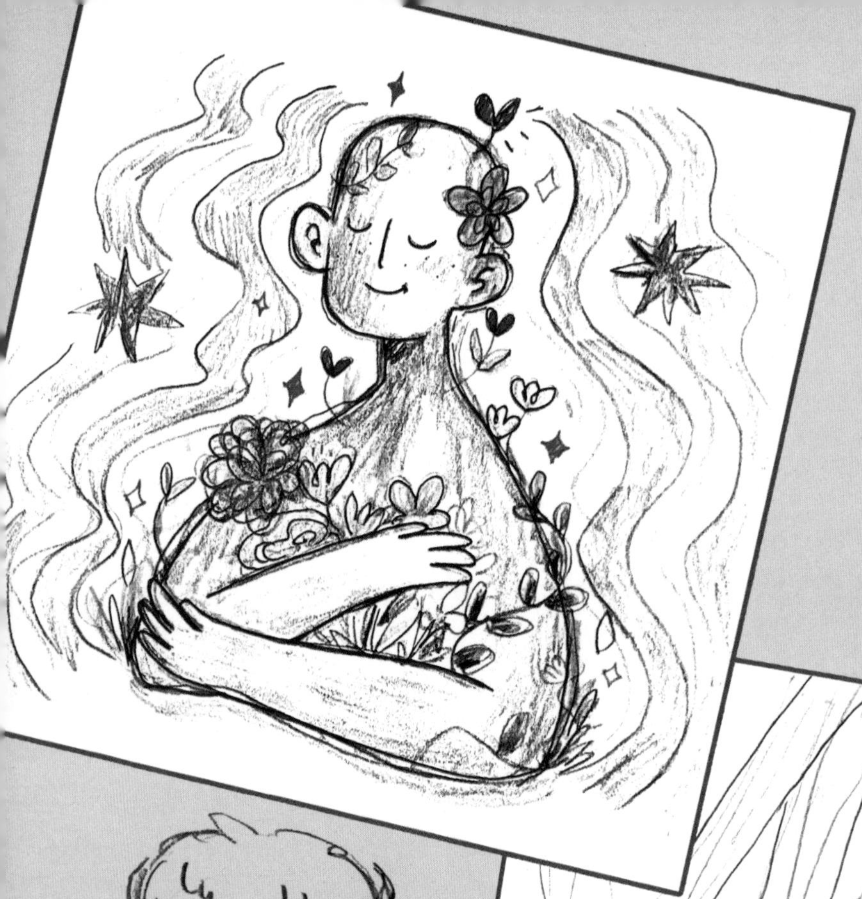

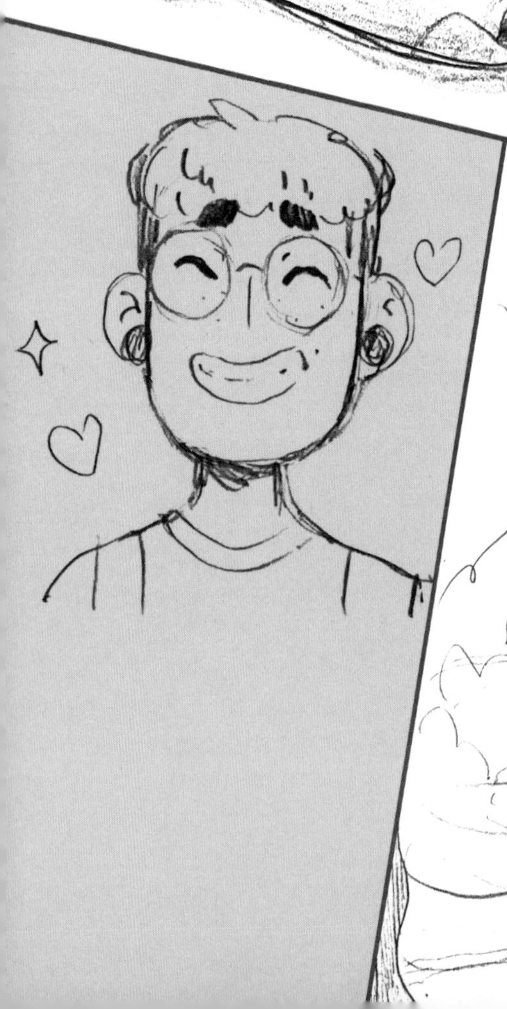

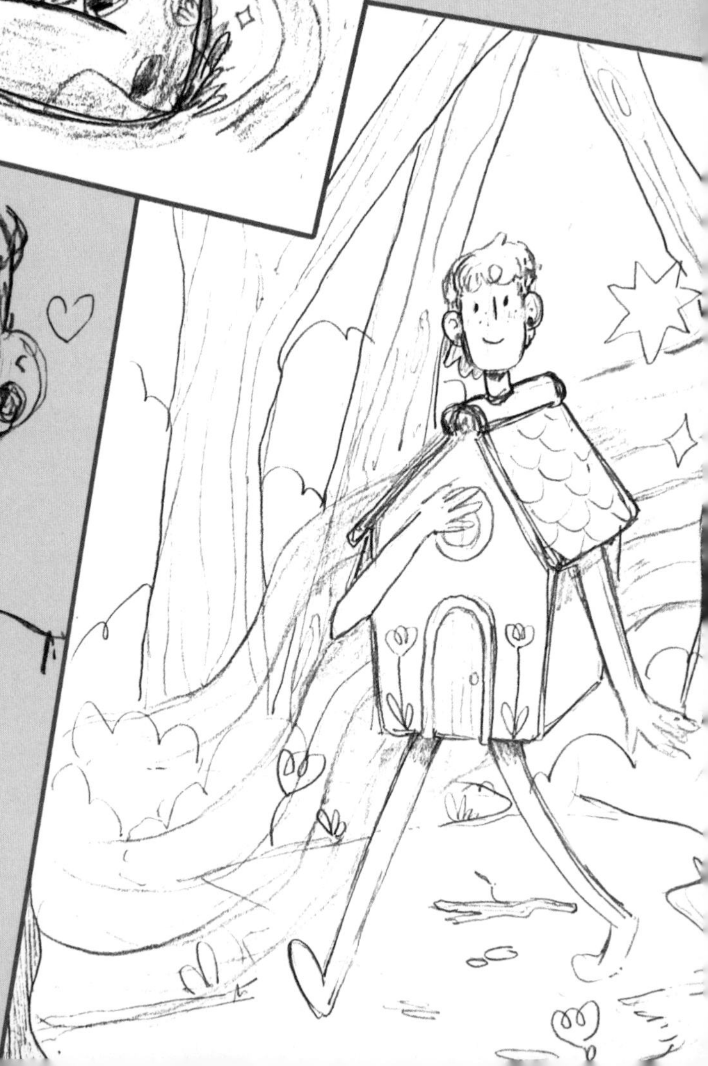

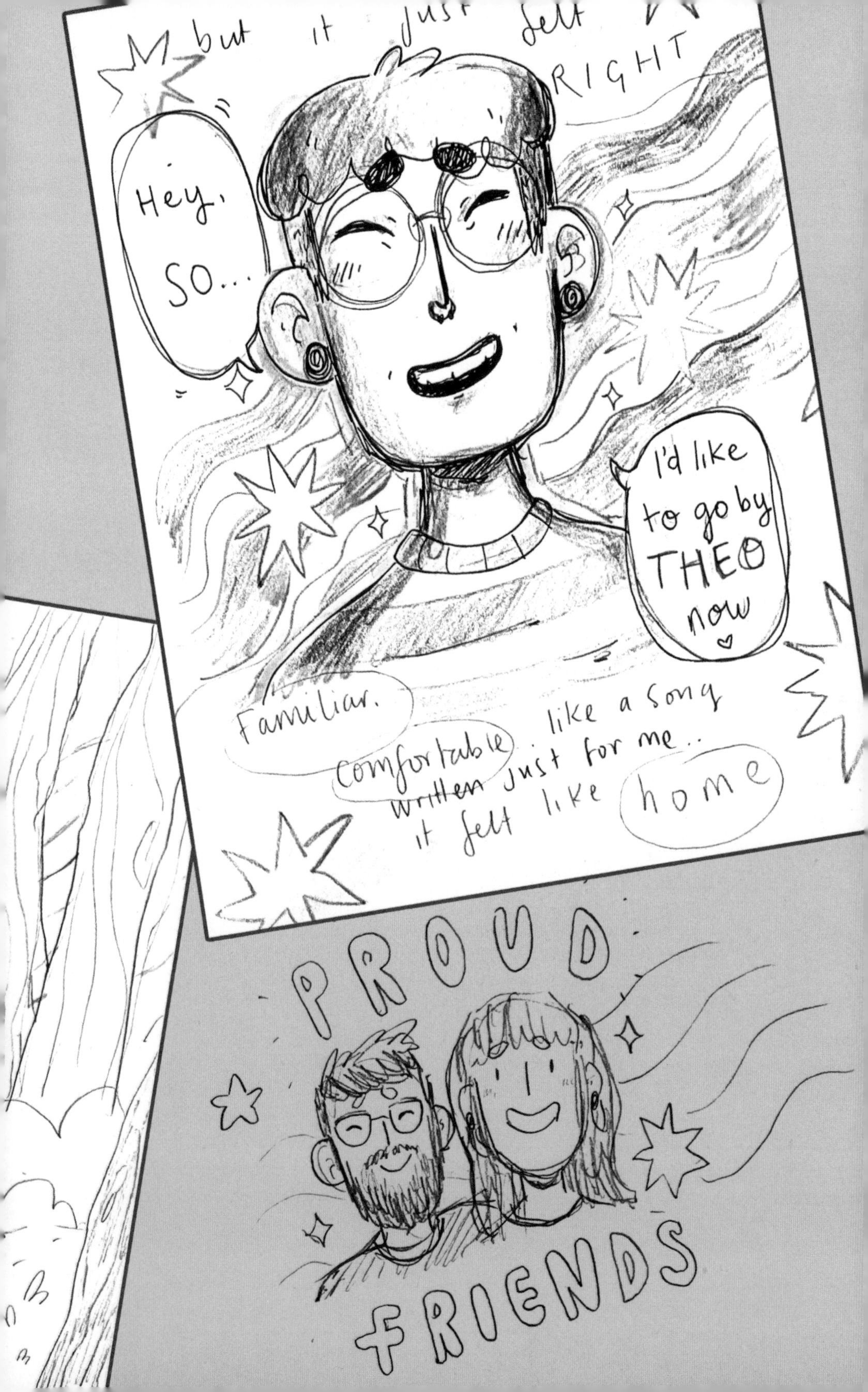
but it just felt RIGHT
Hey, SO...
I'd like to go by THEO now
Familiar.
Comfortable like a song written just for me..
it felt like home
PROUD FRIENDS

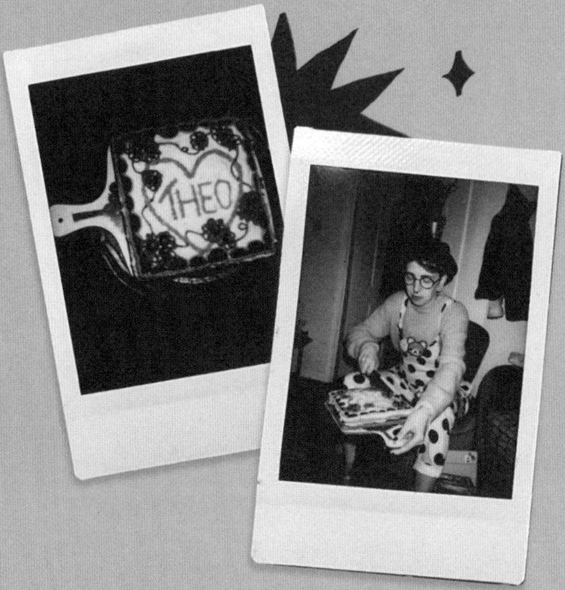
THEO

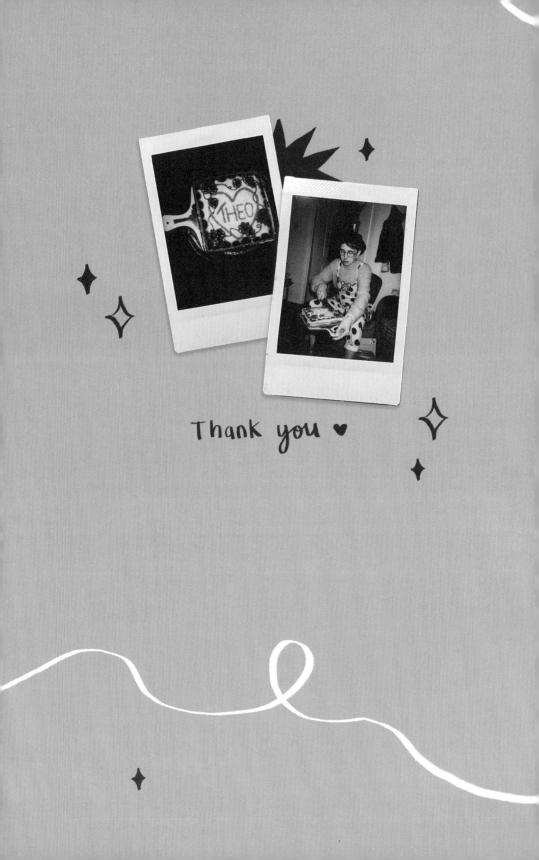

Thank you ♥

THIS BOOK HAS BEEN A WONDERFUL LABOR OF LOVE

and I couldn't have done it without the hard work and support of a whole lot of people.

To my agent Lydia, thank you for championing me from the very beginning, for helping me find my voice, believing in me when I didn't believe in myself, and for always sending me the restaurant menu ahead of time. Huge thank you to my editor Rose Pleuler for all your guidance during this process and your understanding, care, and whole-hearted support of my story from day one. To Andrew Arnold, Maddy Price, and the rest of the team at HarperAlley, thank you so much for providing such a passionate and supportive home for *Homebody* across the pond.

To my family, both chosen and biological, I am so blessed to be surrounded by such a bunch of creative, wonderfully weird, and endlessly supportive people. I wouldn't be the person I am in this moment without your love and care. To everyone who has supported me, both on my journey of finding and expressing my true self and in writing this book, thank you.

Honorable mention to Pura; thank you for being the first to read the comic that later would become this book and encouraging me to share it with the world. Wouldn't be here without you!

To my partner, although often we are on opposite sides of the world, I always feel like I have you right here in my corner. Thank you for always being my loudest supporter!

To Ben, Ollie, and Henry, thank you for keeping me company while I work and for all the "gifts." I mean it when I say "you really shouldn't have," but I appreciate the gesture.

Special thanks to my adventuring party, Charli, Wayne, and Chris. Telling stories with you has been a constant source of comfort and joy. I am so grateful and forever changed by your friendship and support. Thank you for all the pep talks, hugs, coffee, studio biscuits, boba sniffs, belief, and encouragement.

And lastly, thank you for reading. I hope that this book gives you comfort. At the very least, I hope it was a warm hug for you in these uncertain times.

Theo

for you,
whenever and however you need it.

This is a work of nonfiction. The events and experiences detailed here are all true and have been faithfully rendered as the author has remembered them, to the best of their ability. Some names have been changed in order to protect the privacy of the individuals involved. Though conversations from the author's keen recollection of them, they are not written to represent word-for-word documentation; rather, they have retold them in a way that evokes the real feeling and meaning of what was said, in keeping with the spirit of the event.

HarperAlley is an imprint of HarperCollins Publishers.
Homebody
Copyright © 2024 by Theo Parish
All rights reserved. Printed in Malaysia.
No part of this book may be used or reproduced in any manner whatsoever without written permission except in the case of brief quotations embodied in critical articles and reviews.
For information address HarperCollins Children's Books, a division of HarperCollins Publishers, 195 Broadway, New York, NY 10007.
www.harperalley.com
Library of Congress Control Number: 2023937034
ISBN 978-0-06-331959-2 (trade bdg.) — ISBN 978-0-06-331958-5 (pbk.)
24 25 26 27 28 COS 10 9 8 7 6 5 4 3 2 1
First Edition